Hands-On Design Patterns with C# and .NET Core

Write clean and maintainable code by using reusable solutions to common software design problems

Gaurav Aroraa
Jeffrey Chilberto

Packt>

BIRMINGHAM - MUMBAI

Hands-On Design Patterns with C# and .NET Core

Copyright © 2019 Packt Publishing

All rights reserved. No part of this book may be reproduced, stored in a retrieval system, or transmitted in any form or by any means, without the prior written permission of the publisher, except in the case of brief quotations embedded in critical articles or reviews.

Every effort has been made in the preparation of this book to ensure the accuracy of the information presented. However, the information contained in this book is sold without warranty, either express or implied. Neither the authors, nor Packt Publishing or its dealers and distributors, will be held liable for any damages caused or alleged to have been caused directly or indirectly by this book.

Packt Publishing has endeavored to provide trademark information about all of the companies and products mentioned in this book by the appropriate use of capitals. However, Packt Publishing cannot guarantee the accuracy of this information.

Commissioning Editor: Richa Tripathi
Acquisition Editor: Chaitanya Nair
Content Development Editor: Akshita Billava
Senior Editor: Afshaan Khan
Technical Editor: Neha Pande
Copy Editor: Safis Editing
Language Support Editor: Storm Mann
Project Coordinator: Carol Lewis
Proofreader: Safis Editing
Indexer: Tejal Daruwale Soni
Production Designer: Alishon Mendonsa

First published: July 2019

Production reference: 1040719

Published by Packt Publishing Ltd.
Livery Place
35 Livery Street
Birmingham
B3 2PB, UK.

ISBN 978-1-78913-364-6

www.packtpub.com

To my mother, Late Smt. Santosh, and to the memory of my father, the late Sh. Ramkrishan, for their sacrifices and for exemplifying the power of determination. To my youngest sister, the late Baby Kanchan, for her love and always being my lucky charm.

– Gaurav Aroraa

My parents, Francis and Joyce, who tirelessly put their children first, with love, support, and kindness. To my brothers: Jack, for inspiring me to persevere through challenges, and Mike, for reminding me to stop and take the time to enjoy life.

– Jeffrey Chilberto

Packt.com

Subscribe to our online digital library for full access to over 7,000 books and videos, as well as industry leading tools to help you plan your personal development and advance your career. For more information, please visit our website.

Why subscribe?

- Spend less time learning and more time coding with practical eBooks and Videos from over 4,000 industry professionals

- Improve your learning with Skill Plans built especially for you

- Get a free eBook or video every month

- Fully searchable for easy access to vital information

- Copy and paste, print, and bookmark content

Did you know that Packt offers eBook versions of every book published, with PDF and ePub files available? You can upgrade to the eBook version at www.packt.com and as a print book customer, you are entitled to a discount on the eBook copy. Get in touch with us at customercare@packtpub.com for more details.

At www.packt.com, you can also read a collection of free technical articles, sign up for a range of free newsletters, and receive exclusive discounts and offers on Packt books and eBooks.

Foreword

When designing good software, engineers naturally gravitate toward solutions that avoid duplication. We are naturally DRY—Don't Repeat Yourself—often without thinking about it! Developers naturally compartmentalize functionality, create reusable methods, and make helpful classes.

However, many software design patterns have been created over the years. These are useful, general, and reusable solutions to problems you'll see every day. There are more and more developers who are self-taught or who didn't go through a classical software engineer or computer science course at university, and everyone should enjoy the benefits of decades of development of these great design patterns.

Gaurav and Jeffrey have assembled the best and most common patterns and applied them to the open source world of .NET Core and C#. You'll start with OOP, classes, and objects and move your way on to inheritance, encapsulation, and polymorphism. They've covered design principles such as DRY, KISS, and SOLID (these will all make sense very soon!) and applied them to classic patterns that will help you make clear, crisp, and rock-solid (pun intended!) software.

This book is filled with real code that clearly illustrates how to apply all this knowledge to your .NET Core and C# software today. You'll learn how to adopt the Builder pattern, Decorator pattern, Factory pattern, Visitor pattern, and Strategy pattern, and so much more.

These techniques will then be applied to a simple app, then to a web application, and then to more complex problems involving concurrency and parallelism! You'll then apply patterns at a more macro level using solution patterns that will help you move your projects to the cloud in a scalable and maintainable way.

I hope you appreciate this book as much as I did. And I hope you enjoy working with .NET Core and have as much fun as we did making it!

Scott Hanselman

Partner Program Manager—Microsoft

.NET and Open Source Community

This book is a blessing for every developer looking to raise their development skills to the next level, but more importantly, to build scalable, maintainable, and robust solutions. Most industry standards and best practices are covered, using straight-to-the-point examples.

Beyond development design patterns, the book also tackles underlying architecture principles and some key cloud aspects, such as security and scaling.

As a solution architect, I am involved day in day out in, designing end-to-end solutions, from the development aspects to the underlying infrastructure and security bits, and yet I am impressed by the quality contents and the broad scope of this book. It contains a very comprehensive list of patterns that everyone should take a look at when considering the development and deployment of new workloads.

This in-depth immersion into the **Object-oriented programming** (**OOP**) and .NET Core worlds is profitable to anyone interested in writing best-in-class applications.

Stephane Eyskens

Azure MVP

Contributors

About the authors

Gaurav Aroraa has an M.Phil in computer science. He is a former Microsoft MVP, Alibaba Cloud MVP, certified as a Scrum trainer/coach, a lifetime member of **Computer Society of India** (**CSI**), an advisory member of IndiaMentor, XEN for ITIL-F, and APMG for PRINCE-F and PRINCE-P. Gaurav is an open source developer, a contributor to TechNet Wiki, and the founder of Ovatic Systems Private Limited. In a career spanning more than 21 years, he has mentored thousands of students and industry professionals. You can tweet Gaurav using his Twitter handle, `@g_arora`.

> *To my wife, Shuby Aroraa, and my angel (daughter), Aarchi Aroraa, who permitted me to steal time for this book from the time I was supposed to spend with them. Thanks to the entire Packt team, especially Chaitanya, Akshita, and Neha, whose coordination and communication during the period was tremendous, and Denim Pinto, who introduced me for this book.*

Jeffrey Chilberto is a software consultant specializing in the Microsoft technology stack, including Azure, BizTalk, ASP.NET, MVC, WCF, and SQL Server, with experience in a wide range of industries, including banking, telecommunications, and healthcare in New Zealand, Europe, Australia, and the United States. He has a bachelor's degree in information and computer science, and a master's degree in computer science and engineering.

> *I would like to thank my family for their love, inspiration, and support.*

About the reviewers

Sjoukje Zaal is a managing consultant, Microsoft cloud architect, and Microsoft Azure MVP with over 15 years of experience providing architecture, development, consultancy, and design expertise. She works at Capgemini, a global leader in consulting, technology services, and digital transformation. She loves to share her knowledge and is active in the Microsoft community as a cofounder of the Dutch user groups SP&C NL and MixUG. She is also a board member of Azure Thursdays. Sjoukje is a public speaker and is involved in organizing events. She has written several books, writes blogs, and is active in the Microsoft Tech Community. Sjoukje is also part of the Diversity and Inclusion Advisory Board.

Ephraim Kyriakidis has almost 20 years of experience in software development. He got his diploma as an electrical and software engineer from Aristotle University of Thessaloniki in Greece. He has been using .NET since its beginning, from version 1.0. In his career, he has mainly focused on Microsoft technologies. He is currently employed by Siemens AG in Germany as a senior software engineer.

Packt is searching for authors like you

If you're interested in becoming an author for Packt, please visit `authors.packtpub.com` and apply today. We have worked with thousands of developers and tech professionals, just like you, to help them share their insight with the global tech community. You can make a general application, apply for a specific hot topic that we are recruiting an author for, or submit your own idea.

Table of Contents

Preface   1

Section 1: Essentials of Design Patterns in C# and .NET Core

Chapter 1: Overview of OOP in .NET Core and C#   11
  Technical requirements   12
    Installing Visual Studio   12
    Setting up .NET Core   13
    The models used in this book   13
  OOP and how classes and objects work   15
    Explaining OOP   16
    A class   18
    An object   18
      Associations   20
    An interface   22
  Inheritance   23
    Types of inheritance   23
  Encapsulation   25
  Polymorphism   26
    Static polymorphism   27
    Dynamic polymorphism   27
      Interface polymorphism   28
      Inheritance polymorphism   28
      Generics   29
  Summary   30
  Questions   30

Chapter 2: Modern Software Design Patterns and Principles   31
  Technical requirements   32
    Installing Visual Studio   32
    Setting up .NET Core   33
  Design principles   33
    DRY – Don't Repeat Yourself   33
    KISS – Keep It Simple Stupid   34
    YAGNI – You Aren't Gonna Need It   34
    MVP – Minimum Viable Product   34
    SOLID   35
      Single responsibility principle   35
      Open/closed principle   35
      Liskov substitution principle   36

Table of Contents

Interface segregation principle	36
Dependency inversion principle	37
Software patterns	**37**
GoF patterns	37
Creational patterns	38
Structural patterns	38
Decorator patterns	39
Behavioral patterns	42
Chain of responsibility	43
Observer pattern	46
Enterprise integration patterns	49
Topology	49
Patterns	51
Messaging	51
Transformation	52
Routing	54
Software development life cycle patterns	**55**
Waterfall SDLC	56
Agile SDLC	57
Summary	**58**
Questions	**59**

Section 2: Deep Dive into Utilities and Patterns in .NET Core

Chapter 3: Implementing Design Patterns - Basics Part 1	**63**
Technical requirements	**64**
Installing Visual Studio	64
Setting up .NET Core	64
Minimum Viable Product	**65**
Requirements	65
How does MVP fit with future development?	67
Test-driven development	**69**
Why did the team choose TDD?	69
Setting up the projects	70
Initial unit test definitions	74
Abstract Factory design pattern	**76**
InventoryCommand abstract class	77
SOLID principles	**81**
Single responsibility principle (SRP)	81
Open/closed principle (OCP)	82
Liskov substitution principle (LSP)	83
Interface segregation principle (ISP)	84
Dependency inversion principle	85
InventoryCommand unit tests	88
Access modifiers	89
Helper TestUserInterface	91

[ii]

Example unit test – QuitCommand	93
Summary	94
Questions	94

Chapter 4: Implementing Design Patterns - Basics Part 2 — 95

Technical requirements	96
Installing Visual Studio	96
Setting up .NET Core	96
The singleton pattern	97
Processes and threads	98
The repository pattern	99
Unit tests	100
A race condition illustration	108
AddInventoryCommand	111
TestInventoryContext	112
AddInventoryCommandTest	114
UpdateQuantityCommand	115
UpdateQuantityCommandTest	117
GetInventoryCommand	118
GetInventoryCommandTest	119
The factory pattern	120
Unit tests	121
Issue one – UnknownCommand	122
InventoryCommandFactoryTests	123
Issue two – case-insensitive text commands	125
Features in .NET Core	126
IServiceCollection	126
CatalogService	128
IServiceProvider	129
Console application	130
Summary	132
Questions	132

Chapter 5: Implementing Design Patterns - .NET Core — 133

Technical requirements	134
Installing Visual Studio	134
Setting up .NET Core	134
.Net Core service lifetimes	135
Transient	135
Scoped	135
Singleton	136
Back to FlixOne	136
Unit tests	139
Scope	142
Implementation factory	144
IInventoryContext	144

[iii]

Table of Contents

IInventoryReadContext	145
IInventoryWriteContext	145
InventoryCommandFactory	146
InventoryCommand	148
Implementation factory using a function	148
Using services	152
Using third-party containers	155
Summary	157
Questions	158
Chapter 6: Implementing Design Patterns for Web Applications - Part 1	159
Technical requirements	160
Installing Visual Studio	160
Setting up .NET Core	160
Installing SQL Server	161
Creating a .Net Core web application	161
Kicking off the project	161
Developing requirements	162
Crafting a web application	162
Web applications and how they work	163
Coding the web application	165
Implementing CRUD pages	170
Summary	181
Questions	182
Further reading	182
Chapter 7: Implementing Design Patterns for Web Applications - Part 2	183
Technical requirements	183
Installing Visual Studio	184
Setting up .NET Core	184
Installing SQL Server	184
Extending the .NET Core web application	185
Project kickoff	185
Requirements	185
Business requirements	185
Technical requirements	186
Challenges	186
Challenges for developers	186
Challenges for businesses	187
Finding a solution to the problems/challenges	187
Authentication and authorization	188
Authentication in action	193
Why does it make a difference?	203
Authorization in action	204
Creating a web test project	212
Summary	218
Questions	218

Table of Contents

Further reading	218

Section 3: Functional Programming, Reactive Programming, and Coding for the Cloud

Chapter 8: Concurrent Programming in .NET Core	**221**
Technical requirements	222
Installing Visual Studio	222
Setting up .NET Core	222
Installing SQL Server	223
Concurrency in the real world	223
Multithreading and asynchronous programming	225
Async/Await – why is blocking bad?	228
Concurrent collections	230
Patterns and practices – TDD and Parallel LINQ	231
Summary	239
Questions	239
Further reading	239
Chapter 9: Functional Programming Practices	**241**
Technical requirements	242
Installing Visual Studio	242
Setting up .NET Core	242
Installing SQL Server	243
Understanding functional programming	243
Enhancing our inventory application	249
Requirements	249
Back to FlixOne	250
Strategy pattern and functional programming	256
Summary	258
Questions	258
Chapter 10: Reactive Programming Patterns and Techniques	**259**
Technical requirements	260
Installing Visual Studio	260
Setting up .NET Core	261
Installing SQL Server	261
The principles of reactive programming	261
Be reactive with reactive programming	263
Reactive streams in action	265
Reactive and IObservable	271
Observer pattern – implementation using IObservable<T>	272
Reactive extensions – .NET Rx extensions	280
Inventory application use case	282
Starting the project	282

[v]

Requirements	282
Business requirements	282
Getting inventory with a filter, paging, and sorting	283
Patterns and Practices – MVVM	292
Implementation of MVVM	294
Summary	301
Questions	302
Further reading	302
Chapter 11: Advanced Database Design and Application Techniques	303
Technical requirements	304
Installing Visual Studio	304
Setting up .NET Core	304
Installing SQL Server	304
Use case discussion	305
Project kickoff	305
Requirements	306
Business requirements	306
Technical requirements	307
Challenges	307
Challenges for developers	307
Challenges for businesses	308
Providing a solution to the problems/challenges	308
Database discussion	308
Database processing	309
OLTP	309
OLAP	310
Ledger-style databases	311
Implementing the CQRS pattern	313
Summary	331
Questions	332
Chapter 12: Coding for the Cloud	333
Technical requirements	334
Key considerations when building solutions in the cloud	334
Scalability	335
Workload	335
Solution patterns	336
Vertical scaling	336
Horizontal scaling	337
Auto-scaling	339
Microservices	340
Small	340
Business capability	341
Loosely coupled	341
Independently maintainable	342
Isolated state	342
Advantages	343

Resiliency/availability	344
Solution pattern	345
EDA	345
Queue-Based Load Leveling	345
Publisher Subscriber	346
Priority Queue	347
Compensating transaction	347
Security	348
Solution patterns	349
Federated security	349
Application design	350
Solution patterns	350
Cache	350
Cache-aside	351
Write-through cache	351
Static Content Hosting	352
Command and Query Responsibility Segregation	352
Challenges of CQRS	354
Why CQRS?	355
DevOps	355
Solution patterns	356
Telemetry	356
Continuous integration/continuous deployment	356
Summary	358
Questions	359
Further reading	360
Appendix A: Miscellaneous Best Practices	361
Technical requirements	361
Installation of Visual Studio	362
Use case discussion	362
UML diagram	364
Types of UML diagram	364
Best practices	365
Other design patterns	367
Summary	368
Questions	368
Further reading	369
Appendix B: Assessments	371
Chapter 1 – Overview of OOP in .NET Core and C#	371
Chapter 2 – Modern Software Design Patterns and Principles	372
Chapter 3 – Implementing Design Patterns – Basics Part 1	373
Chapter 4 – Implementing Design Patterns – Basics Part 2	374
Chapter 5 – Implementing Design Patterns – .NET Core	375
Chapter 6 – Implementing Design Patterns for Web Applications – Part 1	375

Table of Contents

Chapter 7 – Implementing Design Patterns for Web Applications – Part 2 — 376
Chapter 8 – Concurrent Programming in .NET Core — 377
Chapter 9 – Functional Programming Practices – an Approach — 378
Chapter 10 – Reactive Programming Patterns and Techniques — 379
Chapter 11 – Advanced Database Design and Application Techniques — 380
Chapter 12 – Coding for the Cloud — 381
Appendix A – Miscellaneous Best Practices — 382

Other Books You May Enjoy — 383

Index — 387

Preface

The purpose of this book is to give readers a broad understanding of patterns in modern software development while diving into more detail with specific examples. The number of patterns used when developing solutions is vast, and often, developers use patterns without knowing they are doing so. This book covers patterns from low-level code, to high-level concepts used in solutions that run in the cloud.

Though many of the patterns presented do not require a specific language, C# and .NET Core will be used to illustrate examples for many of them. C# and .NET Core were chosen due to their popularity and design, which supports building solutions from simple console applications to large-enterprise distributed systems.

Covering a large number of patterns, the book serves as a great introduction to many of them, while allowing a deeper, hands-on approach to a selected collection. The specific patterns covered have been selected as they illustrate a specific point or aspect of patterns. References to additional resources are provided to allow the reader to dive deeper into patterns of particular interest.

From simple websites to large-enterprise distributed systems, the right pattern can make the difference between a successful, long-lived solution and a solution viewed as a failure due to its poor performance and high cost. This book covers many patterns that can be applied to build solutions that handle the inevitable change required to stay competitive in business, as well as achieve the robustness and reliability expected of modern applications.

Who this book is for

The target audience is modern application developers working in a collaborative environment. Intentionally, this represents a great number of backgrounds and industries as the patterns can be applied to a wide range of solutions. As this book dives into the code to explain the patterns covered, readers should have a background in software development—this book should not be viewed as a *how to program* book but more of a *how to program **better*** book. Because of this, the target audience will range from junior developers to senior developers, to software architects and designers. For some readers, the content will be new; for others, it will be a refresher.

Preface

What this book covers

Chapter 1, *Overview of OOP in .NET Core and C#*, contains an overview of **Object-oriented-programming** (**OOP**) and how it applies to C#. This chapter serves as a refresher of the important constructs and features of OOP and C#, including inheritance, encapsulation, and polymorphism.

Chapter 2, *Modern Software Design Patterns and Principles*, catalogs and introduces different patterns used in modern software development. This chapter investigates a number of patterns and catalogs, such as SOLID, Gang of Four, and enterprise integration patterns, as well as a discussion of the software development lifecycle and other practices for software development.

Chapter 3, *Implementing Design Patterns - Basics Part 1*, deep dives into design patterns used to build applications in C#. Using the development of an example application, test-driven development, minimum viable product, and other patterns from the Gang of Four will be illustrated.

Chapter 4, *Implementing Design Patterns - Basics Part 2*, continues the deep dive into design patterns used to build applications in C#. The concepts of Dependency Injection and Inversion of Control will be introduced as well, continuing to explore design patterns including the Singleton and Factory patterns.

Chapter 5, *Implementing Design Patterns - .NET Core*, builds upon chapters 3 and 4 by exploring patterns provided by the .NET Core. Several patterns, including Dependency Injection and the Factory pattern, will be revisited using the .NET Core framework.

Chapter 6, *Implementing Design Patterns for Web Applications - Part 1*, continues to explore .NET Core by looking at the features supported in web application development by continuing to build the sample application. This chapter offers guidance on creating an initial web application, discusses the important characteristics of a web application, and introduces how to create CRUD website pages.

Chapter 7, *Implementing Design Patterns for Web Applications - Part 2*, continues the exploration of web application development using .NET Core by looking at different architectural patterns, as well as solution security patterns. Authentication and authorization are covered as well. Unit tests are added including using the Moq mocking framework.

Chapter 8, *Concurrent Programming in .NET Core*, dives deeper into web application development to discuss concurrency in C# and .NET Core application development. The Async/await pattern is explored, as well as a section about multithreading and concurrency. Parallel LINQ is also covered, including delayed execution and thread priorities.

Chapter 9, *Functional Programming Practices*, explores functional programming in .NET Core. This includes illustrating the C# language features that support functional programming and applying them to the sample application, including applying the strategy pattern.

Chapter 10, *Reactive Programming Patterns and Techniques*, continues to build upon .NET Core web application development by exploring reactive programming patterns and techniques used to build responsive and scalable websites. In this chapter, the principles of reactive programming are explored, including the Reactive and IObservable patterns. Different frameworks are also discussed, including the popular .NET Rx Extensions, as well as an illustration of the **Model-view-viewmodel** (**MVVM**) pattern.

Chapter 11, *Advanced Database Design and Application Techniques*, explores patterns used in database design, including a discussion of databases. A practical example of applying the Command Query Responsibility Segregation pattern is shown, including using a ledger-style database design.

Chapter 12, *Coding for the Cloud*, looks at application development as it applies to cloud-based solutions, including the five key concerns of scalability, availability, security, application design, and DevOps. Significant patterns used in cloud-based solutions are explained, including different types of scaling, and patterns used in event-driven architecture, federated security, cache, and telemetry.

Appendix A, *Miscellaneous Best Practices*, wraps up the discussion of patterns by covering additional patterns and best practices. This includes a section about use case modeling, best practices, and additional patterns such as space-based architecture and containerized applications.

To get the most out of this book

This book does assume some familiarity with OOP and C#. Though this book covers advanced topics, it is not designed to be a comprehensive development guide. Instead, the goal of the book is to advance the skill levels of developers and designers by providing a wide array of patterns, practices, and principles. Using a toolbox analogy, the book provides a large number of tools for the modern application developer by progressing from low-level code design to higher-level architecture, as well as important patterns and principles commonly used today.

This book brought the following main points that are additions to readers knowledge:

- To know more about SOLID Principles, best practices with the help of coding examples using C#7.x and .NET Core 2.2.
- In-depth understanding of classic design pattern (Gang of four patterns).
- Functional programming principle and its working examples using C# language.
- Real world examples of Architectural patterns (MVC, MVVM).
- Understanding of native cloud, microservices and more.

Download the example code files

You can download the example code files for this book from your account at `www.packt.com`. If you purchased this book elsewhere, you can visit `www.packt.com/support` and register to have the files emailed directly to you.

You can download the code files by following these steps:

1. Log in or register at `www.packt.com`.
2. Select the **SUPPORT** tab.
3. Click on **Code Downloads & Errata**.
4. Enter the name of the book in the **Search** box and follow the onscreen instructions.

Once the file is downloaded, please make sure that you unzip or extract the folder using the latest version of:

- WinRAR/7-Zip for Windows
- Zipeg/iZip/UnRarX for Mac
- 7-Zip/PeaZip for Linux

Preface

The code bundle for the book is also hosted on GitHub at `https://github.com/PacktPublishing/Hands-On-Design-Patterns-with-C-and-.NET-Core`. In case there's an update to the code, it will be updated on the existing GitHub repository.

We also have other code bundles from our rich catalog of books and videos available at `https://github.com/PacktPublishing/`. Check them out!

Code in Action

Click on the following link to see the Code in Action: `http://bit.ly/2KUuNgQ`.

Download the color images

We also provide a PDF file that has color images of the screenshots/diagrams used in this book. You can download it here: `https://static.packt-cdn.com/downloads/9781789133646_ColorImages.pdf`.

Conventions used

There are a number of text conventions used throughout this book.

`CodeInText`: Indicates code words in text, database table names, folder names, filenames, file extensions, pathnames, dummy URLs, user input, and Twitter handles. Here is an example: "The three `CounterA()`, `CounterB()`, and `CounterC()` methods represent an individual ticket collection counter."

A block of code is set as follows:

```
3-counters are serving...
Next person from row
Person A is collecting ticket from Counter A
Person B is collecting ticket from Counter B
Person C is collecting ticket from Counter C
```

Preface

When we wish to draw your attention to a particular part of a code block, the relevant lines or items are set in bold:

```
public bool UpdateQuantity(string name, int quantity)
{
    lock (_lock)
    {
        _books[name].Quantity += quantity;
    }

    return true;
}
```

Any command-line input or output is written as follows:

```
dotnet new sln
```

Bold: Indicates a new term, an important word, or words that you see onscreen. For example, words in menus or dialog boxes appear in the text like this. Here is an example: "From **Create New Product**, you can add a new product, and **Edit** will give you the facility to update an existing product."

> Warnings or important notes appear like this.

> Tips and tricks appear like this.

Get in touch

Feedback from our readers is always welcome.

General feedback: If you have questions about any aspect of this book, mention the book title in the subject of your message and email us at customercare@packtpub.com.

Errata: Although we have taken every care to ensure the accuracy of our content, mistakes do happen. If you have found a mistake in this book, we would be grateful if you would report this to us. Please visit www.packt.com/submit-errata, selecting your book, clicking on the Errata Submission Form link, and entering the details.

Piracy: If you come across any illegal copies of our works in any form on the Internet, we would be grateful if you would provide us with the location address or website name. Please contact us at `copyright@packt.com` with a link to the material.

If you are interested in becoming an author: If there is a topic that you have expertise in and you are interested in either writing or contributing to a book, please visit `authors.packtpub.com`.

Reviews

Please leave a review. Once you have read and used this book, why not leave a review on the site that you purchased it from? Potential readers can then see and use your unbiased opinion to make purchase decisions, we at Packt can understand what you think about our products, and our authors can see your feedback on their book. Thank you!

For more information about Packt, please visit `packt.com`.

Section 1: Essentials of Design Patterns in C# and .NET Core

In this section, readers will gain a new perspective on design patterns. We will learn about OOP, patterns, practices, and SOLID principles. By the end of this section, readers will be ready to create their own design patterns.

This section consists of the following chapters:

- `Chapter 1`, *Overview of OOP in .NET Core and C#*
- `Chapter 2`, *Modern Software Design Patterns and Principles*

Overview of OOP in .NET Core and C#

For over 20 years, the most popular programming languages have been based on the principles of **object-oriented programming** (**OOP**). The rise in popularity of OOP languages is largely to do with the benefits of being able to abstract complex logic into a structure, called an object, that can be more easily explained, and, more importantly, reused within an application. In essence, OOP is a software design approach, that is, a pattern for developing software using the concept of objects that contain data and functionality. As the software industry matured, patterns appeared in OOP for commonly occurring problems, as they were effective in solving the same problems but across different contexts and industries. As software moved from the mainframe to client servers and then to the cloud, additional patterns have emerged to help in reducing development costs and improving reliability. This book will explore design patterns, from the foundation of OOP to the architecture design patterns for cloud-based software.

> OOP is based on the concept of an object. This object generally contains data, referred to as properties and fields, and code or behavior referred to as methods.

Design patterns are solutions to general problems that software programmers face during development, and are built from the experience of what works and what doesn't. These solutions are trialed and tested by numerous developers in various situations. The benefits of using a pattern based on this previous activity ensure that the same efforts are not repeated again and again. In addition to this, using a pattern adds a sense of reliability that the problem will be solved without introducing a defect or issue.

Overview of OOP in .NET Core and C#

This chapter reviews OOP and how it applies to C#. Note that this is simply intended as a brief introduction and it is not meant to be a complete primer for OOP or C#; instead, the chapter will cover aspects of both in enough detail to introduce you to the design patterns that will be covered in subsequent chapters. This chapter will cover the following topics:

- A discussion of OOP and how classes and objects work
- Inheritance
- Encapsulation
- Polymorphism

Technical requirements

This chapter contains various code examples to explain these concepts. The code is kept simple and is just for demonstration purposes. Most of the examples involve a .NET Core console application written in C#.

To run and execute the code, you will need the following:

- Visual Studio 2019 (you can also run the application using Visual Studio 2017 version 3 or later)
- .NET Core
- SQL Server (the Express Edition is used in this chapter)

Installing Visual Studio

In order to run these code examples, you will need to install Visual Studio or later (you can also use your preferred IDE). To do this, follow these instructions:

1. Download Visual Studio from the following link: `https://docs.microsoft.com/en-us/visualstudio/install/install-visual-studio`.
2. Follow the installation instructions included in the link. Multiple versions of Visual Studio are available; in this chapter, we are using Visual Studio for Windows.

Setting up .NET Core

If you do not have .NET Core installed, you will need to follow these instructions:

1. Download .NET Core from the following link: https://www.microsoft.com/net/download/windows.
2. Follow the installation instructions in the related library: https://dotnet.microsoft.com/download/dotnet-core/2.2.

> The complete source code is available in GitHub. The source code shown in the chapter might not be complete, so it is recommended that you retrieve the source code in order to run the examples (https://github.com/PacktPublishing/Hands-On-Design-Patterns-with-C-and-.NET-Core/tree/master/Chapter1).

The models used in this book

As a learning aid, this book will contain many code samples in C# alongside diagrams and images to help describe specific concepts where possible. This is not a **Unified Modeling Language** (**UML**) book; however, for those with a knowledge of UML, many of the diagrams should seem familiar. This section provides a description of the class diagrams that will be used in this book.

Here, a class will be defined as including both fields and methods separated by a dashed line. If important to the discussion, then accessibility will be indicated as - for private, + for public, # for protected, and ~ for internal. The following screenshot illustrates this by showing a Car class with a private _name variable and a public GetName() method:

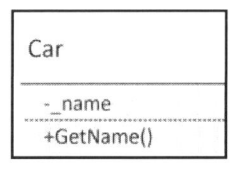

Car
-_name
+GetName()

Overview of OOP in .NET Core and C#

When showing relationships between objects, an association is shown with a solid line, an aggregation is shown with an open diamond, and a composition is shown with a filled diamond. When important to the discussion, multiplicity will be shown next to the class in question. The following diagram illustrates the `Car` class as having a single **Owner**, and up to three **Passengers**; it consists of four **Wheels**:

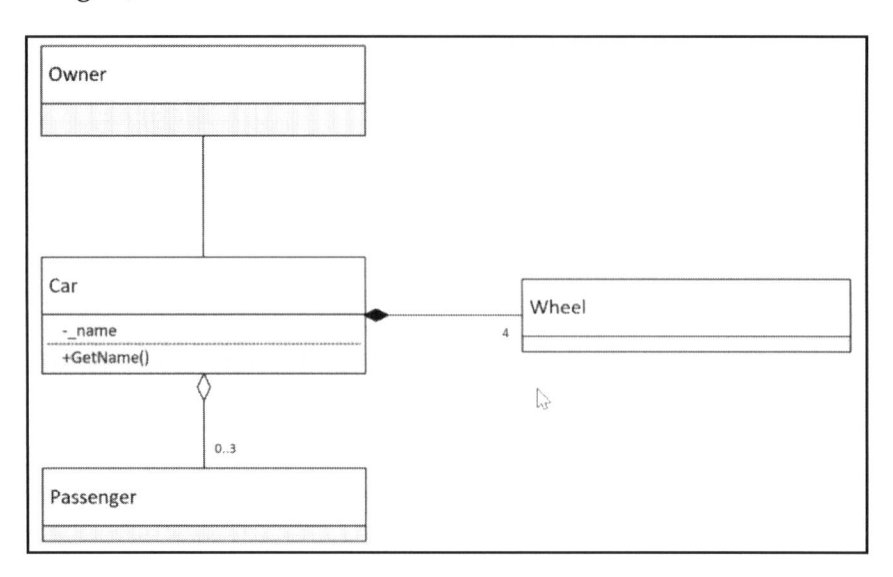

Inheritance is shown using an open triangle on the base class using a solid line. The following diagram shows the relationship between an `Account` base class and the `CheckingAccount` and `SavingsAccount` child classes:

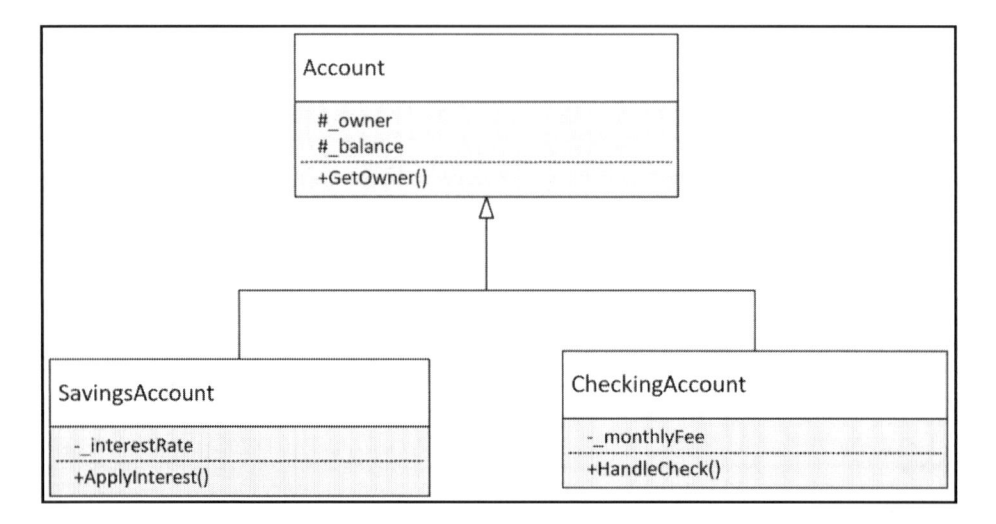

Interfaces are shown in a similar manner to inheritance, but they use a dashed line as well as an additional <<interface>> label, as shown in the following diagram:

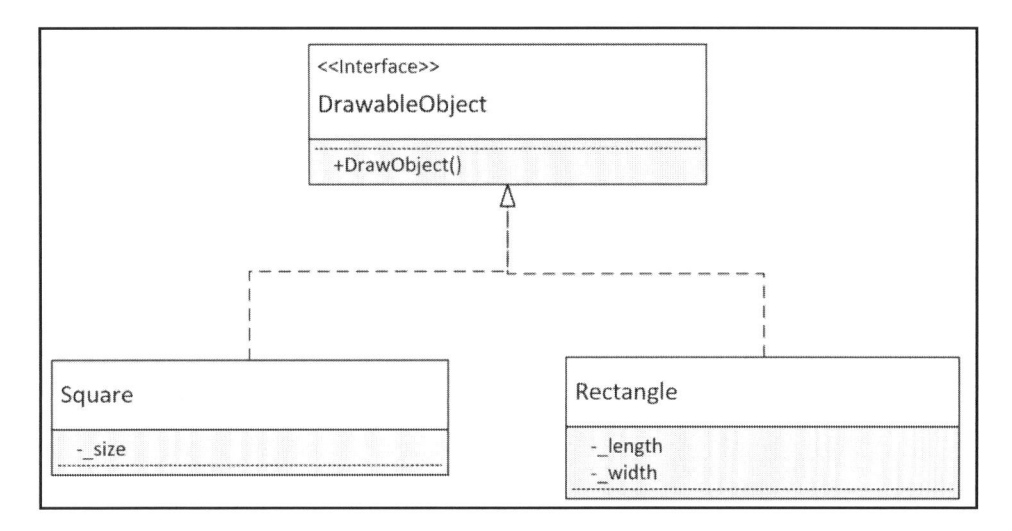

This section provides an overview of the models used in this book. This style/approach was chosen because, hopefully, it will be familiar to the majority of readers.

OOP and how classes and objects work

OOP refers to a software programming approach that uses objects defined as classes. These definitions include fields, sometimes called attributes, to store data and methods in order to provide functionality. The first OOP language was a simulation of real systems known as Simula (https://en.wikipedia.org/wiki/Simula) and was developed at the Norwegian Computing Center in 1960. The first pure OOP language came into existence in 1970 as the Smalltalk (https://en.wikipedia.org/wiki/Smalltalk) language. This language was designed to program the Dynabook (http://history-computer.com/ModernComputer/Personal/Dynabook.html), which is a personal computer created by Alan Kay. Several OOP languages evolved from there, with the most popular being Java, C++, Python, and C#.

> OOP is based on objects that contain data. The OOP paradigm allows developers to arrange/organize code into an abstract or logical structure called an object. An object can contain both data and behavior.

With the use of the OOP approach, we are doing the following:

- **Modularizing**: Here, an application is decomposed into different modules.
- **Reusing the software**: Here, we rebuild or compose an application from different (that is, existing or new) modules.

In the following sections, we will discuss and understand the concepts of OOP in more detail.

Explaining OOP

Earlier, programming approaches had limitations and they often became difficult to maintain. OOP offered a new paradigm in software development that had advantages over other approaches. The concept of organizing code into objects is not difficult to explain and this is a huge advantage for the adoption of a new pattern. Many examples can be taken from the real world in order to explain the concept. Complex systems can also be described using smaller building blocks (that is, an *objects*). These allow developers to look at sections of the solution individually while understanding how they fit into the entire solution.

With this in mind, let's define a program as follows:

> *"A program is a list of instructions that instructs the language compiler on what to do."*

As you can see, an object is a way of organizing a list of instructions in a logical manner. Going back to the example of the house, the architect's instructions help us to build a house, but they are not the house itself. Instead the architect's instructions are an abstract representation of a house. A class is similar as it defines the features of an object. An object is then created from the definition of a class. This is often called **instantiating the object**.

To understand OOP more closely, we should mention two other significant programming approaches:

- **Structured programming**: This is a term coined by Edsger W. Dijkstra in 1966. Structured programming is a programming paradigm that solves a problem to handle 1,000 lines of code and divides these into small parts. These small parts are mostly called **subroutines**, **block structures**, **for** and **while** loops, and more. Languages that use structured programming techniques include ALGOL, Pascal, PL/I, and more.
- **Procedural programming**: This is a paradigm derived from structured programming and is simply based on how we make a call (also known as a **procedural call**). Languages that use procedural programming techniques include COBOL, Pascal, and C. A recent example of the Go programming language was published in 2009.

> **Procedural calls**
> A procedural call is where a collection of statements, known as a *procedure*, is activated. This is sometimes referred to as a procedure that is *invoked*.

The main problem with these two approaches is that programs are not easily manageable once they grow. Programs with more complex and larger code bases strain these two approaches, leading to difficult-to-understand and difficult-to-maintain applications. To overcome such problems, OOP provides the following features:

- Inheritance
- Encapsulation
- Polymorphism

In the following sections, we will discuss these features in more detail.

> Inheritance, encapsulation, and polymorphism are sometimes referred to as the three pillars of OOP.

Before we begin, let's discuss some structures that are found in OOP.

A class

A **class** is a group or template definition of the methods and variables that describe an object. In other words, a class is a blueprint, containing the definition of the variables and the methods that are common to all instances of the class called objects.

Let's take a look at the following code example:

```
public class PetAnimal
{
    private readonly string PetName;
    private readonly PetColor PetColor;

    public PetAnimal(string petName, PetColor petColor)
    {
        PetName = petName;
        PetColor = petColor;
    }

    public string MyPet() => $"My pet is {PetName} and its color is {PetColor}.";
}
```

In the preceding code, we have a `PetAnimal` class that has two private fields called `PetName` and `PetColor`, and one method called `MyPet()`.

An object

In the real world, objects share two characteristics, that is, state and behavior. In other words, we can say that every object has a name, color, and more; these characteristics are simply the state of an object. Let's take the example of any type of pet: a dog and a cat will both have a name by which they called. So, in this way, my dog is named Ace and my cat is named Clementine. Similarly, dogs and cats have specific behaviors, for example, dogs barks and cats meow.

In the *Explaining OOP* section, we discussed that OOP is a programming model that is supposed to combine a state or structure (data) and the behavior (method) to deliver software functionality. In the previous example, the different states of pets make up the actual data, while the behavior of the pets is the method.

Chapter 1

> An object stores the information (which is simply data) in attributes and discloses its behavior through methods.

In terms of an OOP language such as C#, an object is an instance of a class. In our previous example, the real-world object, Dog, would be an object of the PetAnimal class.

> **TIP**: Objects can be concrete (that is, a real-world object, such as a dog or cat, or any type of file, such as physical file or a computer file) or they can be conceptual, such as database schemas or code blueprints.

The following code snippet shows how an object contains data and a method, and how you can use it:

```
namespace OOPExample
{
    class Program
    {
        static void Main(string[] args)
        {
            Console.WriteLine("OOP example");
            PetAnimal dog = new PetAnimal("Ace", PetColor.Black);
            Console.WriteLine(dog.MyPet());
            Console.ReadLine();
            PetAnimal cat = new PetAnimal("Clementine", PetColor.Brown);
            Console.WriteLine(cat.MyPet());
            Console.ReadLine();
        }
    }
}
```

In the previous code snippet, we have created two objects: dog and cat. These objects are two different instances of a PetAnimal class. You can see that the fields or properties that contain data about the animal are given values using the constructor method. The constructor method is a special method used to create an instance of the class.

Let's visualize this example in the following diagram:

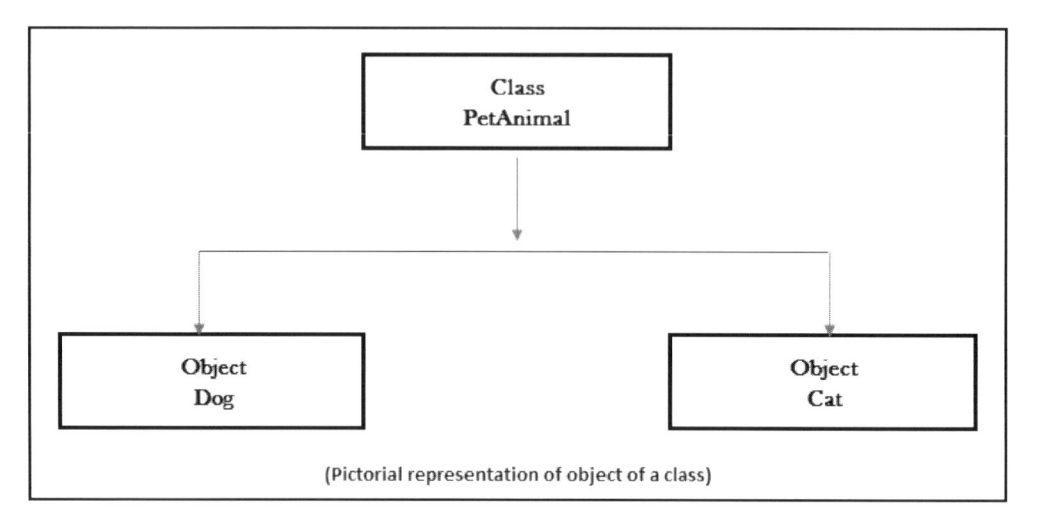

(Pictorial representation of object of a class)

The preceding diagram is a pictorial representation of our previous code example, where we created two different `Dog` and `Cat` objects of the `PetAnimal` class. The diagram is relatively self-explanatory; it tells us that the object of `Dog` class is an instance of the `PetAnimal` class, as is the `Cat` object.

Associations

Object associations are an important feature of OOP. Relationships exist between objects in the real world, and, in OOP, an association allows us to define a *has-a* relationship; for example, a bicycle *has a* rider or a cat *has a* nose.

The types of *has-a* relationship are as follows:

- **Association**: An association is used to describe a relationship between objects so that there is no ownership described, for example, the relationship between a car and a person. The car and person have a relationship described, such as a driver. A person can drive multiple cars and a car can be driven by multiple people.
- **Aggregation**: An aggregation is a specialized form of association. Similar to associations, objects have their own life cycle in aggregations, but it involves ownership. This means that a child object cannot belong to another parent object. Aggregation is a one-way relationship where the lives of the objects are independent from each other. For example, the child and parent relationship is an aggregation, because every child has a parent but it's not necessary that every parent has a child.

- **Composition**: A composition refers to a relationship of death; it represents the relationship between two objects where one object (child) depends on another object (parent). If the parent object is deleted, all its children automatically get deleted. Let's consider a house and a room as an example. One house has multiple rooms, but a single room cannot belong to multiple houses. If we demolished the house, the rooms will automatically be deleted.

Let's illustrate these concepts in C# by extending the previous pet example and introducing a `PetOwner` class. The `PetOwner` class could be associated with one or more `PetAnimal` instances. As the `PetAnimal` class can exist with or without having an owner, the relationship is an aggregation. `PetAnimal` is related to `PetColor` and, in this system, `PetColor` only exists if it is related to `PetAnimal`, making the association a composition.

The following diagram illustrates both aggregation and composition:

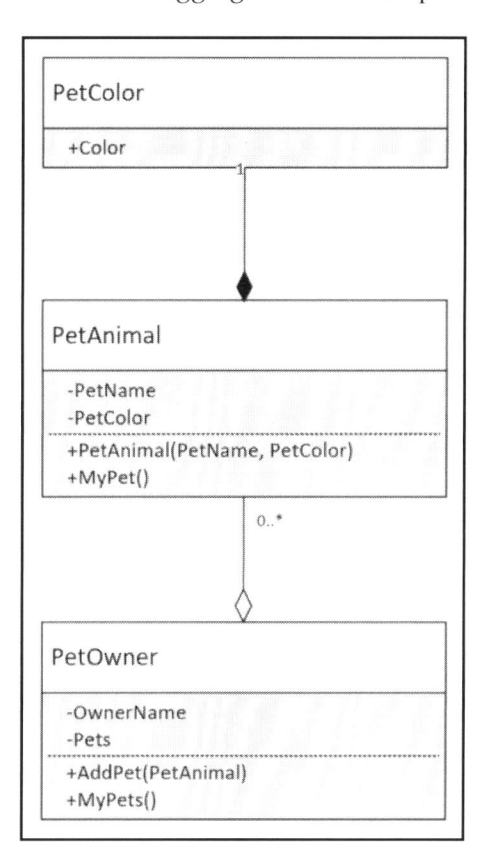

Overview of OOP in .NET Core and C#

The preceding model is based on UML and might not be familiar to you; so, let's point out some important things about the diagram. The class is represented by a box containing the class name as well as its attributes and methods (separated by a dashed line). For now, ignore the symbol before the name, for example, + or –, as we will cover access modifiers when we discuss encapsulation later. The associations are shown with a line connecting the classes. In the case of compositions, a solid diamond on the side of the parent is used, whereas an open diamond on the side of the parent is used to show aggregations. Additionally, note that the diagram supports a multiplicity value that indicates the number of possible children. In the diagram, a `PetOwner` class can have 0 or more `PetAnimal` classes (note that * indicates no enforced limit to the number of associations).

> **UML**
> The UML is a modeling language specifically developed for software engineering. It was developed over 20 years and is managed by the **Object Management Group** (**OMG**). You can refer to http://www.uml.org/ for more details.

An interface

In C#, an **interface** defines what an object contains, or its contract; in particular, the methods, properties, events, or indices of the object. However, the interface does not provide implementation. Interfaces cannot contain attributes. This is in contrast to a base class, where the base class provides both the contract and the implementation. A class that implements an interface must implement everything specified in the interface.

> **An abstract class**
> An abstract class is a bit of a hybrid between the interface and base class as it provides both implementations and attributes as well as methods that must be defined in the child classes.
>
> **Signature**
> The term *signature* can also be used to describe the contract of an object.

[22]

Inheritance

One of the most important concepts in OOP is inheritance. Inheritance between classes allows us to define an *is-a-type-of relationship*; for example, a car *is a type of* vehicle. The importance of this concept is that it allows for objects of the same type to share similar features. Let's say that we have a system for managing different products of an online bookstore. We might have one class for storing information about a physical book and a different one for storing information about a digital or online book. The features that are similar between the two, such as the name, publisher, and author, could be stored in another class. Both the physical and digital book classes could then inherit from the other class.

> There are different terms to describe classes in inheritance: a *child* or *derived* class inherits from another class while the class being inherited from can be called the *parent* or *base* class.

In the following sections, we will discuss inheritance in more detail.

Types of inheritance

Inheritance helps us to define a child class. This child class inherits the behavior of the parent or base class.

> In C#, inheritance is symbolically defined using a colon (:).

Let's take a look at the different types of inheritance:

- **Single inheritance**: As the most common type of inheritance, single inheritance describes a single class that is is derived from another class.

Let's revisit the `PetAnimal` class previously mentioned and, instead, use inheritance to define our `Dog` and `Cat` classes. With inheritance, we can define some attributes that are common for both. For example, the name of the pet and the color of the pet would be common, so they would be located in a base class. The specifics of a cat or a dog would then be defined in a specific class; for example, the sound the cat and dog make. The following diagram illustrates a `PetAnimal` base class with two child classes:

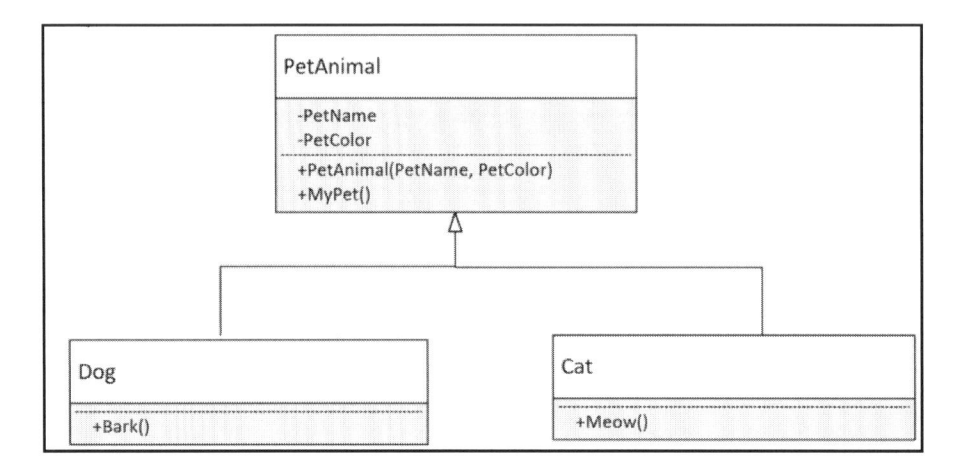

```
                    ┌─────────────────────────────────┐
                    │         PetAnimal               │
                    ├─────────────────────────────────┤
                    │ -PetName                        │
                    │ -PetColor                       │
                    ├─────────────────────────────────┤
                    │ +PetAnimal(PetName, PetColor)   │
                    │ +MyPet()                        │
                    └─────────────────────────────────┘
                                   △
                    ┌──────────────┴──────────────┐
        ┌───────────────────┐           ┌───────────────────┐
        │       Dog         │           │       Cat         │
        ├───────────────────┤           ├───────────────────┤
        │ +Bark()           │           │ +Meow()           │
        └───────────────────┘           └───────────────────┘
```

> **TIP**: C# only supports single inheritance.

- **Multiple inheritance**: Multiple inheritance happens when a derived class inherits multiple base classes. Languages such as C++ support multiple inheritance. C# does not support multiple inheritance, but we can achieve behaviors similar to multiple inheritance with the help of interfaces.

  > You can refer to the following post for more information about C# and multiple inheritance:
  > https://blogs.msdn.microsoft.com/csharpfaq/2004/03/07/why-doesnt-c-supportmultiple-inheritance/.

- **Hierarchical inheritance**: Hierarchical inheritance happens when more than one class inherits from another class.
- **Multilevel inheritance**: When a class is derived from a class that is already a derived class, it is called multilevel inheritance.
- **Hybrid inheritance**: Hybrid inheritance is a combination of more than one inheritance.

> C# does not support hybrid inheritance.

- **Implicit inheritance**: All the types in .NET Core implicitly inherit from the `System.Object` class and its derived classes.

Encapsulation

Encapsulation is another fundamental concept in OOP where the details of a class, that is, the attributes and methods, can be visible or not visible outside the object. With encapsulation, a developer is providing guidance on how a class should be used as well as helping to prevent a class from being handled incorrectly. For example, let's say we wanted to only allow adding `PetAnimal` objects by using the `AddPet(PetAnimal)` method. We would do this by having the `PetOwner` class's `AddPet(PetAnimal)` method available while having the `Pets` attribute restricted to anything outside the `PetAnimal` class. In C#, this is possible by making the `Pets` attribute private. One reason for doing this would be if additional logic was required whenever a `PetAnimal` class was added, such as logging or validating that the `PetOwner` class could have a pet.

C# supports different levels of access that can be set on an item. An item could be a class, a class's attribute or method, or an enumeration:

- **Public**: This indicates that access is available outside the item.
- **Private**: This indicates that only the object has access to the item.
- **Protected**: This indicates that only the object (and objects of classes that extended the class) can access the attribute or method.
- **Internal**: This indicates that only objects within the same assembly have access to the item.
- **Protected Internal**: This indicates that only the object (and objects of classes that extended the class) can access the attribute or method within the same assembly.

In the following diagram, access modifiers have been applied to `PetAnimal`:

```
┌─────────────────────────────────┐
│          PetAnimal              │
├─────────────────────────────────┤
│  -PetName                       │
│  -PetColor                      │
├─────────────────────────────────┤
│  #PetAnimal(PetName, PetColor)  │
│  +MyPet()                       │
└─────────────────────────────────┘
                △
        ┌───────┴───────┐
┌───────────────────────────────┐   ┌───────────────────────────────┐
│            Dog                │   │            Cat                │
├───────────────────────────────┤   ├───────────────────────────────┤
│ +PetAnimal(PetName, PetColor) │   │ +PetAnimal(PetName, PetColor) │
│ +Bark()                       │   │ +Meow()                       │
│ ~RegisterInObedienceSchool()  │   └───────────────────────────────┘
└───────────────────────────────┘
```

As an example, the name of the pet and the color were made private to prevent access from outside the `PetAnimal` class. In this example, we are restricting the `PetName` and `PetColor` properties so only the `PetAnimal` class can access them in order to ensure that only the base class, `PetAnimal`, can change their values. The constructor of `PetAnimal` was protected to ensure only a child class could access it. In this application, only classes within the same library as the `Dog` class have access to the `RegisterInObedienceSchool()` method.

Polymorphism

The ability to handle different objects using the same interface is called polymorphism. This provides developers with the ability to build flexibility into applications by writing a single piece of functionality that can be applied to different forms as long as they share a common interface. There are different definitions of polymorphism in OOP, and we will distinguish between two main types:

- **Static or early binding**: This form of polymorphism happens when the application is compiled.
- **Dynamic or late binding**: This form of polymorphism happens when the application is running.

Static polymorphism

Static or early binding polymorphism happens at compile time and it primarily consists of method overloading, where a class has multiple methods with the same name but with different parameters. This is often useful to convey a meaning behind the method or to simplify the code. For example, in a calculator, it is more readable to have multiple methods for adding different types of number rather than having a different method name for each scenario; let's compare the following code:

```
int Add(int a, int b) => a + b;
float Add(float a, float b) => a + b;
decimal Add(decimal a, decimal b) => a + b;
```

In the following, the code is shown again with the same functionality, but without overloading the `Add()` method:

```
int AddTwoIntegers(int a, int b) => a + b;
float AddTwoFloats(float a, float b) => a + b;
decimal AddTwoDecimals(decimal a, decimal b) => a + b;
```

In the pet example, an owner will use different food to feed objects of the `cat` and `dog` class. We can define this as the `PetOwner` class with two methods for `Feed()`, as follows:

```
public void Feed(PetDog dog)
{
    PetFeeder.FeedPet(dog, new Kibble());
}

public void Feed(PetCat cat)
{
    PetFeeder.FeedPet(cat, new Fish());
}
```

Both methods use a `PetFeeder` class to feed the pet, while the `dog` class is given `Kibble` and the `cat` instance is given `Fish`. The `PetFeeder` class is described in the *Generics* section.

Dynamic polymorphism

Dynamic or late binding polymorphism happens while the application is running. There are multiple situations where this can occur and we'll cover three common forms in C#: interface, inheritance, and generics.

Interface polymorphism

An interface defines the signature that a class must implement. In the `PetAnimal` example, imagine that we define pet food as providing an amount of energy, as follows:

```
public interface IPetFood
{
    int Energy { get; }
}
```

By itself, the interface cannot be instantiated but describes what an instance of `IPetFood` must implement. For example, `Kibble` and `Fish` might provide different levels of energy, as shown in the following code:

```
public class Kibble : IPetFood
{
    public int Energy => 7;
}

public class Fish : IPetFood
{
    int IPetFood.Energy => 8;
}
```

In the preceding code snippet, `Kibble` provides less energy than `Fish`.

Inheritance polymorphism

Inheritance polymorphism allows for functionality to be determined at runtime in a similar way to an interface but applies to class inheritance. In our example, a pet can be fed, so we can define this as having a new `Feed(IPetFood)` method, which uses the interface that was defined previously:

```
public virtual void Feed(IPetFood food)
{
    Eat(food);
}

protected void Eat(IPetFood food)
{
    _hunger -= food.Energy;
}
```

The preceding code indicates that all implementations of `PetAnimal` will have a `Feed(IPetFood)` method and child classes can provide a different implementation. `Eat(IPetFood food)` is not marked as virtual, as it is intended that all `PetAnimal` objects will use the method without needing to override its behavior. It is also marked as protected to prevent it being accessed from outside the object.

> **TIP**
> A virtual method does not have to be defined in a child class; this differs from an interface, where all methods in an interface must be implemented.

`PetDog` will not override the behavior of the base class as a dog will eat both `Kibble` and `Fish`. A cat is more discerning, as shown in the following code:

```
public override void Feed(IPetFood food)
{
    if (food is Fish)
    {
        Eat(food);
    }
    else
    {
        Meow();
    }
}
```

Using the override keyword, `PetCat` will change the behavior of the base class, resulting in a cat only eating fish.

Generics

A generic defines a behavior that can be applied to a class. A commonly used form of this is in collections, where the same approach to handling an object can be applied regardless of the type of object. For example, a list of strings or a list of integers can be handled using the same logic without having to differentiate between the specific types.

Going back to pets, we could define a generic class for feeding a pet. This class simply feeds a pet given both the pet and some food, as shown in the following code:

```
public static class PetFeeder
{
    public static void FeedPet<TP, TF>(TP pet, TF food) where TP : PetAnimal
                                                        where TF : IPetFood
```

```
        {
            pet.Feed(food);
        }
    }
```

There are a couple of interesting thing to point out here. First of all, the class does not have to be instantiated as both the class and method are marked as static. The generic method is described using the method signature, `FeedPet<TP, TF>`. The `where` keyword is used to indicate additional requirements as to what `TP` and `TF` must be. In this example, the `where` keyword defines `TP` as having to be a type of `PetAnimal`, while `TF` must implement the `IPetFood` interface.

Summary

In this chapter, we discussed OOP and its three main features: inheritance, encapsulation, and polymorphism. Using these features, the classes within an application can be abstracted to provide definitions that are both easy to understand and protected against being used in a manner that is inconsistent with its purpose. This is an essential difference between OOP and some earlier types of software development language such as structural and procedural programming. With the ability to abstract functionality, the ability to reuse and maintain code is increased.

In the next chapter, we will discuss various patterns used in enterprise software development. We will cover programming patterns as well as software development principles and patterns used in the **Software Development Life Cycle** (**SDLC**).

Questions

The following questions will allow you to consolidate the information contained in this chapter:

1. What do the terms late and early binding refer to?
2. Does C# support multiple inheritance?
3. In C#, what level of encapsulation could be used to prevent access to a class from outside the library?
4. What is the difference between aggregation and composition?
5. Can interfaces contain properties? (This is a bit of a trick question.)
6. Do dogs eat fish?

2
Modern Software Design Patterns and Principles

In the previous chapter, **object-oriented programming** (**OOP**) was discussed in preparation for exploring different patterns. As many patterns rely on concepts in OOP, it is important to introduce and/or revisit these concepts. Inheritance between classes allows us to define an *is-a-type-of relationship*. This provides a higher degree of abstraction. For example, with inheritance it is possible to perform comparisons such as a *cat* is a type of *animal* and a *dog* is a type of *animal*. Encapsulation provides a way of controlling the visibility and access of details of a class. Polymorphism provides the ability to handle different objects using the same interface. With OOP, a higher level of abstraction can be achieved, providing a more manageable and understandable way to deal with large solutions.

This chapter catalogs and introduces different patterns used in modern software development. This book takes a very broad view of what a pattern is. A pattern in software development is any solution to a general problem that software programmers face during development. They are built from experience on what works and what does not. Also, these solutions are trialed and tested by numerous developers in various situations. The benefit of using a pattern is based on this past activity both in not repeating the effort and in the assurance that the problem will be solved without introducing a defect or issue.

Especially when taking technology-specific patterns into consideration, there are too many to cover in a single book so this chapter will highlight specific patterns to illustrate different types of pattern. We have tried to pick out the commonest and most influential patterns based on our experience. In subsequent chapters, specific patterns will be explored in more detail.

The following topics will be covered in this chapter:

- Design principles, including SOLID
- Pattern catalogs, including **Gang of Four** (**GoF**) patterns and **Enterprise Integration Pattern** (**EIP**)
- Software development life cycle patterns
- Patterns and practices for solution development, cloud development, and service development

Technical requirements

This chapter contains various code examples to explain the concepts. The code is kept simple and is just for demonstration purposes. Most of the examples involve a .NET Core console application written in C#.

To run and execute the code, you need the following:

- Visual Studio 2019 (you can also run the application using Visual Studio 2017 version 3 or later)
- .NET Core
- SQL Server (the Express Edition is used in this chapter)

Installing Visual Studio

To run these code examples, you need to install Visual Studio or you can use your preferred IDE. To do this, follow these instructions:

1. Download Visual Studio from the following link: `https://docs.microsoft.com/en-us/visualstudio/install/install-visual-studio`.
2. Follow the installation instructions included. Multiple versions are available for Visual Studio installation. In this chapter, we are using Visual Studio for Windows.

Setting up .NET Core

If you do not have .NET Core installed, you need to follow these instructions:

1. Download .NET Core from the following link: https://www.microsoft.com/net/download/windows.
2. Follow the Installation instructions and related library: https://dotnet.microsoft.com/download/dotnet-core/2.2.

> The complete source code is available in GitHub. The source code shown in the chapter might not be complete so it is advisable to retrieve the source in order to run the examples: https://github.com/PacktPublishing/Hands-On-Design-Patterns-with-C-and-.NET-Core/tree/master/Chapter2.

Design principles

Arguably, the most important aspect of good software development is software design. Developing software solutions that are both functionally accurate and easy to maintain is challenging and relies considerably on using good development principles. Over time, some decisions that were made early in the project can cause solutions to become too costly to maintain and extend, forcing systems to be rewritten, while others with a good design can be extended and adapted as business requirements and technology change. There are many software development design principles and this section will highlight some popular and important ones you need to be familiar with.

DRY – Don't Repeat Yourself

The guiding thought behind the **Don't Repeat Yourself** (**DRY**) principle is that duplication is a waste of time and effort. The repetition could take the form of processes and code. Handling the same requirement multiple times is a waste of effort and creates confusion within a solution. When first viewing this principle, it might not be clear how a system could end up duplicating a process or code. For example, once someone has determined how to do a requirement, why would someone else take the effort to duplicate the same functionality? There are many circumstances in which this happens in software development, and understanding why this happens is key to understanding the value of this principle.

The following are some common causes of code duplication:

- **Lack of understanding**: In large solutions, a developer might not have a full understanding of an existing solution and/or does not know how to apply abstraction to solve the problem with existing functionality.
- **Copy and paste**: To put this simply, the code is duplicated in multiple classes instead of refactoring the solution to allow for multiple classes to access the shared functionality.

KISS – Keep It Simple Stupid

Similar to DRY, **Keep It Simple Stupid** (**KISS**) has been an important principle in software development for many years. KISS stresses that simplicity should be the goal and complexity should be avoided. The key here is to avoid unnecessary complexity and thus reduce the chances of things going wrong.

YAGNI – You Aren't Gonna Need It

You Aren't Gonna Need It (**YAGNI**) simply states that functionality should only be added when it is required. Sometimes in software development, there is a tendency to *futureproof* a design in case something changes. This can create requirements that are actually not needed currently or in the future:

> *"Always implement things when you actually need them, never when you just foresee that you need them."*

> *- Ron Jeffries*

MVP – Minimum Viable Product

By taking a **Minimum Viable Product** (**MVP**) approach, the scope of a piece of work is limited to the smallest set of requirements in order to produce a functioning deliverable. MVP is often combined with Agile software development (see the *Software development life cycle patterns* section later in the chapter) by limiting requirements to a manageable amount that can be designed, developed, tested, and delivered. This approach lends itself well to smaller website or application development, where a feature set can be progressed all the way to production in a single development cycle.

> In Chapter 3, *Implementing Design Patterns - Basics Part 1*, MVP will be illustrated in a fictitious scenario where the technique will be used to limit the scope of changes as well as to help the team focus during the design and requirement gathering phases.

SOLID

SOLID is one of the most influential design principles and we will cover it in more detail in Chapter 3, *Implementing Design Patterns - Basics Part 1*. Actually made up of five design principles, the intention of SOLID is to encourage designs that are more maintainable and easier to understand. These principles encourage code bases that are easier to modify and they reduce the risk of issues being introduced.

> In Chapter 3, *Implementing Design Patterns - Basics Part 1*, SOLID will be covered in more detail by being applied to a C# application.

Single responsibility principle

A class should have only one responsibility. The goal of this principle is to simplify our classes and logically structure them. Classes with multiple responsibilities are harder to understand and modify, as they are more complex. Responsibility in this circumstance is simply a reason for the change. Another way of looking at responsibility is to define it as a single part of the functionality:

> *"A class should have one, and only one, reason to change."*
>
> - Robert C. Martin

Open/closed principle

The open/closed principle is best described in terms of OOP. A class should be designed with inheritance as a means of extending its functionality. Change, in other words, is planned for and considered while the class is being designed. By defining and using an interface that the class implements, the open/closed principle is applied. The class is *open* for modification, while its description, the interface, is *closed* for modification.

Liskov substitution principle

Being able to substitute objects at runtime is the basis of the Liskov substitution principle. In OOP, if a class inherits from a base class or implements an interface, then it can be referenced as an object of the base class or interface. This is easier to describe with a simple example.

We'll define an interface for an animal and implement two animals, Cat and Dog, as follows:

```
interface IAnimal
{
    string MakeNoise();
}
class Dog : IAnimal
{
   public string MakeNoise()
    {
        return "Woof";
    }
}
class Cat : IAnimal
{
    public string MakeNoise()
    {
        return "Meouw";
    }
}
```

Then we can refer to the Cat and Dog as an animal as follows:

```
var animals = new List<IAnimal> { new Cat(), new Dog() };

foreach(var animal in animals)
{
    Console.Write(animal.MakeNoise());
}
```

Interface segregation principle

Similar to the single responsibility principle, the interface segregation principle states that an interface should be limited to containing only methods that are relevant to a single responsibility. By reducing the complexity of the interface, the code becomes easier to refactor and understand. An important benefit of adhering to this principle in a system is that it aids in decoupling a system by reducing the number of dependencies.

Dependency inversion principle

The **dependency inversion principle** (**DIP**), also referred to as the dependency injection principle, states that modules should not depend on details but on abstractions instead. This principle encourages writing loosely coupled code to enhance readability and maintenance, especially in a large complex code base.

Software patterns

Over the years, many patterns have been compiled into catalogs. This section will use two catalogs as an illustration. The first catalog is a collection of OOP-related patterns by the **GoF**. The second relates to the integration of systems and remains technologically agnostic. At the end of the chapter, there are some references for additional catalogs and resources.

GoF patterns

Potentially, the most influential and well-known OOP collection of patterns comes from the *Design Patterns: Elements of Reusable Object-Oriented Software* book by *GoF*. The aim of the patterns in the book is on a lower level—that is, object creation and interaction—instead of a larger software architecture concern. The collection consists of templates that can be applied to particular scenarios with the goal of producing solid building blocks while avoiding common pitfalls in object-oriented development.

> *Erich Gamma, John Vlissides, Richard Helm*, and *Ralph Johnson* are referred to as the GoF because of their widely influential publications in the 1990s. The book *Design Patterns: Elements of Reusable Object-Oriented Software* has been translated into several languages and contains examples in both C++ and Smalltalk.

The collection is broken into three categories: creational patterns, structural patterns, and behavioral patterns which will be explained in the following sections.

Creational patterns

The following five patterns are concerned with the instantiation of objects:

- **Abstract Factory**: A pattern for the creation of objects belonging to a family of classes. The specific object is determined at runtime.
- **Builder**: A useful pattern for more complex objects where the construction of the object is controlled externally to the constructed class.
- **Factory Method**: A pattern for creating objects derived from a class where the specific class is determined at runtime.
- **Prototype**: A pattern for copying or cloning an object.
- **Singleton**: A pattern for enforcing only one instance of a class.

> In `Chapter 3`, *Implementing Design Patterns - Basics Part 1*, the Abstract Factory pattern will be explored in more detail. In `Chapter 4`, *Implementing Design Patterns - Basics Part 2*, the Singleton and Factory Method patterns will be explored in detail, including using the .NET Core framework support for these patterns.

Structural patterns

The following patterns are concerned with defining relationships between classes and objects:

- **Adapter**: A pattern for providing a match between two different classes
- **Bridge**: A pattern for allowing the implementation details of a class to be replaced without requiring the class to be modified
- **Composite**: Used to create a hierarchy of classes in a tree structure
- **Decorator**: A pattern for replacing the functionality of a class at runtime
- **Facade**: A pattern used to simplify complex systems
- **Flyweight**: A pattern used to reduce the resource usage for complex models
- **Proxy**: A pattern used to represent another object allowing for an additional level of control between the calling and called objects

Decorator patterns

To illustrate a structural pattern, let's take a closer look at the Decorator pattern by using an example. This example will print messages on a console application. First, a base message is defined with a corresponding interface:

```
interface IMessage
{
    void PrintMessage();
}

abstract class Message : IMessage
{
    protected string _text;
    public Message(string text)
    {
        _text = text;
    }
    abstract public void PrintMessage();
}
```

The base class allows for the storage of a text string and requires that child classes implement the `PrintMessage()` method. This will then be extended into two new classes.

The first class is a `SimpleMessage` that writes the given text to the console:

```
class SimpleMessage : Message
{
    public SimpleMessage(string text) : base(text) { }

    public override void PrintMessage()
    {
        Console.WriteLine(_text);
    }
}
```

The second class is an `AlertMessage` that also writes the given text to the console but performs a beep as well:

```
class AlertMessage : Message
{
    public AlertMessage(string text) : base(text) { }
    public override void PrintMessage()
    {
        Console.Beep();
        Console.WriteLine(_text);
    }
}
```

The difference between the two is that the `AlertMessage` class will issue a beep instead of only printing the text to the screen like the `SimpleMessage` class.

Next, a base decorator class is defined that will contain a reference to a `Message` object as follows:

```
abstract class MessageDecorator : IMessage
{
    protected Message _message;
    public MessageDecorator(Message message)
    {
        _message = message;
    }

    public abstract void PrintMessage();
}
```

The following two classes illustrate the Decorator pattern by providing additional functionality for our existing implementation of `Message`.

The first is a `NormalDecorator` that prints the message whose foreground is green:

```
class NormalDecorator : MessageDecorator
{
    public NormalDecorator(Message message) : base(message) { }

    public override void PrintMessage()
    {
        Console.ForegroundColor = ConsoleColor.Green;
        _message.PrintMessage();
        Console.ForegroundColor = ConsoleColor.White;
    }
}
```

`ErrorDecorator` uses a red foreground color to make the message more pronounced when printed to the console:

```
class ErrorDecorator : MessageDecorator
{
    public ErrorDecorator(Message message) : base(message) { }

    public override void PrintMessage()
    {
        Console.ForegroundColor = ConsoleColor.Red;
        _message.PrintMessage();
        Console.ForegroundColor = ConsoleColor.White;
    }
```

}

`NormalDecorator` will print the text in green while the `ErrorDecorator` will print the text in red. The important thing with this example is that the decorator is extending the behavior of the referenced `Message` object.

To complete the example, the following shows how new messages can be used:

```
static void Main(string[] args)
{
    var messages = new List<IMessage>
    {
        new NormalDecorator(new SimpleMessage("First Message!")),
        new NormalDecorator(new AlertMessage("Second Message with a beep!")),
        new ErrorDecorator(new AlertMessage("Third Message with a beep and in red!")),
        new SimpleMessage("Not Decorated...")
    };
    foreach (var message in messages)
    {
        message.PrintMessage();
    }
    Console.Read();
}
```

Running the example will illustrate how the different Decorator patterns can be used to change the referenced functionality as follows:

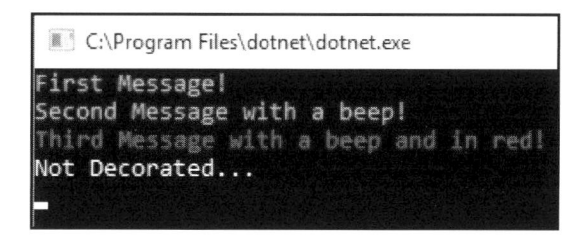

```
C:\Program Files\dotnet\dotnet.exe
First Message!
Second Message with a beep!
Third Message with a beep and in red!
Not Decorated...
```

This is a simplified example but imagine a scenario where a new requirement is added to the project. Instead of using the beep sound, the system sound for exclamation should be played.

```
class AlertMessage : Message
{
    public AlertMessage(string text) : base(text) { }
    public override void PrintMessage()
    {
```

```
            System.Media.SystemSounds.Exclamation.Play();
            Console.WriteLine(_text);
        }
    }
```

As we have a structure in place to handle this, the amendment is a one-line change as shown in the previous code block.

Behavioral patterns

The following behavioral patterns can be used to define the communication between classes and objects:

- **Chain of Responsibility**: A pattern for handling a request between a collection of objects
- **Command**: A pattern used to represent a request
- **Interpreter**: A pattern for defining syntax or language for instructions in a program
- **Iterator**: A pattern for traversing a collection of items without detailed knowledge of the elements in a collection
- **Mediator**: A pattern for simplifying communication between classes
- **Memento**: A pattern for capturing and storing the state of an object
- **Observer**: A pattern for allowing objects to be notified of changes to another object's state
- **State**: A pattern for altering an object's behavior when its state changes
- **Strategy**: A pattern for implementing a collection of algorithms where a specific algorithm can be applied at runtime
- **Template Method**: A pattern for defining the steps of an algorithm while leaving the implementation details in a subclass
- **Visitor**: A pattern promoting loose coupling between data and functionality, allowing for additional operations to be added without requiring changes to the data classes

Chain of responsibility

A useful pattern you need to be familiar with is the Chain of Responsibility pattern so we will use it as an example. With this pattern, we will set up a collection or chain of classes for handling a request. The idea is the request will pass through each class until it is handled. This illustration uses a car service center, where each car will pass through the different sections of the center until the service is complete.

Let's start by defining a collection of flags that will be used to indicate the services required:

```
[Flags]
enum ServiceRequirements
{
    None = 0,
    WheelAlignment = 1,
    Dirty = 2,
    EngineTune = 4,
    TestDrive = 8
}
```

> **TIP:** The `FlagsAttribute` in C# is a great way of using a bit field to hold a collection of flags. The single field will be used to indicate the enum values that are *turned on* by using bitwise operations.

The `Car` will contain a field to capture what servicing is required and a field that returns true when the service has been completed:

```
class Car
{
    public ServiceRequirements Requirements { get; set; }

    public bool IsServiceComplete
    {
        get
        {
            return Requirements == ServiceRequirements.None;
        }
    }
}
```

One thing to point out is that a `Car` is considered to have its service completed once all the requirements have been completed, as represented by the `IsServiceComplete` property.

An abstract base class will be used to represent each of our service technicians in the following manner:

```
abstract class ServiceHandler
{
    protected ServiceHandler _nextServiceHandler;
    protected ServiceRequirements _servicesProvided;

    public ServiceHandler(ServiceRequirements servicesProvided)
    {
        _servicesProvided = servicesProvided;
    }
}
```

Take note that the service provided by the class that extends the `ServiceHandler` class, in other words the technician, is required to be passed in.

The service will then be performed by using the bitwise NOT operation (~) to *turn off* the bit on the given `Car`, indicating the service is required in the `Service` method:

```
public void Service(Car car)
{
    if (_servicesProvided == (car.Requirements & _servicesProvided))
    {
        Console.WriteLine($"{this.GetType().Name} providing {this._servicesProvided} services.");
        car.Requirements &= ~_servicesProvided;
    }

    if (car.IsServiceComplete || _nextServiceHandler == null)
        return;
    else
        _nextServiceHandler.Service(car);
}
```

If all services have been completed on the car and/or there are no more services, the chain is stopped. If there is another service and a car is not ready, then the next service handler is called.

This approach requires the chain to be set and the preceding example shows this being done using the `SetNextServiceHandler()` method to set the next service to be performed:

```
public void SetNextServiceHandler(ServiceHandler handler)
{
    _nextServiceHandler = handler;
}
```

The service specialists include a `Detailer`, `Mechanic`, `WheelSpecialist`, and a `QualityControl` engineer. The `ServiceHandler` representing a `Detailer` is shown in the following code:

```
class Detailer : ServiceHandler
{
    public Detailer() : base(ServiceRequirements.Dirty) { }
}
```

The mechanic, whose specialty is tuning the engine, is shown in the following code:

```
class Mechanic : ServiceHandler
{
    public Mechanic() : base(ServiceRequirements.EngineTune) { }
}
```

The wheel specialist is shown in the following code:

```
class WheelSpecialist : ServiceHandler
{
    public WheelSpecialist() : base(ServiceRequirements.WheelAlignment) { }
}
```

And last is quality control, who will take the car for a test drive:

```
class QualityControl : ServiceHandler
{
    public QualityControl() : base(ServiceRequirements.TestDrive) { }
}
```

The service center technicians have been defined, so the next step is to service a couple of cars. This will be illustrated in the `Main` code block, starting with constructing the required objects:

```
static void Main(string[] args)
{
    var mechanic = new Mechanic();
    var detailer = new Detailer();
    var wheels = new WheelSpecialist();
    var qa = new QualityControl();
```

The next step will be to set up the handling order for the different services:

```
    qa.SetNextServiceHandler(detailer);
    wheels.SetNextServiceHandler(qa);
    mechanic.SetNextServiceHandler(wheels);
```

Then two calls will be made to the mechanic, which is the start of the chain of responsibility:

```
    Console.WriteLine("Car 1 is dirty");
    mechanic.Service(new Car { Requirements = ServiceRequirements.Dirty });

    Console.WriteLine();

    Console.WriteLine("Car 2 requires full service");
    mechanic.Service(new Car { Requirements = ServiceRequirements.Dirty |
ServiceRequirements.EngineTune |
ServiceRequirements.TestDrive |
ServiceRequirements.WheelAlignment });

    Console.Read();
}
```

An important thing to note is the order in which the chain is set. For this service center, the mechanic first performs tuning, followed by the wheels being aligned. Then, a test drive is performed and after that, the car is worked up in detail. Originally, the test drive used to be performed as the last step, but the service center determined that, on rainy days, this required the car details to be repeated. A bit of a silly example, but it illustrates the benefit of having the chain of responsibility defined in a flexible manner.

```
C:\Program Files\dotnet\dotnet.exe
Car 1 is dirty
Detailer providing Dirty services.

Car 2 requires full service
Mechanic providing EngineTune services.
WheelSpecialist providing WheelAlignment services.
QualityControl providing TestDrive services.
Detailer providing Dirty services.
```

The preceding screenshot shows the display after our two cars have been serviced.

Observer pattern

An interesting pattern to explore in more detail is the **Observer pattern**. This pattern allows for instances to be informed of when a particular event happens in another instance. In this way, there are many observers and a single subject. The following diagram illustrates this pattern:

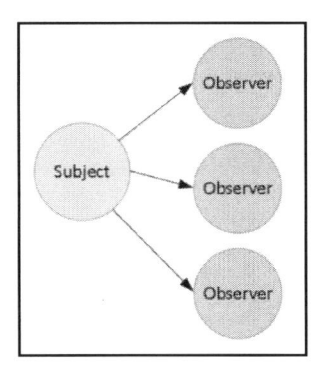

Let's provide an example by creating a simple C# console application that will create a single instance of a `Subject` class and multiple `Observer` instances. When a quantity value changes in the `Subject` class, we want each `Observer` instance to be notified.

The `Subject` class contains a private quantity field that is updated by a public `UpdateQuantity` method:

```
class Subject
{
    private int _quantity = 0;

    public void UpdateQuantity(int value)
    {
        _quantity += value;

        // alert any observers
    }
}
```

In order to alert any observers, we use the C# keywords, `delegate` and `event`. The `delegate` keyword defines the format or handler that will be called. The delegate to be used when the quantity is updated is shown in the following code:

```
public delegate void QuantityUpdated(int quantity);
```

The delegate defines `QuantityUpdated` to be a method that receives an integer and does not return any value. An event is then added to the `Subject` class as follows:

```
public event QuantityUpdated OnQuantityUpdated;
```

And, in the `UpdateQuantity` method, it is called as follows:

```
public void UpdateQuantity(int value)
{
    _quantity += value;

    // alert any observers
    OnQuantityUpdated?.Invoke(_quantity);
}
```

In this example, we will define a method in the `Observer` class that has the same signature as the `QuantityUpdated` delegate:

```
class Observer
{
    ConsoleColor _color;
    public Observer(ConsoleColor color)
    {
        _color = color;
    }

    internal void ObserverQuantity(int quantity)
    {
        Console.ForegroundColor = _color;
        Console.WriteLine($"I observer the new quantity value of {quantity}.");
        Console.ForegroundColor = ConsoleColor.White;
    }
}
```

This implementation will be alerted when the quantity of the `Subject` instance changes and will print a message to the console in a specific color.

Let's put these together in a simple application. At the start of the application, a single `Subject` and three `Observer` objects will be created:

```
var subject = new Subject();
var greenObserver = new Observer(ConsoleColor.Green);
var redObserver = new Observer(ConsoleColor.Red);
var yellowObserver = new Observer(ConsoleColor.Yellow);
```

Next, each `Observer` instance will register to be alerted by the `Subject` when the quantity changes:

```
subject.OnQuantityUpdated += greenObserver.ObserverQuantity;
subject.OnQuantityUpdated += redObserver.ObserverQuantity;
subject.OnQuantityUpdated += yellowObserver.ObserverQuantity;
```

Then, we will update the quantity twice, as shown here:

```
subject.UpdateQuantity(12);
subject.UpdateQuantity(5);
```

When the application is run, we get three messages printed in different colors for each update statement, as shown in the following screenshot:

```
C:\Program Files\dotnet\dotnet.exe
Hello World!
I observer the new quantity value of 12.
I observer the new quantity value of 12.
I observer the new quantity value of 12.
I observer the new quantity value of 17.
I observer the new quantity value of 17.
I observer the new quantity value of 17.
Enter a key to quit.
```

This was a simple sample using the C# `event` keyword, but, hopefully, it illustrates how this pattern could be used. The advantage here is it loosely couples the subject from the observers. The subject does not have to have knowledge of the different observers, or even knowledge of whether any exist.

Enterprise integration patterns

Integration is a discipline of software development that benefits greatly from leveraging the knowledge and experience of others. With this in mind, many catalogs of EIPs exist, some of which are technology agnostic while others are tailored to a particular technology stack. This section will highlight some popular integration patterns.

> *Enterprise Integration Patterns*, by *Gregor Hohpe* and *Bobby Woolf*, provides a solid resource for many integration patterns across a variety of technologies. This book is often referenced when discussing EIPs. The book is available at `https://www.enterpriseintegrationpatterns.com/`.

Topology

An important consideration for enterprise integration is the topology of the systems being connected. In general, there are two distinct topologies: hub-and-spoke and enterprise service bus.

A **hub-and-spoke** (hub) topology describes an integration pattern where a single component, the hub, is centralized and it communicates with each application explicitly. This centralizes the communication so that the hub only needs to know about the other applications, as illustrated in the following diagram:

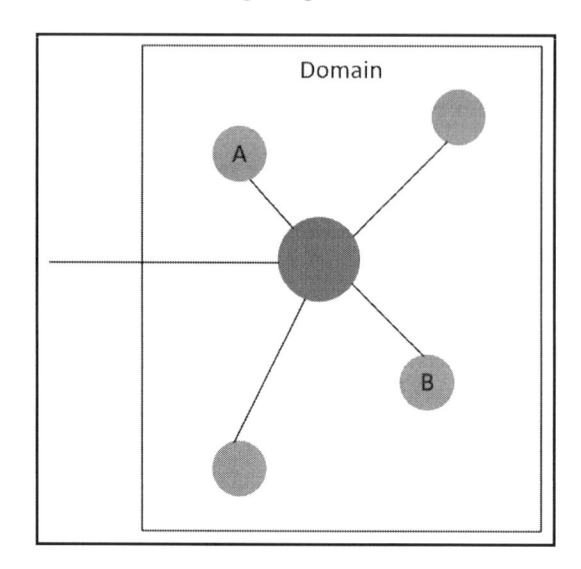

The diagram shows the hub, in blue, as having explicit knowledge of how to communicate with the different applications. This means that, when a message is to be sent from A to B, it is sent from A to the hub and then forwarded on to B. The advantage of this approach for an enterprise is that connectivity to B has to be defined and maintained only in one place, the hub. The significance here is that the security is controlled and maintained in one central location.

An **enterprise service bus** (**ESB**) relies on a messaging model comprising of publishers and subscribers (Pub-Sub). A publisher submits messages to the bus and a subscriber registers to receive published messages. The following diagram illustrates this topology:

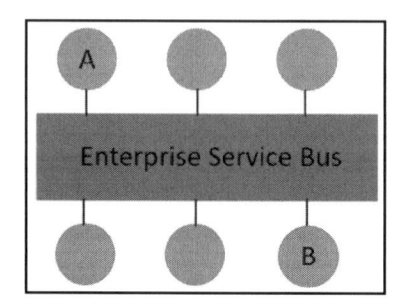

In the preceding diagram, if a message is to be routed from **A** to **B**, **B** subscribes to the ESB for messages published from **A**. When **A** publishes a new message, the message is sent to **B**. In practice, the subscription can be more complex. For example, in an ordering system, there might be two subscribers for priority orders and normal orders. In this situation, priority orders might then be handled differently from normal orders.

Patterns

If we define an integration between two systems as having distinct steps, we can then define patterns in each step. Let's take a look at the following diagram to discuss an integration pipeline:

A → Message → Transform → Routing → Transform → Message → B

This pipeline is simplified as there could be more or fewer steps in a pipeline depending on the technology used. The purpose of the diagram is to provide some context as we look at some common integration patterns. These can be broken into categories as follows:

- **Messaging**: Patterns related to the handling of messages
- **Transformation**: Patterns related to altering message content
- **Routing**: Patterns related to the exchange of messages

Messaging

Patterns related to messaging can take the form of message construction and channels. A channel, in this context, is the endpoint and/or how the message enters and exits the integration pipeline. Some examples of construction-related patterns are the following:

- **Message Sequence**: The message contains a sequence to indicate a particular processing order.
- **Correlation Identifier**: The message contains a medium to identify related messages.
- **Return Address**: The message identifies information about returning a response message.
- **Expiration**: The message has a finite time that it is considered valid.

In the *Topology* section, we covered some patterns related to channels but the following are additional patterns you should consider in integration:

- **Competing Consumers**: Multiple processes could handle the same message.
- **Selective Consumer**: Consumers use criteria to determine the message to process.
- **Dead Letter Channel**: Handles messages that are not successfully processed.
- **Guaranteed Delivery**: Ensures reliable handling of messages, where no message is lost.
- **Event-driven Consumer:** The handling of messages is based on published events.
- **Polling Consumer:** Handles messages that are retrieved from a source system.

Transformation

When integrating complex enterprise systems, transformation patterns allow for flexibility in how messages are handled in the system. With transformation, a message between two applications can be altered and/or enhanced. Here are some transformation-related patterns:

- **Content Enricher**: A message is *enriched* by adding information.
- **Canonical Data Model**: A message is transformed into an application-neutral message format.
- **Message Translator**: A pattern for translating one message to another.

The **Canonical Data Model (CDM)** is a good pattern to highlight. With this pattern, a message can be exchanged between multiple applications without having to perform a translation for each specific message type. This is best shown by an example of multiple systems exchanging messages, as illustrated in the following diagram:

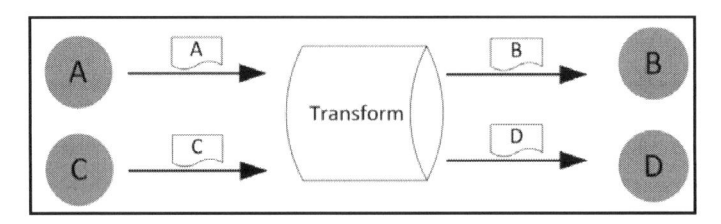

In the diagram, applications **A** and **C** want to send their messages in their format to application **B** and **D**. If we used the Message Translator pattern, only the process, which is handling the transformation, would need to know how to translate from **A** to **B** and from **A** to **D** as well as **C** to **B** and **C** to **D**. This becomes increasingly difficult as the number of applications increases and when the publisher might not know the details of its consumers. With the CDM, source application messages for **A** and **B** are translated into a neutral schema X.

> **Canonical schema**
> A canonical schema is sometimes referred to as a neutral schema, meaning it is not aligned directly with a source or destination system. The schema is then thought of as being impartial.

The message in the neutral schema format is then translated to the message formats for **B** and **D** as shown in the following diagram:

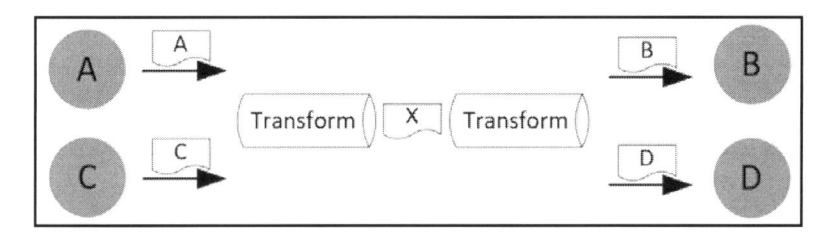

In the enterprise, this becomes unmanageable without some standards, and fortunately, many organizations have been created to produce as well as govern standards in many industries, including the following examples (but there are many more!):

- **Electronic Data Interchange For Administration, Commerce and Transport (EDIFACT)**: An international standard for trade
- **IMS Question and Test Interoperability specification (QTI):** Standards for the representation of assessment content and results produced by the **Information Management System (IMS) Global Learning Consortium (GLC)**
- **Hospitality Industry Technology Integration Standards (HITIS)**: Standards for property management systems maintained by the American Hotel and Motel Association
- **X12 EDI (X12)**: Collection of schemas for health care, insurance, government, finance, transportation, and other industries maintained by the Accredited Standards Committee X12
- **Business Process Framework (eTOM)**: Telecommunications operating model maintained by the TM Forum

Routing

Routing patterns provide different approaches to handling messages. Here are some examples of patterns that fall into this category:

- **Content-based Routing**: The route or destination application(s) is determined by the content in the message.
- **Message Filtering**: Only messages of interest are forwarded on to the destination application(s).
- **Splitter**: Multiple messages are generated from a single message.
- **Aggregator**: A single message is generated from multiple messages.
- **Scatter-Gather**: A pattern for handling a broadcast of multiple messages and aggregating the responses into a single message.

The Scatter-Gather pattern is a very useful pattern and, as it combines both the Splitter and Aggregator patterns, it is a great example to explore. With this pattern, a more complex business process can be modeled.

In our scenario, we will take the fulfillment of an ordering system of widgets. The good news is, several vendors, sell widgets, but the price of widgets fluctuates often. So, which vendor has the best price changes? Using the Scatter-Gather pattern, the ordering system can query multiple vendors, select the best price, and then return the result back to the calling system.

The Splitter pattern will be used to generate multiple messages to the vendors as shown in the following diagram:

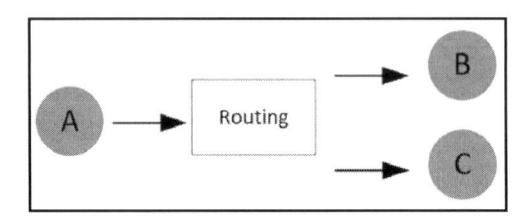

The routing then waits until the vendor responses are received. Once the responses have been received, the Aggregator pattern is used to compile the results into a single message to the calling application:

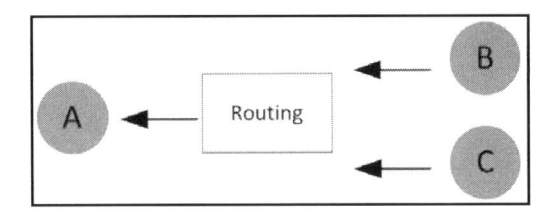

It is worth noting that there are many variations and circumstances for this pattern. The Scatter-Gather pattern might require all vendors to respond or just some of them. Another scenario might require a limit on the amount of time the process should wait for a response from a vendor. Some messages might take milliseconds for a response while other scenarios might take days for a response to be returned.

> An integration engine is software that supports many integration patterns. The integration engine can range from locally installed services to cloud-based solutions. Some of the more popular engines are Microsoft BizTalk, Dell Boomi, MuleSoft Anypoint Platform, IBM WebSphere, and SAS Business Intelligence.

Software development life cycle patterns

There are many approaches to managing software development and the two most common **software development life cycle** (**SDLC**) patterns are **Waterfall** and **Agile**. There are many variations of these two SDLC methodologies and often an organization will adapt a methodology to fit the project and team(s) as well as the company culture.

> The Waterfall and Agile SDLCs patterns are just two examples and there are several other patterns for software development that may suit a company's culture, software maturity, and industry better than others.

Waterfall SDLC

The Waterfall approach comprises distinct phases that a project or piece of work goes through sequentially. Conceptually, it is simple to understand and it follows patterns used in other industries. The following is an example of the different phases:

- **Requirements phase**: All requirements to be implemented are gathered and documented.
- **Design phase**: Using the documentation produced in the previous step, the design that which is to be implemented is completed.
- **Development phase**: Using the design from the previous step, the changes are implemented.
- **Testing phase**: The changes implemented in the previous step are verified against the specified requirements.
- **Deployment phase**: Once the testing has been completed, the changes performed by the project are deployed.

There are many strengths to the Waterfall model. The model is easy to understand and easy to manage, as each phase has a clear definition of what has to be done and what has to be delivered out of each phase. By having a series of phases, milestones can be defined, allowing for easier reporting on progress. Also, with distinct phases, the roles and responsibilities of the resources required can be more easily planned.

But what if something does not go to plan or things change? The Waterfall SDLC does have some disadvantages, and many of the disadvantages stem from its lack of flexibility for change, or the instances when things are discovered, requiring input from a previous step. In Waterfall, if a situation occurs requiring information from a previous phase, the previous phase is repeated. This poses several problems. As phases might be reported, reporting becomes difficult because a project (that had passed a phase or milestone) is now repeating the phase. This could promote a *witch-hunt* company culture, where the effort is diverted to finding blame rather than measures to prevent recurring issues. Also, resources might no longer be available, as they have been moved onto other projects and/or have left the company.

The following diagram illustrates how the cost and time increase the further into the phases that an issue is discovered:

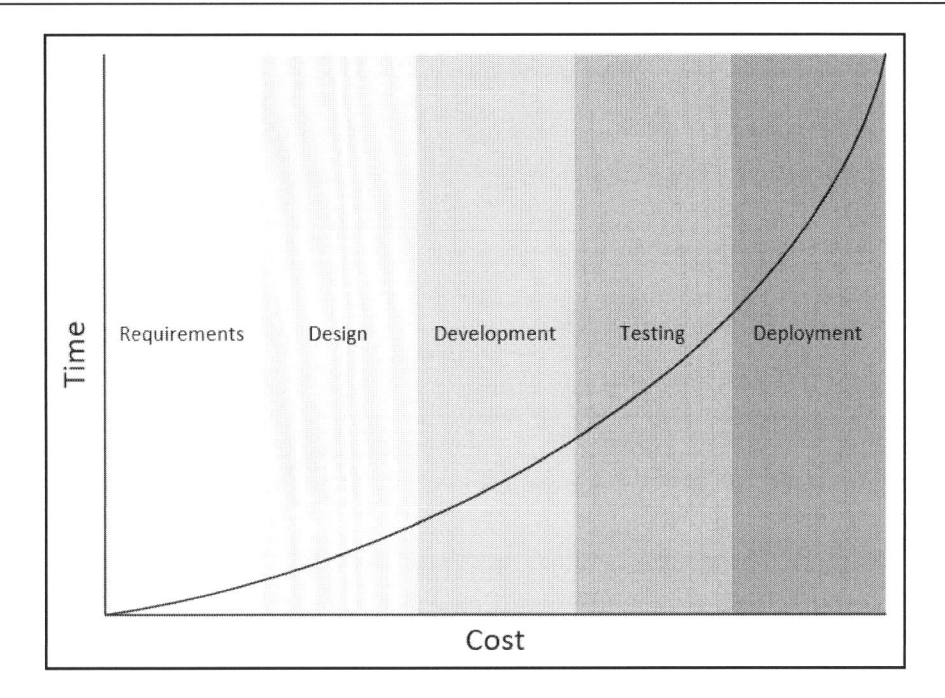

[Graph: Time vs Cost across Requirements, Design, Development, Testing, Deployment phases, showing exponential cost increase]

Because of the cost associated with change, the Waterfall SDLC tends to suit smaller projects with a lower risk of change. Larger and more complex projects increase the potential for change, as requirements might be altered or the business drivers change during the project.

Agile SDLC

The Agile SDLC approach to software development attempts to embrace change and uncertainty. This is achieved by using a pattern that allows for change and/or the occurrence of issues that are discovered during the life of a project or product development. The key concept is to break the project into smaller iterations of development, often referred to as development cycles. In each cycle, the basic Waterfall stages are repeated so each cycle has requirements, design, development, testing, and deployment phase.

This is a simplification but the strategy of breaking the project into cycles has several advantages over Waterfall:

- The impact of shifting business requirements is lessened as the scope is smaller.
- The stakeholders get a visibly working system earlier than with Waterfall. Though not complete, this provides value as it allows for feedback to be incorporated earlier into a product.

- Resourcing might benefit as the type of resources has fewer fluctuations.

The preceding diagram provides a summary of the two approaches.

Summary

In this chapter, we have discussed major design patterns used in modern software development that were introduced in the previous chapter. We started with the discussion of various software development principles such as the DRY, KISS, YAGNI, MVP, and SOLID programming principles. Then, we covered software development patterns including GoF and EIPs. The methodology for SDLC was covered, including Waterfall and Agile. The purpose of this chapter was to illustrate how patterns are used across all levels of software development.

As the software industry matures, patterns emerge as experience evolves, techniques grow, and technology advances. Some patterns have been developed to help different phases of the SDLC. For example in Chapter 3, *Implementing Design Patterns - Basics Part 1*, **Test-driven development** (**TDD**) will be explored, where the definitions of tests are used to provide both measurable progress as well as clear requirements, during the development phase. As the chapters progress, we will discuss higher levels of abstraction in software development, including patterns for web development as well as modern architecture patterns for on-premise and cloud-based solutions.

In the next chapter, we will start by building a fictitious application in .NET Core. Also, we will explain the various patterns discussed in this chapter, including programming principles such as SOLID, and illustrate several GoF patterns.

Questions

The following questions will allow you to consolidate the information contained in this chapter:

1. In SOLID, what does the S stand for? What is meant by a responsibility?
2. Which SDLC method is built around cycles: Waterfall or Agile?
3. Is the Decorator pattern a creational or structural pattern?
4. What does Pub-Sub integration stand for?

Section 2: Deep Dive into Utilities and Patterns in .NET Core

In this section, readers will get hands-on experience with various design patterns. Specific patterns will be illustrated in the process of building a sample application for maintaining an inventory application. An inventory application was chosen as it is conceptually simple but will provide enough complexity to benefit from the use of patterns during development. Certain patterns and principles will be revisited more than once, such as SOLID, **Minimal Viable Product** (**MVP**), and **Test-driven development** (**TDD**). By the end of this section, readers will be able to write neat and clean code with the help of various patterns.

This section consists of the following chapters:

- `Chapter 3`, *Implementing Design Patterns – Basics Part 1*
- `Chapter 4`, *Implementing Design Patterns – Basics Part 2*
- `Chapter 5`, *Implementing Design Patterns – .Net Core*
- `Chapter 6`, *Implementing Design Patterns for Web Applications – Part 1*
- `Chapter 7`, *Implementing Design Patterns for Web Applications – Part 2*

3
Implementing Design Patterns - Basics Part 1

In the previous two chapters, we introduced and defined a wide range of modern patterns and practices pertaining to the **software development life cycle** (**SDLC**), from lower-level development patterns to high-level solution architectural patterns. This chapter applies some of those patterns in a sample scenario in order to provide context and further understanding of the definitions. The scenario is the creation of a solution to manage the inventory of an e-commerce bookseller.

The scenario was chosen as it provides enough complexity to illustrate the patterns while the concept is relatively simple. The company needs a way of managing their inventory, including allowing users to order their products. The organization needs to get an application in place, as soon as possible, to allow them to track their inventory, but there are many additional features, including allowing customers to order products and provide reviews. As the scenario plays out, the number of features requested grows to the point where the development team does not know where to start. Fortunately, by applying some good practices to help manage the expectations and requirements, the development team is able to simplify their initial delivery and get back on track. Also, by using patterns, they are able to build a solid foundation in order to help the expansion of the solution as new features are added.

This chapter will cover the kickoff of a new project and the creation of the first release of the application. The following patterns are illustrated in this chapter:

- **Minimal Viable Product** (**MVP**)
- **Test-driven development** (**TDD**)
- Abstract Factory pattern (Gang of Four)
- SOLID principles

Technical requirements

This chapter contains various code examples to explain the concepts. The code is kept simple and is just for demonstration purposes. Most of the examples involve a .NET Core console application written in C#.

To run and execute the code, you need the following:

- Visual Studio 2019 (you can also run the application using Visual Studio 2017 version 3 or later)
- .NET Core
- SQL Server (Express Edition is used in this chapter)

Installing Visual Studio

To run these code examples, you need to install Visual Studio or you can use your preferred IDE. To do this, follow these instructions:

1. Download Visual Studio from the following link: https://docs.microsoft.com/en-us/visualstudio/install/install-visual-studio.
2. Follow the installation instructions included. Multiple versions are available for Visual Studio installation. In this chapter, we are using Visual Studio for Windows.

Setting up .NET Core

If you do not have .NET Core installed, you need to follow these instructions:

1. Download .NET Core from the following link: https://www.microsoft.com/net/download/windows.
2. Follow the installation instructions and related library: https://dotnet.microsoft.com/download/dotnet-core/2.2.

> The complete source code is available in GitHub. The source code shown in the chapter might not be complete, so it is advisable to retrieve the source in order to run the examples: https://github.com/PacktPublishing/Hands-On-Design-Patterns-with-C-and-.NET-Core/tree/master/Chapter3.

Minimum Viable Product

This section covers the initial phase of starting a new project to build a software application. This is sometimes referred to as a project kickoff or project launch, where the initial features and capabilities of the application are collected (in other words, requirement gathering).

> Many approaches, which can be viewed as patterns, exist for the determining the features of a software application. Best practices around how to effectively model, conduct interviews and workshops, brainstorm and other techniques are outside the scope of this book. Instead, one approach, Minimum Viable Product, is described to provide an example of what these patterns might contain.

The project is for a hypothetical situation where a company, FlixOne, wants to use an inventory management application to manage its growing collection of books. This new application will be used both by the staff to manage the inventory, and by customers to browse and create new orders. The application will need to be scalable, and, as an essential system to the business, it is planned to be used for a foreseeable future.

The company is broadly broken down into *business users* and the *development team*, where business users are primarily concerned with the functionality of the system and the development team is concerned about satisfying the requirements, as well as keeping a tab on the maintainability of the system. This is a simplification; however, organizations are not necessarily so tidily organized, and individuals might not fit correctly into one classification or another. For example, a **Business Analyst** (**BA**) or **Subject Matter Expert** (**SME**) often represent both a business user and a member of the development team.

As this is a technical book, we will mostly view the scenario from the development team's perspective and discuss the patterns and practices used to implement the inventory management application.

Requirements

Over the course of several meetings, the business and the development teams discussed the requirements of the new inventory management system. Progress toward defining a clear set of requirements was slow and the vision of the final product was not clear. The development team decided to pare down the enormous list of requirements to enough functionality that a key individual could start to record some inventory information. This would allow for simple inventory management and provide a basis that the business could extend upon. Each new set of requirements could then be added to the initial release.

Minimum Viable Product (MVP)
A Minimum Viable Product is the smallest set of features of an application that can still be released and have enough value for a user base.

An advantage of the MVP approach is it gives the business and development teams a simplified vision of what needs to be delivered by narrowing the scope of an application. By reducing the features that will be delivered, the effort in determining what needs to be done becomes more focused. In the FlixOne scenario, a meeting's value would often degrade into discussing the particulars of a feature that, although important for the final version of the product, would require several features to be released before it. For example, the design around a customer-facing website was distracting the team from focusing on the data to be stored in the inventory management system.

MVP is very useful in situations where the complexity of requirements is not fully understood and/or the final vision is not well defined. It is important though to still maintain a product vision to avoid the risk of developing functionality that may not be required in the final version of the application.

The business and development teams were able to define the following functional requirements for the initial inventory management application:

- The application should be a console application:
    - It should print a welcome message that includes the version of the assembly.
    - It should loop until a quit command is given.
    - If a given command is not successful or not understood, then it should print a helpful message.
- The application should respond to simple case-insensitive text commands.
- Each command should have a short form, of a single character, and a long form.
- If a command has additional parameters:
    - Each one should be entered in sequence and submitted with the return key.
    - Each one should have a prompt `Enter {parameter}:` where `{parameter}` is the name of the parameter.
- A help command (?) should be available:
    - Prints a summary of the commands available.
    - Prints example usage of each command.

- A quit command (`q`, `quit`) should be available:
    - Prints a farewell message
    - Ends the application
- An add inventory command (`"a"`, `"addinventory"`) should be available:
    - The `name` parameter of type string.
    - It should add an entry into the database with the given name and a 0 quantity.
- An update quantity command (`"u"`, `"updatequantity"`) should be available :
    - The `name` parameter of type string.
    - The `quantity` parameter of a positive or negative integer.
    - It should update the quantity value of the book with the given name by adding the given quantity.
- A get inventory command (`"g"`, `"getinventory"`) should be available:
    - Returns all the books and their quantities in the database.

And the following non-functional requirements were defined:

- No security is required other than what was supplied by the operating system.
- The short form of a command is for usability while the long form of a command is for readability.

The FlixOne example is an illustration of how MVP could be used to help focus and streamline the SDLC. It is worth emphasizing that the difference between a **Proof of Concept** (**PoC**) and an MVP will differ with each organization. In this book, a PoC is different from MVP in that the resulting application is not viewed as disposable or incomplete. For a commercial product, this would mean the end product could be sold, and for an internal enterprise solution, the application could add value to the organization.

How does MVP fit with future development?

Another benefit to using MVP to focus and contain requirements is its synergy with Agile software development. Breaking development cycles into smaller cycles of development is a software development technique that has gained popularity over traditional Waterfall development. The driving concept is that requirements and solutions evolve during the life cycle of an application and involve a collaboration between the development team and the end users. Typically, the agile software development framework has a short release cycle where new functionality is designed, developed, tested, and released. Release cycles are then repeated as the application includes additional functionality. MVP fits well within agile development when the scope of work fits within a release cycle.

Implementing Design Patterns - Basics Part 1

> Scrum and Kanban are popular software development frameworks based on agile software development.

The scope of the initial MVP requirements was kept to a size that could be designed, developed, tested, and released with an agile cycle. In the next cycle, additional requirements will be added to the application. The challenge is to limit the scope of new functionality to what can be accomplished within a cycle. Each new release of functionality is limited to essential requirements or to its MVP. The principle here is that, by using an iterative approach to software development, the final version of the application will have a greater benefit to the end user than by using a single release that requires all requirements to be defined up front.

The following diagram sums up the difference between Agile and Waterfall software development methods:

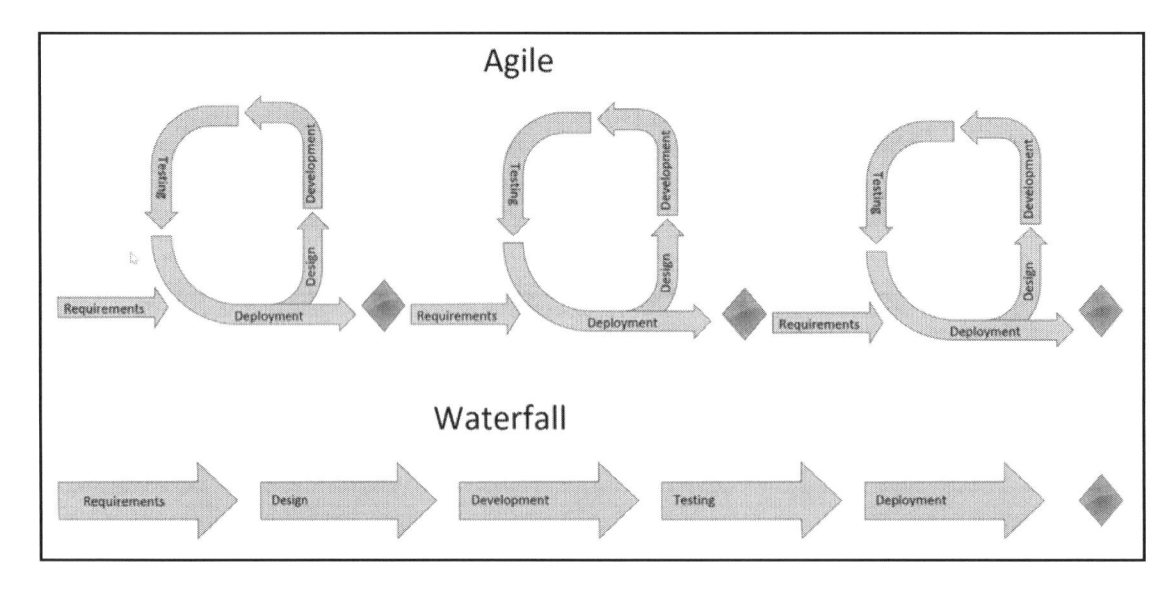

Test-driven development

Different approaches to **test-driven development** (**TDD**) exist, and a *test* can vary from a unit test that is run on demand during development, to a unit test that is run during the build of a project, to a test script that will be run as a part of **user acceptance testing** (**UAT**). Similarly, a *test* can be code or a document describing the steps to be performed by a user in order to verify a requirement. A reason for this is that there are different views as to what TDD is trying to achieve. TDD for some teams is a technique to refine requirements before writing code, while others view TDD as a way of measuring or validating the code that is delivered.

> **UAT**
> UAT is a term used for the activity during the SDLC where the product or project is verified to fulfill specified requirements. This is typically performed by members of the business or a selection of customers. Depending on the circumstances, this phase can be broken further into alpha and beta stages where alpha testing is performed by the development team and beta by the end users.

Why did the team choose TDD?

The development team decided to use TDD for several reasons. First, the team wanted a way to clearly measure progress during the development process. Second, they wanted to be able to reuse the tests in subsequent development cycles in order to continue to validate existing functionality while new functionality is added. For these reasons, the team will use unit tests to verify that the functionality written satisfies the given requirements of the team.

The following diagram illustrates the basics of TDD:

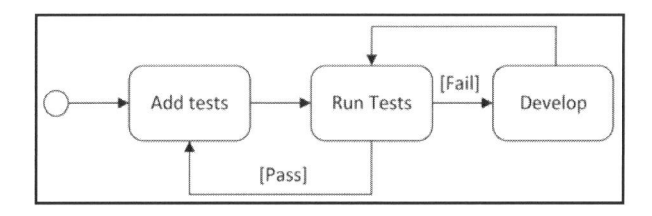

Tests are added and the code base is updated until all the defined tests pass. It is important to note that this is repeated. In each iteration, new tests are added and the tests are not considered passed until all tests, new and existing, pass.

The FlixOne development team decided to incorporate both unit tests and UAT into a single agile cycle. At the beginning of each cycle, new acceptance criteria would be determined. This would include the functionality to be delivered, as well as how it would be verified or accepted at the end of the development cycle. These acceptance criteria would then be used to add tests to the project. The development team would then build the solution until the new and existing tests passed, and then prepare a build for acceptance testing. Then, the acceptance testing would be run, and if any issues were detected, the development team would define new tests or amend existing tests based on the failures. The application would be developed again until all tests passed and a new build would be prepared. This would be repeated until acceptance testing passed. Then, the application would be deployed and a new development cycle would begin.

The following diagram illustrates this approach:

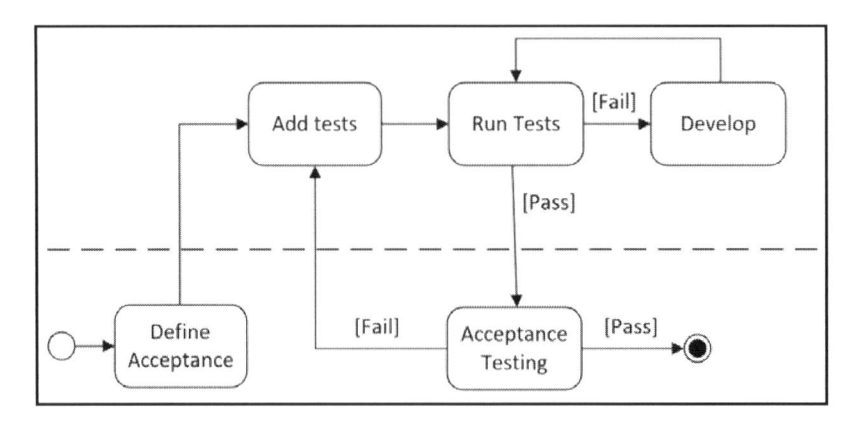

The team now has a plan, so let's start coding!

Setting up the projects

In this scenario, we will use the **Microsoft Unit Test (MSTest)** framework. This section provides some instructions to create the initial project using the .NET Core **command-line interface (CLI)** tools. These steps could have been completed using an **integrated development environment (IDE)** such as Visual Studio or Visual Studio Code. The instructions are supplied here to illustrate how the CLI can be used to complement the IDE.

> **CLI**
> .NET Core CLI tools are cross-platform utilities for developing .NET applications and are the basis for more sophisticated tooling, such as IDEs. Please see the documentation for more information: `https://docs.microsoft.com/en-us/dotnet/core/tools`.

The solution for this chapter will consist of three projects: a console application, a class library, and a test project. Let's create the solution directory, FlixOne, to contain the solution and sub-directories for the three projects. Within the created directory, the following command will create a new solution file:

```
dotnet new sln
```

The following screenshot illustrates creating the directory and solution (note: only an empty solution file has been created so far):

```
Administrator: Windows PowerShell
PS J:\git> mkdir FlixOne


    Directory: J:\git


Mode                LastWriteTime         Length Name
----                -------------         ------ ----
d-----       24/05/2018     2:51 PM                FlixOne


PS J:\git> cd .\FlixOne\
PS J:\git\FlixOne> dotnet new sln
The template "Solution File" was created successfully.
PS J:\git\FlixOne> dir


    Directory: J:\git\FlixOne


Mode                LastWriteTime         Length Name
----                -------------         ------ ----
-a----       24/05/2018     2:51 PM            540 FlixOne.sln


PS J:\git\FlixOne>
```

The class library, `FlixOne.InventoryManagement`, will contain our business entities and logic. In later chapters, we will split these into separate libraries but, as our application is still small, they are contained in a single assembly. The `dotnet` core CLI command to create the project is shown here:

```
dotnet new classlib --name FlixOne.InventoryManagement
```

Note, in the following screenshot, that a new directory is created containing the new class library project file:

```
PS J:\git\FlixOne> dotnet new classlib --name FlixOne.InventoryManagement
The template "Class library" was created successfully.

Processing post-creation actions...
Running 'dotnet restore' on FlixOne.InventoryManagement\FlixOne.InventoryManagement.csproj...
  Restoring packages for J:\git\FlixOne\FlixOne.InventoryManagement\FlixOne.InventoryManagement.csproj...
  Generating MSBuild file J:\git\FlixOne\FlixOne.InventoryManagement\obj\FlixOne.InventoryManagement.csproj.nuget.g.props.
  Generating MSBuild file J:\git\FlixOne\FlixOne.InventoryManagement\obj\FlixOne.InventoryManagement.csproj.nuget.g.targets.
  Restore completed in 113.91 ms for J:\git\FlixOne\FlixOne.InventoryManagement\FlixOne.InventoryManagement.csproj.

Restore succeeded.
```

References should be made from the solution to the new class library with the following command:

```
dotnet sln add .\FlixOne.InventoryManagement\FlixOne.InventoryManagement.csproj
```

To create a new console application project, the following command should be used:

```
dotnet new console --name FlixOne.InventoryManagementClient
```

The following screenshot shows the `console` template being restored:

```
PS J:\git\FlixOne> dotnet new console --name FlixOne.InventoryManagementClient
The template "Console Application" was created successfully.

Processing post-creation actions...
Running 'dotnet restore' on FlixOne.InventoryManagementClient\FlixOne.InventoryManagementClient.csproj...
  Restoring packages for J:\git\FlixOne\FlixOne.InventoryManagementClient\FlixOne.InventoryManagementClient.csproj...
  Generating MSBuild file J:\git\FlixOne\FlixOne.InventoryManagementClient\obj\FlixOne.InventoryManagementClient.csproj.nuget.g.props.
  Generating MSBuild file J:\git\FlixOne\FlixOne.InventoryManagementClient\obj\FlixOne.InventoryManagementClient.csproj.nuget.g.targets.
  Restore completed in 197.76 ms for J:\git\FlixOne\FlixOne.InventoryManagementClient\FlixOne.InventoryManagementClient.csproj.

Restore succeeded.
```

The console application requires a reference to the class library (note: the command needs to be run in the directory with the project file that will have the reference added to it):

```
dotnet add reference
..\FlixOne.InventoryManagement\FlixOne.InventoryManagement.csproj
```

A new `MSTest` project will be created using the following command:

```
dotnet new mstest --name FlixOne.InventoryManagementTests
```

The following screenshot shows the creation of the MSTest project and should be run in the same folder as the solution, FlixOne (note the packages restored as part of the command containing the required MSTest NuGet packages):

```
PS J:\git\FlixOne> dotnet new mstest --name FlixOne.InventoryManagementTests
The template "Unit Test Project" was created successfully.

Processing post-creation actions...
Running 'dotnet restore' on FlixOne.InventoryManagementTests\FlixOne.InventoryManagementTests.csproj...
  Restoring packages for J:\git\FlixOne\FlixOne.InventoryManagementTests\FlixOne.InventoryManagementTests.csproj...
  Installing Microsoft.TestPlatform.ObjectModel 15.7.0.
  Installing Microsoft.TestPlatform.TestHost 15.7.0.
  Installing MSTest.TestFramework 1.2.1.
  Installing MSTest.TestAdapter 1.2.1.
  Installing Microsoft.NET.Test.Sdk 15.7.0.
  Generating MSBuild file J:\git\FlixOne\FlixOne.InventoryManagementTests\obj\FlixOne.InventoryManagementTests.csproj.nuget.g.props.
  Generating MSBuild file J:\git\FlixOne\FlixOne.InventoryManagementTests\obj\FlixOne.InventoryManagementTests.csproj.nuget.g.targets.
  Restore completed in 2.71 sec for J:\git\FlixOne\FlixOne.InventoryManagementTests\FlixOne.InventoryManagementTests.csproj.

Restore succeeded.
```

The test project also requires a reference to the class library (note: this command needs to be run in the same folder as the MSTest project file):

```
dotnet add reference
..\FlixOne.InventoryManagement\FlixOne.InventoryManagement.csproj
```

Finally, both the console application and the MSTest project should be added to the solution by running the following commands in the same directory as the solution file:

```
dotnet sln add
.\FlixOne.InventoryManagementClient\FlixOne.InventoryManagementClient.csproj
dotnet sln add
.\FlixOne.InventoryManagementTests\FlixOne.InventoryManagementTests.csproj
```

Visually, the solution is shown as follows:

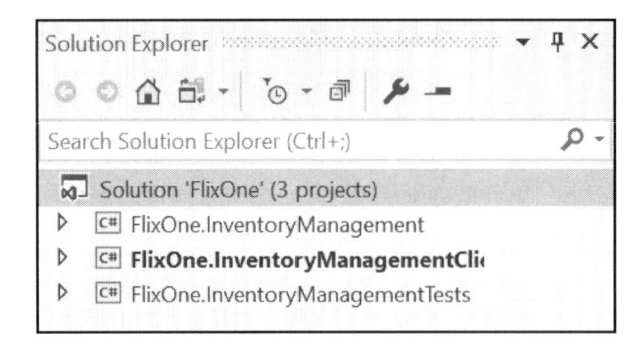

Now that the initial structure of our solution is ready, let's first start by adding to our unit test definitions.

Initial unit test definitions

The development team first transcribed the requirements into some basic unit tests. As nothing had been designed or written yet, these mostly take the form of noting what functionality should be validated. As the design and development progress, these tests will also evolve toward completion; for example, there is a requirement for adding inventory:

> An add inventory command ("a", "addinventory") is available:
> - The name parameter of type string.
> - Add an entry into the database with the given name and a 0 quantity.

To capture this requirement, the development team created the following unit test to serve as a placeholder:

```
[TestMethod]
private void AddInventoryCommand_Successful()
{
  // create an instance of the command
  // add a new book with parameter "name"
  // verify the book was added with the given name with 0 quantity

  Assert.Inconclusive("AddInventoryCommand_Successful has not been implemented.");
}
```

As the application design becomes known and development starts, the existing tests will expand and new tests will be created, as follows:

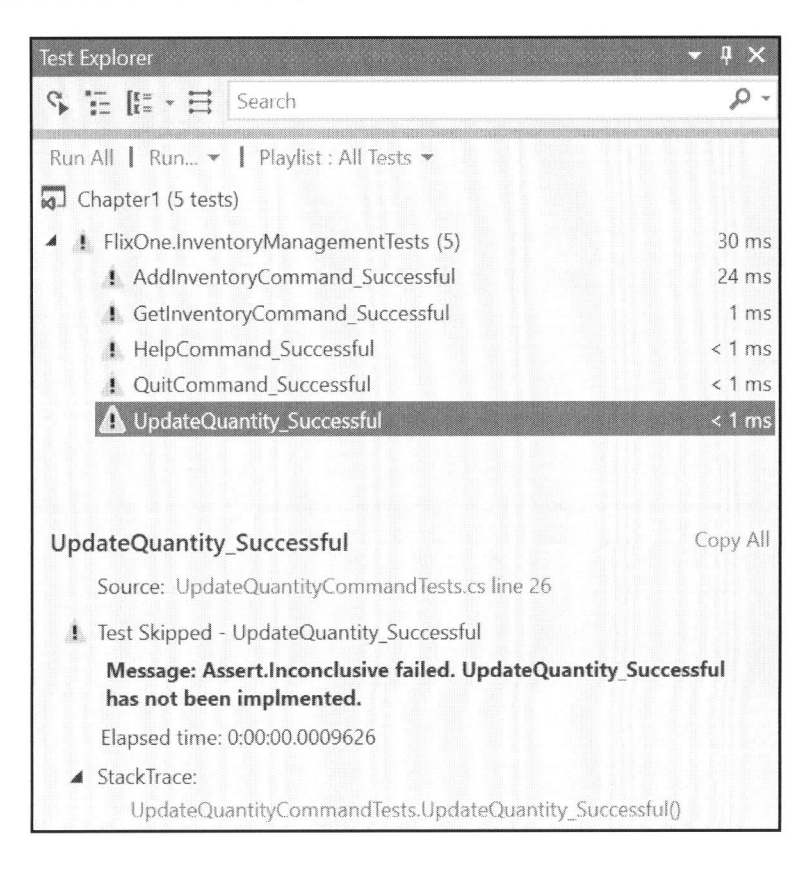

```
Test Explorer
Run All | Run... ▼ | Playlist : All Tests ▼
Chapter1 (5 tests)
  FlixOne.InventoryManagementTests (5)          30 ms
    AddInventoryCommand_Successful              24 ms
    GetInventoryCommand_Successful               1 ms
    HelpCommand_Successful                     < 1 ms
    QuitCommand_Successful                     < 1 ms
    UpdateQuantity_Successful                  < 1 ms

UpdateQuantity_Successful                              Copy All
    Source: UpdateQuantityCommandTests.cs line 26
    Test Skipped - UpdateQuantity_Successful
    Message: Assert.Inconclusive failed. UpdateQuantity_Successful
    has not been implmented.
    Elapsed time: 0:00:00.0009626
    StackTrace:
        UpdateQuantityCommandTests.UpdateQuantity_Successful()
```

The importance of the inconclusive tests is that they communicate what needs to be accomplished to the team and provide a measure as the development proceeds. As the development progresses, inconclusive and failing tests will indicate work to be undertaken and successful tests will indicate progress toward completing the current set of tasks.

Abstract Factory design pattern

To illustrate our first pattern, let's walk through the development of the help command and the initial console application. The initial version of the console application is shown as follows:

```
private static void Main(string[] args)
{
    Greeting();
    // note: inline out variable introduced as part of C# 7.0
    GetCommand("?").RunCommand(out bool shouldQuit);

    while (!shouldQuit)
    {
        // handle the commands
        ...
    }

    Console.WriteLine("CatalogService has completed.");
}
```

When the application starts, both a greeting and the result of a help command are shown. The application will then process entered commands until the quit command is entered.

The following shows the detail of handling commands:

```
while (!shouldQuit)
{
    Console.WriteLine(" > ");
    var input = Console.ReadLine();
    var command = GetCommand(input);

    var wasSuccessful = command.RunCommand(out shouldQuit);

    if (!wasSuccessful)
    {
        Console.WriteLine("Enter ? to view options.");
    }
}
```

Until the application solution quits, the application will continue to prompt the user for command and, if a command was not successfully handled, then help text is shown.

> **RunCommand(out bool shouldQuit)**
> C# 7.0 introduces a more fluid syntax for creating `out` parameters. This will declare the variables in the scope of the command block. This is illustrated with the following, where the `shouldQuit` Boolean is not declared ahead of time.

InventoryCommand abstract class

The first thing to point out about the initial console application is that the team is using **object-oriented programming** (**OOP**) to create a standard way of handling commands. What the team learned from this initial design is that all commands will contain a `RunCommand()` method that will return two Booleans indicating whether the command was successful and whether the program should terminate. For example, the `HelpCommand()` will simply display a help message to the console and should not cause the program to end. The two return Booleans would then be *true*, to indicate that the command ran successfully and *false*, to indicate that the application should not terminate. The following shows the initial version:

> The ... indicates additional statements and, in this particular example, additional `Console.WriteLine()` statements.

```
public class HelpCommand
{
    public bool RunCommand(out bool shouldQuit)
    {
        Console.WriteLine("USAGE:");
        Console.WriteLine("\taddinventory (a)");
        ...
        Console.WriteLine("Examples:");
        ...

        shouldQuit = false;
        return true;
    }
}
```

Implementing Design Patterns - Basics Part 1

The `QuitCommand` will display a message and then cause the program to end. The initial `QuitCommand` was as follows:

```
public class QuitCommand
{
    public bool RunCommand(out bool shouldQuit)
    {
        Console.WriteLine("Thank you for using FlixOne Inventory Management System");
        shouldQuit = true;
        return true;
    }
}
```

The team decided to either create an interface that both classes implement, or an abstract class that both classes inherit from. Both could have achieved the desired dynamic polymorphism but the team chose to use an abstract class as all commands will have shared functionality.

> In OOP and in particular C#, polymorphism is supported in three main ways: function overloading, generics, and subtyping or dynamic polymorphism.

Using the Abstract Factory Design pattern, the team created an abstract class that commands would inherit from, `InventoryCommand`. The `InventoryCommand` class has a single method, `RunCommand`, that will perform the command and return whether the command was successfully executed and whether the application should quit. The class is abstract, meaning the class contains one or more abstract methods. In this case, the `InternalCommand()` method is abstract and the intent is that classes deriving from the `InventoryCommand` class will implement the `InternalCommand` method with the specific command functionality. For example, `QuitCommand` will extend `InventoryCommand` and provide a concrete implementation for the `InternalCommand()` method. The following snippet shows the `InventoryCommand` abstract class with the abstract `InternalCommand()` method:

```
public abstract class InventoryCommand
{
    private readonly bool _isTerminatingCommand;
    internal InventoryCommand(bool commandIsTerminating)
    {
        _isTerminatingCommand = commandIsTerminating;
    }
    public bool RunCommand(out bool shouldQuit)
    {
```

```
            shouldQuit = _isTerminatingCommand;
            return InternalCommand();
        }

        internal abstract bool InternalCommand();
    }
```

The abstract method would then be implemented in each derived class, as illustrated with the `HelpCommand`. The `HelpCommand` simply prints some information to the console and then returns `true`, indicating that the command was executed successfully:

```
    public class HelpCommand : InventoryCommand
    {
        public HelpCommand() : base(false) { }

        internal override bool InternalCommand()
        {
            Console.WriteLine("USAGE:");
            Console.WriteLine("\taddinventory (a)");
            ...
            Console.WriteLine("Examples:");
            ...
            return true;
        }
    }
```

The development team then decided on making two additional changes to the `InventoryCommand`. The first thing they did not like was how the `shouldQuit` Boolean was being returned as an *out* variable. Thus, they decided to use the new tuples feature of C# 7 to instead return a single `Tuple<bool,bool>` object as follows:

```
    public (bool wasSuccessful, bool shouldQuit) RunCommand()
    {
        /* additional code hidden */

        return (InternalCommand(), _isTerminatingCommand);
    }
```

> **Tuple**
>
> The tuple is a C# type that provides a lightweight syntax for packaging multiple values into a single object easily. The disadvantage over defining a class is you lose inheritance and other object-oriented functionality. For more information, please see https://docs.microsoft.com/en-us/dotnet/csharp/tuples.

The other change was to introduce another abstract class to indicate whether the command was a non-terminating command; in other words, a command that does not cause the solution to quit or end.

As shown in the following code, this command is still abstract as it does not implement the `InternalCommand` method of `InventoryCommand`, but it passes a false value to the base class:

```
internal abstract class NonTerminatingCommand : InventoryCommand
{
    protected NonTerminatingCommand() : base(commandIsTerminating: false)
    {
    }
}
```

The advantage here is now commands that do not cause the application to end – in other words, are non-terminating – now have a simpler definition:

```
internal class HelpCommand : NonTerminatingCommand
{
    internal override bool InternalCommand()
    {
        Interface.WriteMessage("USAGE:");
        /* additional code hidden */

        return true;
    }
}
```

The following class diagram shows the inheritance of the `InventoryCommand` abstract class:

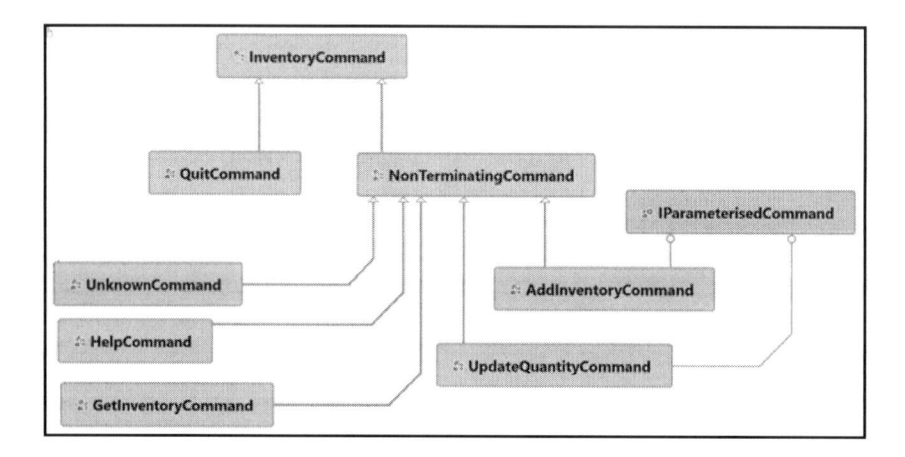

There is only one terminating command, `QuitCommand`, while the other commands extend the `NonTerminatingCommand` abstract class. It is also worth noting that only the `AddInventoryCommand` and `UpdateQuantityCommand` require parameters and the use of the `IParameterisedCommand` is explained later in the *Liskov Substitution Principle* section. Another subtle point in the diagram is that all the types, other than the base `InventoryCommand`, are not public (visible to external assemblies). This will become relevant in the *Access modifiers* section later in the chapter.

SOLID principles

As the team simplifies the code by using patterns, they also use SOLID principles to help identify problems. By simplifying the code, the team aims to make the code more maintainable and easier for new team members to understand. This approach of reviewing the code with a set of principles is very useful in writing concise classes that only do what they need to achieve, and putting in a layer of abstraction that helps to write code that is easier to modify and understand.

Single responsibility principle (SRP)

The first principle that the team applies is the **single responsibility principle** (**SRP**). The team identified that the actual mechanism of writing to the console is not the responsibility of the `InventoryCommand` classes. Because of this, a `ConsoleUserInterface` class is introduced that is responsible for the interaction with the user. SRP will help keep the `InventoryCommand` classes smaller and avoid situations where the same code is duplicated. For example, the application should have a uniform way of prompting the user for information and displaying messages and warnings. Instead of repeating this in the `InventoryCommand` classes, this logic is encapsulated in the `ConsoleUserInterface` class.

The `ConsoleUserInteraface` will consist of three methods, as indicated in the following:

```
public class ConsoleUserInterface
{
    // read value from console

    // message to the console

    // writer warning message to the console
}
```

Implementing Design Patterns - Basics Part 1

The first method will be used to read input from the console:

```
public string ReadValue(string message)
{
    Console.ForegroundColor = ConsoleColor.Green;
    Console.Write(message);
    return Console.ReadLine();
}
```

The second method will print a message to the console using the color green:

```
public void WriteMessage(string message)
{
    Console.ForegroundColor = ConsoleColor.Green;
    Console.WriteLine(message);
}
```

The final method will print a message to the console using a dark yellow color indicating a warning message:

```
public void WriteWarning(string message)
{
    Console.ForegroundColor = ConsoleColor.DarkYellow;
    Console.WriteLine(message);
}
```

With the `ConsoleUserInterface` class, we can reduce the impact of changes to how we interact with the user. As our solution develops, we might find that the interface changes from a console to a web application. In theory, we would replace the `ConsoleUserInterface` with a `WebUserInterface`. If we had not reduced the user interface to a single class, the impact of such a change would most likely be more disruptive.

Open/closed principle (OCP)

The **open/closed principle**, the O in SOLID, is represented by the different `InventoryCommand` classes. Instead of having an implementation of the `InventoryCommand` class per command, the team could have defined a single class containing multiple `if` statements. Each `if` statement would determine what functionality to execute. For example, the following illustrates how the team could have broken this principle:

```
internal bool InternalCommand(string command)
{
    switch (command)
```

```
{
    case "?":
    case "help":
        return RunHelpCommand();
    case "a":
    case "addinventory":
        return RunAddInventoryCommand();
    case "q":
    case "quit":
        return RunQuitCommand();
    case "u":
    case "updatequantity":
        return RunUpdateInventoryCommand();
    case "g":
    case "getinventory":
        return RunGetInventoryCommand();
}
return false;
}
```

The above method breaks this principle because adding a new command would alter the behavior of the code. The idea of the principle is that it is **closed** to modification that would *alter* its behavior and instead is **open** to extend the class to support additional behavior. This is what is accomplished by having the abstract `InventoryCommand` and derived classes (for example, `QuitCommand`, `HelpCommand`, and `AddInventoryCommand`). A compelling reason for this, especially when combined with the other principles, is that it leads to succinct code that is easier to maintain and understand.

Liskov substitution principle (LSP)

The commands for quit, help, and get inventory do not require parameters, while the `AddInventory` and `UpdateQuantityCommand` do. There are several ways to handle this and the team decided to introduce an interface to identify those commands as follows:

```
public interface IParameterisedCommand
{
    bool GetParameters();
}
```

Implementing Design Patterns - Basics Part 1

By applying the **Liskov substitution principle (LSP)**, only those commands that require parameters should implement the `GetParameters()` method. For example, on the `AddInventory` command, the `IParameterisedCommand` is implemented using a method defined on the base `InventoryCommand`:

```
public class AddInventoryCommand : InventoryCommand, IParameterisedCommand
{
    public string InventoryName { get; private set; }

    /// <summary>
    /// AddInventoryCommand requires name
    /// </summary>
    /// <returns></returns>
    public bool GetParameters()
    {
        if (string.IsNullOrWhiteSpace(InventoryName))
            InventoryName = GetParameter("name");

        return !string.IsNullOrWhiteSpace(InventoryName);
    }
}
```

The `GetParameter` method on the `InventoryCommand` class simply uses the `ConsoleUserInterface` to read a value from the console. The method will be shown later in this chapter. In C#, there is handy syntax that shows well how LSP can be used to apply functionality to only objects of a specific interface. On the first line of the `RunCommand` method, the `is` keyword is used to both test whether the current object implements the `IParameterisedCommand` interface as well as cast the object as a new object: `parameterisedCommand`. This is shown in bold in the following code snippet:

```
public (bool wasSuccessful, bool shouldQuit) RunCommand()
{
    if (this is IParameterisedCommand parameterisedCommand)
    {
        var allParametersCompleted = false;

        while (allParametersCompleted == false)
        {
            allParametersCompleted = parameterisedCommand.GetParameters();
        }
    }

    return (InternalCommand(), _isTerminatingCommand);
}
```

Interface segregation principle (ISP)

One approach to handling commands with and without parameters would have been to define another method, `GetParameters`, on the `InventoryCommand` abstract class, and for those that do not require parameters to just return true to indicate that all, in this case no, parameters have been received. For example, the `QuitCommand`, **HelpCommand**, and `GetInventoryCommand` would all have an implementation similar to the following:

```
internal override bool GetParameters()
{
    return true;
}
```

This would work but it does break the **interface segregation principle (ISP)**, which states that an interface should only contain methods and properties that are required. Similar to SRP, which applies to classes, ISP applies to interfaces and is effective in keeping interfaces small and focused. In our example, only the `AddInventoryCommand` and `UpdateQuantityCommand` classes will implement the `InventoryCommand` interface.

Dependency inversion principle

The **dependency inversion principle (DIP)**, also referred to as the **dependency injection principle (DIP)**, modules should not depend on details but, instead, on abstractions. This principle encourages writing loosely coupled code to enhance both readability as well as maintenance, especially in a large complex code base.

If we revisit the `ConsoleUserInterface` class that was introduced earlier (in the *Single responsibility principle* section), we could use the class without the `QuitCommand` as follows:

```
internal class QuitCommand : InventoryCommand
{
    internal override bool InternalCommand()
    {
        var console = new ConsoleUserInterface();
        console.WriteMessage("Thank you for using FlixOne Inventory Management System");
        return true;
    }
}
```

Implementing Design Patterns - Basics Part 1

This breaks several SOLID principles, but in regards to DIP, it makes a tight coupling between the `QuitCommand` and the `ConsoleUserInterface`. Imagine the scenario where the console is no longer the means to display information to the user, or what if the constructor of the `ConsoleUserInterface` requires additional parameters?

By applying the DIP principle, the following refactor was performed. First a new interface, `IUserInterface`, was introduced that contained the definitions of the methods implemented in the `ConsoleUserInterface`. Next, the interface, and not the concrete class, is used in the `InventoryCommand` classes. Finally, a reference to an object implementing the `IUserInterface` is passed into the constructor of the `InventoryCommand` classes. This approach protects the `InventoryCommand` classes from changes to the implementation details of `IUserInterface` classes, as well as providing a mechanism for more easily replacing different implementations of `IUserInterface` as the code base evolves.

The DIP is illustrated as follows with the `QuitCommand` and is our final version of the class for this chapter:

```
internal class QuitCommand : InventoryCommand
{
    public QuitCommand(IUserInterface userInterface) :
            base(commandIsTerminating: true, userInteface: userInterface)
    {
    }

    internal override bool InternalCommand()
    {
        Interface.WriteMessage("Thank you for using FlixOne Inventory Management System");
        return true;
    }
}
```

Note that the class extends the `InventoryCommand` abstract class, providing both a common way of handling commands, as well as providing shared functionality. The constructor requires the `IUserInterface` dependency to be injected when the object is instantiated. Also note the `QuitCommand` implements a single method, `InternalCommand()`, keeping the `QuitCommand` lean and easy to read and understand.

To complete the picture, let's view the final `InventoryCommand` base class. The following shows the constructor and properties:

```
public abstract class InventoryCommand
{
    private readonly bool _isTerminatingCommand;
    protected IUserInterface Interface { get; }

    internal InventoryCommand(bool commandIsTerminating, IUserInterface userInteface)
    {
        _isTerminatingCommand = commandIsTerminating;
        Interface = userInteface;
    }
    ...
}
```

Note the `IUserInterface` is passed into the constructor as well as a Boolean indicating whether the command is terminating or not. The `IUserInterface` is then made available to all implementation of `InventoryCommand` as the `Interface` property.

The `RunCommand` is the only public method on the class:

```
public (bool wasSuccessful, bool shouldQuit) RunCommand()
{
    if (this is IParameterisedCommand parameterisedCommand)
    {
        var allParametersCompleted = false;

        while (allParametersCompleted == false)
        {
            allParametersCompleted = parameterisedCommand.GetParameters();
        }
    }

    return (InternalCommand(), _isTerminatingCommand);
}

internal abstract bool InternalCommand();
```

Furthermore, the `GetParameter` method is a method common to all implementations of `InventoryCommand`, so it is made internal:

```
internal string GetParameter(string parameterName)
{
    return Interface.ReadValue($"Enter {parameterName}:");
}
```

DIP and IoC

The DIP and **Inversion of Control** (**IoC**) are closely related and all address the same issues but in slightly different ways. IoC and its specialized form, the **Service Locator Pattern** (**SLP**), use a mechanism to supply an implementation of an abstraction on demand. So, instead of injecting the implementation, IoC acts as a proxy to supply the details that are required. In the next chapter, .NET Core support for these patterns will be explored.

InventoryCommand unit tests

With the `InventoryCommand` classes taking shape, let's revisit the unit tests so we can start to validate what has been written so far and identify any missing requirements. The SOLID principles will show their value here. Because we kept our classes (SRP) and interfaces (ISP) small, and focused on just the minimum amount of functionality required (LSP), our tests should also be simpler to write and validate. For example, a test regarding one of the commands will not need to validate the display of the messages on the console (for example, color or text size) as that is not the responsibility of the `InventoryCommand` classes but of the implementation of the `IUserInterface`. Also, with dependency injection, we will be able to isolate the test to just the inventory command. The following diagram illustrates this, as the unit test will only validate what is contained in the green box:

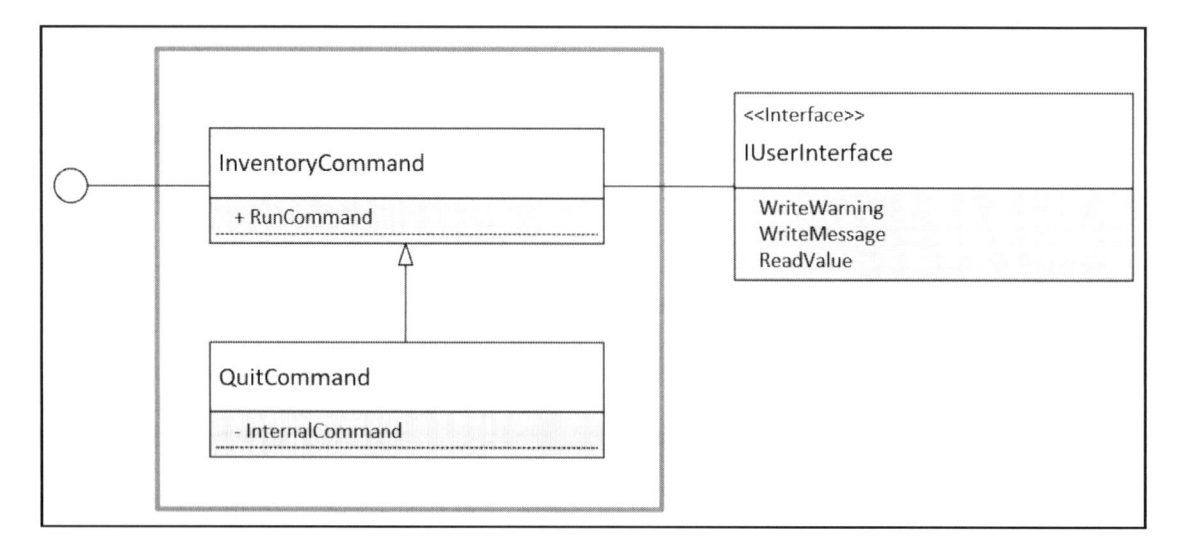

> By keeping the unit test's scope limited, it will be easier to handle change as the application changes. In some situations where it is more difficult to separate the functionality due to interdependencies within classes (in other words, when SOLID is not followed), a test can span a larger section of the application including repositories. These tests are usually referred to as integration tests instead of unit tests.

Access modifiers

Access modifiers are an important way of handling the visibility of types and type members by encapsulating code. By using a clear access strategy, the intent of how an assembly and its types should be used can be communicated and enforced. For example, in the FlixOne application, only types that should be accessed directly by the console are marked as public. This means that the console application should have visibility of a limited number of types and methods. These types and methods have been marked as public while types and methods that the console should not have access to, have been marked as internal, private, or protected.

> Please see the Microsoft docs programming guide for more information on access modifiers:
> https://docs.microsoft.com/en-us/dotnet/csharp/programming-guide/classes-and-structs/access-modifiers

The `InventoryCommand` abstract class is made public as the console application will use the `RunCommand` method to handle the command.

In the following snippet, note how the constructor and interface are made protected to give access to the sub-classes:

```
public abstract class InventoryCommand
{
    private readonly bool _isTerminatingCommand;
    protected IUserInterface Interface { get; }

    protected InventoryCommand(bool commandIsTerminating, IUserInterface userInteface)
    {
        _isTerminatingCommand = commandIsTerminating;
        Interface = userInteface;
    }
    ...
}
```

Implementing Design Patterns - Basics Part 1

In the following snippet, note that the `RunCommand` method is made public while the `InternalCommand` is made internal:

```
public (bool wasSuccessful, bool shouldQuit) RunCommand()
{
    if (this is IParameterisedCommand parameterisedCommand)
    {
        var allParametersCompleted = false;

        while (allParametersCompleted == false)
        {
            allParametersCompleted = parameterisedCommand.GetParameters();
        }
    }

    return (InternalCommand(), _isTerminatingCommand);
}

internal abstract bool InternalCommand();
```

Similarly, the implementations of `InventoryCommand` are marked as internal to prevent them from being directly referenced outside of the assembly. This is illustrated as follows with the `QuitCommand`:

```
internal class QuitCommand : InventoryCommand
{
    internal QuitCommand(IUserInterface userInterface) : base(true, userInterface) { }

    protected override bool InternalCommand()
    {
        Interface.WriteMessage("Thank you for using FlixOne Inventory Management System");
        return true;
    }
}
```

Because the access of the different implementations will not be visible directly to the unit test project, an additional step is required to make the internal types visible. The `assembly` directive could be placed in any compiled file and, for the FlixOne application, an `assembly.cs` was added containing the assembly attribute:

```
using System.Runtime.CompilerServices;
[assembly: InternalsVisibleTo("FlixOne.InventoryManagementTests")]
```

> In situations where the assembly is signed, the `InternalsVisibleTo()` requires a public key. Please see the Microsoft Docs C# Guide for more information: https://docs.microsoft.com/en-us/dotnet/csharp/programming-guide/concepts/assemblies-gac/how-to-create-signed-friend-assemblies.

Helper TestUserInterface

As part of a unit test of one of the `InventoryCommand` implementations, we do not want to test the referenced dependencies. Fortunately, because the commands adhere to the DIP, we can create a `helper` class to validate the implementation interactions with the dependencies. One of the dependencies is the `IUserInterface`, which is passed into the implementation in the constructor. The following is a reminder of the methods of the interface:

```
public interface IUserInterface : IReadUserInterface, IWriteUserInterface {
}

public interface IReadUserInterface
{
    string ReadValue(string message);
}

public interface IWriteUserInterface
{
    void WriteMessage(string message);
    void WriteWarning(string message);
}
```

By implementing a `helper` class, we can supply the information required by the `ReadValue` method as well as verify that the appropriate messages are received in the `WriteMessage` and `WriteWarning` methods. In the test project, a new class called `TestUserInterface` was created that implements the `IUserInterface` interface. The class contains three lists containing the expected `WriteMessage`, `WriteWarning`, and `ReadValue` calls, and keeps track of the number of times it has been called.

For example, the `WriteWarning` method is shown as follows:

```
public void WriteWarning(string message)
{
    Assert.IsTrue(_expectedWriteWarningRequestsIndex <
_expectedWriteWarningRequests.Count,
                "Received too many command write warning requests.");
```

```
    Assert.AreEqual(_expectedWriteWarningRequests[_expectedWriteWarningRequests
    Index++], message,                        "Received unexpected command
    write warning message");
    }
```

The `WriteWarning` method performs two asserts. The first verifies that the method is not called more times than expected and the second verifies that the message received matches the expected message.

The `ReadValue` method is similar but it additionally returns a value back to the calling `InventoryCommand` implementation. This will simulate the user entering information into the console:

```
    public string ReadValue(string message)
    {
        Assert.IsTrue(_expectedReadRequestsIndex < _expectedReadRequests.Count,
                    "Received too many command read requests.");
    Assert.AreEqual(_expectedReadRequests[_expectedReadRequestsIndex].Item1,
    message,
                      "Received unexpected command read message");

        return _expectedReadRequests[_expectedReadRequestsIndex++].Item2;
    }
```

As an extra validation step, at the end of a test method, the `TestUserInterface` is called to verify that the expected number of `ReadValue`, `WriteMessage`, and `WriteWarning` requests were received:

```
    public void Validate()
    {
        Assert.IsTrue(_expectedReadRequestsIndex ==
    _expectedReadRequests.Count,
                    "Not all read requests were performed.");
        Assert.IsTrue(_expectedWriteMessageRequestsIndex ==
    _expectedWriteMessageRequests.Count,
                    "Not all write requests were performed.");
        Assert.IsTrue(_expectedWriteWarningRequestsIndex ==
    _expectedWriteWarningRequests.Count,
                    "Not all warning requests were performed.");
    }
```

The `TestUserInterface` class illustrates how a dependency can be mocked to provide stubbed functionality as well as provide assertions to help verify the expected behavior. In later chapters, we will use a third-party package to provide a more sophisticated framework for mocking the dependencies.

Example unit test – QuitCommand

Starting with the `QuitCommand`, the requirements are pretty straightforward: the command should print a farewell message and then cause the application to end. We have designed the `InventoryCommand` to return two Booleans to indicate whether the application should quit and whether the command ended successfully:

```
[TestMethod]
public void QuitCommand_Successful()
{
    var expectedInterface = new Helpers.TestUserInterface(
        new List<Tuple<string, string>>(), // ReadValue()
        new List<string> // WriteMessage()
        {
            "Thank you for using FlixOne Inventory Management System"
        },
        new List<string>() // WriteWarning()
    );

    // create an instance of the command
    var command = new QuitCommand(expectedInterface);

    var result = command.RunCommand();

    expectedInterface.Validate();

    Assert.IsTrue(result.shouldQuit, "Quit is a terminating command.");
    Assert.IsTrue(result.wasSuccessful, "Quit did not complete Successfully.");
}
```

The test uses the `TestUserInterface` to verify that the text `"Thank you for using FlixOne Inventory Management System"` is sent to the `WriteMessage` method and no `ReadValue` or `WriteWarning` requests are received. These last two criteria are verified by the `expectedInterface.Validate()` call. The result of the `QuitCommand` is verified by checking that the `shouldQuit` and `wasSuccessful` Booleans are true.

> **TIP**
> In the FlixOne scenario, the text to be shown is *hardcoded* in the solution for simplicity. A better approach would be to use resource files. Resource files provide a way of maintaining the text separate from the functionality as well as supporting localizing the data for different cultures.

Summary

This chapter introduced the scenario of an online bookseller, FlixOne, wanting to build an application for managing their inventory. The chapter covered a range of patterns and practices that the development team can use while developing the application. The team used MVP to help keep the scope of the initial delivery to a manageable level and to help focus the business onto determining the requirements that had the maximum benefit to the organization. The team decided to use TDD to validate that the delivery matches the requirements and to help the team measure progress. The basic project, as well as the unit testing framework, MSTest, was created. The team also used SOLID principles to help structure the code in a way that will both help readability as well as the maintenance of the code base, as new enhancements to the application are added. The first Gang of Four pattern, the Abstract Factory design pattern, was used to provide a base for all inventory commands.

In the next chapter, the team will continue to build the initial inventory management project to fit the requirements defined in the MVP. The Gang of Four's Singleton pattern and the Factory Method pattern will be used by the team. These will be shown both with and without the mechanisms supported in .NET Core for these features.

Questions

The following questions will allow you to consolidate the information contained in this chapter:

1. In developing software for an organization, why is it sometimes difficult to determine requirements?
2. What are two advantages and disadvantages of Waterfall software development versus Agile software development?
3. How does dependency injection help when writing unit tests?
4. Why is the following statement false? With TDD, you no longer need people to test a new software deployment.

4
Implementing Design Patterns - Basics Part 2

In the previous chapter, we introduced FlixOne and the initial development of a new inventory management application. Several patterns were used by the development team, ranging from patterns designed to limit the scope of a deliverable such as a **Minimum Viable Product** (**MVP**) to patterns to assist in the development of the project such as **Test Driven Development** (**TDD**). Several patterns from the **Gang of Four** (**GoF**) were also applied as a solution to leverage how others have solved similar problems in the past so that we don't repeat common mistakes. Single responsibility principle, Open–closed principle, Liskov substitution principle, Interface Segregation principle, and Dependency inversion principle (SOLID principles) were applied to ensure we are creating a stable code base that will help in the management and future development of our application.

This chapter will continue to explain the building of the FlixOne inventory management application by incorporating more patterns. More of the GoF patterns will be used, including the singleton and factory patterns. A singleton pattern will be used to illustrate the repository pattern that is used to maintain the FlixOne collection of books. The factory pattern will further the understanding of the **Dependency Injection** (**DI**). Finally, we will use the .NET Core framework to facilitate an **Inversion of Control** (**IoC**) container that will be used to complete the initial inventory management console application.

The following topics will be covered in this chapter:

- The singleton pattern
- The factory pattern
- Features of .NET Core
- Console application

Technical requirements

This chapter contains various code examples to explain these concepts. The code is kept simple and is just for demonstration purposes. Most of the examples involve a .NET Core console application written in C#.

To run and execute the code, you will need the following:

- Visual Studio 2019 (you can also run the application using Visual Studio 2017 version 3 or later)
- .NET Core
- SQL Server (the Express Edition is used in this chapter)

Installing Visual Studio

To run these code examples, you need to install Visual Studio or later. You can use your preferred IDE. To do this, follow these instructions:

1. Download Visual Studio from the following link: https://docs.microsoft.com/en-us/visualstudio/install/install-visual-studio.
2. Follow the installation instructions included. Multiple versions are available for the installation of Visual Studio; in this chapter, we are using Visual Studio for Windows.

Setting up .NET Core

If you do not have .NET Core installed, you will need to follow these instructions:

1. Download .NET Core from the following link: https://www.microsoft.com/net/download/windows.
2. Follow the installation instructions for the related library: https://dotnet.microsoft.com/download/dotnet-core/2.2.

> The complete source code is available in GitHub. The source code that is shown in this chapter might not be complete, so it is recommended that you retrieve the source code in order to run the examples (https://github.com/PacktPublishing/Hands-On-Design-Patterns-with-C-and-.NET-Core/tree/master/Chapter4).

The singleton pattern

The singleton pattern is another GoF design pattern that is used to restrict the instantiation of a class to one object. It is used in situations where actions within a system need to be coordinated or access to data needs to be limited. For example, if access to a file needs to be restricted within an application to a single writer, then a singleton could be used to prevent multiple objects from trying to write to the file at the same time. In our scenario, we are going to use a singleton to maintain the collection of books and their inventory.

The value of the singleton pattern is more apparent when it is illustrated using examples. This section will start with a basic class and then go on to identify the different issues that the singleton pattern addresses. These issues will be identified, and the class will be updated and then verified by unit tests.

The singleton pattern should only be used when necessary as it can introduce a potential bottleneck for the application. Sometimes, the pattern is viewed as an anti-pattern as it introduces global state. With global state, unknown dependencies within an application are introduced and it then becomes unclear as to how many types might depend on the information. Additionally, many frameworks and repositories already limit access when required, so introducing an additional mechanism might limit the performance unnecessarily.

> .NET Core provides support for a number of the patterns discussed. In the next chapter, we will take advantage of the `ServiceCollection` class's support for both the factory method and the singleton pattern.

In our scenario, the singleton pattern will be used to hold an in-memory repository containing a collection of books. The singleton will prevent the collection of books from being updated by more than one thread at a time. This will require us to *lock* a section of the code to prevent unpredictable updates.

The complexity of introducing a singleton into an application can be subtle; so, to gain a solid understanding of the pattern, we will cover the following topics:

- .Net Framework's handling of processes and threads
- The repository pattern
- Race conditions
- Unit testing to identify race conditions

Processes and threads

To understand the singleton pattern, we need to provide a little context. In the .Net Framework, an application will be composed of lightweight, managed subprocesses called application domains that can comprise one or more managed threads. For the purpose of understanding the singleton pattern, let's define this as a multithreaded application that contains one or more threads running simultaneously. Technically, the threads are actually not running simultaneously, but this is achieved by dividing the available processor time between the threads, so that each thread will execute for a small amount of time and then the thread will suspend activity, allowing for another thread to execute.

Going back to the singleton pattern, in a multithreaded application, special care needs to be taken to ensure that access to the singleton is limited so that only one thread enters specific areas of logic at a time. Because of this synchronization of threads, it is possible for one thread to retrieve a value and update it, and, before it can be stored, another thread also updates the value.

> The potential for more than one thread to access the same shared data and update it with unpredictable results can be referred to as a **race condition**.

To avoid data being updated incorrectly, some restriction is required to prevent more than one thread from executing the same block of logic at the same time. There are several mechanisms supported in the .Net Framework and, in the singleton pattern, the `lock` keyword is used. In the following code, the `lock` keyword is illustrated to show that only one thread at a time can execute the highlighted code while all other threads will be blocked:

```csharp
public class Inventory
{
    int _quantity;
    private Object _lock = new Object();

    public void RemoveQuantity(int amount)
    {
        lock (_lock)
        {
            if (_quantity - amount < 0)
            {
                throw new Exception("Cannot remove more than we have!");
            }
            _quantity -= amount;
        }
    }
}
```

}

The lock is a simple way of restricting access to a section of code and can be applied to both object instances, as our previous example shows, and to the sections of code marked as static.

The repository pattern

The singleton pattern that is introduced to the project is applied to a class being used to maintain the inventory's collection of books. The singleton will prevent access from multiple threads being handled incorrectly, and, another pattern, the repository pattern, will be used to create a facade over the data that is being managed.

The repository pattern provides an abstraction over a repository to provide a layer between the business logic of an application and the underlying data. This provides several advantages. By having a clean separation, our business logic can be maintained and unit tested independently of the underlying data. Often, the same repository pattern class can be reused by multiple business objects. An example of this could be `GetInventoryCommand`, `AddInventoryCommand`, and `UpdateInventoryCommand` objects; all of these objects use the same repository class. This allows us to test the logic in these commands in isolation from the repository. Another advantage of the pattern is that it enables centralized data-related policies to be more easily implemented, such as caching.

To begin, let's consider the following interface that describes the methods that the repository will implement; it contains a method for retrieving the books, adding a book, and updating the quantity of the book:

```
internal interface IInventoryContext
{
    Book[] GetBooks();
    bool AddBook(string name);
    bool UpdateQuantity(string name, int quantity);
}
```

The initial version of the repository is as follows:

```
internal class InventoryContext : IInventoryContext
{
    public InventoryContext()
    {
        _books = new Dictionary<string, Book>();
    }
    private readonly IDictionary<string, Book> _books;
```

Implementing Design Patterns - Basics Part 2

```
public Book[] GetBooks()
{
    return _books.Values.ToArray();
}

public bool AddBook(string name)
{
    _books.Add(name, new Book { Name = name });
    return true;
}

public bool UpdateQuantity(string name, int quantity)
{
    _books[name].Quantity += quantity;
    return true;
}
```

> In this chapter, the book collection is being maintained in the form of an in-memory cache, and, in later chapters, this will be moved to a repository providing persistent data. Of course, this implementation is not ideal, as, once the application ends, all the data will be lost. However, it serves to illustrate the singleton pattern.

Unit tests

To illustrate the issues that the singleton pattern addresses, let's start with a simple unit test that adds 30 books to the repository, updates the quantity of the different books, and then verifies the result. The following code shows the overall unit test, and we will explain each step individually:

```
[TestClass]
public class InventoryContextTests
{
    [TestMethod]
    public void MaintainBooks_Successful()
    {
        var context = new InventoryContext();

        // add thirty books
        ...

        // let's update the quantity of the books by adding 1, 2, 3, 4, 5
...
        ...
```

```
            // let's update the quantity of the books by subtracting 1, 2, 3,
    4, 5 ...
            ...
            // all quantities should be 0
            ...
        }
    }
```

To add 30 books, the `context` instance is used to add books from `Book_1` to `Book_30`:

```
            // add thirty books
            foreach(var id in Enumerable.Range(1, 30))
            {
                context.AddBook($"Book_{id}");
            }
```

The next section updates the book quantity by adding the numbers from 1 to 10 to the quantity of each book:

```
            // let's update the quantity of the books by adding 1, 2, 3, 4, 5
    ...
            foreach (var quantity in Enumerable.Range(1, 10))
            {
                foreach (var id in Enumerable.Range(1, 30))
                {
                    context.UpdateQuantity($"Book_{id}", quantity);
                }
            }
```

Then, in the next section, we will subtract the numbers from 1 to 10 from the quantity of each book:

```
            foreach (var quantity in Enumerable.Range(1, 10))
            {
                foreach (var id in Enumerable.Range(1, 30))
                {
                    context.UpdateQuantity($"Book_{id}", -quantity);
                }
            }
```

As we have added and removed the same quantity for each book, the last part of our test will verify that the ending quantity is 0:

```
            // all quantities should be 0
            foreach (var book in context.GetBooks())
            {
                Assert.AreEqual(0, book.Quantity);
```

}

After running the test, we can see that the test passes:

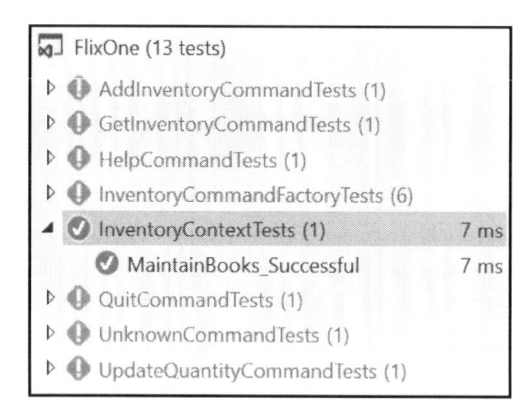

```
FlixOne (13 tests)
    ▷ AddInventoryCommandTests (1)
    ▷ GetInventoryCommandTests (1)
    ▷ HelpCommandTests (1)
    ▷ InventoryCommandFactoryTests (6)
    ▲ ✓ InventoryContextTests (1)                7 ms
           ✓ MaintainBooks_Successful            7 ms
    ▷ QuitCommandTests (1)
    ▷ UnknownCommandTests (1)
    ▷ UpdateQuantityCommandTests (1)
```

So, when the test is run in a single process, the repository works as desired. However, what if the update requests are performed in separate threads? In order to test this, the unit test will be refactored to perform calls to the `InventoryContext` class in separate threads.

The addition of the books is moved to a method that performs adding a book as a task (that is, in its own thread):

```
public Task AddBook(string book)
{
    return Task.Run(() =>
    {
        var context = new InventoryContext();
        Assert.IsTrue(context.AddBook(book));
    });
}
```

Additionally, the update quantity step is moved into another method with a similar approach:

```
public Task UpdateQuantity(string book, int quantity)
{
    return Task.Run(() =>
    {
        var context = new InventoryContext();
        Assert.IsTrue(context.UpdateQuantity(book, quantity));
    });
}
```

The unit test is then updated to call the new methods. It is worth noting that the unit test will wait until all books are added before updating the quantity.

The `add thirty books` section now looks as follows:

```
// add thirty books
foreach (var id in Enumerable.Range(1, 30))
{
    tasks.Add(AddBook($"Book_{id}"));
}

Task.WaitAll(tasks.ToArray());
tasks.Clear();
```

Similarly, the update quantity is changed to call both the `Add` and `subtract` method in the tasks:

```
// let's update the quantity of the books by adding 1, 2, 3, 4, 5 ...
foreach (var quantity in Enumerable.Range(1, 10))
{
    foreach (var id in Enumerable.Range(1, 30))
    {
        tasks.Add(UpdateQuantity($"Book_{id}", quantity));
    }
}

// let's update the quantity of the books by subtractin 1, 2, 3, 4, 5 ...
foreach (var quantity in Enumerable.Range(1, 10))
{
    foreach (var id in Enumerable.Range(1, 30))
    {
        tasks.Add(UpdateQuantity($"Book_{id}", -quantity));
    }
}

// wait for all adds and subtracts to finish
Task.WaitAll(tasks.ToArray());
```

Implementing Design Patterns - Basics Part 2

After the refactor, the unit test no longer successfully completes, and, when the unit test runs now, an error is reported indicating that the book was not found in the collection. This will be reported as "`The given key was not present in the dictionary.`". This is because each time the context is instantiated, a new books collection is created. The first step is to restrict the creation of the context. This is done by changing the access of the constructor so that the class can no longer be instantiated directly. Instead, a new public `static` property that only supports a `get` operation is added. This property will return an underlying `static` instance of the `InventoryContext` class and, if the instance is missing, will create it:

```
internal class InventoryContext : IInventoryContext
{
    protected InventoryContext()
    {
        _books = new Dictionary<string, Book>();
    }

    private static InventoryContext _context;
    public static InventoryContext Singleton
    {
        get
        {
            if (_context == null)
            {
                _context = new InventoryContext();
            }

            return _context;
        }
    }
    ...
}
```

This is still not enough to fix the broken unit test, but this is due to a different reason. To identify the issue, the unit test is run in debug mode with a breakpoint set in the `UpdateQuantity` method. The first time this is run, we can see that 28 books have been created and loaded in the book collection, as shown in the following screenshot:

Chapter 4

```
public bool UpdateQuantity(string name, int quantity)
{
    _books[name].Quantity += quantity;      ⊞●_books Count = 28
    return true;
}
```

At this point in the unit test, we would expect 30 books; however, before we start investigating, let's run the unit test a second time. This time, we get an **Object reference not set to an instance of an object** error when we try to access the books collection for adding a new book, as shown in the following screenshot:

```
public bool AddBook(string name)
{
    _books.Add(name, new Book { Name = name });
    return true;
}

3 references
public bool UpdateQuantity(string name, int quan
{
▶   _books[name].Quantity += quantity;       ⊞●_bo
    return true;
}
```

Exception User-Unhandled

System.NullReferenceException: 'Object reference not set to an instance of an object.'

View Details | Copy Details
▷ Exception Settings

Moreover, when the unit test is run a third time, the **Object reference not set to an instance of an object** error is not encountered, but there are only 27 books in our collection, as shown in the following screenshot:

```
public bool UpdateQuantity(string name, int quantity)
{
    _books[name].Quantity += quantity;      ⊞●_books Count = 27
    return true;
}
```

This type of unpredictable behavior is typical of race conditions and indicates that the shared resource, that is, the `InventoryContext` singleton, is being handled by multiple threads without synchronizing the access. The construction of the static object still allows more than one instance of the `InventoryContext` singleton to be created:

```
public static InventoryContext Singleton
{
    get
```

Implementing Design Patterns - Basics Part 2

```
    {
        if (_context == null)
        {
            _context = new InventoryContext();
        }

        return _context;
    }
}
```

The race condition is where multiple threads evaluate the `if` statement as true and they all try to construct the `_context` object. All will succeed, but they will overwrite the previously constructed value by doing so. Of course, this is inefficient, especially when the constructor is a costly operation, but the issue discovered with the unit test is that the `_context` object is actually constructed by a thread after another thread or threads have updated the books collection. That is why the books collection, `_books`, has a different number of elements between runs.

To prevent this issue, the pattern uses a lock around the constructor as follows:

```
private static object _lock = new object();
public static InventoryContext Singleton
{
    get
    {
        if (_context == null)
        {
            lock (_lock)
            {
                _context = new InventoryContext();
            }
        }
        return _context;
    }
}
```

Unfortunately, the unit tests still fail. This is because although one thread at a time can enter the lock, all blocked instances will still enter the lock once the blocking thread has completed. The pattern handles this situation by having an additional check inside the lock in case the construction has already been completed:

```
public static InventoryContext Singleton
{
    get
    {
        if (_context == null)
        {
```

```
        lock (_lock)
        {
            if (_context == null)
            {
                _context = new InventoryContext();
            }
        }
    }
    return _context;
}
```

The preceding lock is essential as it prevents the static `InventoryContext` object from getting instantiated multiple times. Unfortunately, our test still does not consistently pass; with each change, the unit test becomes closer to passing. Some unit test runs will complete without error but, occasionally, the test completes with a failed result, as indicated in the following screenshot:

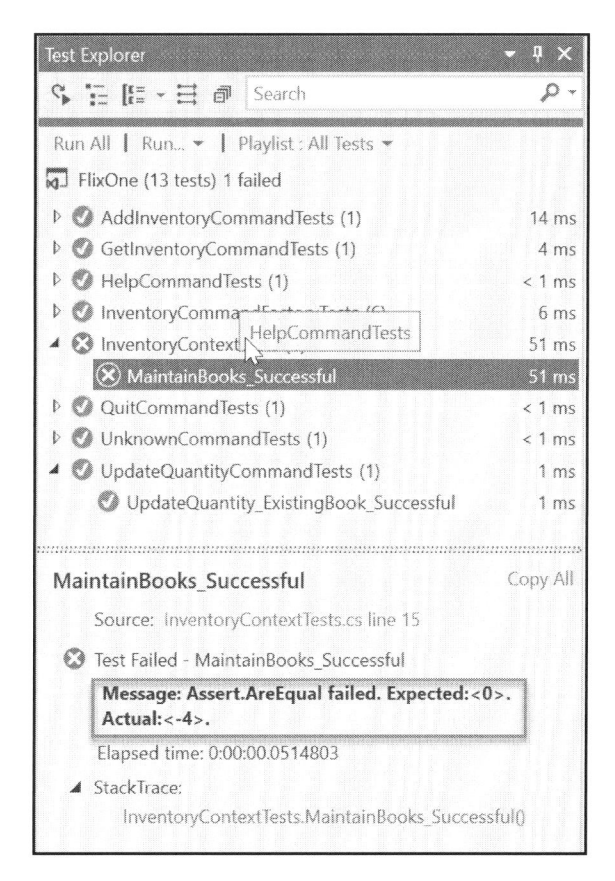

Our instantiation of the static repository is now thread safe, but our access to the books collection is not. One thing to note is that the `Dictionary` class being used is not thread-safe. Fortunately, there are thread-safe collections available as part of the .Net Framework. These classes ensure that **adds and removals** from the collection are written for a multithreaded process. Note that only adds and removals are thread safe as this will become important a little bit later. The updated constructor is shown in the following code:

```
protected InventoryContext()
{
    _books = new ConcurrentDictionary<string, Book>();
}
```

> **TIP**
> Microsoft recommends using the thread-safe collections in `System.Collections.Concurrent` over the corresponding collections in `System.Collections`, unless the application is targeting .Net Framework 1.1 or earlier.

After running the unit test again, introducing a `ConcurrentDictionary` class is still not enough to prevent incorrectly maintaining the books. The unit test is still failing. The concurrent dictionary protects from multiple threads being added and removed unpredictably, but does not offer any protection on the items in the collection themselves. This means that updates to the objects in the collection are not thread safe.

Let's take a closer look at race conditions in a multithreaded environment to understand why this is the case.

A race condition illustration

The following sequence of diagrams visualize what is happening conceptually between two threads: **ThreadA** and **ThreadB**. The first diagram shows both threads without any values from the collection:

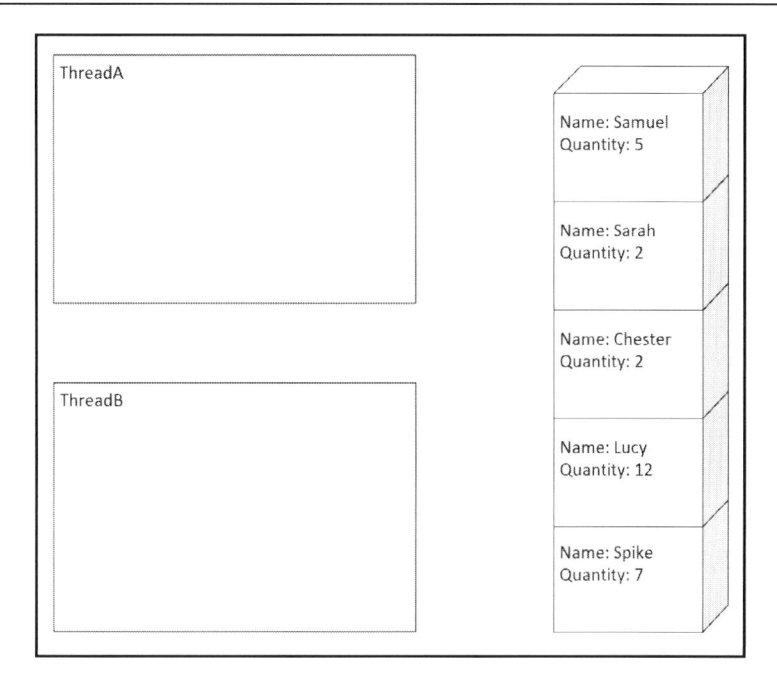

The following diagram shows that both threads read from the collection of the book with the name of `Chester`:

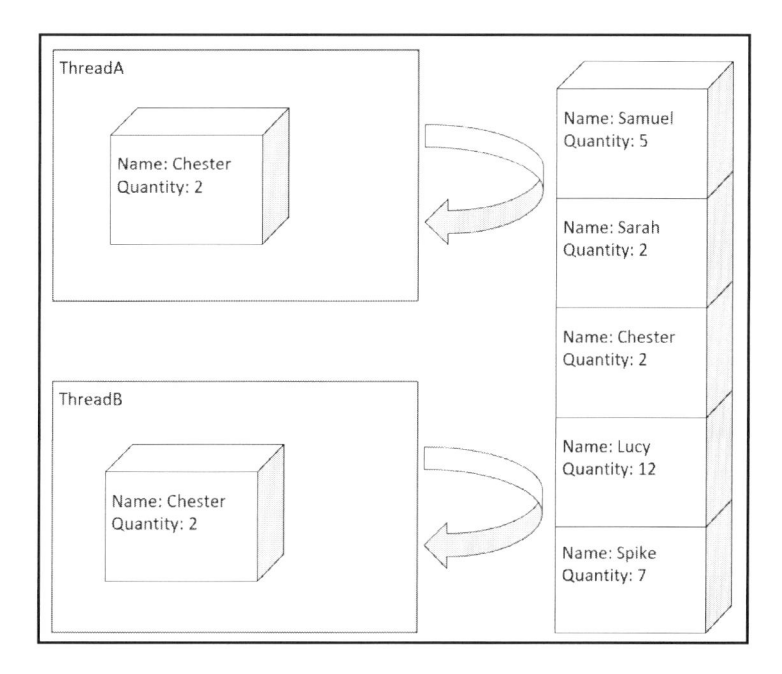

Implementing Design Patterns - Basics Part 2

The following diagram shows that **ThreadA** updates the book by increasing the quantity by 4, while **ThreadB** updates the book by increasing the quantity by 3:

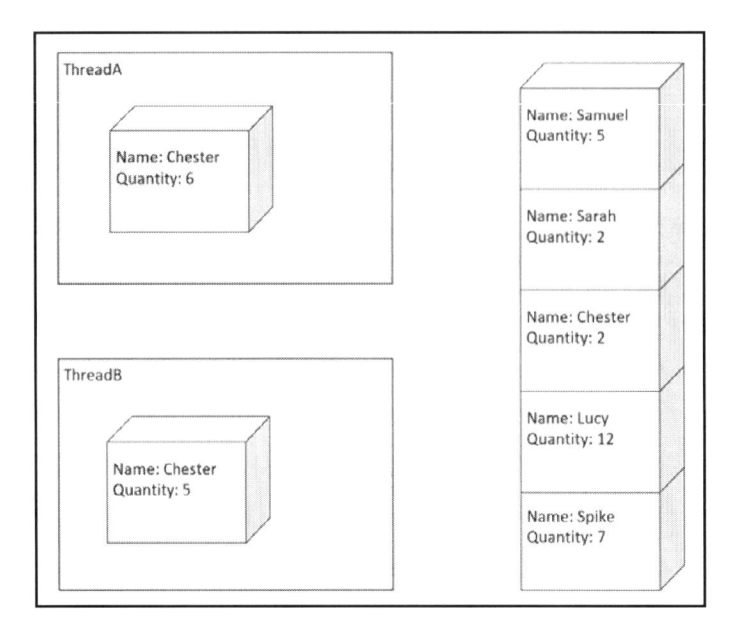

Then, when the updated book is persisted back to the collection, we have an unknown quantity as the result, as shown in the following diagram:

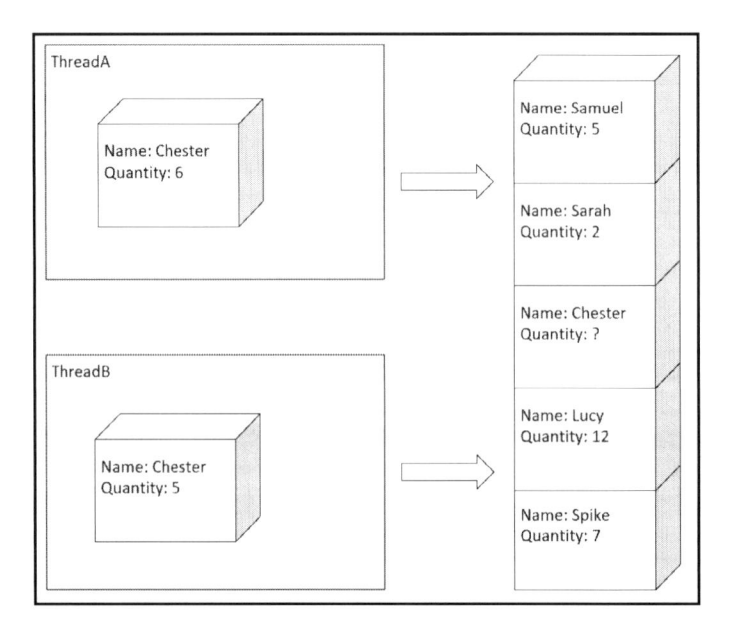

To avoid this race condition, we need to block other threads while an update operation is taking place. In `InventoryContext`, blocking other threads takes the form of a lock around the update of the book quantity:

```
public bool UpdateQuantity(string name, int quantity)
{
    lock (_lock)
    {
        _books[name].Quantity += quantity;
    }

    return true;
}
```

The unit test now completes without error, as the additional locks prevent unpredictable race conditions.

> The `InventoryContext` class is still not complete as it has been completed just enough to illustrate the singleton and repository patterns. In later chapters, the `InventoryContext` class will be adapted to use Entity Framework, an **Object Relational Mapping** (**ORM**) framework. At this point, the `InventoryContext` class will be improved to support additional functionality.

AddInventoryCommand

With our repository available, the three `InventoryCommand` classes can be completed. The first, `AddInventoryCommand`, is shown as follows:

```
internal class AddInventoryCommand : NonTerminatingCommand,
IParameterisedCommand
{
    private readonly IInventoryContext _context;

    internal AddInventoryCommand(IUserInterface userInterface,
IInventoryContext context)
                                                        :
base(userInterface)
    {
        _context = context;
    }

    public string InventoryName { get; private set; }

    /// <summary>
```

```
        /// AddInventoryCommand requires name
        /// </summary>
        /// <returns></returns>
        public bool GetParameters()
        {
            if (string.IsNullOrWhiteSpace(InventoryName))
                InventoryName = GetParameter("name");

            return !string.IsNullOrWhiteSpace(InventoryName);
        }

        protected override bool InternalCommand()
        {
            return _context.AddBook(InventoryName);
        }
    }
```

The first thing to note is that the repository, `IInventoryContext`, is injected in the constructor along with the `IUserInterface` interface described in the previous chapter. The command also requires a single parameter, `name`, to be supplied. This is retrieved in the `GetParameters` method that implements the `IParameterisedCommand` interface, which was also covered in the previous chapter. The command is then run in the `InternalCommand` method, which simply executes the `AddBook` method on the repository and returns a bool indicating whether the command has executed successfully.

TestInventoryContext

Similar to `TestUserInterface` used in the previous chapter, the `TestInventoryContext` class will be used to mock the behavior of our repository by implementing the `IInventoryContext` interface. This class will support the three methods of the interface, as well as supporting two additional methods for retrieving the books that have been added to the collection during the unit test and for retrieving the books that have been updated during the unit test.

To support the `TestInventoryContext` class, two collections will be used:

```
    private readonly IDictionary<string, Book> _seedDictionary;
    private readonly IDictionary<string, Book> _books;
```

The first is used to store the starting collection of the books, while the second is used to store the final collection of the books. The constructor is shown in the following code; note how the dictionaries are copies of each other:

```
public TestInventoryContext(IDictionary<string, Book> books)
{
    _seedDictionary = books.ToDictionary(book => book.Key,
                                        book => new Book { Id = book.Value.Id,
                                                           Name = book.Value.Name,
                                                           Quantity = book.Value.Quantity });
    _books = books;
}
```

The `IInventoryContext` methods are written to update and return just one of the collections, as follows:

```
public Book[] GetBooks()
{
    return _books.Values.ToArray();
}

public bool AddBook(string name)
{
    _books.Add(name, new Book() { Name = name });

    return true;
}

public bool UpdateQuantity(string name, int quantity)
{
    _books[name].Quantity += quantity;

    return true;
}
```

At the end of the unit test, the two remaining methods can be used to determine the difference between the starting and ending collections:

```
public Book[] GetAddedBooks()
{
    return _books.Where(book => !_seedDictionary.ContainsKey(book.Key))
                 .Select(book => book.Value).ToArray();
}
```

```
public Book[] GetUpdatedBooks()
{
    return _books.Where(book => _seedDictionary[book.Key].Quantity != book.Value.Quantity)
                                                            .Select(book => book.Value).ToArray();
}
```

> There is some confusion in the software industry around the differences between mocks, stubs, fakes, and other terms used to identify and/or categorize types or services used in testing that are not suitable for production but are necessary for the unit test. These dependencies may have functionality that is different, missing, and/or the same as their *real* counterparts.
>
> For example, the `TestUserInterface` class could be referred to as a mock as it provides some expectation (for example, assert statements) of the unit test while the `TestInventoryContext` class would be a fake, as it provides a working implementation. In this book, we will not follow these classifications too strictly.

AddInventoryCommandTest

`AddInventoryCommandTest` was updated by the team to verify the `AddInventoryCommand` functionality. This test will verify the adding of a single book to an existing inventory. The first part of the test is to define what is expected of the interface, which is only a single prompt to receive the new book name (remember that the `TestUserInterface` class takes three parameters: expected input, expected messages, and expected warnings):

```
const string expectedBookName = "AddInventoryUnitTest";
var expectedInterface = new Helpers.TestUserInterface(
    new List<Tuple<string, string>>
    {
        new Tuple<string, string>("Enter name:", expectedBookName)
    },
    new List<string>(),
    new List<string>()
);
```

The `TestInventoryContext` class will be initialized with a single book simulating an existing book collection:

```
var context = new TestInventoryContext(new Dictionary<string, Book>
{
    { "Gremlins", new Book { Id = 1, Name = "Gremlins", Quantity = 7 } }
});
```

The following code snippet shows the creation of `AddInventoryCommand`, the running of the command, and the assert statements used to validate that the command ran successfully:

```
// create an instance of the command
var command = new AddInventoryCommand(expectedInterface, context);

// add a new book with parameter "name"
var result = command.RunCommand();

Assert.IsFalse(result.shouldQuit, "AddInventory is not a terminating command.");
Assert.IsTrue(result.wasSuccessful, "AddInventory did not complete Successfully.");

// verify the book was added with the given name with 0 quantity
Assert.AreEqual(1, context.GetAddedBooks().Length, "AddInventory should have added one new book.");

var newBook = context.GetAddedBooks().First();
Assert.AreEqual(expectedBookName, newBook.Name, "AddInventory did not add book successfully.");
```

After the command is run, the result is verified to have run without error and that the command is not a terminating command. The rest of the `Assert` statements validate the expectation that only one book was added with the expected name.

UpdateQuantityCommand

`UpdateQuantityCommand` is very similar to `AddInventoryCommand` and its source is as follows:

```
internal class UpdateQuantityCommand : NonTerminatingCommand,
IParameterisedCommand
{
    private readonly IInventoryContext _context;
```

```
        internal UpdateQuantityCommand(IUserInterface userInterface,
IInventoryContext context)
: base(userInterface)
    {
        _context = context;
    }

    internal string InventoryName { get; private set; }

    private int _quantity;
    internal int Quantity { get => _quantity; private set => _quantity =
value; }

        ...
}
```

Like `AddInventoryCommand`, the `UpdateInventoryCommand` command is a non-terminating command with parameters. Therefore, it extends the `NonTerminatingCommand` base class and implements the `IParameterisedCommand` interface. Similarly, the dependencies for `IUserInterface` and `IInventoryContext` are injected in the constructor:

```
        /// <summary>
        /// UpdateQuantity requires name and an integer value
        /// </summary>
        /// <returns></returns>
        public bool GetParameters()
        {
            if (string.IsNullOrWhiteSpace(InventoryName))
                InventoryName = GetParameter("name");

            if (Quantity == 0)
                int.TryParse(GetParameter("quantity"), out _quantity);

            return !string.IsNullOrWhiteSpace(InventoryName) && Quantity != 0;
        }
```

The `UpdateQuantityCommand` class does have an additional parameter, *quantity*, which is determined as part of the `GetParameters` method.

Finally, the quantity of a book is updated via the repository's `UpdateQuantity` method in the `InternalCommand` override method:

```
        protected override bool InternalCommand()
        {
            return _context.UpdateQuantity(InventoryName, Quantity);
        }
```

Now that the `UpdateQuantityCommand` class has been defined, the following section will add a unit test to validate the command.

UpdateQuantityCommandTest

`UpdateQuantityCommandTest` contains a test to validate a scenario where a book is updated in an existing collection. The creation of the expected interface and existing collection are shown in the following code (note that the test involves adding 6 to the quantity of an existing book):

```
const string expectedBookName = "UpdateQuantityUnitTest";
var expectedInterface = new Helpers.TestUserInterface(
    new List<Tuple<string, string>>
    {
        new Tuple<string, string>("Enter name:", expectedBookName),
        new Tuple<string, string>("Enter quantity:", "6")
    },
    new List<string>(),
    new List<string>()
);

var context = new TestInventoryContext(new Dictionary<string, Book>
{
    { "Beavers", new Book { Id = 1, Name = "Beavers", Quantity = 3 } },
    { expectedBookName, new Book { Id = 2, Name = expectedBookName, Quantity = 7 } },
    { "Ducks", new Book { Id = 3, Name = "Ducks", Quantity = 12 } }
});
```

The following code block shows the running of the command and the initial validation of the successful run of the non-terminating command:

```
// create an instance of the command
var command = new UpdateQuantityCommand(expectedInterface, context);
var result = command.RunCommand();

Assert.IsFalse(result.shouldQuit, "UpdateQuantity is not a terminating command.");
Assert.IsTrue(result.wasSuccessful, "UpdateQuantity did not complete Successfully.");
```

The expectation of the test is that no new books would be added and that the existing book's quantity of 7 will be increased by 6, resulting in a new quantity of 13:

```
Assert.AreEqual(0, context.GetAddedBooks().Length,
            "UpdateQuantity should not have added one new book.");
```

[117]

Implementing Design Patterns - Basics Part 2

```
var updatedBooks = context.GetUpdatedBooks();
Assert.AreEqual(1, updatedBooks.Length,
                "UpdateQuantity should have updated one new book.");
Assert.AreEqual(expectedBookName, updatedBooks.First().Name,
                "UpdateQuantity did not update the correct book.");
Assert.AreEqual(13, updatedBooks.First().Quantity,
                "UpdateQuantity did not update book quantity successfully.");
```

With the `UpdateQuantityCommand` class added, the ability to retrieve the inventory will be added in the next section.

GetInventoryCommand

The `GetInventoryCommand` command differs from the previous two commands because it does not require any parameters. It does use the `IUserInterface` dependency and the `IInventoryContext` dependency to write the content of the collection. This is shown as follows:

```
internal class GetInventoryCommand : NonTerminatingCommand
{
    private readonly IInventoryContext _context;
    internal GetInventoryCommand(IUserInterface userInterface, IInventoryContext context) :
base(userInterface)
    {
        _context = context;
    }

    protected override bool InternalCommand()
    {
        foreach (var book in _context.GetBooks())
        {
Interface.WriteMessage($"{book.Name,-30}\tQuantity:{book.Quantity}");
        }

        return true;
    }
}
```

With the `GetInventoryCommand` command implemented, the next step is to add a new test.

GetInventoryCommandTest

`GetInventoryCommandTest` covers a scenario when the `GetInventoryCommand` command is used to retrieve the collection of books. The test will define the expected messages (remember that the first parameter is for the parameters, the second parameter is for messages, and the third parameter is for warnings) that will occur when testing the user interface:

```
var expectedInterface = new Helpers.TestUserInterface(
    new List<Tuple<string, string>>(),
    new List<string>
    {
        "Gremlins                        \tQuantity:7",
        "Willowsong                      \tQuantity:3",
    },
    new List<string>()
);
```

These messages will correspond to the mock repository, as follows:

```
var context = new TestInventoryContext(new Dictionary<string, Book>
{
    { "Gremlins", new Book { Id = 1, Name = "Gremlins", Quantity = 7 } },
    { "Willowsong", new Book { Id = 2, Name = "Willowsong", Quantity = 3 } },
});
```

The unit test runs the command with the mock dependencies. It verifies that the command executed without error and that the command is not a terminating command:

```
// create an instance of the command
var command = new GetInventoryCommand(expectedInterface, context);
var result = command.RunCommand();

Assert.IsFalse(result.shouldQuit, "GetInventory is not a terminating command.");
```

The expected messages are validating in `TestUserInterface` and, hence, the only thing that remains for the unit test to do is to make sure that no books were mysteriously added or updated by the command:

```
Assert.AreEqual(0, context.GetAddedBooks().Length, "GetInventory should not have added any books.");
Assert.AreEqual(0, context.GetUpdatedBooks().Length, "GetInventory should not have updated any books.");
```

Implementing Design Patterns - Basics Part 2

Now that suitable unit tests for the `GetInventoryCommand` class have been added, we'll introduce the factory pattern in order to manage the creation of specific commands.

The factory pattern

The next pattern applied by the team is the GoF factory pattern. The pattern introduces a **creator** whose responsibility is the instantiation of implementations of a specific type. Its purpose is to encapsulate the complexity around constructing types. The factory pattern allows for more flexibility as the application changes, by limiting the amount of required change compared to whether the construction was in the calling class. This is because the complexity of the construction is in one location, instead of distributed in multiple locations across the application.

In the FlixOne example, `InventoryCommandFactory` implements the pattern and shields the details of constructing each of the different `InventoryCommand` instances. In this scenario, the input received from the console application will be used to determine the concrete implementation of `InventoryCommand` to return. It is important to note that the return type is the `InventoryCommand` abstract class, thus shielding the calling class from the details of the concrete class.

`InventoryCommandFactory` is shown in the following code block. But, for now, focus on the `GetCommand` method as this implements the factory pattern:

```
public class InventoryCommandFactory : IInventoryCommandFactory
{
    private readonly IUserInterface _userInterface;
    private readonly IInventoryContext _context = InventoryContext.Instance;

    public InventoryCommandFactory(IUserInterface userInterface)
    {
        _userInterface = userInterface;
    }

    ...
}
```

`GetCommand` uses a given string to determine the specific implementation of `InventoryCommand` to return:

```
public InventoryCommand GetCommand(string input)
{
    switch (input)
    {
        case "q":
        case "quit":
            return new QuitCommand(_userInterface);
        case "a":
        case "addinventory":
            return new AddInventoryCommand(_userInterface, _context);
        case "g":
        case "getinventory":
            return new GetInventoryCommand(_userInterface, _context);
        case "u":
        case "updatequantity":
            return new UpdateQuantityCommand(_userInterface, _context);
        case "?":
            return new HelpCommand(_userInterface);
        default:
            return new UnknownCommand(_userInterface);
    }
}
```

All commands require `IUserInterface` to be supplied, but some also require access to the repository. These will be supplied with the singleton instance of `IInventoryContext`.

> The factory pattern is often used with an Interface as the return type. It is illustrated here as the `InventoryCommand` base class.

Unit tests

At first glance, the idea of building unit tests for such a simple class seemed like a waste of the team's time. Two important issues were uncovered by constructing the unit tests that might have gone undetected.

Implementing Design Patterns - Basics Part 2

Issue one – UnknownCommand

The first issue was what to do when a command is received that does not match any of the defined `InventoryCommand` inputs. After reviewing the requirements, the team noticed they missed this requirement, as shown in the following screenshot:

> - The application is a console application
>   - print a welcome message that includes the version of the assembly
>   - loops until a quit command is given
>   - if a given command is not successful or not understood, then print a helpful message
> - The application is driven by simple case-insensitive text commands
> - Each command has a short form of a single character and a long form

The team decided to introduce a new `InventoryCommand` class, `UnknownCommand`, to handle this situation. The `UnknownCommand` class should print a warning message to the console (via the `IUserInterface WriteWarning` method), should not cause the application to end, and should return false to indicate that the command was not run successfully. The implementation details are shown in the following code:

```
internal class UnknownCommand : NonTerminatingCommand
{
    internal UnknownCommand(IUserInterface userInterface) :
base(userInterface)
    {
    }

    protected override bool InternalCommand()
    {
        Interface.WriteWarning("Unable to determine the desired command.");

        return false;
    }
}
```

The unit test created for `UnknownCommand` will test for the warning message as well as the two Boolean values returned by the `InternalCommand` method:

```
[TestClass]
public class UnknownCommandTests
{
    [TestMethod]
    public void UnknownCommand_Successful()
    {
```

```
            var expectedInterface = new Helpers.TestUserInterface(
                new List<Tuple<string, string>>(),
                new List<string>(),
                new List<string>
                {
                    "Unable to determine the desired command."
                }
            );

            // create an instance of the command
            var command = new UnknownCommand(expectedInterface);
            var result = command.RunCommand();

            Assert.IsFalse(result.shouldQuit, "Unknown is not a terminating
command.");
            Assert.IsFalse(result.wasSuccessful, "Unknown should not complete
Successfully.");
        }
    }
```

`UnknownCommandTests` covers the commands that require testing. Next, tests around `InventoryCommandFactory` will be implemented.

InventoryCommandFactoryTests

`InventoryCommandFactoryTests` contains unit tests related to `InventoryCommandFactory`. Because each test will have a similar pattern of constructing `InventoryCommandFactory` and its `IUserInterface` dependency and then running the `GetCommand` method, a shared method is created that will run when the test initializes:

```
[TestInitialize]
public void Initialize()
{
    var expectedInterface = new Helpers.TestUserInterface(
        new List<Tuple<string, string>>(),
        new List<string>(),
        new List<string>()
    );

    Factory = new InventoryCommandFactory(expectedInterface);
}
```

Implementing Design Patterns - Basics Part 2

The `Initialize` method constructs a stubbed `IUserInterface` and sets the `Factory` property. The individual unit tests then take a simple form of validating that the object returned is the correct type. First, an instance of the `QuitCommand` class should be returned when the user enters "q" or "quit", as follows:

```
[TestMethod]
public void QuitCommand_Successful()
{
    Assert.IsInstanceOfType(Factory.GetCommand("q"), typeof(QuitCommand),
                                                                "q should be
QuitCommand");
    Assert.IsInstanceOfType(Factory.GetCommand("quit"),
typeof(QuitCommand),
                                                             "quit should be
QuitCommand");
}
```

The `QuitCommand_Successful` test method validates that when the `InventoryCommandFactory` method, `GetCommand`, is run, the object returned is a specific instance of the `QuitCommand` type. `HelpCommand` is only available when "?" is submitted:

```
[TestMethod]
public void HelpCommand_Successful()
{
    Assert.IsInstanceOfType(Factory.GetCommand("?"), typeof(HelpCommand),
"h should be HelpCommand");
}
```

The team did add a test for `UnknownCommand` that validated how `InventoryCommand` would respond when given a value not matching an existing command:

```
[TestMethod]
public void UnknownCommand_Successful()
{
    Assert.IsInstanceOfType(Factory.GetCommand("add"),
typeof(UnknownCommand),
                                                          "unmatched command
should be UnknownCommand");
    Assert.IsInstanceOfType(Factory.GetCommand("addinventry"),
typeof(UnknownCommand),
                                                          "unmatched command
should be UnknownCommand");
    Assert.IsInstanceOfType(Factory.GetCommand("h"),
typeof(UnknownCommand),
                                                          "unmatched command
should be UnknownCommand");
    Assert.IsInstanceOfType(Factory.GetCommand("help"),
```

```
typeof(UnknownCommand),
                                            "unmatched command
should be UnknownCommand");
}
```

With the test methods in place, we can now cover a scenario where a command is given that does not match a known command in the application.

Issue two – case-insensitive text commands

The second issue was uncovered when the requirements were reviewed again, stating that the commands should not be case-sensitive:

- The application is a console application
    - print a welcome message that includes the version of the assembly
    - loops until a quit command is given
    - if a given command is not successful or not understood, then print a helpful message
- The application is driven by simple case-insensitive text commands
- Each command has a short form of a single character and a long form

With the test for `UpdateInventoryCommand`, `InventoryCommandFactory` was found to be case-sensitive using the following test:

```
[TestMethod]
public void UpdateQuantityCommand_Successful()
{
    Assert.IsInstanceOfType(Factory.GetCommand("u"),
                        typeof(UpdateQuantityCommand),
                        "u should be UpdateQuantityCommand");
    Assert.IsInstanceOfType(Factory.GetCommand("updatequantity"),
                        typeof(UpdateQuantityCommand),
                        "updatequantity should be
UpdateQuantityCommand");
    Assert.IsInstanceOfType(Factory.GetCommand("UpdaTEQuantity"),
                        typeof(UpdateQuantityCommand),
                        "UpdaTEQuantity should be
UpdateQuantityCommand");
}
```

Fortunately, this test was easy to solve by applying a `ToLower()` method to the input before determining the command, as follows:

```
public InventoryCommand GetCommand(string input)
{
    switch (input.ToLower())
    {
        ...
    }
}
```

This scenario highlights both the value of the `Factory` method and the value of leveraging unit tests to help validate requirements during development and not relying on user testing.

Features in .NET Core

`Chapter 3`, *Implementing Design Patterns – Basics Part 1*, and the first part of this chapter have illustrated the GoF patterns without using any frameworks. It is worth covering this as, sometimes, a framework is not available for a specific pattern or applicable in a particular scenario. Additionally, it is important to understand what functionality the framework is providing in order to know when a pattern should be used. The rest of this chapter will look at a couple of features that .NET Core provides that support some of the patterns we have covered so far.

IServiceCollection

.NET Core was designed with **Dependency Injection** (**DI**) built-in to the framework. Typically, the start of a .NET Core application contains the set up of the DI for an application that primarily contains the creation of a collection of services. The framework uses these services to supply the dependencies when the application requires them. The services provide the foundation of a robust **Inversion of Control** (**IoC**) framework and are arguably one of the coolest features of .NET Core. This section will complete the console application and demonstrate how .NET Core supports building a sophisticated IoC framework based on the `IServiceCollection` interface.

The `IServiceCollection` interface is used to define the services available to the container that implements `IServiceProvider` interface. The services themselves are types that will be injected at runtime when required by the application. For example, `ConsoleUserInterface` interface, which was defined previously, will be a service injected at runtime. This is shown in the following code:

```
IServiceCollection services = new ServiceCollection();
services.AddTransient<IUserInterface, ConsoleUserInterface>();
```

In the preceding code, `ConsoleUserInterface` interface is being added as a service that implements the `IUserInterface` interface. If the DI is providing another type that requires a `IUserInterface` interface dependency, then `ConsoleUserInterface` interface will be used. For example, `InventoryCommandFactory` is also added to the services, as shown in the following code:

```
services.AddTransient<IInventoryCommandFactory, InventoryCommandFactory>();
```

`InventoryCommandFactory` has a constructor that requires an implementation of the `IUserInterface` interface:

```
public class InventoryCommandFactory : IInventoryCommandFactory
{
    private readonly IUserInterface _userInterface;

    public InventoryCommandFactory(IUserInterface userInterface)
    {
        _userInterface = userInterface;
    }
    ...
}
```

Later, an instance of `InventoryCommandFactory` is requested, as follows:

```
IServiceProvider serviceProvider = services.BuildServiceProvider();
var service = serviceProvider.GetService<IInventoryCommandFactory>();
service.GetCommand("a");
```

Then, an instance of `IUserInterface` (in this application it is the registered `ConsoleUserInterface`) is instantiated and supplied to the constructor of `InventoryCommandFactory`.

There are different types of service *lifetimes* that can be specified when registering a service. A lifetime governs how the types will be instantiated and include Transient, Scoped, and Singleton. Transient means the service is created each time it is requested. Scope will be covered later when we look at website-related patterns and in particular where services are created per web request. Singleton behaves like the singleton pattern we covered earlier, and will also be covered later in this chapter.

CatalogService

The `CatalogService` interface represents the console application the team is building and is described as having a single `Run` method, as shown in the `ICatalogService` interface:

```
interface ICatalogService
{
    void Run();
}
```

The service has two dependencies, `IUserInterface` and `IInventoryCommandFactory`, and they will be injected into the constructor and stored as local variables:

```
public class CatalogService : ICatalogService
{
    private readonly IUserInterface _userInterface;
    private readonly IInventoryCommandFactory _commandFactory;

    public CatalogService(IUserInterface userInterface,
IInventoryCommandFactory commandFactory)
    {
        _userInterface = userInterface;
        _commandFactory = commandFactory;
    }
    ...
}
```

The `Run` method is based on the earlier design by the team shown in Chapter 3, *Implementing Design Patterns – Basics Part 1*. It prints a greeting and then loops until the quit inventory command is entered by the user. Each loop will perform the command and, if the command is not successful, it will print a help message:

```
public void Run()
{
    Greeting();

    var response = _commandFactory.GetCommand("?").RunCommand();

    while (!response.shouldQuit)
    {
        // look at this mistake with the ToLower()
        var input = _userInterface.ReadValue("> ").ToLower();
        var command = _commandFactory.GetCommand(input);

        response = command.RunCommand();

        if (!response.wasSuccessful)
        {
            _userInterface.WriteMessage("Enter ? to view options.");
        }
    }
}
```

Now that we have the `CatalogService` interface ready, the next step will be to put everything together. The next section will do this using .NET Core.

IServiceProvider

With `CatalogService` defined, the team is finally able to put everything together in .NET Core. The start of all applications, that is, EXE programs, is the `Main` method, and .NET Core is no exception. The program is shown in the following code:

```
class Program
{
    private static void Main(string[] args)
    {
        IServiceCollection services = new ServiceCollection();
        ConfigureServices(services);
        IServiceProvider serviceProvider = services.BuildServiceProvider();

        var service = serviceProvider.GetService<ICatalogService>();
        service.Run();
```

```
        Console.WriteLine("CatalogService has completed.");
    }

    private static void ConfigureServices(IServiceCollection services)
    {
        // Add application services.
        services.AddTransient<IUserInterface, ConsoleUserInterface>();
        services.AddTransient<ICatalogService, CatalogService>();
        services.AddTransient<IInventoryCommandFactory,
InventoryCommandFactory>();
    }
}
```

In the `ConfigureServices` method, different types are added to the IoC container including `ConsoleUserInterface`, `CatalogService`, and `InventoryCommandFactory` classes. The `ConsoleUserInterface` and `InventoryCommandFactory` class will be injected as required and the `CatalogService` class will be explicitly retrieved from the `IServiceProvider` interface built from the `ServiceCollection` object containing the added types. The program *runs* until the `CatalogService Run` method completes.

> In Chapter 5, *Implementing Design Patterns - .NET Core*, the singleton pattern will be revisited to use the .NET Core built-in capabilities by using the `IServiceCollection`, `AddSingleton` method to control the `InventoryContext` instance.

Console application

The console application, when running from the command line, is simple, but it is a foundation of well-designed code adhering to the SOLID principles discussed in Chapter 3, *Implementing Design Patterns – Basics Part 1*. When run, the application provides a simple greeting and displays a help message, including the command's supports and examples:

Chapter 4

```
*******************************************************************************
*                                                                             *
*            Welcome to FlixOne Inventory Management System                   *
*                                                                  v1.0.0.0   *
*******************************************************************************
USAGE:
        addinventory (a)
        getinventory (g)
        updatequantity (u)
        quit (q)
        ?
Examples:
        New Inventory
        > addinventory
        Enter name:The Meaning of Life

        Get Inventory
        > getinventory
        The Meaning of Life        Quantity:10
        The Life of a Ninja        Quantity:2

        Update Quantity (Increase)
        > updatequantity
        Enter name:The Meaning of Life
        11
        11 added to quantity

        Update Quantity (Decrease)
        > updatequantity
        Enter name:The Life of a Ninja
        -3
        3 removed from quantity

> _
```

The application then loops through the commands until a quit command is received. The following screenshot illustrates its functionality:

```
> addinventory
Enter name:Godfather
> u
Enter name:Godfather
Enter quantity:12
> g
Godfather                        Quantity:12
> notsurecommand
Unable to determine the desired command.
Enter ? to view options.
> q
Thank you for using FlixOne Inventory Management System
CatalogService has completed.
```

This was not the most impressive of console applications, but it served to illustrated many principles and patterns.

Summary

Similar to Chapter 3, *Implementing Design Patterns – Basics Part 1*, this chapter continued the description of building an inventory management console application for FlixOne, in order to show practical examples of using **Object-Oriented Programming** (**OOP**) design patterns. In this chapter, the GoF's singleton and factory patterns were the focus. These two patterns have a particularly important role to play in .NET Core applications and will be used often in the following chapters. An introduction to using the built-in framework to provide an IoC container was also covered in this chapter.

This chapter finished with a working inventory management console application based on the requirements determined in Chapter 3, *Implementing Design Patterns – Basics Part 1*. These requirements were the basis of the unit tests created in both chapters and were used to illustrate TDD. The team has a higher level of confidence that the application will pass the **User Acceptance Testing** (**UAT**) by having a suite of tests that verify the features required for this phase of development.

In the next chapter, we will continue with the description of building the inventory management application. The focus will move from basic OOP patterns to using the .NET Core framework to implement different patterns. For example, the singleton pattern introduced in this chapter will be refactored to use the capability of `IServiceCollection` to create a singleton, and we will also take a closer look at its DI capabilities. Additionally, the application will be extended to support logging using a variety of logging providers.

Questions

The following questions will allow you to consolidate the information contained in this chapter:

1. Provide an example why using a singleton **would not** be a good mechanism for limiting access to a shared resource.
2. Is the following statement true? Why or why not? `ConcurrentDictionary` prevents items in the collection from being updated by more than one thread at a time.
3. What is a race condition and why should it be avoided?
4. How does the factory pattern help to simplify code?
5. Do .NET Core applications require third-party IoC containers?

Implementing Design Patterns - .NET Core

The previous chapter continued the building of the FlixOne inventory management application by incorporating additional patterns. More of the Gang of Four patterns were used, including the Singleton and Factory patterns. The Singleton pattern was used to illustrate the Repository pattern that was used to maintain the FlixOne collection of books. The Factory pattern was used to further explore the **dependency injection** (**DI**). The .Net Core framework was used to complete the initial inventory management console application, in order to facilitate an **inversion of control** (**IoC**) container.

This chapter will continue building upon the inventory management console application, while also exploring features of .Net Core. The Singleton pattern, which was covered in the previous chapter, will be revisited and created, using the Singleton service lifetime built into the .Net Core framework. Using the framework's DI, the Configuration pattern will be shown, as well as **constructor injection (CI)** explained, using different examples.

The following topics will be covered in this chapter:

- .Net Core service lifetimes
- Implementation factory

Technical requirements

This chapter contains various code examples that are used to explain the concepts. The code is kept simple, and is just for demonstration purposes. Most of the examples involve a .NET Core console application written in C#.

To run and execute the code, you need the following:

- Visual Studio 2019 (you can also run the application using Visual Studio 2017 Version 3 or later).
- Setting up .NET Core.
- SQL server (express edition is used in this chapter).

Installing Visual Studio

To run these code examples, you need to install Visual Studio 2010, or later. You can use your preferred IDE. To do this, follow these instructions:

1. Download Visual Studio from the following link: https://docs.microsoft.com/en-us/visualstudio/install/install-visual-studio.
2. Follow the installation instructions included. Multiple versions are available for Visual Studio installation. In this chapter, we are using Visual Studio for Windows.

Setting up .NET Core

If you do not have .NET Core installed, you need to follow these instructions:

1. Download .NET Core from the following link: https://www.microsoft.com/net/download/windows.
2. The installation instructions and the related library can be found at the following link: https://dotnet.microsoft.com/download/dotnet-core/2.2.

> The complete source code is available in the GitHub repository. The source code shown in the chapter might not be complete, so it is advisable to retrieve the source in order to run the examples. Please refer to https://github.com/PacktPublishing/Hands-On-Design-Patterns-with-C-and-.NET-Core/tree/master/Chapter5.

.Net Core service lifetimes

A fundamental concept to understand when working with .Net Core's DI, is service lifetimes. A service lifetime defines how a dependency is managed in regards to how often it is created. As an illustration of this process, think of DI as managing a container of dependencies. Dependency is just a class that the DI knows about, because the class was *registered* with it. For .Net Core's DI, this is done with the following three methods of `IServiceCollection`:

- `AddTransient<TService, TImplementation>()`
- `AddScoped<TService, TImplementation>()`
- `AddSingleton<TService, TImplementation>()`

The `IServiceCollection` interface is a collection of registered service descriptions, basically containing the dependency, and when the DI should supply the dependency. For example, when `TService` is requested, `TImplementation` is supplied (that is, injected).

In this section, we will look at the three service lifetimes, and provide an illustration of the different lifetimes via unit tests. We will also look at how implementation factories can be used to create instances of the dependencies.

Transient

A `transient` dependency means each time the DI receives a request for a dependency, then a new instance of the dependency will be created. In most situations, this is the service lifetime that makes the most sense to use, as most classes should be designed to be lightweight, stateless services. In situations where the state needs to be persisted between references and/or if there is considerable effort in instantiating a new instance, then another service lifetime might make more sense.

Scoped

In .Net Core, there is the concept of a scope, which can be thought of as a context or boundary for the executing process. In some .Net Core implementations, the scope is implicitly defined, so you might not be aware that it is being put in place. For example, in ASP.Net Core, a scope is created for each web request that is received. This means that, if a dependency has a Scoped lifetime, then it will only be constructed once per web request, so, if the same dependency is used multiple times for the same web request, it will be shared.

Later in this chapter, we will explicitly create a scope in order to illustrate a Scoped lifetime, and the same concept applies in the unit test as it will in an ASP.Net Core application.

Singleton

In .Net Core, the Singleton pattern is implemented so that dependency is only ever instantiated once, just like the Singleton pattern that was implemented in the previous chapter. Similar to the Singleton pattern in the previous chapter, the `singleton` class needs to be thread safe, and only the factory method that is used to create the singleton class is guaranteed to be called only once by a single thread.

Back to FlixOne

To illustrate .Net Core's DI, we need to make some modifications to the FlixOne inventory management application. The first thing to do will be to update the `InventoryContext` class, which was defined earlier, in order to no longer implement the Singleton pattern (as we will do this using .Net Core's DI):

```
public class InventoryContext : IInventoryContext
{
    public InventoryContext()
    {
        _books = new ConcurrentDictionary<string, Book>();
    }

    private readonly static object _lock = new object();

    private readonly IDictionary<string, Book> _books;

    public Book[] GetBooks()
    {
        return _books.Values.ToArray();
    }

    ...
}
```

The detail of the `AddBook` and `UpdateQuantity` methods are shown in the following code:

```
public bool AddBook(string name)
{
    _books.Add(name, new Book {Name = name});
    return true;
```

```
    }

    public bool UpdateQuantity(string name, int quantity)
    {
        lock (_lock)
        {
            _books[name].Quantity += quantity;
        }

        return true;
    }
```

There are a couple of things to note. The constructor has been changed from protected to public. This will allow the class to be instantiated by objects outside of the class. Also, note that the static `Instance` property and the private static `_instance` field have been removed, while the private `_lock` field remains. Similar to the Singleton pattern defined in the previous chapter, this only guarantees how the class is instantiated; it does not prevent methods from being accessed in parallel.

> Both the `IInventoryContext` interface and the `InventoryContext` and `Book` classes were made public, as our DI is being defined in an external project.

Subsequently, the `InventoryCommandFactory` class, which is used to return commands, has been updated to have an instance of the `InventoryContext` injected into its constructor:

```
    public class InventoryCommandFactory : IInventoryCommandFactory
    {
        private readonly IUserInterface _userInterface;
        private readonly IInventoryContext _context;

        public InventoryCommandFactory(IUserInterface userInterface,
    IInventoryContext context)
        {
            _userInterface = userInterface;
            _context = context;
        }

        // GetCommand()
        ...
    }
```

The `GetCommand` method uses the input provided to determine the specific command:

```
public InventoryCommand GetCommand(string input)
{
    switch (input.ToLower())
    {
        case "q":
        case "quit":
            return new QuitCommand(_userInterface);
        case "a":
        case "addinventory":
            return new AddInventoryCommand(_userInterface, _context);
        case "g":
        case "getinventory":
            return new GetInventoryCommand(_userInterface, _context);
        case "u":
        case "updatequantity":
            return new UpdateQuantityCommand(_userInterface, _context);
        case "?":
            return new HelpCommand(_userInterface);
        default:
            return new UnknownCommand(_userInterface);
    }
}
```

As noted, the `IInventoryContext` interface will now be supplied by the DI container that is defined in the client project. The console application now has an additional line to create a Singleton of the `IInventoryContext` interface using the `InventoryContext` class:

```
class Program
{
    private static void Main(string[] args)
    {
        IServiceCollection services = new ServiceCollection();
        ConfigureServices(services);
        IServiceProvider serviceProvider = services.BuildServiceProvider();

        var service = serviceProvider.GetService<ICatalogService>();
        service.Run();

        Console.WriteLine("CatalogService has completed.");
        Console.ReadLine();
    }

    private static void ConfigureServices(IServiceCollection services)
    {
        // Add application services.
        services.AddTransient<IUserInterface, ConsoleUserInterface>();
```

```
        services.AddTransient<ICatalogService, CatalogService>();
        services.AddTransient<IInventoryCommandFactory,
InventoryCommandFactory>();

        services.AddSingleton<IInventoryContext, InventoryContext>();
    }
}
```

The console application can now be run with the same manual test as that performed in the previous chapter, but unit tests are a great way to understand what is being achieved using .Net Core's DI.

> The example code provided for this chapter shows the completed project. The following section concentrates on the `InventoryContext` tests. The `InventoryCommandFactory` tests were also modified, but, as the changes are trivial, they will not be covered here.

Unit tests

With the changes to the `InventoryContext` class, we no longer have a convenient property for getting the only instance of the class. This means that `InventoryContext.Instance` will need to be replaced, and, as a first attempt, let's create a method to return a new instance of `InventoryContext`, and use `GetInventoryContext()` instead of `InventoryContext.Instance`:

```
    private IInventoryContext GetInventoryContext()
    {
        return new InventoryContext();
    }
```

As expected, the unit tests fail with an error message: *The given key was not present in the dictionary*:

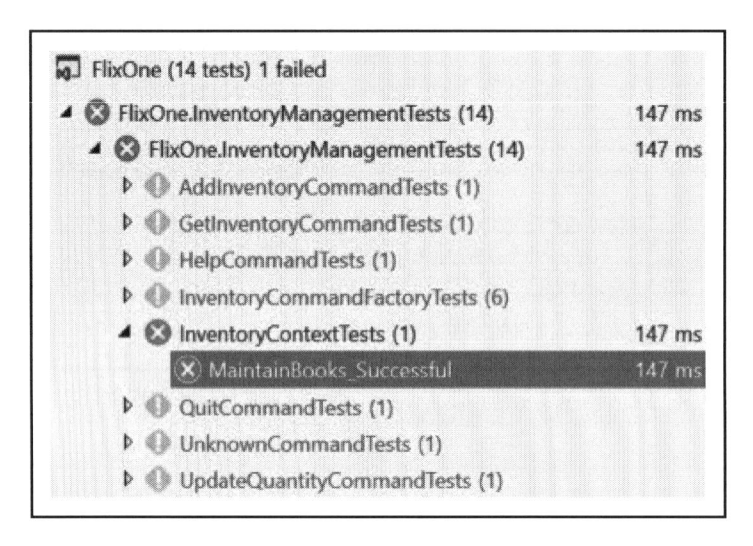

```
FlixOne (14 tests) 1 failed
  FlixOne.InventoryManagementTests (14)                    147 ms
    FlixOne.InventoryManagementTests (14)                  147 ms
      AddInventoryCommandTests (1)
      GetInventoryCommandTests (1)
      HelpCommandTests (1)
      InventoryCommandFactoryTests (6)
      InventoryContextTests (1)                            147 ms
        MaintainBooks_Successful                           147 ms
      QuitCommandTests (1)
      UnknownCommandTests (1)
      UpdateQuantityCommandTests (1)
```

As we saw in the previous chapter, this is because the `InventoryContext` list of books is empty each time the `InventoryContext` class is created. This is why we need to create a context using a Singleton.

Let's update the `GetInventoryContext()` method to now supply an instance of the `IInventoryContext` interface using .Net Core's DI:

```
private IInventoryContext GetInventoryContext()
{
    IServiceCollection services = new ServiceCollection();
    services.AddSingleton<IInventoryContext, InventoryContext>();
    var provider = services.BuildServiceProvider();

    return provider.GetService<IInventoryContext>();
}
```

In the updated method, an instance of the `ServiceCollection` class is created, which will be used to contain all the registered dependencies. The `InventoryContext` class is registered as a Singleton to be supplied when the `IInventoryContext` dependency is requested. A `ServiceProvider` instance is then generated, which will actually perform the DI based on the registrations in the `IServiceCollection` interface. The final step is to supply the `InventoryContext` class when the `IInventoryContext` interface is requested.

Chapter 5

> The `Microsoft.Extensions.DependencyInjection` library will need to be added to the `InventoryManagementTests` project in order to be able to reference the .Net Core DI components.

Unfortunately, the unit test still does not pass, and results in the same error: *The given key was not present in the dictionary.* This is because we are creating a new instance of the DI framework each time `IInventoryContext` is requested. This means that even though our dependency is a Singleton, each instance of `ServiceProvider` will supply a new instance of the `InventoryContext` class. To get around this, we will create `IServiceCollection` when the test first starts up, and then we will use the same reference during the test:

```
ServiceProvider Services { get; set; }

[TestInitialize]
public void Startup()
{
    IServiceCollection services = new ServiceCollection();
    services.AddSingleton<IInventoryContext, InventoryContext>();
    Services = services.BuildServiceProvider();
}
```

> Using the `TestInitialize` attribute is a great way to separate the functionality required by multiple `TestMethod` tests within a `TestClass` class. The method will be run before every test is run.

Now that there is a reference to the same `ServiceProvider` instance, we can update to retrieve the dependency. The following illustrates how the `AddBook()` method has been updated:

```
public Task AddBook(string book)
{
    return Task.Run(() =>
    {
Assert.IsTrue(Services.GetService<IInventoryContext>().AddBook(book));
    });
}
```

Our unit test now passes successfully, as only one instance of the `InventoryContext` class is created during the execution of the test:

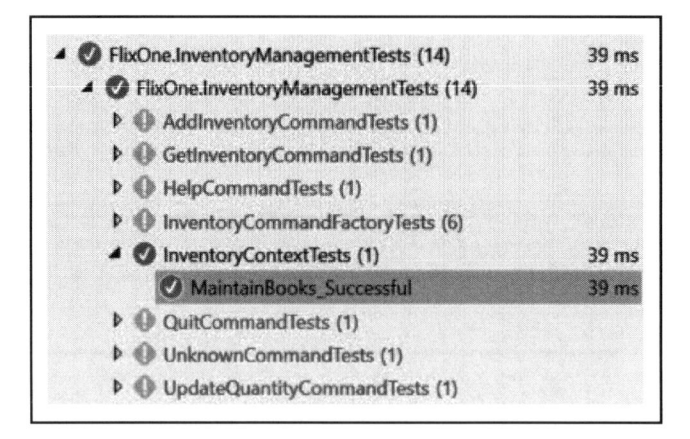

```
▲ ✓ FlixOne.InventoryManagementTests (14)                    39 ms
    ▲ ✓ FlixOne.InventoryManagementTests (14)                39 ms
        ▷ ⊘ AddInventoryCommandTests (1)
        ▷ ⊘ GetInventoryCommandTests (1)
        ▷ ⊘ HelpCommandTests (1)
        ▷ ⊘ InventoryCommandFactoryTests (6)
        ▲ ✓ InventoryContextTests (1)                        39 ms
            ✓ MaintainBooks_Successful                       39 ms
        ▷ ⊘ QuitCommandTests (1)
        ▷ ⊘ UnknownCommandTests (1)
        ▷ ⊘ UpdateQuantityCommandTests (1)
```

The Singleton pattern is relatively easy to implement using the built-in DI, as illustrated in this section. Understanding when to use the pattern is an important concept. The next section will explore the concept of scope in more detail, in order to gain a further understanding of service lifetimes.

Scope

In applications that have multiple processes executing simultaneously, understanding service lifetime is very important to both functional and non-functional requirements. As illustrated in the previous unit test without the correct service lifetime, `InventoryContext` did not function as desired, and led to an invalid situation. Likewise, the incorrect use of service lifetimes could lead to applications that do not scale well. In general, the use of a lock-and-shared state should be avoided in multi-process solutions.

To illustrate this concept, imagine the FlixOne inventory management application was supplied to multiple staff members. The challenge now is how to perform a lock across multiple applications, and how to have a single collected state. In our terms, this would be a single `InventoryContext` class shared by multiple applications. Of course, this is where changing our solution to use a shared repository (for example, a database) would make sense, and/or changing our solution to a web application. We will cover databases and web application patterns in later chapters, but, as we are discussing service lifetimes, it does make sense to describe these in terms of a web application in more detail now.

The following diagram depicts a web app receiving two requests:

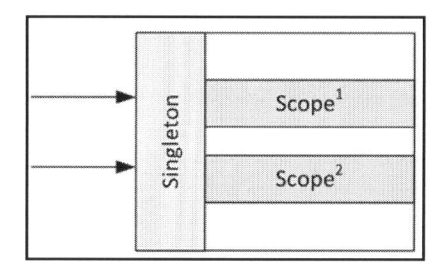

In terms of service lifetimes, a Singleton service lifetime will be available to both requests, while each request receives its own Scope lifetime. The important thing to note is around garbage collection. Dependencies that are created with a Transient service lifetime are marked to be released once the object is no longer referenced, while dependencies created with a Scope service lifetime are not marked to be released until the web request completes. And, dependencies created with a Singleton service lifetime are not marked to be released until the application ends.

Also, as shown in the following diagram, it is important to remember that dependencies in .Net Core are not shared between server instances in a web garden or web farm:

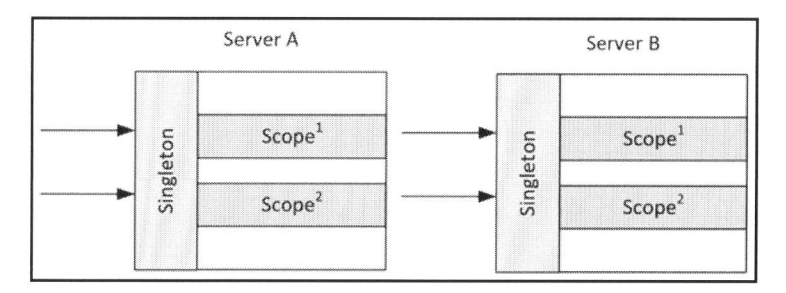

In the following chapters, different approaches to the shared state will be shown, including using a shared cache, databases, and other forms of repositories.

Implementation factory

The .Net Core DI supports the ability to specify an *implementation factory* when registering a dependency. This allows for control over the creation of the dependency that is supplied by the service provided. This is done when registering by using the following extension of the `IServiceCollection` interface:

```
public static IServiceCollection AddSingleton<TService,
TImplementation>(this IServiceCollection services,
Func<IServiceProvider, TImplementation> implementationFactory)
            where TService : class
            where TImplementation : class, TService;
```

The `AddSingleton` extension receives both a class to be registered as well as the class to be supplied when the dependency is required. An interesting thing to note is the .Net Core DI framework will maintain the registered services and either deliver the implementation when requested, or as part of instantiating one of the dependencies. This automatic instantiation is called **constructor injection** (**CI**). We will see examples of both in the following sections.

IInventoryContext

As an example, let's revisit the `InventoryContext` class that is used to manage the inventory of books, by segregating the read and the write operations performed on our collection of books. `IInventoryContext` is split into `IInventoryReadContext` and `IInventoryWriteContext`:

```
using FlixOne.InventoryManagement.Models;

namespace FlixOne.InventoryManagement.Repository
{
    public interface IInventoryContext : IInventoryReadContext,
IInventoryWriteContext { }

    public interface IInventoryReadContext
    {
        Book[] GetBooks();
    }
```

```
public interface IInventoryWriteContext
{
    bool AddBook(string name);
    bool UpdateQuantity(string name, int quantity);
}
}
```

IInventoryReadContext

The `IInventoryReadContext` interface contains the operation to read the books, while `IInventoryWriteContext` contains the operations that modify the collection of books. The original `IInventoryContext` interface was created for convenience for when a class requires both dependency types.

> In later chapters, we will cover patterns that take advantage of splitting the context, including the **Command and Query Responsibility Segregation (CQRS)** pattern.

With this refactor, some changes are required. First classes only requiring to read the collection of books have their constructor updated with the `IInventoryReadContext` interface, as illustrated in the `GetInventoryCommand` class:

```
internal class GetInventoryCommand : NonTerminatingCommand
{
    private readonly IInventoryReadContext _context;
    internal GetInventoryCommand(IUserInterface userInterface,
IInventoryReadContext context) : base(userInterface)
    {
        _context = context;
    }

    protected override bool InternalCommand()
    {
        foreach (var book in _context.GetBooks())
        {
Interface.WriteMessage($"{book.Name,-30}\tQuantity:{book.Quantity}");
        }

        return true;
    }
}
```

IInventoryWriteContext

Likewise, classes requiring to modify the collection of books are updated to the `IInventoryWriteContext` interface, as illustrated with `AddInventoryCommand`:

```
internal class AddInventoryCommand : NonTerminatingCommand,
IParameterisedCommand
{
    private readonly IInventoryWriteContext _context;

    internal AddInventoryCommand(IUserInterface userInterface,
IInventoryWriteContext context) : base(userInterface)
    {
        _context = context;
    }

    public string InventoryName { get; private set; }

    ...
}
```

The following shows the detail of the `GetParameters` and `InternalCommand` methods:

```
/// <summary>
/// AddInventoryCommand requires name
/// </summary>
/// <returns></returns>
public bool GetParameters()
{
    if (string.IsNullOrWhiteSpace(InventoryName))
        InventoryName = GetParameter("name");
    return !string.IsNullOrWhiteSpace(InventoryName);
}

protected override bool InternalCommand()
{
    return _context.AddBook(InventoryName);
}
```

Note the `InternalCommand` method, where the book is added to the inventory with the given name of the book held in the `InventoryName` parameter.

Next, we will look at the factory for the inventory commands.

InventoryCommandFactory

The `InventoryCommandFactory` class is an implementation of the Factory pattern using .Net classes, which requires both readings of, and writing to, the collection of books:

```
public class InventoryCommandFactory : IInventoryCommandFactory
{
    private readonly IUserInterface _userInterface;
    private readonly IInventoryContext _context;

    public InventoryCommandFactory(IUserInterface userInterface,
IInventoryContext context)
    {
        _userInterface = userInterface;
        _context = context;
    }

    public InventoryCommand GetCommand(string input)
    {
        switch (input.ToLower())
        {
            case "q":
            case "quit":
                return new QuitCommand(_userInterface);
            case "a":
            case "addinventory":
                return new AddInventoryCommand(_userInterface, _context);
            case "g":
            case "getinventory":
                return new GetInventoryCommand(_userInterface, _context);
            case "u":
            case "updatequantity":
                return new UpdateQuantityCommand(_userInterface, _context);
            case "?":
                return new HelpCommand(_userInterface);
            default:
                return new UnknownCommand(_userInterface);
        }
    }
}
```

An interesting thing to note, is that the class actually did not require modifying from the previous chapter's version, as polymorphism handles the casting from `IInventoryContext` to the `IInventoryReadContext` and `IInventoryWriteContext` interfaces.

With these changes, we need to change the registration of the dependencies that are related to `InventoryContext`, in order to use an implementation factory:

```
private static void ConfigureServices(IServiceCollection services)
{
    // Add application services.
    ...

    var context = new InventoryContext();
    services.AddSingleton<IInventoryReadContext, InventoryContext>(p => context);
    services.AddSingleton<IInventoryWriteContext, InventoryContext>(p => context);
    services.AddSingleton<IInventoryContext, InventoryContext>(p => context);
}
```

For all three interfaces, the same instance of `InventoryContext` will be used, and this is instantiated once using the implementation factory extension. This is supplied when a `IInventoryReadContext`, `IInventoryWriteContext`, or `IInventoryContext` dependency is requested.

InventoryCommand

`InventoryCommandFactory` was useful to illustrate how the Factory pattern could be achieved using .Net, but let's revisit this now that we are using the .Net Core framework. Our requirement is given a string value; we want to return a particular implementation of `InventoryCommand`. This can be achieved in several ways, and, in this section, three examples will be given:

- Implementation factory using a function
- Using services
- Using third-party containers

Implementation factory using a function

The implementation factory of the `GetService()` method can be used to determine the type of `InventoryCommand` class to be returned. For this example, a new static method is created in the `InventoryCommand` class:

```
public static Func<IServiceProvider, Func<string, InventoryCommand>> GetInventoryCommand =>
```

```
provider => input =>
{
    switch (input.ToLower())
    {
        case "q":
        case "quit":
            return new QuitCommand(provider.GetService<IUserInterface>());
        case "a":
        case "addinventory":
            return new
AddInventoryCommand(provider.GetService<IUserInterface>(),
provider.GetService<IInventoryWriteContext>());
        case "g":
        case "getinventory":
            return new
GetInventoryCommand(provider.GetService<IUserInterface>(),
provider.GetService<IInventoryReadContext>());
        case "u":
        case "updatequantity":
            return new
UpdateQuantityCommand(provider.GetService<IUserInterface>(),
provider.GetService<IInventoryWriteContext>());
        case "?":
            return new HelpCommand(provider.GetService<IUserInterface>());
        default:
            return new
UnknownCommand(provider.GetService<IUserInterface>());
    }
};
```

This is a little tricky to read if you are not familiar with lambda expression bodies, so we will explain the code in a bit of detail. First of all, let's revisit the syntax of the `AddSingleton`:

```
public static IServiceCollection AddSingleton<TService,
TImplementation>(this IServiceCollection services, Func<IServiceProvider,
TImplementation> implementationFactory)
            where TService : class
            where TImplementation : class, TService;
```

This shows that the parameter of the `AddSingleton` extension is a function:

Func<IServiceProvider, TImplementation> implementationFactory

Implementing Design Patterns - .NET Core

This means that the following code is equivalent:

```
services.AddSingleton<IInventoryContext, InventoryContext>(provider => new InventoryContext());

services.AddSingleton<IInventoryContext, InventoryContext>(GetInventoryContext);
```

The `GetInventoryContext` method is defined as follows:

```
static Func<IServiceProvider, InventoryContext> GetInventoryContext =>
provider =>
{
    return new InventoryContext();
};
```

In our particular example, the specific `InventoryCommand` types have been marked as internal to the `FlixOne.InventoryManagement` project, so the `FlixOne.InventoryManagementClient` project is not able to access them directly. This is why a new static method was created in the `FlixOne.InventoryManagement.InventoryCommand` class that returned the following type:

```
Func<IServiceProvider, Func<string, InventoryCommand>>
```

What this means is, when the service is requested, a string will be supplied to determine the specific type. Because the dependency changed, this means the `CatalogService` constructor requires updating:

```
public CatalogService(IUserInterface userInterface, Func<string, InventoryCommand> commandFactory)
{
    _userInterface = userInterface;
    _commandFactory = commandFactory;
}
```

When the service is requested, a string will be supplied to determine the specific. Because the dependency changed, the `CatalogueService` constructor requires updating:

Chapter 5

Now when the string the user has entered is supplied to the `CommandFactory` dependency, the correct command is supplied:

```
while (!response.shouldQuit)
{
    // look at this mistake with the ToLower()
    var input = _userInterface.ReadValue("> ").ToLower();
    var command = _commandFactory(input);

    response = command.RunCommand();

    if (!response.wasSuccessful)
    {
        _userInterface.WriteMessage("Enter ? to view options.");
    }
}
```

The unit tests associated with the command factory were also updated. As a comparison, a new `test` class was created from the existing `InventoryCommandFactoryTests` class, and named `InventoryCommandFunctionTests`. The initialization step is shown in the following code, with the changes highlighted:

```
ServiceProvider Services { get; set; }

[TestInitialize]
public void Startup()
{
    var expectedInterface = new Helpers.TestUserInterface(
        new List<Tuple<string, string>>(),
        new List<string>(),
        new List<string>()
    );

    IServiceCollection services = new ServiceCollection();
    services.AddSingleton<IInventoryContext, InventoryContext>();
    services.AddTransient<Func<string, InventoryCommand>>(InventoryCommand.GetInventoryCommand);

    Services = services.BuildServiceProvider();
}
```

The individual tests were also updated to supply the string as part of the get service call, as shown in the following code with `QuitCommand`:

```
[TestMethod]
public void QuitCommand_Successful()
{
```

[151]

```
    Assert.IsInstanceOfType(Services.GetService<Func<string,
InventoryCommand>>().Invoke("q"),
                    typeof(QuitCommand),
                    "q should be QuitCommand");

    Assert.IsInstanceOfType(Services.GetService<Func<string,
InventoryCommand>>().Invoke("quit"),
                    typeof(QuitCommand),
                    "quit should be QuitCommand");
}
```

The two tests verify that the services that are returned are of the `QuitCommand` type, when the service provider is given `"q"` or `"quit"`.

Using services

The `ServiceProvider` class provides a `Services` method that can be used to determine the appropriate service, when there are multiple dependencies registered for the same type. This example will take a different tack with `InventoryCommands`, and, because of the extent of the refactor, this will be done with new classes that will be created just to illustrate this approach.

In the unit test project, a new folder, `ImplementationFactoryTests`, was created, to contain the classes for this section. In the folder, a new base class for `InventoryCommand` was created:

```
public abstract class InventoryCommand
{
    protected abstract string[] CommandStrings { get; }
    public virtual bool IsCommandFor(string input)
    {
        return CommandStrings.Contains(input.ToLower());
    }
}
```

The concept behind this new class is that child classes will define the strings that they respond to. For example, `QuitCommand` will respond to the `"q"` and `"quit"` strings:

```
public class QuitCommand : InventoryCommand
{
    protected override string[] CommandStrings => new[] { "q", "quit" };
}
```

Chapter 5

The following shows the `GetInventoryCommand`, `AddInventoryCommand`, `UpdateQuantityCommand`, and `HelpCommand` classes, which follow a similar approach:

```
public class GetInventoryCommand : InventoryCommand
{
    protected override string[] CommandStrings => new[] { "g", "getinventory" };
}

public class AddInventoryCommand : InventoryCommand
{
    protected override string[] CommandStrings => new[] { "a", "addinventory" };
}

public class UpdateQuantityCommand : InventoryCommand
{
    protected override string[] CommandStrings => new[] { "u", "updatequantity" };
}

public class HelpCommand : InventoryCommand
{
    protected override string[] CommandStrings => new[] { "?" };
}
```

The `UnknownCommand` class, though, will be used as a default, so it will always evaluate to true, by overriding the `IsCommandFor` method:

```
public class UnknownCommand : InventoryCommand
{
    protected override string[] CommandStrings => new string[0];

    public override bool IsCommandFor(string input)
    {
        return true;
    }
}
```

Because the `UnknownCommand` class is being treated as a default, the order of registration is important, and is shown below in the initialization of the unit `test` class:

```
[TestInitialize]
public void Startup()
{
    var expectedInterface = new Helpers.TestUserInterface(
        new List<Tuple<string, string>>(),
```

[153]

```
        new List<string>(),
        new List<string>()
    );

    IServiceCollection services = new ServiceCollection();
    services.AddTransient<InventoryCommand, QuitCommand>();
    services.AddTransient<InventoryCommand, HelpCommand>();
    services.AddTransient<InventoryCommand, AddInventoryCommand>();
    services.AddTransient<InventoryCommand, GetInventoryCommand>();
    services.AddTransient<InventoryCommand, UpdateQuantityCommand>();
    // UnknownCommand should be the last registered
    services.AddTransient<InventoryCommand, UnknownCommand>();

    Services = services.BuildServiceProvider();
}
```

For convenience, a new method has been created in order to return an instance of the `InventoryCommand` class when given a matching input string:

```
public InventoryCommand GetCommand(string input)
{
    return Services.GetServices<InventoryCommand>().First(svc => svc.IsCommandFor(input));
}
```

This method will traverse the collection of dependencies that are registered for the `InventoryCommand` service, until a match is found by using the `IsCommandFor()` method.

The unit test then uses the `GetCommand()` method to determine the dependency, as shown below for `UpdateQuantityCommand`:

```
[TestMethod]
public void UpdateQuantityCommand_Successful()
{
    Assert.IsInstanceOfType(GetCommand("u"),
                            typeof(UpdateQuantityCommand),
                            "u should be UpdateQuantityCommand");

    Assert.IsInstanceOfType(GetCommand("updatequantity"),
                            typeof(UpdateQuantityCommand),
                            "updatequantity should be UpdateQuantityCommand");

    Assert.IsInstanceOfType(GetCommand("UpdaTEQuantity"),
                            typeof(UpdateQuantityCommand),
                            "UpdaTEQuantity should be UpdateQuantityCommand");
}
```

Using third-party containers

The .Net Core framework provides great flexibility and functionality, but some features might not be supported, and a third-party container might be a more appropriate choice. Fortunately .Net Core is extensible and allows for the built-in service container to be replaced by a third-party container. To provide an example, we will use `Autofac` as our IoC container of the .Net Core DI.

> `Autofac` has a ton of great features, and is shown here as an example; but of course, there are other IoC containers that could have been used. For example, Castle Windsor and Unit are great alternatives that should also be considered.

The first step is to add the required `Autofac` package to the project. Using the package manager console, add the package using the following command (only required on the test project):

```
install-package autofac
```

This example will again support our `InventoryCommand` factory by using an `Autofac` feature of naming registered dependencies. These named dependencies will be used to retrieve the correct `InventoryCommand` instance, based on the supplied input.

Similar to the previous example, the registration of dependencies will be done in the `TestInitialize` method. The registrations will be named based on the command that will be used to determine the command. The following shows the `Startup` method structure that creates the `ContainerBuilder` object which will build the `Container` instance:

```
[TestInitialize]
public void Startup()
{
    IServiceCollection services = new ServiceCollection();

    var builder = new ContainerBuilder();

    // commands
    ...

    Container = builder.Build();
}
```

The commands are registered as follows:

```
// commands
builder.RegisterType<QuitCommand>().Named<InventoryCommand>("q");
builder.RegisterType<QuitCommand>().Named<InventoryCommand>("quit");
builder.RegisterType<UpdateQuantityCommand>().Named<InventoryCommand>("u");
builder.RegisterType<UpdateQuantityCommand>().Named<InventoryCommand>("updatequantity");
builder.RegisterType<HelpCommand>().Named<InventoryCommand>("?");
builder.RegisterType<AddInventoryCommand>().Named<InventoryCommand>("a");
builder.RegisterType<AddInventoryCommand>().Named<InventoryCommand>("addinventory");
builder.RegisterType<GetInventoryCommand>().Named<InventoryCommand>("g");
builder.RegisterType<GetInventoryCommand>().Named<InventoryCommand>("getinventory");
builder.RegisterType<UpdateQuantityCommand>().Named<InventoryCommand>("u");
builder.RegisterType<UpdateQuantityCommand>().Named<InventoryCommand>("u");
builder.RegisterType<UnknownCommand>().As<InventoryCommand>();
```

Unlike the previous example, the container that is generated is an instance of `Autofac.IContainer`. This will be used to retrieve each registered dependency. `QuitCommand`, for example, will be named both "q" and "quit", which indicates the two commands that can be used to execute the command. Also, note the last registered type is not named, and belongs to `UnknownCommand`. This will act as a default if no command is found by name.

To determine a dependency, a new method will be used to retrieve the dependency by name:

```
public InventoryCommand GetCommand(string input)
{
    return Container.ResolveOptionalNamed<InventoryCommand>(input.ToLower()) ??
            Container.Resolve<InventoryCommand>();
}
```

The `Autofac.IContainer` interface has a `ResolveOptionalNamed<T>(string)` method name, which will return the dependency with the given name, or null, if no matching registrations are found. If the dependency is not registered with the given name, then an instance of the `UnknownCommand` class will be returned. This is done by using the null-coalescing operation, `??`, and the `IContainer.Resolve<T>` method.

> `Autofac.IContainer.ResolveNamed<T>(string)` will throw a `ComponentNotRegisteredException` exception if the dependency resolution fails.

A test method is written for each command in order to ensure that the commands are resolved correctly. Again, using `QuitCommand` as an example, we can see the following:

```
[TestMethod]
public void QuitCommand_Successful()
{
    Assert.IsInstanceOfType(GetCommand("q"), typeof(QuitCommand), "q should be QuitCommand");
    Assert.IsInstanceOfType(GetCommand("quit"), typeof(QuitCommand), "quit should be QuitCommand");
}
```

Please view the `InventoryCommandAutofacTests` class in the source for the other `InventoryCommand` examples.

Summary

The goal of this chapter was to explore the .Net Core framework in more detail, and, in particular, the .Net Core DI. Three types of service lifetimes are supported: Transient, Scoped, and Singleton. A Transient service will create a new instance of a registered dependency for each request. A Scoped service will be generated once with a defined scope, while a Singleton service will be performed once for the lifetime of the DI service collection.

As the .Net Core DI is central to confidently building .Net Core applications, it is important to understand its capabilities and its limitations. It is important to use the DI effectively, as well as to avoid duplicating functionality that is already supplied. Just as crucial, it is also wise to know the limits of the .Net Core DI framework, as well as the strengths of other DI frameworks, for situations where replacing the basic .Net Core DI framework with a third-party DI framework could be beneficial for an application.

The next chapter will build upon the previous chapters and explore, common patterns in .Net Core ASP.Net web applications.

Questions

The following questions will allow you to consolidate the information contained in this chapter:

1. If you are not sure what type of service lifetime to use, which type is it best to register a class as? Why?
2. In .Net Core ASP.Net solutions, is a Scope defined per web request, or per session?
3. Does registering a class as a Singleton in the .Net Core DI framework make it thread-safe?
4. Is it true that the .Net Core DI framework can only be replaced with other Microsoft-supplied DI frameworks?

6
Implementing Design Patterns for Web Applications - Part 1

In this chapter, we will continue building the **FlixOne** Inventory Management application (see `Chapter 3`, *Implementing Design Patterns Basics – Part 1*), and we will discuss the conversion of a console application to a web application. The web application should be more appealing to users, as opposed to a console application; Here, we will also discuss why we are going for this change.

The following topics will be covered in this chapter:

- Creating a .NET Core web application
- Crafting a web application
- Implementing CRUD pages

> If you have not looked at the earlier chapters yet, please note that the **FlixOne Inventory Management** web application is an imaginary product. We are creating this application to discuss the various design patterns required in web projects.

Implementing Design Patterns for Web Applications - Part 1

Technical requirements

This chapter contains various code examples to explain the concepts. The code is kept simple and is just for demonstration purposes. Most of the examples involve a **.NET Core** console application written in C#.

To run and execute the code, you need the following:

- Visual Studio 2019 (you can also run the application using Visual Studio 2017 Update 3 or later)
- Environment Setup for .NET Core
- SQL Server (the Express edition is used in this chapter)

Installing Visual Studio

To run these code examples, you need to install Visual Studio (2017), or later version such as 2019 (or you can use your preferred IDE). To do this, follow these steps:

1. Download Visual Studio from: `https://docs.microsoft.com/en-us/visualstudio/install/install-visual-studio`.
2. Follow the installation instructions included. Multiple versions are available for the Visual Studio installation. In this chapter, we are using Visual Studio for Windows.

Setting up .NET Core

If you do not have .NET Core installed, you need to follow these steps:

1. Download .NET Core from: `https://www.microsoft.com/net/download/windows`.
2. Follow the installation instructions and follow the related library: `https://dotnet.microsoft.com/download/dotnet-core/2.2`.

Installing SQL Server

If you do not have SQL Server installed, you need to follow these instructions:

1. Download SQL Server from: `https://www.microsoft.com/en-in/download/details.aspx?id=1695`.
2. You can find the installation instructions at: `https://docs.microsoft.com/en-us/sql/ssms/download-sql-server-management-studio-ssms?view=sql-server-2017`.

> For troubleshooting and for more information, refer to: `https://www.blackbaud.com/files/support/infinityinstaller/content/installermaster/tkinstallsqlserver2008r2.htm`.

This section is meant to provide the prerequisite information to get started with web applications. We'll look at more details in the subsequent sections. In this chapter, we will use code examples to elaborate on various terms and sections.

> The complete source code is available at: `https://github.com/PacktPublishing/Hands-On-Design-Patterns-with-C-and-.NET-Core/tree/master/Chapter6`.

Creating a .Net Core web application

At the beginning of this chapter, we discussed our FlixOne console-based application, and there are various reasons to go with a web application as identified by the business team. Now it's time to make changes in the application. In this section, we will start the creation of a new UI of our existing FlixOne application with a new look and feel. We will also discuss all the requirements and initialization.

Kicking off the project

In continuation of our existing FlixOne console application, management has decided to revamp our FlixOne Inventory console application with a lot of features. Management came to the conclusion that we have to convert our existing console application into a web-based solution.

The tech team and the business team sat down together and identified the various reasons why the decision was made to scrap the current console application:

- The interface is not interactive.
- The application is not available everywhere.
- It is complex to maintain.
- The growing business needs a scalable system with higher performance and adaptability.

Developing requirements

The following list of requirements was produced as the outcome of the discussions. The high-level requirements identified are as follows:

- Product categorization
- Product addition
- Product updating
- Product deletion

The actual requirements that the business demands fall on the developers. These technical requirements include the following:

- **A landing or home page**: This should be a dashboard that contains various widgets, and it should show a summary of the store.
- **A product page**: This should have the ability to add, update, and delete products and categories.

Crafting a web application

According to the requirements just discussed, our main goal is to convert our existing console application to a web application. In the process of this conversion, we will discuss various design patterns for web applications, and the importance of these design patterns in the context of web applications.

Web applications and how they work

Web applications are one of the best implementations of the client-server architecture. A web application can be a small piece of code, a program, or a complete solution for a problem or a business scenario in which users interact with one another or with the server, using browsers. A web application serves requests and responses via browsers, mainly through the use of **HyperText Transfer Protocol** (**HTTP**).

> Whenever any communication occurs between the client and the server, two things happen: the client initiates the request and the server generates the response. This communication is made up of HTTP requests and HTTP responses. For more information, refer to the documentation at: https://www.w3schools.com/whatis/whatis_http.asp.

In the following diagram, you can see an overview of a web application and how it works:

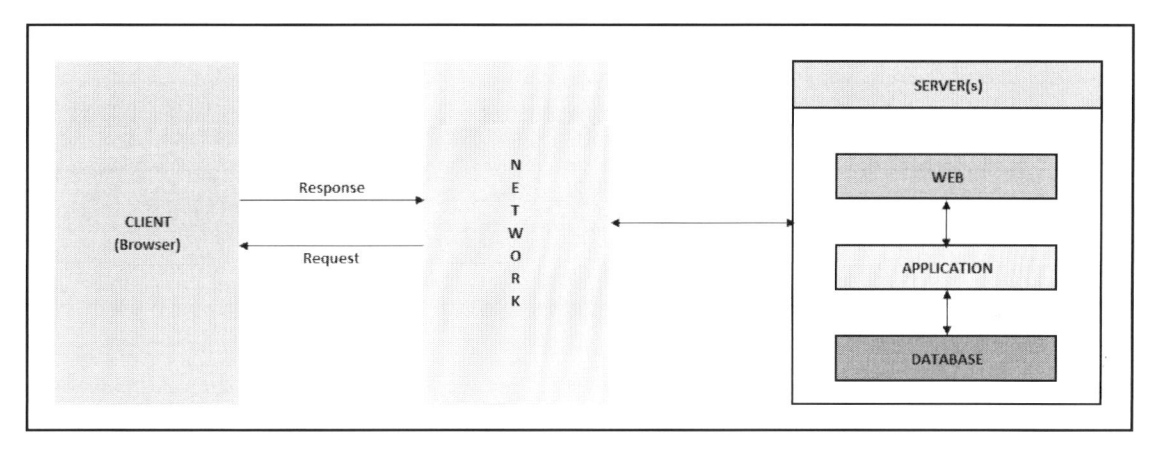

From this diagram, you can easily see that with the use of a browser (as a client), you're opening doors for millions of users who can access the website from anywhere in the world and can interact with you as a user. With a web application, you and your customers can communicate easily. Generally, effective engagement is only possible when you capture and store the data with all the necessary information required for your business and your users. This information is then processed, and the results are presented to your users.

Implementing Design Patterns for Web Applications - Part 1

> In general, web applications use a combination of server-side code to handle the storage and retrieval of the information, and client-side scripts to present the information to the users.

The web application requires a web server (such as **IIS** or **Apache**) to manage requests coming from the client (from the browser, as can be seen in the previous diagram). An application server (such as IIS or Apache Tomcat) is also required to perform the tasks requested. A database is sometimes needed to store the information as well.

> Put simply, both a web server and an application server are designed to serve HTTP content, but with certain variations. Web servers serve static HTTP content, such as HTML pages. Application servers can, apart from serving static HTTP content, also serve dynamic content, using different programming languages. For more information, refer to `https://stackoverflow.com/questions/936197/what-is-the-difference-between-application-server-and-web-server`.

We can elaborate on the workflow of a web application as follows. These are known as the five-step working processes of a web application:

1. A request is triggered by the client (browser) to the web server using HTTP (in most cases) over the internet. This usually happens through a web browser or the application's user interface.
2. The request arises at the web server, and the web server forwards the request to the application server (for different requests, there would be different application servers).
3. In the application server, the requested tasks are completed. This might involve querying the database server, retrieving information from the database, processing information, and building results.
4. The generated results (the requested information or the processed data) are sent to the web server.
5. Finally, the response is sent back to the requester (the client) from the web server with the requested information. This appears on the user's display.

The following diagram shows a pictorial overview of these five steps:

```
Client requests
      ↓ ↑
Requests come to the web server and
are forwarded to the application server  ←┐
      ↓                                    │
The application server processes the      │ Results
requests with the required operations  ──┐│
and builds the results                    ││
      ↑↓                                   ││
The database server executes the          ││
queries, when requested                ───┘┘
```

In the following sections, I will describe the working process of the web application using the **Model-View-Controller** (**MVC**) pattern.

Coding the web application

Up until now, we have gone through the requirements and looked at our aim, which is to convert a console application into a web-based platform or application. In this section, we will develop the actual web application using Visual Studio.

Implementing Design Patterns for Web Applications - Part 1

Carry out the following steps to create a web application using Visual Studio:

1. Open the Visual Studio instance.
2. Click on **File|New|Project** or press *Ctrl + Shift + N*, as shown in the following screenshot:

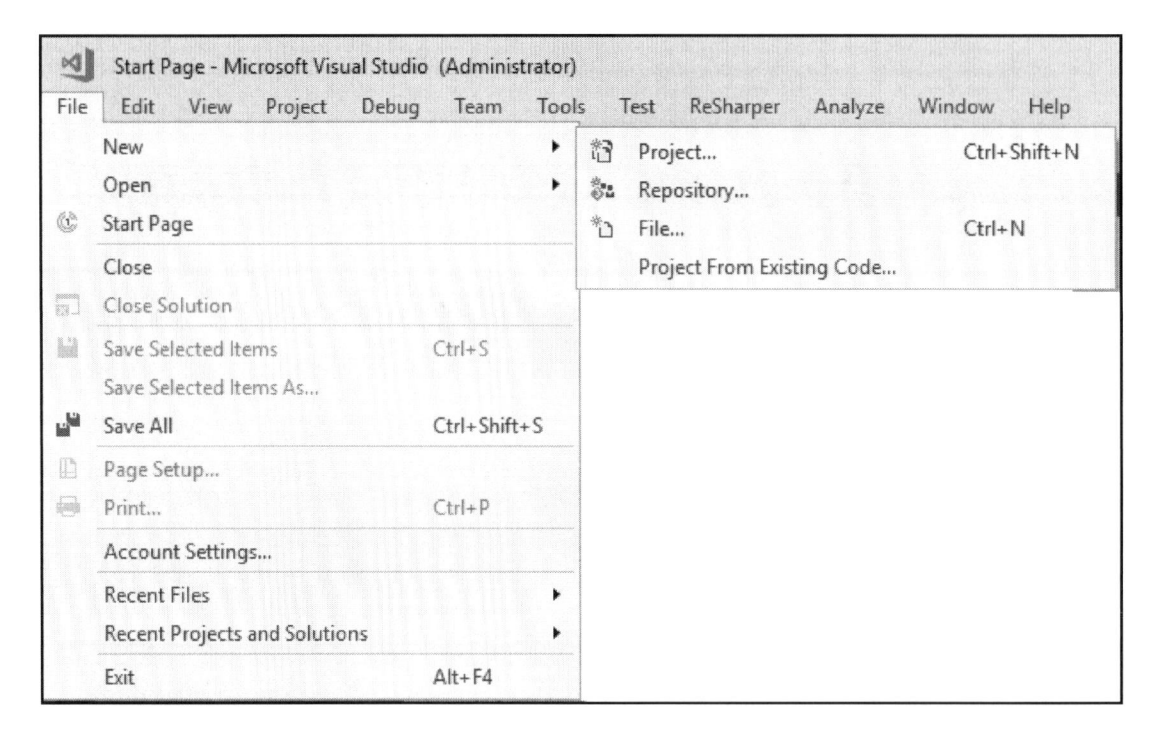

3. From the **New Project** window, select **Web|.NET Core|ASP.NET Core Web Application**.

4. Name it (for example, `FlixOne.Web`), select the location, and then you can update the solution name. By default, the solution name will be the same as the project name. Check the **Create directory for solution** checkbox. You can also choose to check the **Create new Git repository** checkbox (if you want to create a new repository for this, you need a valid Git account).

The following screenshot shows the creation process of a **New project**:

Implementing Design Patterns for Web Applications - Part 1

5. The next step is to select the proper template for your web application and the **.NET Core** version. We are not going to enable Docker support for this project, as we are not going to deploy our application using Docker as the container. We will go with the HTTP protocol only, instead of HTTPS. Both the **Enable Docker Support** and **Configure HTTPs** checkboxes should, therefore, remain unchecked, as shown in the following screenshot:

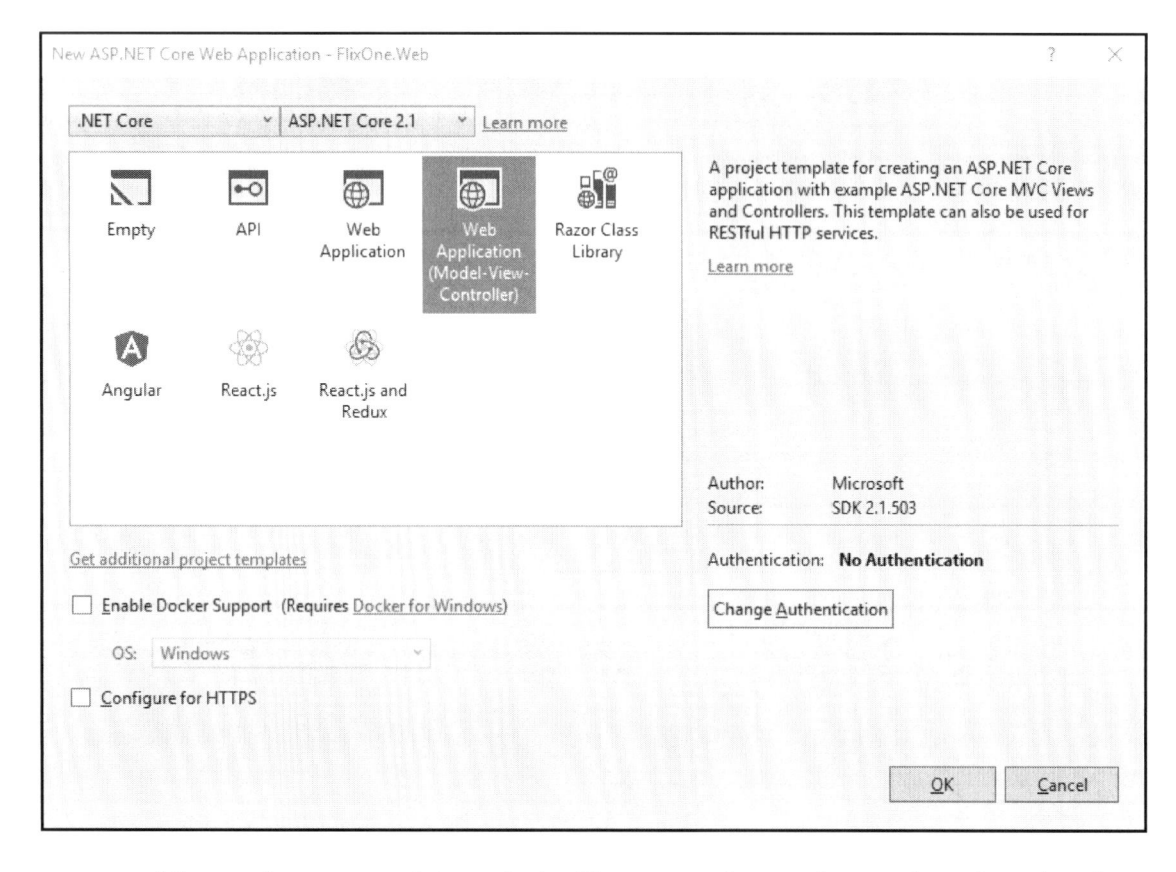

We now have a complete project with our template and example code, using the MVC framework. The following screenshot shows our solution so far:

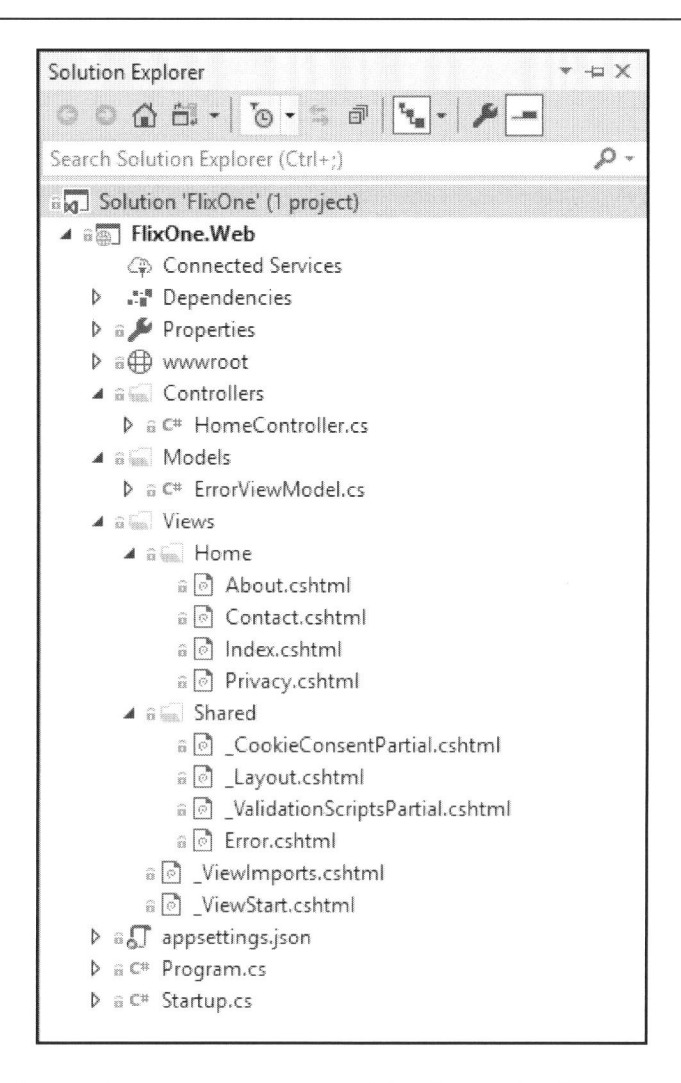

```
Solution Explorer                    ▼ ⌐ X
○ ○ ⌂ ⌐ ▾ | ⌐ ▾ ⊰ ⊜ | ⌐ ▾ | ⌁ ⎯
Search Solution Explorer (Ctrl+;)         ⌕ ▾
⌐ Solution 'FlixOne' (1 project)
▲ ⌐ FlixOne.Web
      ☁ Connected Services
   ▷ ⌑ Dependencies
   ▷ ⌐ Properties
   ▷ ⌐ wwwroot
   ▲ ⌐ Controllers
      ▷ C# HomeController.cs
   ▲ ⌐ Models
      ▷ C# ErrorViewModel.cs
   ▲ ⌐ Views
      ▲ ⌐ Home
            About.cshtml
            Contact.cshtml
            Index.cshtml
            Privacy.cshtml
      ▲ ⌐ Shared
            _CookieConsentPartial.cshtml
            _Layout.cshtml
            _ValidationScriptsPartial.cshtml
            Error.cshtml
         _ViewImports.cshtml
         _ViewStart.cshtml
   ▷ ⌐ appsettings.json
   ▷ C# Program.cs
   ▷ C# Startup.cs
```

Architectural patterns are a way of implementing best practices within the design of the user interface and application itself. They provide us with reusable solutions to common problems. These patterns also allow us to easily implement a separation of concerns.

The most popular architectural patterns are as follows:

- **Model-View-Controller (MVC)**
- **Model-view-presenter (MVP)**
- **Model-view-viewmodel (MVVM)**

Implementing Design Patterns for Web Applications - Part 1

You can try to run the application by hitting *F5*. The following screenshot shows the default home page of the web application:

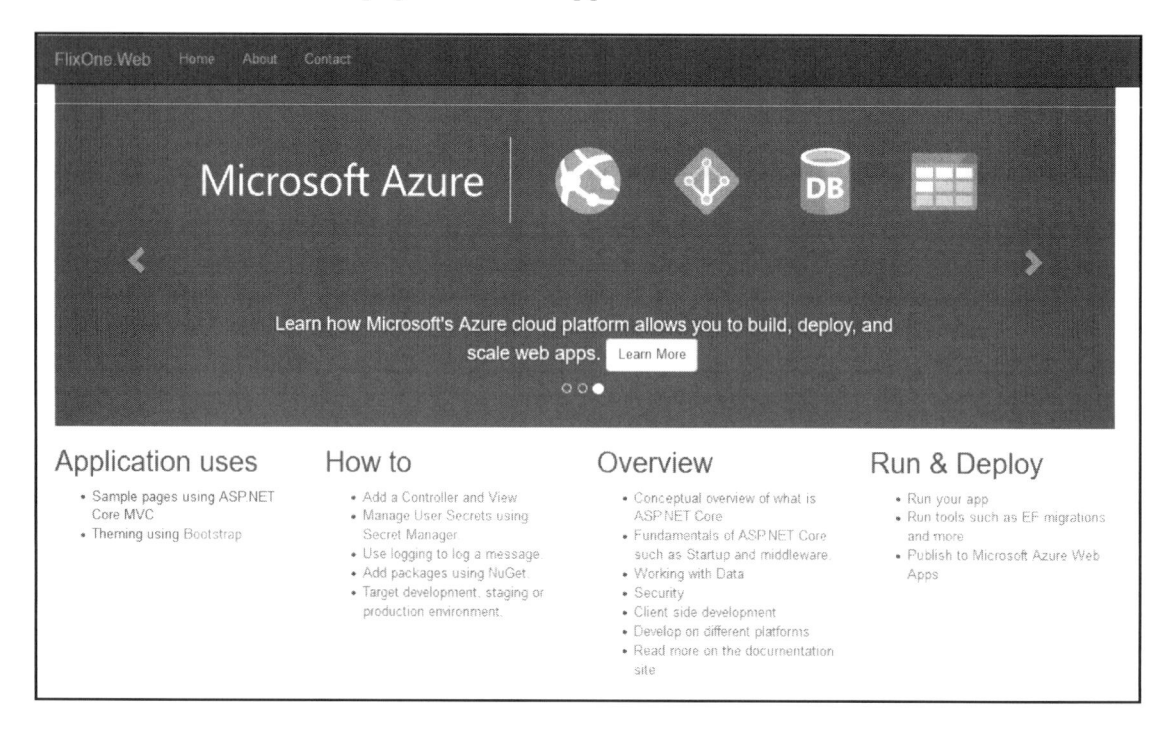

In the coming sections, I will discuss MVC patterns and create **CRUD** (**Create**, **Update**, and **Delete**) pages to interact with the users.

Implementing CRUD pages

In this section, we will start creating functional pages to create, update, and delete products. To get started, open your `FlixOne` solution, and add the following classes into the specified folders:

`Models`: Add the following files in the `Models` folder of the solution:

- `Product.cs`: The code snippet of the `Product` class is as follows:

    ```
    public class Product
    {
        public Guid Id { get; set; }
        public string Name { get; set; }
    ```

```
        public string Description { get; set; }
        public string Image { get; set; }
        public decimal Price { get; set; }
        public Guid CategoryId { get; set; }
        public virtual Category Category { get; set; }
    }
```

The `Product` class represents almost all the elements of the product. It has a `Name`, a complete `Description`, an `Image`, a `Price`, and a unique `ID` so that our system recognizes it. The `Product` class also has a `Category ID` to which this product belongs. It also includes a complete definition of the `Category`.

> **Why should we define a `virtual` property?**
> In our `Product` class, we have defined a `virtual` property. This is because, in the **Entity Framework** (**EF**), this property helps to create a proxy for the virtual property. In this way, the property can support lazy loading and more efficient change tracking. This means that data is available on demand. EF loads the data when you request to use the `Category` property.

- `Category.cs`: The code snippet of the `Category` class is as follows:

    ```
    public class Category
    {
        public Category()
        {
            Products = new List<Product>();
        }

        public Guid Id { get; set; }
        public string Name { get; set; }
        public string Description { get; set; }
        public virtual IEnumerable<Product> Products { get; set; }
    }
    ```

Our `Category` class represents the actual category of the product. A category has a unique `ID`, a `Name`, a complete `Description`, and a collection of `Products` that belong to this category. Whenever we initialize our `Category` class, it initializes our `Product` class.

- `ProductViewModel.cs`: The code snippet of the `ProductViewModel` class is as follows:

    ```
    public class ProductViewModel
    {
    ```

[171]

Implementing Design Patterns for Web Applications - Part 1

```
        public Guid ProductId { get; set; }
        public string ProductName { get; set; }
        public string ProductDescription { get; set; }
        public string ProductImage { get; set; }
        public decimal ProductPrice { get; set; }
        public Guid CategoryId { get; set; }
        public string CategoryName { get; set; }
        public string CategoryDescription { get; set; }
}
```

Our `ProductViewModel` class represents a complete `Product` which is having attributes like a unique `ProductId`, a `ProductName`, a complete `ProductDescription`, a `ProductImage`, a `ProductPrice`, a unique `CategoryId`, a `CategoryName`, and a complete `CategoryDescription`.

`Controllers`: Add the following files to the `Controllers` folder of the solution:

- `ProductController` is responsible for all operations related to products. Let's take a look at the code and the operations that we are trying to achieve in this controller:

```
public class ProductController : Controller
{
    private readonly IInventoryRepositry _repositry;
    public ProductController(IInventoryRepositry 
inventoryRepositry) => _repositry = inventoryRepositry;

    ...
}
```

Here, we defined the `ProductController` that inherits from a `Controller` class. We used **dependency injection**, which is built-in support from the ASP.NET Core MVC framework.

> We discussed the inversion of control in detail in Chapter 5, *Implementing Design Patterns - .Net Core*; `Controller` is a base class for an MVC controller. For more information, refer to: https://docs.microsoft.com/en-us/dotnet/api/microsoft.aspnetcore.mvc.controller.

We have created our main controller, `ProductController`. Let's now start adding functionalities for our CRUD operations.

The following code is simply a `Read` or `Get` operation that requests the repository (`_inventoryRepository`) to list all available products, and then transposes this product list to the `ProductViewModel` type and returns an `Index` view:

```
    public IActionResult Index() =>
View(_repositry.GetProducts().ToProductvm());
    public IActionResult Details(Guid id) =>
View(_repositry.GetProduct(id).ToProductvm());
```

In the preceding code snippet, the `Details` method returns the details of a specific `Product` based on its unique `Id`. This is also a `Get` operation that is similar to our `Index` method, but it provides a single object instead of a list.

> The methods of the **MVC controller** are also called **action methods** and have the return type of `ActionResult`. In this case, we are using `IActionResult`. In general, you can say that `IActionResult` is an interface of the `ActionResult` class. It also provides us a way to return many things, including the following:
> - `EmptyResult`
> - `FileResult`
> - `HttpStatusCodeResult`
> - `ContentResult`
> - `JsonResult`
> - `RedirectToRouteResult`
> - `RedirectResult`
>
> We are not going to discuss all of these in detail, as these are beyond the scope of this book. To find out more about return types, refer to: https://docs.microsoft.com/en-us/aspnet/core/web-api/action-return-types.

In the following code, we are creating a new product. The following code snippet has two action methods. One has the `[HttpPost]` attribute, and the other is without the attribute:

```
public IActionResult Create() => View();
[HttpPost]
[ValidateAntiForgeryToken]
public IActionResult Create([FromBody] Product product)
{
    try
    {
        _repositry.AddProduct(product);
```

[173]

Implementing Design Patterns for Web Applications - Part 1

```
        return RedirectToAction(nameof(Index));
    }
    catch
    {
        return View();
    }
}
```

The first method simply returns a `View`. This will return a `Create.cshtml` page.

> **TIP**
>
> If any of the action methods in the **MVC framework** do not have any attribute, it will use the `[HttpGet]` attribute by default. In other views, by default, action methods are `Get` requests. Whenever a user views a page, we use `[HttpGet]`, or a `Get` request. Whenever a user submits a form or performs an action, we use `[HttpPost]`, or a `Post` request.
>
> If we did not explicitly mention the view name in our action method, then the MVC framework looks like a view name in this format: `actionmethodname.cshtml` or `actionmethodname.vbhtml`. In our case, the view name is `Create.cshtml` because we are using the C# language. It would be `vbhtml` if we used Visual Basic. It first looks in the folder that has a name that is similar to the controller's folder name. If it does not find a file in this folder, it looks in the `shared` folder.

The second action method in the previous code snippet uses the `[HttpPost]` attribute, which means it handles `Post` requests. This action method simply adds the product by calling the `AddProduct` method of `_repository`. In this action method, we have used the `[ValidateAntiForgeryToken]` attribute and `[FromBody]`, which is a model binder.

The MVC framework provides a lot of security to protect our application from **Cross-Site Scripting/Cross-Site Request Forgery** (**XSS/CSRF**) attacks by providing the `[ValidateAntiForgeryToken]` attribute. These type of attacks generally include some dangerous client-side script code.

Model binding in MVC maps data from `HTTP` requests to action method parameters. Frequently used model binding attributes with action methods are as follows:

- `[FromHeader]`
- `[FromQuery]`
- `[FromRoute]`
- `[FromForm]`

We are not going to discuss these in more detail, as this is beyond the scope of this book. However, you can find complete details from the official documentation at https://docs.microsoft.com/en-us/aspnet/core/mvc/models/model-binding.

In the previous code snippets, we discussed the Create and Read operations. It's now time to write a code for the Update operation. In the following code, we have two action methods: one is Get, and the other is a Post request:

```
public IActionResult Edit(Guid id) => View(_repository.GetProduct(id));

[HttpPost]
[ValidateAntiForgeryToken]
public IActionResult Edit(Guid id, [FromBody] Product product)
{
    try
    {
        _repository.UpdateProduct(product);
        return RedirectToAction(nameof(Index));
    }
    catch
    {
        return View();
    }
}
```

The first action method of the previous code gets a Product based on the ID and returns a View. The second action method takes the data from the view and updates the requested Product based on its ID:

```
public IActionResult Delete(Guid id) => View(_repository.GetProduct(id));

[HttpPost]
[ValidateAntiForgeryToken]
public IActionResult Delete(Guid id, [FromBody] Product product)
{
    try
    {
        _repository.RemoveProduct(product);
        return RedirectToAction(nameof(Index));
    }
    catch
    {
        return View();
    }
}
```

Implementing Design Patterns for Web Applications - Part 1

Finally, the previous code represents the `Delete` operation from our CRUD operations. It also has two action methods; one retrieves the data from the repository and serves it to the view, and another takes the data request and deletes the specific `Product` based on its ID.

`CategoryController` is responsible for all the operations of the `Product` category. Add the following code to the controller, it represents the `CategoryController`, where we have used dependency injections to initialize our `IInventoryRepository`:

```
public class CategoryController: Controller
{
  private readonly IInventoryRepositry _inventoryRepositry;
  public CategoryController(IInventoryRepositry inventoryRepositry) =>
_inventoryRepositry = inventoryRepositry;
  //code omitted
}
```

The following code contains two action methods. The first gets a list of categories, and the second is a specific category based on its unique ID:

```
public IActionResult Index() => View(_inventoryRepositry.GetCategories());
public IActionResult Details(Guid id) =>
View(_inventoryRepositry.GetCategory(id));
```

The following code is for the `Get` and the `Post` request to create a new category in the system:

```
public IActionResult Create() => View();
    [HttpPost]
    [ValidateAntiForgeryToken]
    public IActionResult Create([FromBody] Category category)
    {
        try
        {
            _inventoryRepositry.AddCategory(category);

            return RedirectToAction(nameof(Index));
        }
        catch
        {
            return View();
        }
    }
```

In the following code, we are updating our existing category. The code contains the Edit action methods with Get and Post requests:

```
public IActionResult Edit(Guid id) =>
View(_inventoryRepositry.GetCategory(id));
    [HttpPost]
    [ValidateAntiForgeryToken]
    public IActionResult Edit(Guid id, [FromBody]Category category)
    {
        try
        {
            _inventoryRepositry.UpdateCategory(category);

            return RedirectToAction(nameof(Index));
        }
        catch
        {
            return View();
        }
    }
```

Finally, we have a Delete action method. This is the final operation of our CRUD pages for Category deletion as shown in the following code:

```
public IActionResult Delete(Guid id) =>
View(_inventoryRepositry.GetCategory(id));

    [HttpPost]
    [ValidateAntiForgeryToken]
    public IActionResult Delete(Guid id, [FromBody] Category category)
    {
        try
        {
            _inventoryRepositry.RemoveCategory(category);

            return RedirectToAction(nameof(Index));
        }
        catch
        {
            return View();
        }
    }
```

Views: Add the following views to their respective folders:

- Index.cshtml
- Create.cshtml

Implementing Design Patterns for Web Applications - Part 1

- Edit.cshtml
- Delete.cshtml
- Details.cshtml

Contexts: Add the InventoryContext.cs file to the Contexts folder with the following code:

```
public class InventoryContext : DbContext
{
    public InventoryContext(DbContextOptions<InventoryContext> options)
        : base(options)
    {
    }

    public InventoryContext()
    {
    }

    public DbSet<Product> Products { get; set; }
    public DbSet<Category> Categories { get; set; }
}
```

The preceding code provides the various methods needed to interact with the database using EF. You might face the following exception while running the code:

```
An unhandled exception occurred while processing the request.

InvalidOperationException: Unable to resolve service for type 'FlixOne.Web.Persistance.IInventoryRepositry' while attempting to activate 'FlixOne.Web.Controllers.ProductController'.
Microsoft.Extensions.DependencyInjection.ActivatorUtilities.GetService(IServiceProvider sp, Type type, Type requiredBy, bool isDefaultParameterRequired)
```

To fix this exception, you should map to the IInventoryRepository in the Startup.cs file, as shown in the following screenshot:

```
// This method gets called by the runtime. Use this method to add services to the container.
public void ConfigureServices(IServiceCollection services)
{
    services.AddTransient<IInventoryRepository, InventoryRepository>();
    services.AddDbContext<InventoryContext>(o => o.UseSqlServer(Configuration.GetConnectionString("FlixOneDbConnection")));
    services.Configure<CookiePolicyOptions>(options =>
    {
        // This lambda determines whether user consent for non-essential cookies is needed for a given request.
        options.CheckConsentNeeded = context => true;
        options.MinimumSameSitePolicy = SameSiteMode.None;
    });

    services.AddMvc().SetCompatibilityVersion(CompatibilityVersion.Version_2_1);
}
```

We have now added various functionalities to our web application, and our solution now looks as shown in the following screenshot:

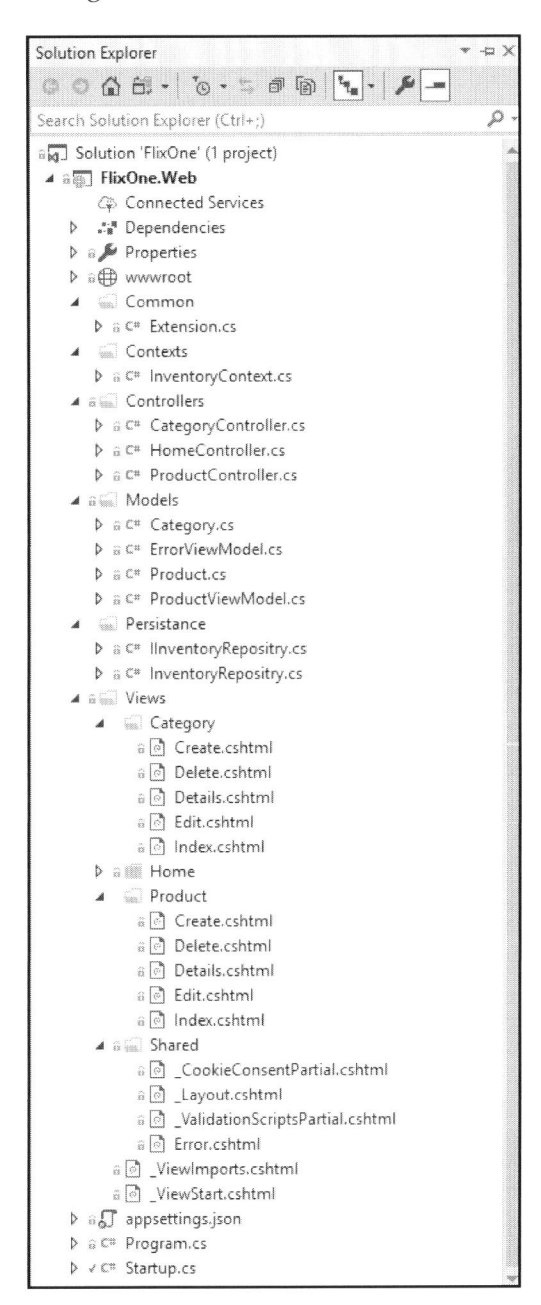

Refer to the GitHub repository for this chapter (`https://github.com/PacktPublishing/Hands-On-Design-Patterns-with-C-and-.NET-Core/tree/master/Chapter6`).

If we were to visualize the MVC model, then it would work as shown in the following diagram:

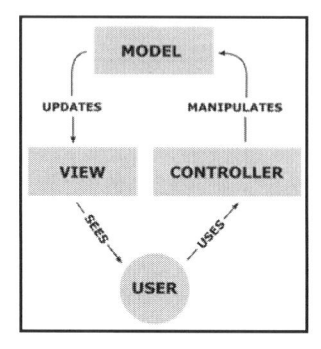

The preceding image was adapted from `https://commons.wikimedia.org/wiki/File:MVC-Process.svg`

As shown in the previous diagram, whenever a user raises a request, it comes to the controller and triggers the action method to be further manipulated or updated, if required, to the model, and then serves the view to the user.

In our case, whenever a user requests `/Product`, the request goes to the `Index` action method of `ProductController` and serves the `Index.cshtml` view after fetching the list of products. You will get the product listing as shown in the following screenshot:

Product Name	Description	Image	Price (INR)	Category Name	Action
Mango	A juicy mango		40.00	Fruit	Edit | Details | Delete
Apple	Red apple		100.00	Fruit	Edit | Details | Delete
Orange	Fruity oranges		35.00	Fruit	Edit | Details | Delete

© 2019 - FlixOne.Web

The preceding screenshot is a simple product listing, and it represents the `Read` section of the `CRUD` operations. On this screen, the application shows the total available products and their categories.

The following diagram depicts how our application interacts:

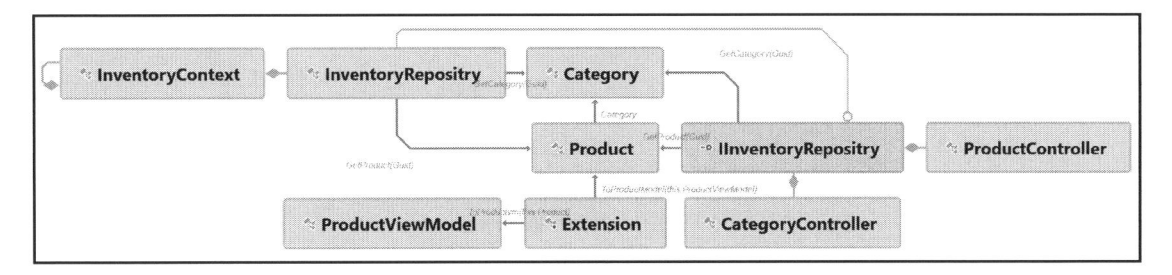

[Diagram showing InventoryContext, InventoryRepositry, Category, Product, IInventoryRepository, ProductController, ProductViewModel, Extension, and CategoryController and their relationships]

It shows the pictorial overview of the process of our application.
The `InventoryRepository` depends on the `InventoryContext` for database operations and interacts with our model classes, `Category` and `Product`. Our controllers for `Product` and `Category` use the `IInventoryRepository` interface to interact with the repository for CRUD operations.

Summary

The main goal of this chapter was to start a basic web application.

We started the chapter by discussing business requirements, why we needed a web application, and why we wanted to upgrade our console application. We then covered the step-by-step creation of a web application using Visual Studio in the MVC pattern. We also discussed how a web application can work as a client-server model, and looked at user interface patterns. We also started building CRUD pages.

In the next chapter, we will continue with the web application and discuss more design patterns for web applications.

Questions

The following questions will allow you to consolidate the information contained in this chapter:

1. What is a web application?
2. Craft a web application of your choice, and depict how it works.
3. What is inversion of control?
4. What are the architectural patterns that we've covered in this chapter? Which one do you like and why?

Further reading

Congratulations! You've completed this chapter. We have covered a lot of things related to authentication, authorization, and testing projects. This is not the end of your learning; it is just the beginning, and there are more books you can refer to increase your understanding. The following books provide an in-depth look at RESTful web services and test-driven development:

- *Building RESTful Web services with .NET Core,* by *Gaurav Aroraa, Tadit Dash,* from *Packt Publishing,* at: https://www.packtpub.com/application-development/building-restful-web-services-net-core
- *C# and .NET Core Test Driven Development,* by *Ayobami Adewole,* from *Packt Publishing,* at: https://www.packtpub.com/application-development/c-and-net-core-test-driven-development

7
Implementing Design Patterns for Web Applications - Part 2

In the previous chapter, we extended our FlixOne inventory management console application to a web application while illustrating different patterns. We also covered **User Interface** (**UI**) architectural patterns such as **Model-View-Controller** (**MVC**), **Model View Presenter** (**MVP**), and others. The previous chapter aimed to discuss patterns such as MVC. We now need to extend our existing application to incorporate more patterns.

In this chapter, we will continue with our existing FlixOne web application and extend the application by working on code to see the implementation of authentication and authorization. In addition to this, we will discuss **Test-Driven Development** (**TDD**).

In this chapter, we will cover the following topics:

- Authentication and authorization
- Creating a .NET Core web test project

Technical requirements

This chapter contains various code examples to explain the concepts. The code is kept simple and is just for demonstration purposes. Most of the examples involve a .NET Core console application that is written in C#.

To run and execute the code, Visual Studio 2019 is a prerequisite (you can also use Visual Studio 2017 to run the application).

Installing Visual Studio

To run these code examples, you need to install Visual Studio (the preferred **Integrated Development Environment** (**IDE**)). To do so, follow these instructions:

1. Download Visual Studio from the following download link, which contains installation instructions: `https://docs.microsoft.com/en-us/visualstudio/install/install-visual-studio`.
2. Follow the installation instructions you find there. Multiple versions are available for Visual Studio installation. Here, we are using Visual Studio for Windows.

Setting up .NET Core

If you do not have .NET Core installed, you need to follow these instructions:

1. Download .NET Core for Windows using `https://www.microsoft.com/net/download/windows`.
2. For multiple versions and a related library, visit `https://dotnet.microsoft.com/download/dotnet-core/2.2`.

Installing SQL Server

If you do not have SQL Server installed, you need to follow these instructions:

1. Download SQL Server from the following link: `https://www.microsoft.com/en-in/download/details.aspx?id=1695`.
2. You can find installation instructions here: `https://docs.microsoft.com/en-us/sql/ssms/download-sql-server-management-studio-ssms?view=sql-server-2017`.

> For troubleshooting and for more information, refer to the following link: `https://www.blackbaud.com/files/support/infinityinstaller/content/installermaster/tkinstallsqlserver2008r2.htm`.
>
> The complete source code is available from the following link: `https://github.com/PacktPublishing/Hands-On-Design-Patterns-with-C-and-.NET-Core/tree/master/Chapter7`.

Extending the .NET Core web application

In this chapter, we will continue with our FlixOne inventory application. Throughout this chapter, we will discuss web application patterns and extend the web application that we developed in the previous chapter.

> This chapter continues with the web application developed in the previous chapter. If you skipped the previous chapter, please revisit it to Synchronization with the current chapter.

In this section, we will go through the process of requirement gathering, and then discuss the various challenges with our web application that we developed before now.

Project kickoff

In `Chapter 6`, *Implementing Design Patterns for Web Applications – Part 1*, we extended our FlixOne inventory console application and developed a web application. We extended the application after considering the following points:

- Our business needs a rich UI.
- New opportunities demand a responsive web application.

Requirements

After several meetings and discussions with the management, **Business Analysts** (**BAs**), and presales folks, management decided to work on the following high-level requirements: **business requirements** and **technical requirements**.

Business requirements

The business team eventually came up with the following business requirements:

- **Product categorization**: There are several products, but if a user wants to search for a specific product, they can do so by filtering all products by their categories. For example, products such as mangoes, bananas, and more should come under a category called `Fruits`.
- **Product addition**: There should be an interface that provides us with a feature to add new products. This feature should only be available to users who have the `Add Products` privilege.

- **Product updation**: There should be a new interface where product updates should be possible.
- **Product deletion**: There is a requirement for administrators to delete products.

Technical requirements

The actual requirements for meeting the business needs are now ready for development. After several discussions with business folks, we concluded that the following are the requirements:

- **You should have a landing or home page**:
    - Should be a dashboard that contains various widgets
    - Should show an at-a-glance picture of the store
- **You should have a product page**:
    - Should have the capability to add, update, and delete products
    - Should have the capability to add, update, and delete product categories

> The FlixOne Inventory Management web application is an imaginary product. We are creating this application to discuss the various design patterns required/used in web projects.

Challenges

Although we have extended our existing console application to a new web application, it has various challenges for both developers and businesses. In this section, we will discuss these challenges, and then we will find out the solution to overcome these challenges.

Challenges for developers

The following are the challenges that arose due to a big change in the application. These were also a result of major extensions to upgrading a console application to a web application:

- **No support for TDD**: Currently, there is no test project incorporated in the solution. Consequently, developers can't follow the TDD approach, which could lead to more bugs in the application.

- **Security**: In the current application, there is no mechanism to restrict or permit the user from providing access to a particular screen or module of the application. There is also nothing related to authentication and authorization.
- **UI and User Experience (UX)**: Our app is promoted from a console-based application, so the UI is not very rich.

Challenges for businesses

It takes time to achieve the final output, which delays the product, resulting in a loss for the business. The following challenges occur as we adapt a new technology stack, and there are plenty of changes in the code:

- **Loss of clients**: Here, we are still in the stage of development but the demand for our business is very high; however, the development team is taking longer than expected to deliver the product.
- **It takes more time to roll out the production updates**: Development efforts are time-consuming at the moment, which delays the subsequent activities and leads to a delay in production.

Finding a solution to the problems/challenges

After several meetings and brainstorming sessions, the development team came to the conclusion that we have to stabilize our web-based solution. To overcome these challenges and provide the solution, the tech team and the business team got together to identify the various solutions and points.

The following points are supported by the solution:

- Implementing authentication and authorization
- Following TDD
- Redesigning the UI to meet the UX

Authentication and authorization

In the previous chapter—where we started upgrading our console application to a web application—we added **Create, Read, Update, and Delete** (**CRUD**) operations, which are available publicly to any user who is able to perform them. There is nothing coded to restrict a particular user from performing these operations. The risk with this is that users who are not supposed to perform these operations can easily do so. The consequences of this are as follows:

- Unattended access
- An open door for hackers/attackers
- Data leakage issues

Now, if we are keen to safeguard our application and restrict the operations to permitted users only, then we have to implement a design that only allows these users to perform operations. There may be scenarios in which we could allow open access for a few operations. In our case, most operations are only for restricted access. In simple terms, we can try something that tells our application that the incoming user is the one who belongs to our application and can perform the specified task.

> **Authentication** is simply a process in which a system verifies or identifies the incoming requests through credentials (generally a user ID and password). If the system finds that the provided credentials are wrong, then it notifies the user (generally via a message on the GUI screen) and terminates the authorization process.
>
> **Authorization** always comes after authentication. This is a process that allows the authenticated user who raised the request to access resources or data after verifying that they have access to the specific resources or data.

In the previous paragraph, we have discussed some mechanisms that stop unattended access to our application's operations. Let's refer to the following diagram and discuss what it shows:

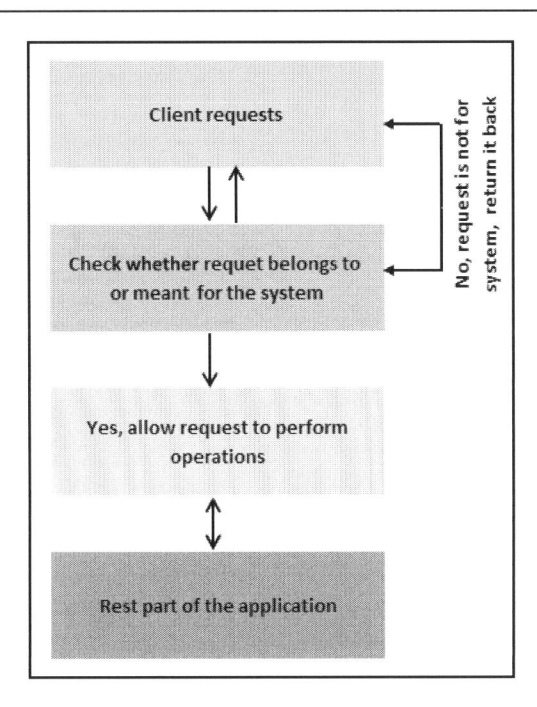

The preceding diagram depicts a scenario in which the system does not allow unattended access. This is simply defined as follows: an incoming request is received and the internal system (an authentication mechanism) checks whether a request is authenticated or not. If a request is authenticated, then a user is allowed to perform the operations for which they are authorized. This is not only the single check, but for a typical system, authorization comes in place after authentication. We will discuss this in the upcoming sections.

To understand this in a better way, let's write a simple login application. Let's follow the steps given here:

1. Open **Visual Studio 2018.**
2. Open **File | New | New project.**
3. From the **Project** window, give a name to your project.

4. Select **ASP.NET Core 2.2** for the Web Application (**Model-View-Controller**) template:

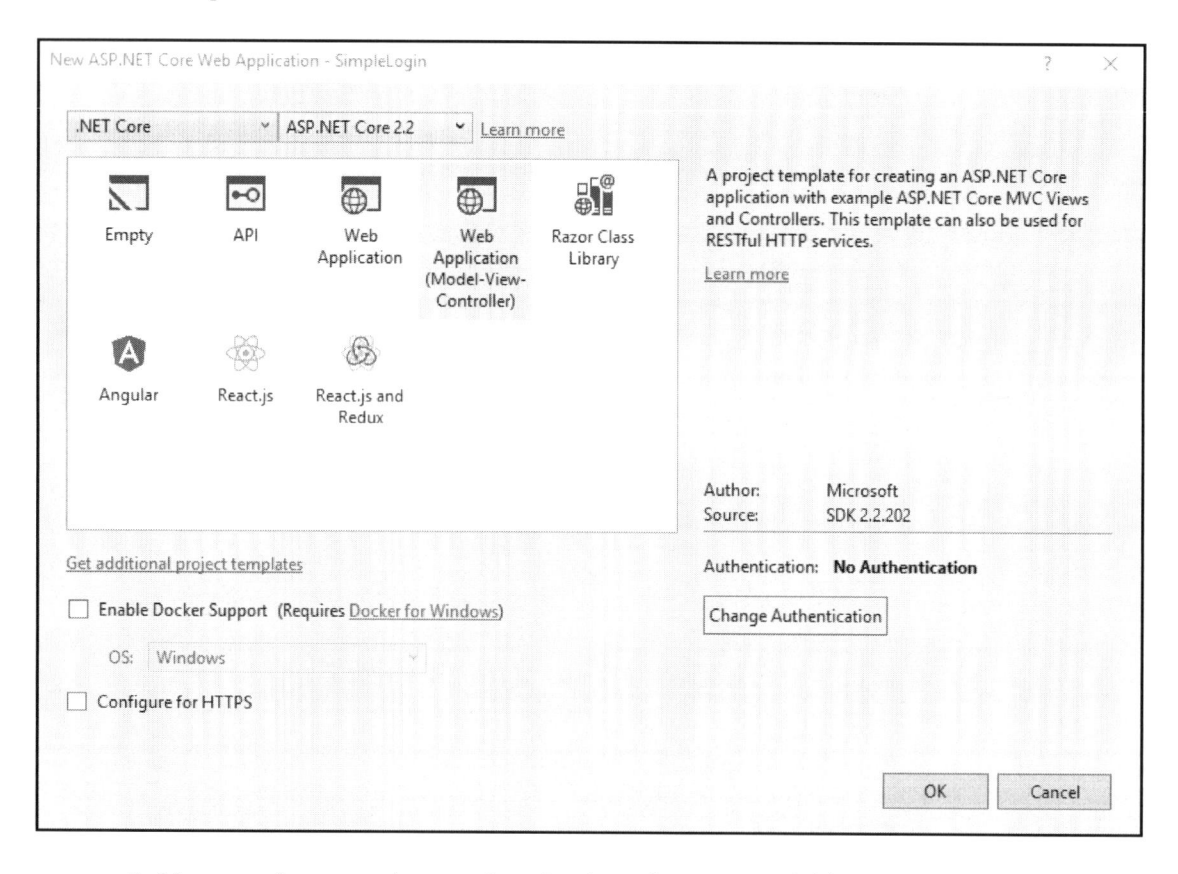

5. You can choose various authentications that are available as part of the selected template.
6. By default, the template provides an option named **No Authentication**, as shown here:

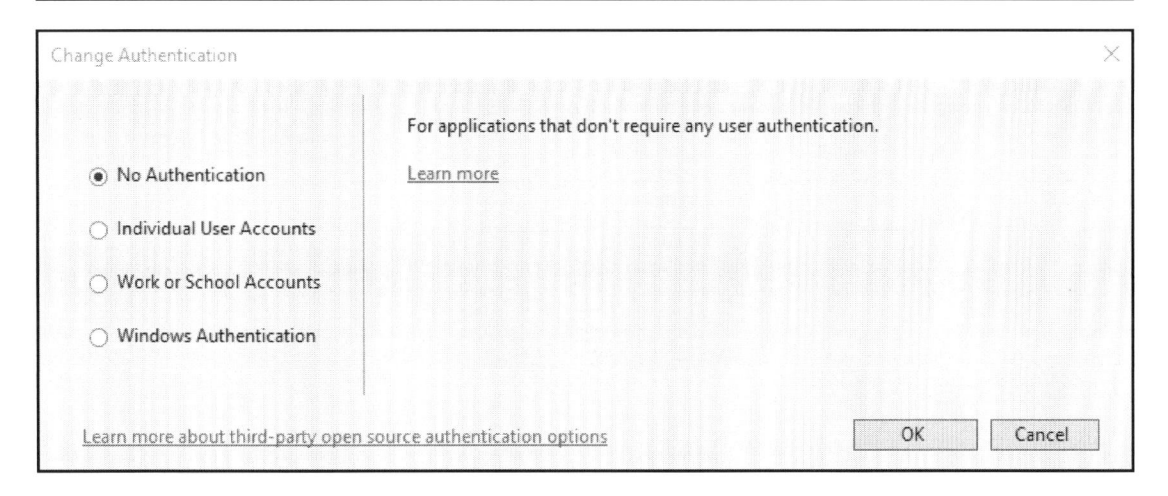

[Screenshot of the "Change Authentication" dialog in Visual Studio with options: No Authentication (selected), Individual User Accounts, Work or School Accounts, Windows Authentication.]

7. Press *F5* and run the application. From here, you will see the default home page:

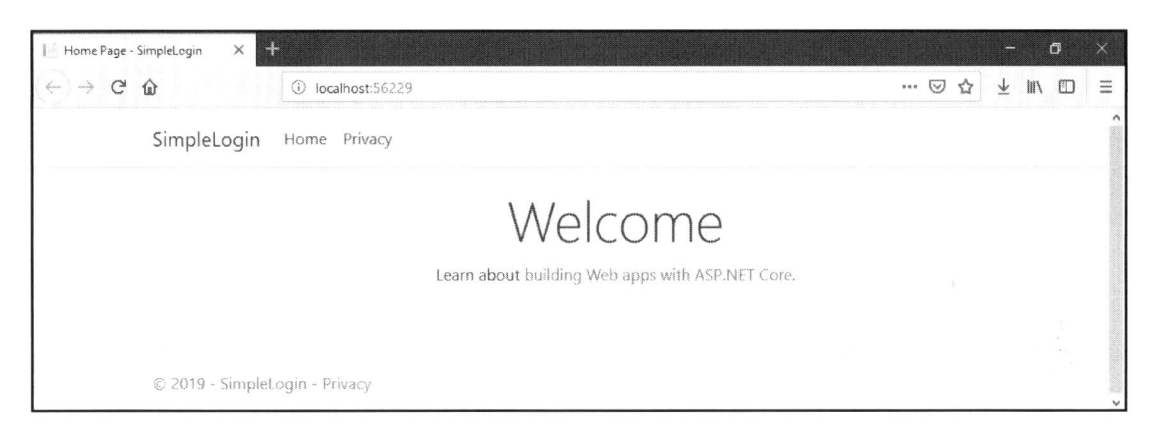

[Screenshot of the SimpleLogin home page in a browser showing "Welcome — Learn about building Web apps with ASP.NET Core."]

You will now notice that you can navigate every page without any restrictions. This is obvious and makes sense as these pages are available as open access. The **Home** and **Privacy** pages are open access and do not require any authentication, meaning that anyone can access/view these pages. On the other hand, we may have a few pages that are meant for unattended access, such as the **User Profile**, and **Admin** pages.

> **TIP:** Refer to the GitHub repository for the chapter at `https://github.com/PacktPublishing/Hands-On-Design-Patterns-with-C-and-.NET-Core/tree/master/Chapter6`, and go through the entire application that we have built using ASP.NET Core MVC.

Implementing Design Patterns for Web Applications - Part 2

To continue with our **SimpleLogin** application, let's add a screen that is meant for restricted access: the **Products** screen. In this chapter, we are not going to discuss how to add a new controller or views to an existing project. If you want to know how we can add these to our project, revisit `Chapter 6`, *Implementing Design Patterns for Web Applications – Part 1*.

We have added new functionality to our project to showcase products with CRUD operations. Now, hit *F5* and check the output:

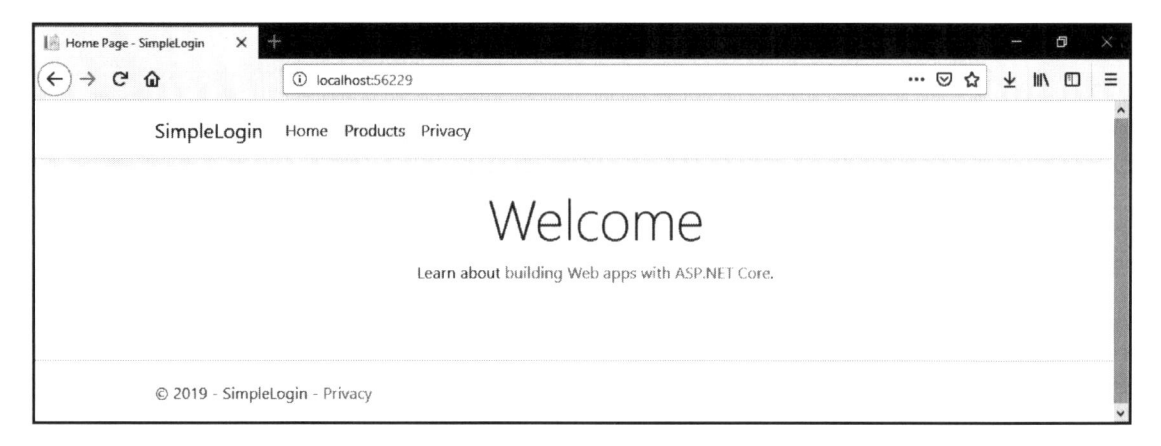

You will get the output that is shown in the previous screenshot. You might notice that we now have a new menu named **Products**.

Let's navigate through the new menu options. Click on the **Products** menu:

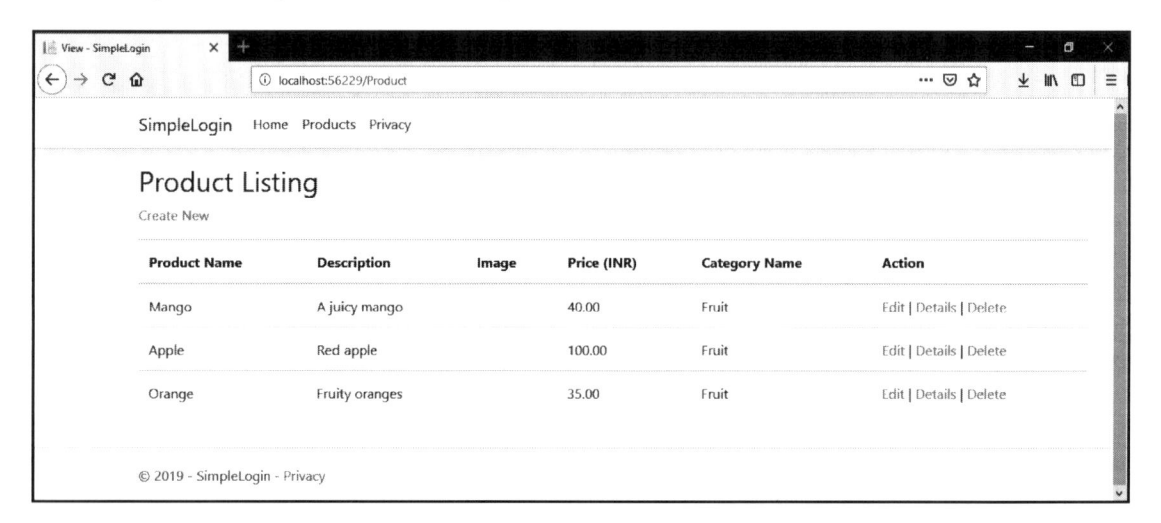

The previous screenshot shows our **Product** page. This page is available to all and anyone can view it without any restrictions. You might have a look and observe that this page has the feature to **Create New** products, and to **Edit** and **Delete** existing products. Now, imagine a scenario where one unknown user came and deleted a specific product that is very important and attracts a high sales volume. You can imagine the scenario and how much this hampers a business. There might even be a chance that customers are lost.

In our scenario, we can protect our **Product** page in two ways:

- **Prior Authenticate**: On this page, the link to **Products** is not available for everyone; it is only available for authenticated requests/users.
- **Post Authenticate**: On this page, the link to **Products** is available for everyone. However, once someone requests to access the page, the system performs an authentication check.

Authentication in action

In this section, we will see how to implement authentication and make our web pages restricted for unauthenticated requests.

To achieve authentication, we should adopt some sort of mechanism that provides us with a way to authenticate a user. In general cases, if a user is logged in, that means they are already authenticated.

In our web application, we will also follow the same approach and make sure that the user is logged in before accessing the restricted pages, views, and operations:

```
public class User
{
    public Guid Id { get; set; }
    public string UserName { get; set; }
    public string EmailId { get; set; }
    public string FirstName { get; set; }
    public string LastName { get; set; }
    public byte[] PasswordHash { get; set; }
    public byte[] PasswordSalt { get; set; }
    public string SecretKey { get; set; }
    public string Mobile { get; set; }
    public string EmailToken { get; set; }
    public DateTime EmailTokenDateTime { get; set; }
    public string OTP { get; set; }
    public DateTime OtpDateTime { get; set; }
    public bool IsMobileVerified { get; set; }
    public bool IsEmailVerified { get; set; }
```

```
            public bool IsActive { get; set; }
            public string Image { get; set; }
}
```

The previous class is a typical `User` model/entity that represents our database `User` table. This table will persist all the information regarding `User`. Here is what every field looks like:

- `Id` is a **Globally Unique Identifier** (**GUID**) and primary key in the table.
- `UserName` is typically used during login and other related operations. It is a programmatically generated field.
- `FirstName` and `LastName` combine the full name of the user.
- `Emailid` is the valid email ID of the user. It should be a valid email because we will validate this after/during the registration process.
- `PasswordHash` and `PasswordSalt` are the byte arrays that are based on a **Hash-Based Message Authentication Code, Secure Hash Algorithm** (**HMACSHA**) 512. A value for `PasswordHash` attribute is 64 bytes and `PasswordSalt` is 128 bytes.
- `SecretKey` is a Base64-encoded string.
- `Mobilie` is a valid mobile number that depends on the validity check by the system.
- `EmailToken` and `OTP` are the **One-Time Passwords** (**OTPs**) that are randomly generated to validate `emailId` and `Mobile number`.
- `EmailTokenDateTime` and `OtpDateTime` are the properties of the `datetime` data type; they represent the date and time in which `EmailToken` and `OTP` are issued for the user.
- `IsMobileVerified` and `IsEmailverified` are Boolean values (`true/false`) that tell the system whether the mobile number and/or email ID are verified or not.
- `IsActive` is a Boolean value (`true/false`) that tells the system whether a `User` model is active or not.
- `Image` is a Base64-encoded string of an image. It represents the profile picture of a user.

We need to add our new class/entity to our `Context` class. Let's add what we can see in the following screenshot:

```csharp
public class InventoryContext : DbContext
{
    public InventoryContext(DbContextOptions<InventoryContext> options)
        : base(options)
    {
    }

    public InventoryContext()
    {
    }

    public DbSet<Product> Products { get; set; }
    public DbSet<Category> Categories { get; set; }
    public DbSet<User>Users { get; set; }
}
```

By adding the previous line in our `Context` class, we can access our `User` table directly using **Entity Framework** (**EF**) functionality:

```csharp
public class LoginViewModel
{
    [Required]
    public string Username { get; set; }
    [Required]
    [DataType(DataType.Password)]
    public string Password { get; set; }
    [Display(Name = "Remember Me")]
    public bool RememberMe { get; set; }
    public string ReturnUrl { get; set; }
}
```

`LoginViewModel` is used to authenticate the user. The values of this `viewmodel` come from the **Login** page (we will discuss and create this page in the upcoming section). It contains the following:

- `UserName`: This is a unique name that is used to identify the user. This is a human-readable value that can be easily identified. It is not like the GUID value.
- `Password`: This is a secret and sensitive value for any user.
- `RememberMe`: This tells us whether the user wants to allow the current system to persist cookies which store values in cookies at the client browser.

To perform the CRUD operations, let's add the following code to the `UserManager` class:

```
public class UserManager : IUserManager
{
    private readonly InventoryContext _context;

    public UserManager(InventoryContext context) => _context = context;

    public bool Add(User user, string userPassword)
    {
        var newUser = CreateUser(user, userPassword);
        _context.Users.Add(newUser);
        return _context.SaveChanges() > 0;
    }

    public bool Login(LoginViewModel authRequest) => FindBy(authRequest) != null;

    public User GetBy(string userId) => _context.Users.Find(userId);
```

The following is the code snippet from the rest of the methods of the `UserManager` class:

```
    public User FindBy(LoginViewModel authRequest)
    {
        var user = Get(authRequest.Username).FirstOrDefault();
        if (user == null) throw new ArgumentException("You are not registered with us.");
        if (VerifyPasswordHash(authRequest.Password, user.PasswordHash, user.PasswordSalt)) return user;
        throw new ArgumentException("Incorrect username or password.");
    }
    public IEnumerable<User> Get(string searchTerm, bool isActive = true)
    {
        return _context.Users.Where(x =>
            x.UserName == searchTerm.ToLower() || x.Mobile == searchTerm ||
            x.EmailId == searchTerm.ToLower() && x.IsActive == isActive);
    }
    ...
}
```

The preceding code is the `UserManager` class, which gives us the ability to interact with our `User` table using EF:

The following code shows the View of the **Login** screen:

```
<form asp-action="Login" asp-route-returnurl="@Model.ReturnUrl">
    <div asp-validation-summary="ModelOnly" class="text-danger"></div>

    <div class="form-group">
        <label asp-for="Username" class="control-label"></label>
        <input asp-for="Username" class="form-control" />
        <span asp-validation-for="Username" class="text-danger"></span>
    </div>

    <div class="form-group">
        <label asp-for="Password" class="control-label"></label>
        <input asp-for="Password" class="form-control"/>
        <span asp-validation-for="Password" class="text-danger"></span>
    </div>

    <div class="form-group">
        <label asp-for="RememberMe" ></label>
        <input asp-for="RememberMe" />
        <span asp-validation-for="RememberMe"></span>
    </div>
    <div class="form-group">
        <input type="submit" value="Login" class="btn btn-primary" />
    </div>
</form>
```

The previous code snippet is from our `Login.cshtml` page/view. This page provides a form to enter the `Login` details. These details come to our `Account` controller and are then validated to authenticate the user:

The following is the `Login` action method:

```
[HttpGet]
public IActionResult Login(string returnUrl = "")
{
    var model = new LoginViewModel { ReturnUrl = returnUrl };
    return View(model);
}
```

Implementing Design Patterns for Web Applications - Part 2

The preceding code snippet is a `Get /Account/Login` request that displays the empty login page, which is shown in the following screenshot:

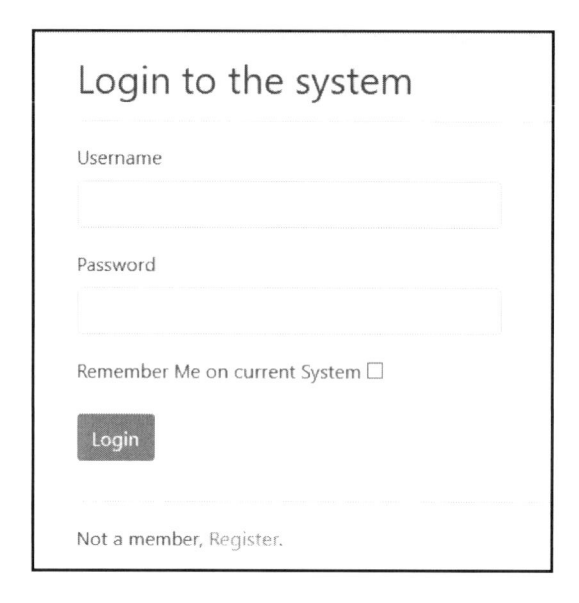

Login to the system

Username

Password

☐ Remember Me on current System

[Login]

Not a member, Register.

The previous screenshot appears as soon as the user clicks on the **Login** menu option. This is a simple form used to enter the **Login** details.

The following code shows the `Login` action method that handles the `Login` functionality of the application:

```
[HttpPost]
public IActionResult Login(LoginViewModel model)
{
    if (ModelState.IsValid)
    {
        var result = _authManager.Login(model);

        if (result)
        {
            return !string.IsNullOrEmpty(model.ReturnUrl) &&
Url.IsLocalUrl(model.ReturnUrl)
                ? (IActionResult)Redirect(model.ReturnUrl)
                : RedirectToAction("Index", "Home");
        }
    }
    ModelState.AddModelError("", "Invalid login attempt");
    return View(model);
}
```

The preceding code snippet is a `Post /Account/Login` request from a login page that posts the entire `LoginViewModel` class:

The following is the screenshot of our Login view:

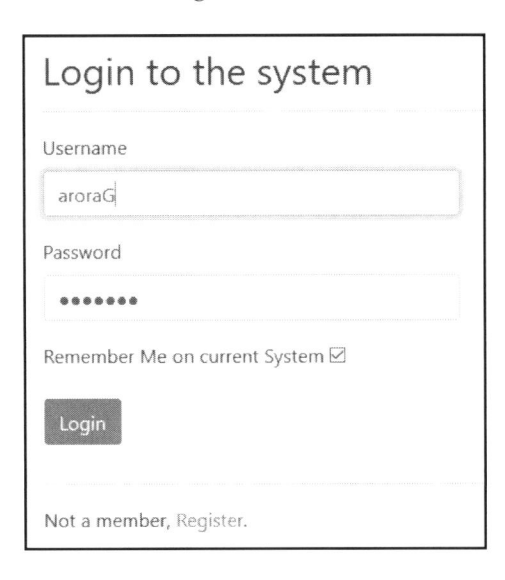

![Login to the system screenshot showing Username aroraG, Password field, Remember Me on current System checkbox checked, Login button, and "Not a member, Register." link]

In the previous screenshot, we are trying to log in using our default user credentials (**Username**: `aroraG` and **Password**: `test123`). The information related to this login is being persisted in cookies, but only if the **Remember Me** checkbox is checked by the user. The system remembers the logged-in session on the current computer until the user hits the **Logout** button.

As soon as the user hits the **Login** button, the system authenticates their login details and redirects them to the home page, as shown in the following screenshot:

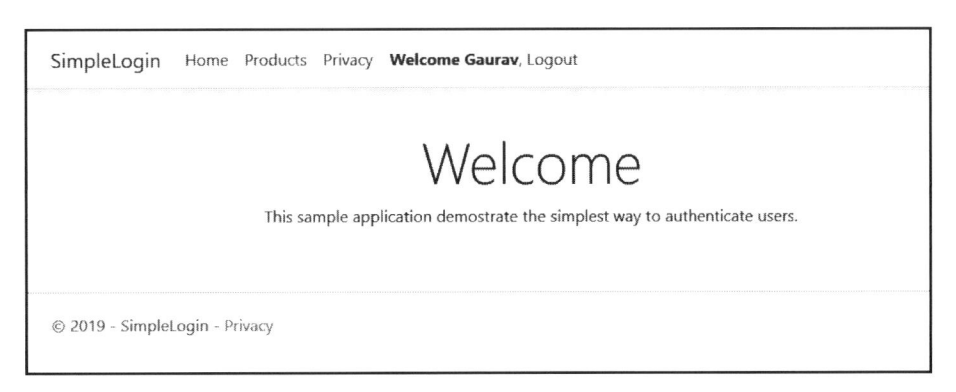

![Home page screenshot showing SimpleLogin navigation with Home, Products, Privacy, Welcome Gaurav, Logout, and Welcome heading with text "This sample application demostrate the simplest way to authenticate users." Footer: © 2019 - SimpleLogin - Privacy]

Implementing Design Patterns for Web Applications - Part 2

You might observe text in the menu, such as `Welcome Gaurav`. This welcome text is not coming automatically, but we did instruct our system to show this text by adding a few lines of code, as shown in the following code:

```
<li class="nav-item">
    @{
        if (AuthManager.IsAuthenticated)
        {
            <a class="nav-link text-dark" asp-area="" asp-controller="Account" asp-action="Logout"><strong>Welcome @AuthManager.Name</strong>, Logout</a>

        }
        else
        {
            <a class="nav-link text-dark" asp-area="" asp-controller="Account" asp-action="Login">Login</a>
        }
    }
</li>
```

The previous code snippet is taken from the `_Layout.cshtml` view/page. In the previous code snippet, we are checking whether `IsAuthenticated` returns true. If so, then the welcome message is displayed. This welcome message comes along with the **Logout** option, but it displays the `Login` menu when `IsAuthenticated` returns the `false` value:

```
public bool IsAuthenticated
{
    get { return User.Identities.Any(u => u.IsAuthenticated); }
}
```

`IsAuthenticated` is a `ReadOnly` property of the `AuthManager` class that checked whether the request is authenticated or not. Before we move ahead, let's revisit our `Login` method:

```
public IActionResult Login(LoginViewModel model)
{
    if (ModelState.IsValid)
    {
        var result = _authManager.Login(model);

        if (result)
        {
            return !string.IsNullOrEmpty(model.ReturnUrl) && Url.IsLocalUrl(model.ReturnUrl)
                ? (IActionResult)Redirect(model.ReturnUrl)
                : RedirectToAction("Index", "Home");
```

```
            }
        }
        ModelState.AddModelError("", "Invalid login attempt");
        return View(model);
    }
```

The previous `Login` method simply validates the user. Take a look at this statement—`var result = _authManager.Login(model);`. This calls a `Login` method from `AuthManager`:

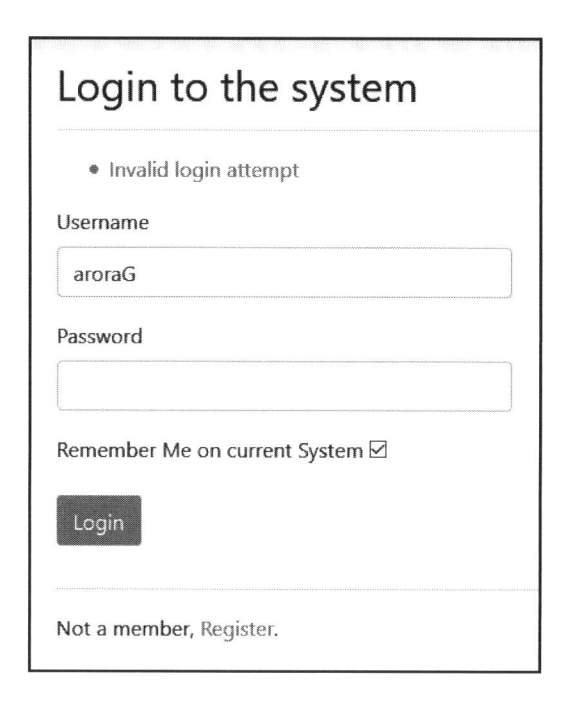

Login to the system

- Invalid login attempt

Username

aroraG

Password

Remember Me on current System ☑

Login

Not a member, Register.

If the `Login` method returns `true`, then it redirects the current **Login** page to the **Home** page. Otherwise, it remains on the same **Login** page by complaining about an **Invalid login attempt**. The following is the code of the `Login` method:

```
    public bool Login(LoginViewModel model)
    {
        var user = _userManager.FindBy(model);
        if (user == null) return false;
        SignInCookie(model, user);
        return true;
    }
```

The `Login` method is a typical method of the `AuthManager` class, which calls the `FindBy(model)` method of `UserManager` and checks whether it exists or not. If it exists, then it further calls the `SignInCookie(model, user)` method of the `AuthManager` class, otherwise, it simply returns as `false`, meaning that the **Login** is unsuccessful:

```
private void SignInCookie(LoginViewModel model, User user)
{
    var claims = new List<Claim>
    {
        new Claim(ClaimTypes.Name, user.FirstName),
        new Claim(ClaimTypes.Email, user.EmailId),
        new Claim(ClaimTypes.NameIdentifier, user.Id.ToString())
    };

    var identity = new ClaimsIdentity(claims, CookieAuthenticationDefaults.AuthenticationScheme);
    var principal = new ClaimsPrincipal(identity);
    var props = new AuthenticationProperties { IsPersistent = model.RememberMe };
    _httpContext.SignInAsync(CookieAuthenticationDefaults.AuthenticationScheme, principal, props).Wait();
}
```

The following code snippet makes sure that if the user is authenticated, then their details should be persisted in `HttpContext` so that the system can authenticate each and every incoming request from users. You might observe the `_httpContext.SignInAsync(CookieAuthenticationDefaults.AuthenticationScheme, principal, props).Wait();` statement that actually signed in and enabled the cookie authentication:

```
//Cookie authentication
services.AddAuthentication(CookieAuthenticationDefaults.AuthenticationScheme).AddCookie();
//For claims
services.AddSingleton<IHttpContextAccessor, HttpContextAccessor>();
services.AddTransient<IAuthManager, AuthManager>();
```

The previous statements help us to enable cookie authentication and claims for incoming requests for our application. Finally, the `app.UseAuthentication();` statement adds the authentication mechanism ability into our application. These statements should be added to the `Startup.cs` class.

Why does it make a difference?

We have added plenty of code into our web application, but does this really help us to restrict our pages/views from unattended requests? The **Products** page/view is still open; therefore, I can perform any available actions from the **Products** page/view:

SimpleLogin   Home   Products   Privacy   Login

As a user, I can see the **Products** option whether I am logged in or not:

SimpleLogin   Home   Products   Privacy   **Welcome Gaurav**, Logout

The previous screenshot shows the same **Products** menu option after login as before login.

We can restrict the access of the **Products** page like this:

```
<li class="nav-item">
    @{
        if (AuthManager.IsAuthenticated)
        {
            <a class="nav-link text-dark" asp-area="" asp-controller="Product" asp-action="Index">Products</a>
        }
    }
</li>
```

The following is the home screen of the application:

SimpleLogin   Home   Privacy   Login

Welcome
This sample application demostrate the simplest way to authenticate users.

© 2019 - SimpleLogin - Privacy

Implementing Design Patterns for Web Applications - Part 2

The previous code helps systems to only display the **Products** menu option once the user is logged in/authenticated. The **Products** menu options will not get displayed on the screen. Like this, we can restrict the unattended access. However, this approach has its own cons. The biggest one is that if someone knows the URL of the **Products** page—which will lead you to /Product/Index—then they can perform restricted operations. These operations are restricted as they are not meant to be used by a user who is not logged in.

Authorization in action

In the previous section, we discussed how to avoid unattended access to a particular or restricted screen/page. We have seen that **Login** actually authenticates the user and allows them to make a request to the system. On the other hand, authentication does not mean that if a user is authenticated, then they are authorized to access a particular section, page, or screen.

The following depicts a typical authorization and authentication process:

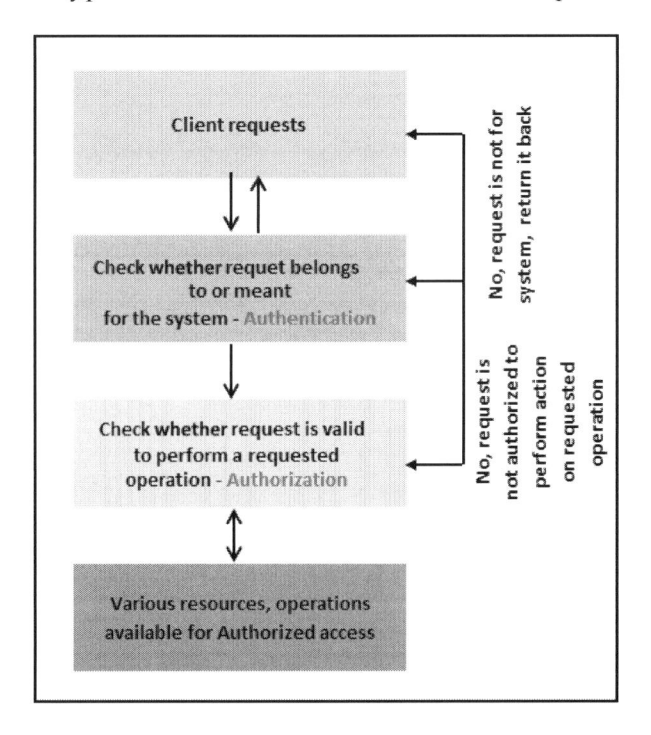

In this process, the first request/user gets authenticated (typically, it is a login form), then a request is authorized to perform a particular/requested operation(s). There may be many scenarios where a request is authenticated but not authorized to access a specific resource or perform a specific operation.

In our application (created in the previous section), we have a `Products` page with CRUD operations. The `Products` page is not a public page, which means that this page is not available for all; it is available with restricted access.

We come back to the following main problem that we left within the previous section: "What if a user is authenticated but they are not authorized to access a particular page/resource? It does not matter whether we hide the page from the unauthorized user because they can easily access or view it by entering its URL." To overcome this challenge/issue, we can implement the following steps:

1. Check the authorization on each access of the restricted resource, which means that whenever a user tries to access the resource (by entering a direct URL in the browser), the system checks for authorization, so that incoming requests to access the resource can be authorized. If the incoming request of the user is not authorized, then they would not be able to perform the specified operation.
2. Checking authorization on each operation of the restricted resource means that if the user is authenticated, they would be able to access the restricted page/view, but the operations of this page/view can only be accessible if the user is authorized.

> The `Microsoft.AspNetCore.Authorization` namespace provides built-in functions to authorize specific resources.

Implementing Design Patterns for Web Applications - Part 2

To restrict access and avoid unattended access to a particular resource, we can use the `Authorize` attribute:

```csharp
namespace SimpleLogin.Controllers
{
    [Authorize]
    public class ProductController : Controller
    {
        private readonly IInventoryRepositry _inventoryRepositry;

        public ProductController(IInventoryRepositry inventoryRepositry) => _inventoryRepositry = inventoryRepositry;

        public IActionResult Index() => View(_inventoryRepositry.GetProducts().ToProductvm());

        public IActionResult Details(Guid id) => View(_inventoryRepositry.GetProduct(id).ToProductvm());

        public IActionResult Create() => View();
```

The previous screenshot shows that we are putting the `Authorize` attribute into our `ProductController`. Now, hit *F5* and run the application.

> **TIP**
> If the user is not logged in to the system, they would not able to see the **Product** page as we have already added the condition. If the user is validated, then display **Products** in the menu bar.

Do not log in to the system and enter the product URL, `http://localhost:56229/Product`, directly to your browser. This will redirect the user to the **Login** screen. Please see the following screenshot and check the URL; you might notice that the URL contains a **ReturnUrl** part that will instruct the system on where to be redirected upon a successful login attempt.

See the following screenshot; note that the URL contains the **ReturnUrl** part. The system redirects the application to this URL once the user is logged in:

[Login screenshot]

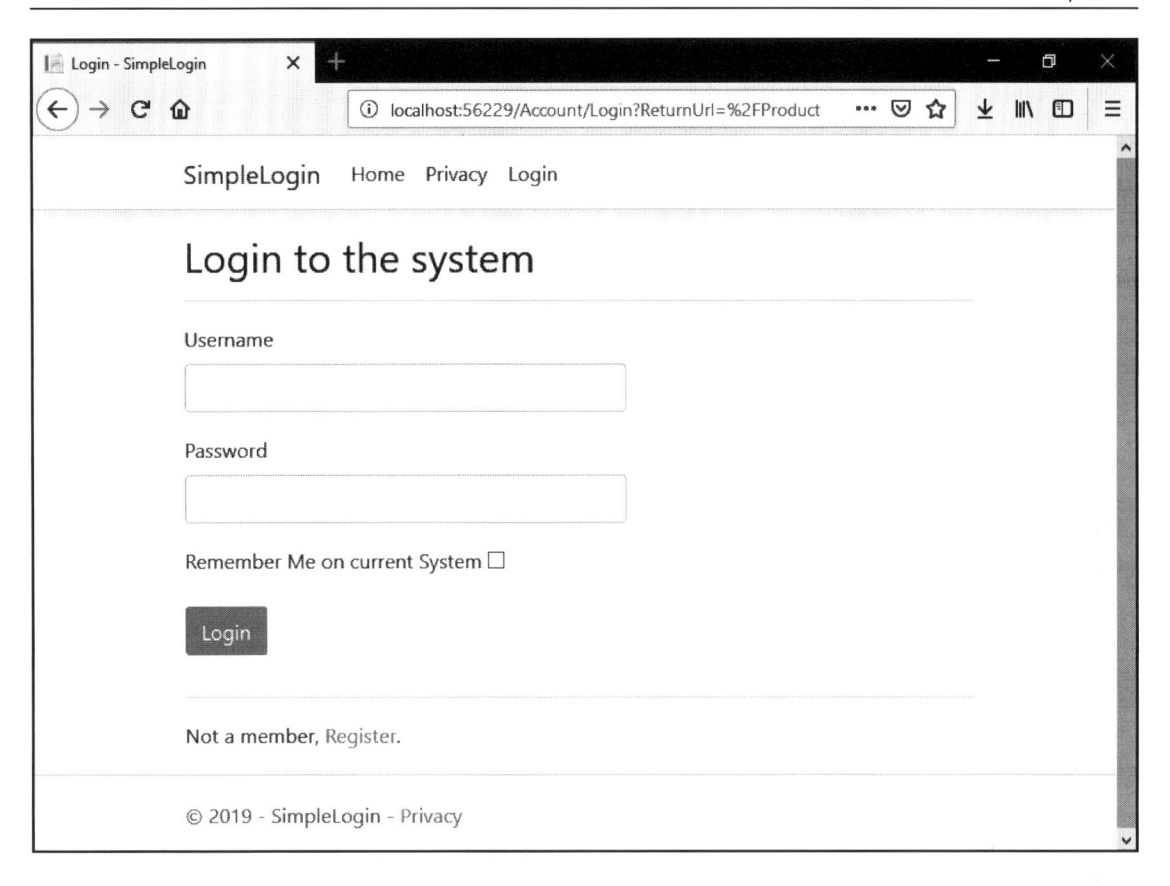

The following screenshot shows **Product Listing**:

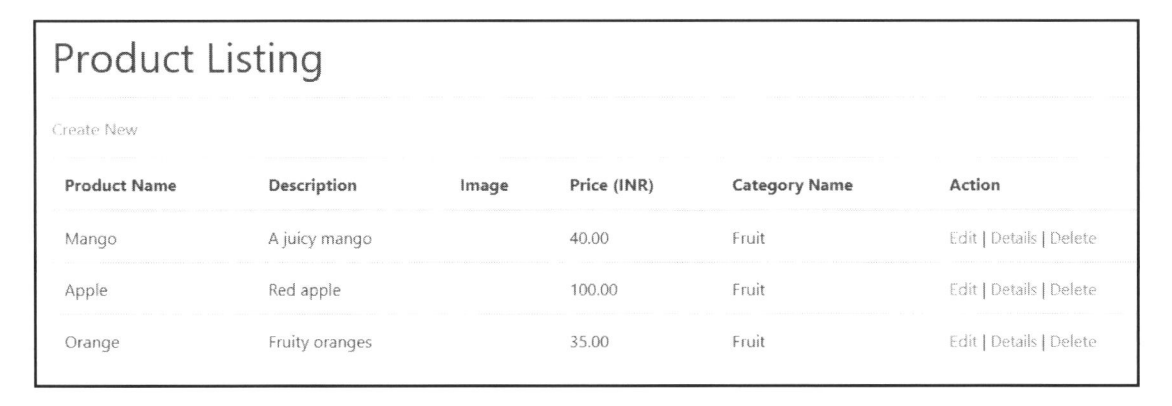

[Product Listing screenshot]

Our **Product Listing** screen provides operations such as **Create New**, **Edit**, **Delete**, and **Details**. The current application allows the user to perform these operations. Therefore, does it make sense that any visiting and authenticated user can create, update, and delete a product? If we allow this for every user, the consequences can be as follows:

- We can have many products that have been already added to the system.
- Unavoidable removal/deletion of products.
- Unavoidable updating of products.

Can we have something such as user types that differentiate all users of the `Admin` type from normal users, allowing only users with admin rights—not the normal users—to perform these operations? A better idea is to add roles for users; therefore, we would need to make a user of a specific type.

Let's add a new entity into our project and name it `Role`:

```
public class Role
{
    public Guid Id { get; set; }
    public string Name { get; set; }
    public string ShortName { get; set; }
}
```

The previous code snippet that defines the `Role` class for a user has properties, as explained in the following list:

- `Id`: This uses `GUID` as a primary key.
- `Name`: A `Role` name of a `string` type.
- `ShortName`: A short or abbreviated name of the role that is of a `string` type.

Chapter 7

We need to add our new class/entity to our `Context` class. Let's add this as follows:

```csharp
public class InventoryContext : DbContext
{
    public InventoryContext(DbContextOptions<InventoryContext> options)
        : base(options)
    {
    }

    public InventoryContext()
    {
    }

    public DbSet<Product> Products { get; set; }
    public DbSet<Category> Categories { get; set; }
    public DbSet<User> Users { get; set; }
    public DbSet<Role> Roles { get; set; }
}
```

The previous code provides the ability to work various DB operations using EF:

```csharp
public IEnumerable<Role> GetRoles() => _context.Roles.ToList();

public IEnumerable<Role> GetRolesBy(string userId) =>
_context.Roles.Where(x => x.UserId.ToString().Equals(userId));

public string RoleNamesBy(string userId)
{
    var listofRoleNames =
GetRolesBy(userId).Select(x=>x.ShortName).ToList();
    return string.Join(",", listofRoleNames);
}
```

The three methods of the `UserManager` class that appeared in the previous code snippet provide us with the ability to get `Roles` from the database:

```csharp
private void SignInCookie(LoginViewModel model, User user)
{
    var claims = new List<Claim>
    {
        new Claim(ClaimTypes.Name, user.FirstName),
        new Claim(ClaimTypes.Email, user.EmailId),
        new Claim(ClaimTypes.NameIdentifier, user.Id.ToString())
    };

    if (user.Roles != null)
    {
        string[] roles = user.Roles.Split(",");
```

Implementing Design Patterns for Web Applications - Part 2

```
        claims.AddRange(roles.Select(role => new Claim(ClaimTypes.Role,
role)));
    }

    var identity = new ClaimsIdentity(claims,
CookieAuthenticationDefaults.AuthenticationScheme);

    var principal = new ClaimsPrincipal(identity);
    var props = new AuthenticationProperties { IsPersistent =
model.RememberMe };
    _httpContext.SignInAsync(CookieAuthenticationDefaults.AuthenticationScheme,
principal, props).Wait();
}
```

We have added `Roles` to our `Claims` by modifying the `SigningCookie` method of the `AuthManager` class:

```
private void SignInCookie(LoginViewModel model, User user)    model = {LoginViewModel}, user = {User}
{
    var claims = new List<Claim>    claims = Count = 5
    {
        new Claim(ClaimTypes.Name, user.FirstName),
        new Claim(ClaimTypes.Email, user.EmailId),
        new Claim(ClaimTypes.NameIdentifier, user.Id.ToString())
    };

    if (user.Roles != null)
    {
        string[] roles = user.Roles.Split(",");    roles = {string[2]}

        claims.AddRange(roles.Select(role => new Claim(ClaimTypes.Role, role)));
    }
                        claims  Count = 5
                        ▶ ● [0]    {http://schemas.xmlsoap.org/ws/2005/05/identity/claims/name: Gaurav}
    var identity       ▶ ● [1]    {http://schemas.xmlsoap.org/ws/2005/05/identity/claims/emailaddress: gaurav@gaurav-arora.com}
                        ▶ ● [2]    {http://schemas.xmlsoap.org/ws/2005/05/identity/claims/nameidentifier: db38ab09-b499-496a-979f-08d6c745083c}
                        ▶ ● [3]    {http://schemas.microsoft.com/ws/2008/06/identity/claims/role: Admin}
    var principa       ▶ ● [4]    {http://schemas.microsoft.com/ws/2008/06/identity/claims/role: Manager}
                        ▶ ● Raw View
    var props = new AuthenticationProperties { IsPersistent = model.RememberMe };

    _httpContext.SignInAsync(CookieAuthenticationDefaults.AuthenticationScheme, principal, props).Wait();
}
```

The previous screenshot shows that a user named `Gaurav` has two roles: `Admin` and `Manager`:

```
[Authorize(Roles = "Admin,Manager")]
```

Chapter 7

We restrict `ProductController` for the user(s) with the `Admin` and `Manager` roles only. Now, try to log in with user `aroraG` and you will see `Product Listing`, as shown in the following screenshot:

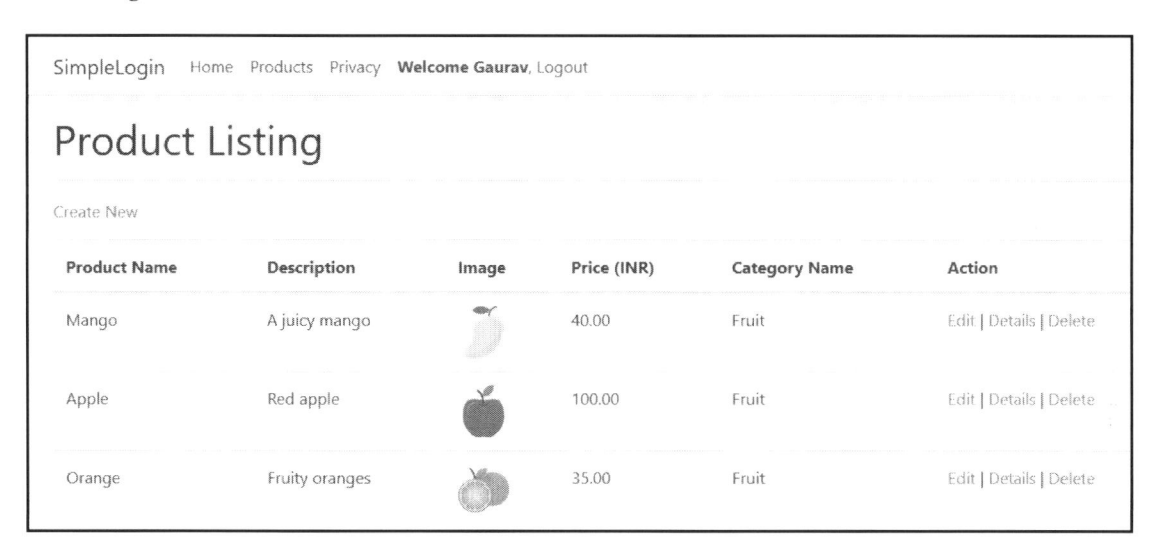

Product Name	Description	Image	Price (INR)	Category Name	Action
Mango	A juicy mango		40.00	Fruit	Edit	Details	Delete
Apple	Red apple		100.00	Fruit	Edit	Details	Delete
Orange	Fruity oranges		35.00	Fruit	Edit	Details	Delete

Now, let's try to log in with a second user, `aroraG1`, which has the role of `Editor`. This will throw an `AccessDenied` error. For this, see the following screenshot:

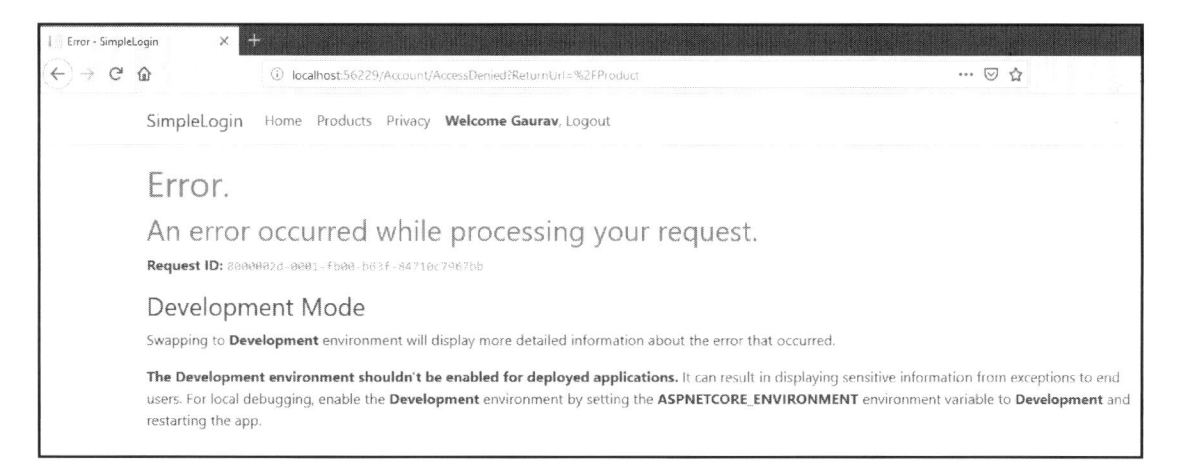

Error.

An error occurred while processing your request.

Request ID: 8000802d-0001-fb00-b63f-84710c7967bb

Development Mode

Swapping to **Development** environment will display more detailed information about the error that occurred.

The Development environment shouldn't be enabled for deployed applications. It can result in displaying sensitive information from exceptions to end users. For local debugging, enable the **Development** environment by setting the **ASPNETCORE_ENVIRONMENT** environment variable to **Development** and restarting the app.

[211]

Implementing Design Patterns for Web Applications - Part 2

In this way, we can safeguard our restricted resources. There are a lot of ways to achieve this. .NET Core MVC provides built-in functionality to achieve this, and you can also do so in a customizable way. If you do not want to use these available built-in features, you can easily draft your own functionality of required features by adding to the existing code. If you want to do this, you need to start from scratch. Furthermore, if something is available, then there is no sense in creating something similar again. If you do not find the functionality for available components, then you should customize the existing functionality/features rather than writing the entire code from scratch.

> **A developer should implement an authentication mechanism that can't be tampered with.** In this section, we have discussed a lot to do with authentication and authorization, as well as writing code and creating our web application. In regard to authentication, we should use a good mechanism for the authentication so that no one can tamper with or bypass it. There are two more designs you can start with:
> - Authentication filters
> - Authenticating individual requests/endpoints

After the implementation of the previous steps, every request that comes via any mode should be authenticated and authorized before the system responds to the user or the client that made the call. This process mainly includes the following:

- **Confidentiality**: The secured system makes sure that any sensitive data is not exposed to unauthenticated and unauthorized access requests.
- **Availability**: The security measures in the system make sure that the system is available for users who are genuine, as confirmed through the system's authentication and authorization mechanism.
- **Integrity**: In a secured system, data tampering is not possible, so the data is secure.

Creating a web test project

Unit testing is the one that checks code health. This means that if the code is buggy (unhealthy), that would be the basis of many unknown and unwanted issues in the application. To overcome this approach, we could follow the TDD approach.

> You can practice TDD with Katas. You can refer to `https://www.codeproject.com/Articles/886492/Learning-Test-Driven-Development-with-TDD-Katas` to find out more about TDD katas. If you want to practice this approach, use this repository: `https://github.com/garora/TDD-Katas`.

We have already discussed a lot about TDD in previous chapters, so we are not going to discuss this in detail here. Instead, let's create a test project as follows:

1. Open our web application.
2. From **Solution Explorer** in **Visual Studio**, right-click on **Solution** and click on **Add | New Project...**, as shown in the following screenshot:

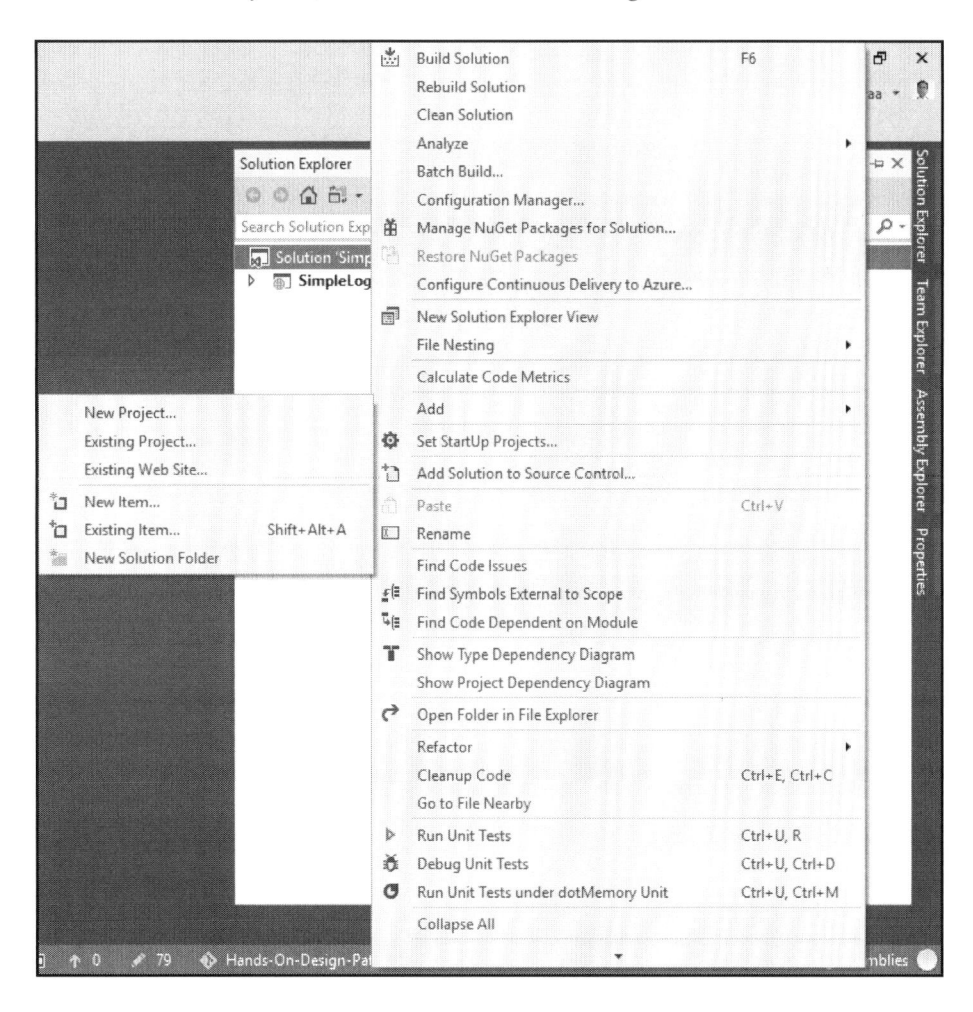

Implementing Design Patterns for Web Applications - Part 2

3. From the **Add New Project** template, select **.NET Core and xUnit Test Project (.NET Core)** and provide a meaningful name:

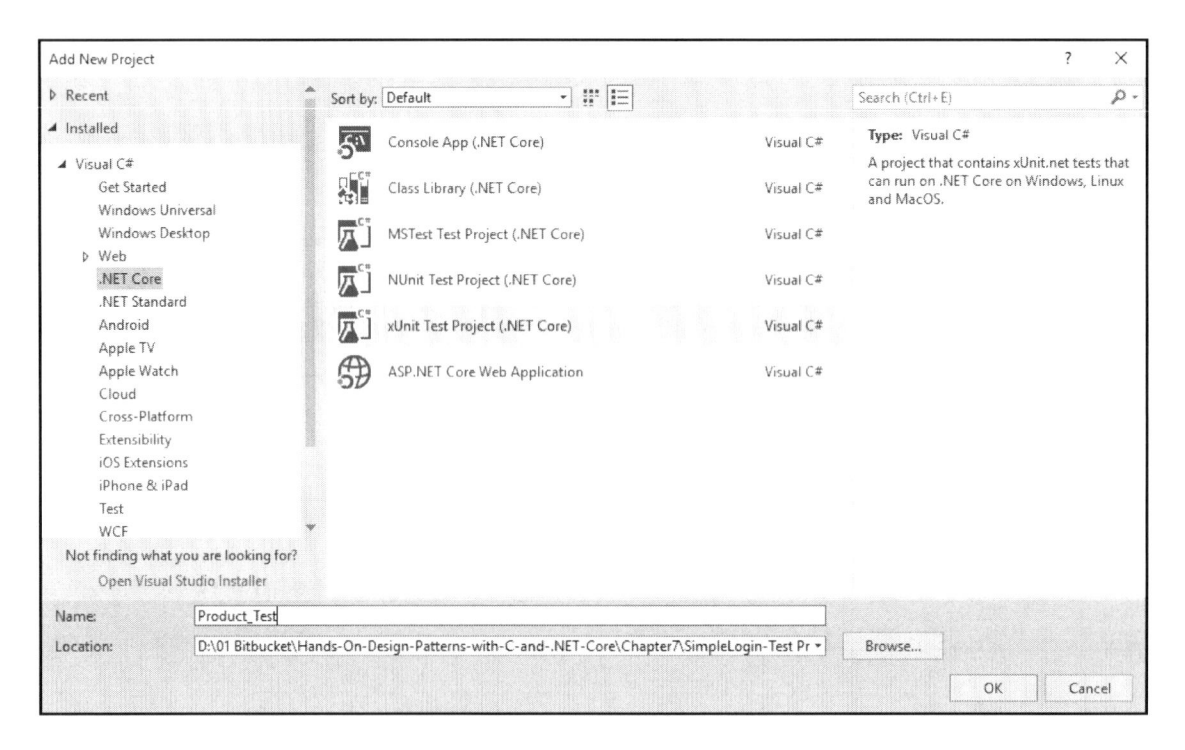

You will get a default unit `test` class with an empty test code, as shown in the following code snippet:

```
namespace Product_Test
{
    public class UnitTest1
    {
        [Fact]
        public void Test1()
        {
        }
    }
}
```

Chapter 7

You can change the name of this class or discard this class if you want to write your own `test` class:

```
public class ProductData
{
    public IEnumerable<ProductViewModel> GetProducts()
    {
        var productVm = new List<ProductViewModel>
        {
            new ProductViewModel
            {
                CategoryId = Guid.NewGuid(),
                CategoryDescription = "Category Description",
                CategoryName = "Category Name",
                ProductDescription = "Product Description",
                ProductId = Guid.NewGuid(),
                ProductImage = "Image full path",
                ProductName = "Product Name",
                ProductPrice = 112M
            },
            ...
        };

        return productVm;
    }
}
```

4. The previous code is from our newly added `ProductDate` class. Please add this to a new folder called `Fake`. This class just creates dummy data so that we can test our web application for the product:

```
public class ProductTests
{
    [Fact]
    public void Get_Returns_ActionResults()
    {
        // Arrange
        var mockRepo = new Mock<IProductRepository>();
        mockRepo.Setup(repo => repo.GetAll()).Returns(new ProductData().GetProductList());
        var controller = new ProductController(mockRepo.Object);

        // Act
        var result = controller.GetList();

        // Assert
        var viewResult = Assert.IsType<OkObjectResult>(result);
        var model =
```

[215]

Implementing Design Patterns for Web Applications - Part 2

```
        Assert.IsAssignableFrom<IEnumerable<ProductViewModel>>(viewResult.V
alue);
            Assert.NotNull(model);
            Assert.Equal(2, model.Count());
        }
    }
```

5. Add a new file called `ProductTests` in the `Services` folder. Please note that we are using `Stubs` and `Mocks` in this code.

   Our previous code will complain about the error using red squiggly lines, as shown in the following screenshot:

```
namespace Product_Test.Services
{
    public class ProductTests
    {
        [Fact]
        public void Get_Returns_ActionResults()
        {
            // Arrange
            var mockRepo = new Mock<IProductRepository>();
            mockRepo.Setup(repo => repo.
            var controller = new ProductContr

            // Act
            var result = controller.GetList();

            // Assert
            var viewResult = Assert.IsType<OkObjectResult>(result);
            var model = Assert.IsAssignableFrom<IEnumerable<ProductViewModel>>(viewResult.Value);
            Assert.NotNull(model);
            Assert.Equal(2, model.Count());
        }
    }
}
```

The type or namespace name 'Mock<>' could not be found (are you missing a using directive or an assembly reference?)
The type or namespace name 'IProductRepository' could not be found (are you missing a using directive or an assembly reference?)
Cannot resolve symbol 'IProductRepository'
Show potential fixes (Ctrl+.)

6. The previous code has errors as we did not add certain packages that were required for us to perform tests. To overcome these errors, we should install `moq` support to our `test` project. Pass the following command in your **Package Manager Console**:

   `install-package moq`

7. The preceding command will install the `moq` framework in the test project. Please note that while firing the preceding command, you should select the test project that we have created:

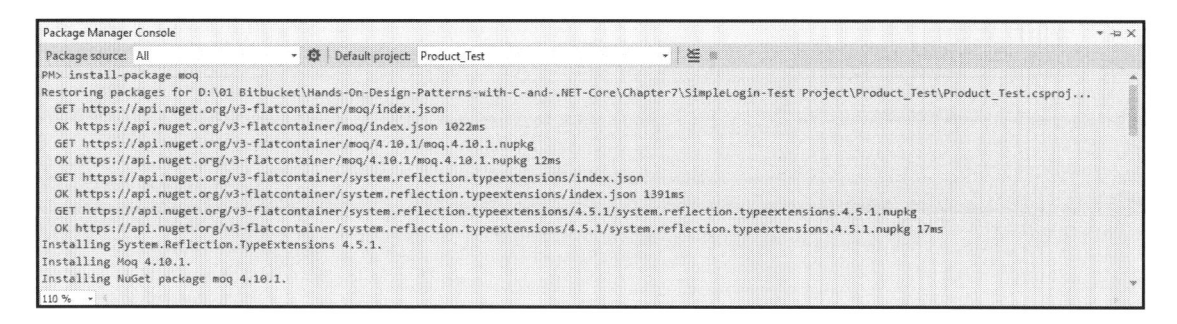

Once `moq` is installed, you can go ahead and start testing.

> **TIP**
>
> Important points to note while you're working with the `xUnit` test projects are as follows:
>
> - **Fact** is an attribute and is used for a normal test method that is without parameters.
> - **Theory** is an attribute and is used for a parameterized test method.

8. All set. Now, click on **Test explorer** and run your tests:

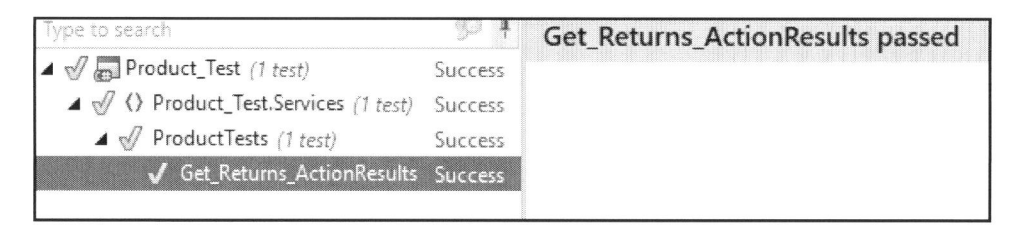

Finally, our tests have passed! This means that our controller methods are good, and we do not have any issues or bugs in our code that can break the functionality of the application/system.

Summary

The main goal of this chapter was to make it possible for our web application to safeguard against unattended requests. This chapter covered a step-by-step creation of a web application using Visual Studio and discussed authentication and authorization. We also discussed TDD and created a new xUnit web test project where we used `Stubs` and `Mocks`.

In the next chapter, we will discuss the best practices and patterns while using concurrent programming in .NET Core.

Questions

The following questions will allow you to consolidate the information contained in this chapter:

1. What are authentication and authorization?
2. Is it safe to use authentication at the first level of request and then allow incoming requests for restricted areas?
3. How can you prove that authorization always comes after authentication?
4. What is TDD and why do developers care about it?
5. Define TDD katas. How do they help us to improve our TDD approach?

Further reading

Congratulations, you've completed this chapter! To learn more about the topics covered in this chapter, refer to the following books:

- *Building RESTful Web services with .NET Core,* by *Gaurav Aroraa, Tadit Dash*, published by *Packt Publishing*: `https://www.packtpub.com/application-development/building-restful-web-services-net-core`
- *C# and .NET Core Test Driven Development,* by *Ayobami Adewole*, published by *Packt Publishing*: `https://www.packtpub.com/in/application-development/c-and-net-core-test-driven-development`

Section 3: Functional Programming, Reactive Programming, and Coding for the Cloud

This is the most important section of the book. In this section, readers who are already familiar with the .NET Framework can correlate their learning with .NET Core, and readers who are familiar with .NET Core can enhance their knowledge through practical examples. We will use patterns to address some of the more challenging aspects of modern software development.

This section consists of the following chapters:

- `Chapter 8`, *Concurrent Programming in .NET Core*
- `Chapter 9`, *Functional Programming Practices – an Approach*
- `Chapter 10`, *Reactive Programming Patterns and Techniques*
- `Chapter 11`, *Advanced Database Design and Application Techniques*
- `Chapter 12`, *Coding for the Cloud*

8
Concurrent Programming in .NET Core

In the previous chapter (Chapter 7, *Implementing Design Patterns for Web Applications - Part 2*), we created a sample web application with the help of various patterns for the web. We adapted authorization and authentication mechanisms to secure a web application and discussed **Test-driven development** (**TDD**) to make sure that our code has been tested and is working.

This chapter will discuss the best practices to adopt while performing concurrent programming in .NET Core. In the upcoming sections of this chapter, we will learn about the design patterns relevant for well-organized concurrency in C# and .NET Core applications.

The following topics will be covered in this chapter:

- Async/Await – Why is blocking bad?
- Multithreading and asynchronous programming
- Concurrent collections
- Patterns and practices – TDD and Parallel LINQ

Technical requirements

This chapter contains various code examples to explain the concepts. The code is kept simple and is only for demonstration purposes. Most of the examples involve a .NET Core console application written in C#.

> The complete source code is available at the following link: `https://github.com/PacktPublishing/Hands-On-Design-Patterns-with-C-and-.NET-Core/tree/master/Chapter8`.

To run and execute the code, you will require the following:

- Visual Studio 2019 (you can also use Visual Studio 2017)
- Setting up .NET Core
- SQL Server (the Express Edition is used in this chapter)

Installing Visual Studio

To run the code examples, you will need to install Visual Studio (preferred IDE). To do so, you can follow these instructions:

1. Download Visual Studio from the download link mentioned with the installation instructions: `https://docs.microsoft.com/en-us/visualstudio/install/install-visual-studio`.
2. Follow the installation instructions mentioned.
3. Multiple options are available for the Visual Studio installation. Here, we are using Visual Studio for Windows.

Setting up .NET Core

If you do not have .NET Core installed, you will need to follow these instructions:

1. Download .NET Core for Windows at `https://www.microsoft.com/net/download/windows`.
2. For multiple versions and a related library, visit `https://dotnet.microsoft.com/download/dotnet-core/2.2`.

Installing SQL Server

If you do not have SQL Server installed, you can follow these instructions:

1. Download SQL Server from the following link: `https://www.microsoft.com/en-in/download/details.aspx?id=1695`.
2. You can find installation instructions here: `https://docs.microsoft.com/en-us/sql/ssms/download-sql-server-management-studio-ssms?view=sql-server-2017`.

> For troubleshooting and for more information, refer to the following link: `https://www.blackbaud.com/files/support/infinityinstaller/content/installermaster/tkinstallsqlserver2008r2.htm`.

Concurrency in the real world

Concurrency is a part of our life: it exists in the real world. When we are discussing concurrency, we are referring to multitasking.

In the real world, many of us perform multitasking frequently. For example, we can write a program while speaking on a mobile phone, we can watch a movie while having dinner, and we can sing while reading notations. There are a lot of examples of how we as humans can multitask. Without going into too much scientific detail, we can look at our brain trying to grasp new things while also commanding the other organs of the body to work, such as the heart or our sense of smell, as a form of multitasking.

The same approach applies to our systems (computers). If we think about today's computers, every computer that is available has a CPU of multiple cores (more than one core). This is to allow multiple instructions simultaneously, and let us perform multiple tasks at once.

True parallelism is not possible on a single CPU machine because tasks are not switchable, as the CPU has a single core. It is only possible on a machine with multiple CPUs (multiple cores). In simple terms, concurrent programming involves two things:

- **Task management**: Managing/distributing work units to available threads.
- **Communication**: This sets up the initial parameter of the task and gets the results.

> Whenever things/tasks are happening at the same time, we call this *concurrency*. In our programming language, whenever any parts of our program run at the same time, this is called concurrent programming. You can also use **parallel programming** as a synonym for concurrent programming.

As an example, imagine a big conference that you need a ticket for, to gain entry into a specific conference hall. At the gate of a conference hall, you have to buy a ticket, making a payment with cash or by card. While you're making a payment, the counter assistant could enter your details into the system, print an invoice, and provide you with the ticket. Now consider that there are more people who want to buy a ticket. Each person has to perform the required activities to collect the ticket from the ticket counter. In this case, only one person can be served at a time from one counter, and the rest of the people wait for their turn. Let's assume that one person takes two minutes to collect their ticket from the counter; the next person, therefore, needs to wait for two minutes for their turn. Consider the wait time of the last person in line if it is a queue of 50 people. Things can be changed here. If there were two more ticket counters and every counter is performing the tasks in two minutes, this means that every two minutes, three people will be able to collect three tickets—or three counters are selling two tickets every two minutes. In other words, every ticket counter is performing the same task (that is, ticket selling) at the same point in time. This means all counters are served in parallel; therefore, they are concurrent. This is depicted in the following diagram:

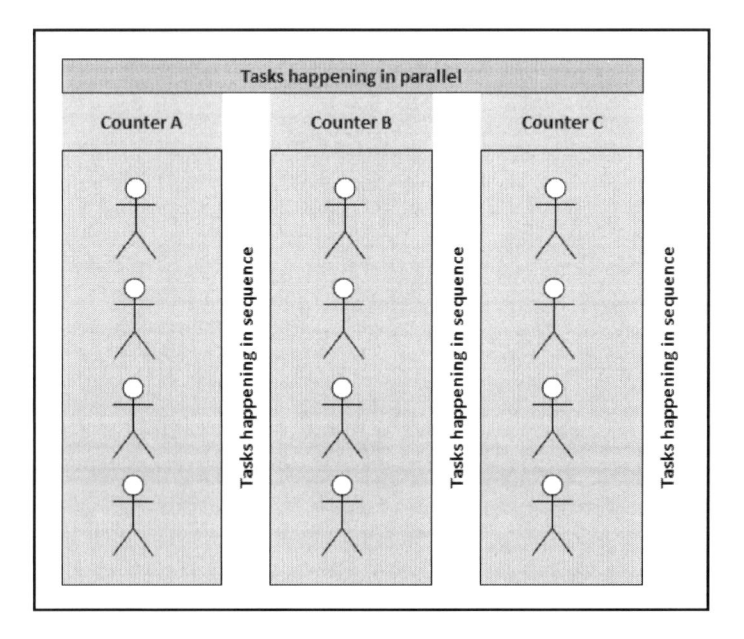

In the preceding diagram, it is clearly shown that every person who is in the queue is either in the wait position or is active at the counter, and there are three queues in which tasks are happening in a sequence. All three counters (`CounterA`, `CounterB`, and `CounterC`) are performing tasks at the same point in time—they are doing the activities in parallel.

> **Concurrency** is when two or more tasks start, run, and complete in overlapping time periods.
> **Parallelism** is when two or more tasks run at the same time.

These are concurrent activities, but think of a scenario in which a huge amount of people are in the queue (for example, 10,000 people); there is no use in performing parallelism here, as this would not resolve the issue of a likely bottleneck in this operation. On the other hand, you can increase the number of counters to 50. Will they resolve this problem? These kinds of problems would occur while we work with any software. This is an issue that is related to blocking. In the upcoming sections, we will discuss concurrent programming in more detail.

Multithreading and asynchronous programming

To put it simply, we can say that multithreading means that a program is running parallel on multiple threads. In asynchronous programming, a unit of work runs separately from the main application thread, and it tells the calling thread that the task has completed, failed, or is in progress. The interesting issues to consider around asynchronous programming are when we should use it and what its benefits are.

> The potential for more than one thread to access the same shared data and update it with unpredictable results can be referred to as a **race condition**. We have already discussed race condition in `Chapter 4`, *Implementing Design Patterns - Basics Part 2*.

Consider the scenario we discussed in the previous section, in which people from a queue are collecting their tickets. Let's try to capture this scenario in a multithreading program:

```
internal class TicketCounter
{
    public static void CounterA() => Console.WriteLine("Person A is collecting ticket from Counter A");
    public static void CounterB() => Console.WriteLine("Person B is collecting ticket from Counter B");
```

```
        public static void CounterC() => Console.WriteLine("Person C is
    collecting ticket from Counter C");
    }
```

Here, we have a `TicketCounter` class that represents our whole set up of ticket collecting counters (we discussed these in the previous section). The three methods: `CounterA()`, `CounterB()`, and `CounterC()` represent an individual ticket collection counter. These methods are simply writing a message to the console, as shown in the following code:

```
internal class Program
{
    private static void Main(string[] args)
    {
        var counterA = new Thread(TicketCounter.CounterA);
        var counterB = new Thread(TicketCounter.CounterB);
        var counterC = new Thread(TicketCounter.CounterC);
        Console.WriteLine("3-counters are serving...");
        counterA.Start();
        counterB.Start();
        counterC.Start();
        Console.WriteLine("Next person from row");
        Console.ReadLine();
    }
}
```

The preceding code is our `Program` class that is initiating the activities from within the `Main` method. Here, we declared and started three threads for all the counters. Note that we have started these threads in a sequence/order. As we are expect that these threads will execute in the same sequence, let's run the program and see the output, as shown in the following screenshot:

```
3-counters are serving...
Next person from row
Person A is collecting ticket from Counter A
Person C is collecting ticket from Counter C
Person B is collecting ticket from Counter B
```

The preceding program is not executed as per the given sequence in the code. As per our code, the execution sequence should be as follows:

```
3-counters are serving...
Next person from row
Person A is collecting ticket from Counter A
Person B is collecting ticket from Counter B
Person C is collecting ticket from Counter C
```

This is due to threads, and these threads are working simultaneously without the guarantee that these should execute in the order/sequence that they have been declared/started in.

Once again, run the program and see whether we get the same output:

```
3-counters are serving...
Person A is collecting ticket from Counter A
Person B is collecting ticket from Counter B
Next person from row
Person C is collecting ticket from Counter C
```

The preceding snapshot is showing a different output from the previous results, so now we have the output in sequence/order:

```
3-counters are serving...
Person A is collecting ticket from Counter A
Person B is collecting ticket from Counter B
Next person from row
Person C is collecting ticket from Counter C
```

So, the threads are working, but not in the sequence we defined them.

> **TIP**: You can set the priorities of threads like this: `counterC.Priority = ThreadPriority.Highest;`, `counterB.Priority = ThreadPriority.Normal;`, and `counterA.Priority = ThreadPriority.Lowest;`.

To run the threads in a synchronized way, let's modify our code as follows:

```
internal class SynchronizedTicketCounter
{
    public void ShowMessage()
    {
        int personsInQueue = 5; //assume maximum persons in queue
        lock (this)
        {
            Thread thread = Thread.CurrentThread;
            for (int personCount = 0; personCount < personsInQueue; personCount++)
            {
                Console.WriteLine($"\tPerson {personCount + 1} is collecting ticket from counter {thread.Name}.");
            }
        }
    }
}
```

We created a new `SynchronizedTicketCounter` class with the `ShowMessage()` method; please note the `lock(this){...}` in the preceding code. Run the program and check the output:

```
Person 1 is collecting ticket from counter A.
Person 2 is collecting ticket from counter A.
Person 3 is collecting ticket from counter A.
Person 4 is collecting ticket from counter A.
Person 5 is collecting ticket from counter A.
Person 1 is collecting ticket from counter B.
Person 2 is collecting ticket from counter B.
Person 3 is collecting ticket from counter B.
Person 4 is collecting ticket from counter B.
Person 5 is collecting ticket from counter B.
Person 1 is collecting ticket from counter C.
Person 2 is collecting ticket from counter C.
Person 3 is collecting ticket from counter C.
Person 4 is collecting ticket from counter C.
Person 5 is collecting ticket from counter C.
```

We have the output we expected now that our counters are serving in the right sequence/order.

Async/Await – why is blocking bad?

Asynchronous programming is very helpful in cases where we are expecting various activities at the same point in time. With the `async` keyword, we define our method/operation as asynchronous. Consider the following code snippet:

```
internal class AsyncAwait
{
    public async Task ShowMessage()
    {
        Console.WriteLine("\tServing messages!");
        await Task.Delay(1000);
    }
}
```

Here, we have a `AsyncAwait` class with an `async` method, `ShowMessage()`. This method is simply printing a message that would show in the console window. Now, whenever we call/consume this method in another code, that part of the code could wait/hold/block the operation until the `ShowMessage()` method executes and completes its task. Refer to the following snapshot:

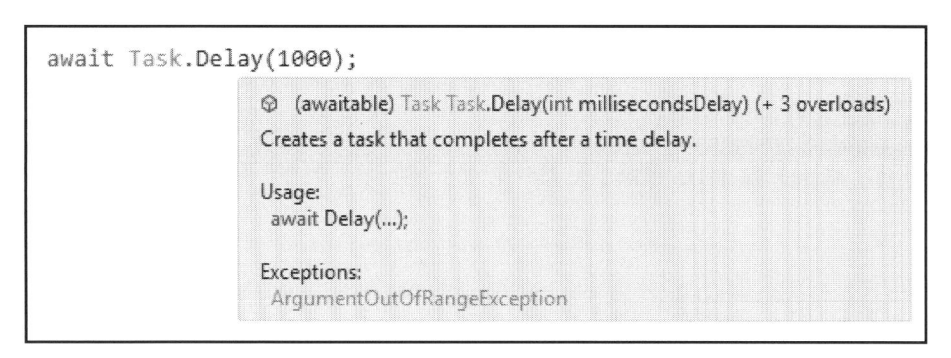

```
await Task.Delay(1000);
```
(awaitable) Task Task.Delay(int millisecondsDelay) (+ 3 overloads)
Creates a task that completes after a time delay.

Usage:
  await Delay(...);

Exceptions:
  ArgumentOutOfRangeException

Our previous screenshot says that we have set a delay of 1,000 milliseconds for our `ShowMessage()` method. Here, we instructed the program to complete after 1,000 milliseconds. If we try to remove `await` from the previous code, Visual Studio will immediately give the warning to put `await` back in; see the following snapshot:

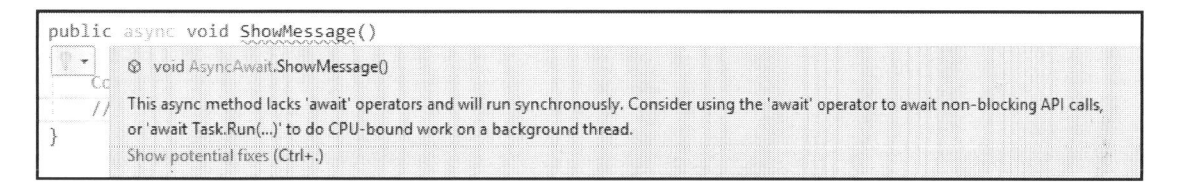

```
public async void ShowMessage()
```
void AsyncAwait.ShowMessage()
This async method lacks 'await' operators and will run synchronously. Consider using the 'await' operator to await non-blocking API calls, or 'await Task.Run(...)' to do CPU-bound work on a background thread.
Show potential fixes (Ctrl+.)

With the help of the `await` operator, we are using non-blocking API calls. Run the program and see the following output:

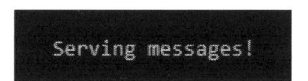

```
Serving messages!
```

We will get the output that is shown in the preceding snapshot.

Concurrent collections

The .NET Core framework provides a variety of collections with which we can use LINQ queries. As a developer, there are far fewer options when looking for thread-safe collections. Without thread-safe collections, it can become difficult for developers when they have to perform multiple operations. In this case, we would meet the race condition that we have already discussed in Chapter 4, *Implementing Design Patterns - Basics Part 2*. To overcome such situations, we need to use the `lock` statement, as we have used in the previous section. For example, we can write a code of a simplified implementation of the `lock` statement—refer to the following code snippet, where we have used the `lock` statement and collection class, `Dictionary`:

```
public bool UpdateQuantity(string name, int quantity)
{
    lock (_lock)
    {
        _books[name].Quantity += quantity;
    }

    return true;
}
```

The preceding code is from `InventoryContext`; in this code, we are blocking other threads from locking the operation in which we are trying to update the quantity.

> **TIP**
> The main drawback of the `Dictionary` collection class is that it is not thread-safe. We have to use this in the `lock` statement while we're using `Dictionary` with multiple threads. To make our code thread-safe, we can use the `ConcurrentDictionary` collection class.

`ConcurrentDictionary` is a thread-safe collection class and stores key-value pairs. This class has the implementation for the `lock` statement and provides a thread-safe class. Consider the following code:

```
private readonly IDictionary<string, Book> _books;
protected InventoryContext()
{
    _books = new ConcurrentDictionary<string, Book>();
}
```

The preceding code snippet is from the `InventoryContext` class of our FlixOne console application. In this code, we have the _books field, and it is initialized as a `ConcurrentDictionary` collection class.

As we are using the `UpdateQuantity()` method of the `InventoryContext` class in multithreads, there is a chance that one thread adds the quantity, while the other thread resets the quantity to its initial level. This happens because our object is from a single collection, and any changes to the collection in one thread are not visible to the other threads. All threads are referencing the original unmodified collection, and, in simple terms, our method is not thread-safe, unless we use the `lock` statement or the `ConcurretDictionary` collection class.

Patterns and practices – TDD and Parallel LINQ

While we work with multithreading, we should follow best practices to write a **smooth code**. A smooth code is where a developer doesn't face deadlock. In other words, multithreading requires a lot of care during the writing process.

> **TIP**
> While multiple threads are running in a class/program, deadlock occurs when each thread approaches the object or resource written under a `lock` statement. The actual deadlock occurs when each thread approaches to lock an object/resource that is already locked by another thread.

A small mistake can result in developers having to tackle unknown bugs that occur due to threads that are blocked. In addition to this, a bad implementation of a few words in the code can impact 100 lines of code.

Let's go back to our example of conference tickets, which we discussed at the beginning of this chapter. What would happen if ticket counters are unable to serve their purpose and distribute tickets? In this scenario, each person would try to reach a ticket counter and obtain a ticket, which could jam the ticket counter. This could cause the ticket counter to become blocked. The same logic applies to our program. We'd meet a deadlock situation in which multiple threads would try to lock our object/resource. The best practice to use to avoid such a condition is using a mechanism that synchronizes access to the object/resource. The .NET Core framework provides a `Monitor` class to achieve this. I have rewritten our old code to avoid a deadlock situation—see the following code:

```
private static void ProcessTickets()
{
    var ticketCounter = new TicketCounter();
    var counterA = new Thread(ticketCounter.ShowMessage);
    var counterB = new Thread(ticketCounter.ShowMessage);
    var counterC = new Thread(ticketCounter.ShowMessage);
    counterA.Name = "A";
```

```
        counterB.Name = "B";
        counterC.Name = "C";
        counterA.Start();
        counterB.Start();
        counterC.Start();
    }
```

Here, we have the `ProcessTicket` method; it starts three threads (each thread represents each ticket counter). Every thread is reaching to `ShowMessage` of the `TicketCounter` class. There will be a problem of deadlock if our `ShowMessage` method is not written well to handle this situation. All three threads will try to acquire a lock for the respective object/resource related to the `ShowMessage` method.

The following code is the implementation of the `ShowMessage` method, and I have written this code to handle a deadlock situation:

```
private static readonly object Object = new object();
public void ShowMessage()
{
    const int personsInQueue = 5;
    if (Monitor.TryEnter(Object, 300))
    {
        try
        {
            var thread = Thread.CurrentThread;
            for (var personCount = 0; personCount < personsInQueue; personCount++)
                Console.WriteLine(
                    $"\tPerson {personCount + 1} is collecting ticket from counter {thread.Name}.");
        }
        finally
        {
            Monitor.Exit(Object);
        }
    }
}
```

The preceding is the ShowMessage() method of our TicketCounter class. In this method, whenever a thread will try to lock Object, if Object is already locked, it tries for 300 milliseconds. The Monitor class handles this situation automatically. When using the Monitor class, the developer does not need to worry about a situation in which multiple threads are running, and each of these threads is trying to acquire the lock. Run the program to see the following output:

```
Person 1 is collecting ticket from counter A.
Person 2 is collecting ticket from counter A.
Person 3 is collecting ticket from counter A.
Person 4 is collecting ticket from counter A.
Person 5 is collecting ticket from counter A.
Person 1 is collecting ticket from counter C.
Person 2 is collecting ticket from counter C.
Person 3 is collecting ticket from counter C.
Person 4 is collecting ticket from counter C.
Person 5 is collecting ticket from counter C.
Person 1 is collecting ticket from counter B.
Person 2 is collecting ticket from counter B.
Person 3 is collecting ticket from counter B.
Person 4 is collecting ticket from counter B.
Person 5 is collecting ticket from counter B.
```

In the preceding snapshot, you will notice that after counterA, counterC is serving and then counter B. This means that after thread A, thread C was initiated, and then thread B. In other words, thread A acquires the lock first, and after 300 milliseconds, thread C tries to lock, and then thread B tries to lock the object. If you want to set the order or priorities of the thread, you can add the following lines of code:

```
counterC.Priority = ThreadPriority.Highest
counterB.Priority = ThreadPriority.Normal;
counterA.Priority = ThreadPriority.Lowest;
```

When you add the preceding lines to the `ProcessTickets` method, all the threads will work: first `Thread C`, then `Thread B`, and, finally, `Thread A`.

> Thread priorities are an enum that tells us how to schedule the thread and `System.Threading.ThreadPriority` with the following values:
>
> - **Lowest**: This is the least priority, which means threads with the `Lowest` priority can be scheduled after the threads of any other priority.
> - **BelowNormal**: Threads with a `BelowNormal` priority can be scheduled after threads having a `Normal` priority, but before threads having the `Lowest` priority.
> - **Normal**: All threads are having the default priority as `Normal`. Threads with a `Normal` priority can be scheduled after threads having an `AboveNormal` priority, but before those threads that have a `BelowNormal` priority.
> - **AboveNormal**: Threads with an `AboveNormal` priority can be scheduled before threads having a `Normal` priority, but after threads having the `Highest` priority.
> - **Highest**: This is the top-most priority level of threads. Threads with the `Highest` priority can be scheduled before threads having any other priority.

After setting a priority level for the threads, execute the program and see the following output:

```
Person 1 is collecting ticket from counter C.
Person 2 is collecting ticket from counter C.
Person 3 is collecting ticket from counter C.
Person 4 is collecting ticket from counter C.
Person 5 is collecting ticket from counter C.
Person 1 is collecting ticket from counter B.
Person 2 is collecting ticket from counter B.
Person 3 is collecting ticket from counter B.
Person 4 is collecting ticket from counter B.
Person 5 is collecting ticket from counter B.
Person 1 is collecting ticket from counter A.
Person 2 is collecting ticket from counter A.
Person 3 is collecting ticket from counter A.
Person 4 is collecting ticket from counter A.
Person 5 is collecting ticket from counter A.
```

As per the preceding snapshot, after setting the priority, the counters are serving in the order C, B, and A. With a little caution and simple implementation, we can handle a deadlock situation as well as schedule our threads to be served in a specific order/priority.

The .Net Core framework also provides a **Task Parallel Library** (**TPL**) that is a set of public APIs that belong to the `System.Threading` and `System.Threading.Tasks` namespaces. With the help of TPL, developers can make applications concurrent by adapting its simplification implementation.

Considering the following code, we can see the simplest implementation of a TPL:

```
public void PallelVersion()
{
    var books = GetBooks();
    Parallel.ForEach(books, Process);
}
```

The preceding is a simple `ForEach` loop using a `Parallel` keyword. In the preceding code, we are just iterating a collection of `books` and processing it with the use of the `Process` method:

```
private void Process(Book book)
{
    Console.WriteLine($"\t{book.Id}\t{book.Name}\t{book.Quantity}");
}
```

The preceding code is our `Process` method (again, the simplest one), and it prints the details of the `books`. As per their requirement, users can perform as many actions as they want:

```
private static void ParallelismExample()
{
    var parallelism = new Parallelism();
    parallelism.GenerateBooks(19);
    Console.WriteLine("\n\tId\tName\tQty\n");
    parallelism.PallelVersion();
    Console.WriteLine($"\n\tTotal Processes Running on the
machine:{Environment.ProcessorCount}\n");
    Console.WriteLine("\tProcessing complete. Press any key to exit.");
    Console.ReadKey();
}
```

As you can see, we have the `ParallelismExample` method, and it generates the book list and processes the books by executing the `PallelVersion` method.

Before you execute the program to see the following output, first consider the following code snippet of sequential implementation:

```
public void Sequential()
{
    var books = GetBooks();
    foreach (var book in books) { Process(book); }
}
```

The preceding code is a `Sequential` method; it uses a simple `foreach` loop to process the book collections. Execute the program and see the following output:

```
Id       Name      Qty

1        Book#1    10
2        Book#2    20
3        Book#3    30
4        Book#4    40
5        Book#5    50
6        Book#6    60
7        Book#7    70
8        Book#8    80
9        Book#9    90
13       Book#13   130
10       Book#10   100
14       Book#14   140
15       Book#15   150
11       Book#11   110
16       Book#16   160
12       Book#12   120
17       Book#17   170
18       Book#18   180
19       Book#19   190

Total Processes Running on the machine:4

Processing complete. Press any key to exit.
```

Take note of the preceding snapshot. First, there are four processes running in the system on which I am running this demo. The second iterated collection is in a sequence/order from 1 to 19. The program does not divide the tasks into different processes running on the machine. Press any key to exit from the current process, execute the program for the `ParallelismVersion` method, and see the following output:

```
Id        Name     Qty

1         Book#1   10
2         Book#2   20
3         Book#3   30
4         Book#4   40
5         Book#5   50
6         Book#6   60
7         Book#7   70
8         Book#8   80
9         Book#9   90
10        Book#10  100
11        Book#11  110
12        Book#12  120
13        Book#13  130
14        Book#14  140
15        Book#15  150
16        Book#16  160
17        Book#17  170
18        Book#18  180
19        Book#19  190

Total Processes Running on the machine:4

Processing complete. Press any key to exit.
```

The preceding screenshot is of an output from a parallel code; you may notice that the code is not processed in sequence and the IDs are not coming through in sequence/order, as we can see `Id` 13 comes after 9 but before 10. If these were running in sequence, then the order of the `Id`s would be 9, 10, and then 13.

LINQ was in the .NET world a long time before the birth of .NET Core. `LINQ-to-Objects` allows us to perform in-memory query operations by using arbitrary sequences of objects. `LINQ-to-Objects` is a collection of extension methods on top of `IEnumerable<T>`.

> **Deferred execution** means execution happens once the data is enumerated.

PLINQ can be used as an alternative to TPL. It is a parallel implementation of LINQ. The PLINQ query operates on in-memory `IEnumerable` or `IEnumerable<T>` data sources. Also, it has a deferred execution. The LINQ query performs operations in sequence, while PLINQ executes operations in parallel and makes full use of all the processors on the machine. Consider the following code to see the implementation of PLINQ:

```
public void Process()
{
    var bookCount = 50000;
    _parallelism.GenerateBooks(bookCount);
    var books = _parallelism.GetBooks();
    var query = from book in books.AsParallel()
        where book.Quantity > 12250
        select book;
    Console.WriteLine($"\n\t{query.Count()} books out of {bookCount} total books," +
                    "having Qty in stock more than 12250.");
    Console.ReadKey();
}
```

The preceding code is the process method of our PLINQ class. Here, we are using PLINQ to query any books in stock with a quantity of more than `12250`. Execute the code to see this output:

```
48775 books out of 50000 total books,having Qty in stock more than 12250.
```

PLINQ uses all the processors of a machine, but we can limit the processors in PLINQ by using the `WithDegreeOfParallelism()` method. We can use the following code in our `Process ()` method of the `Linq` class:

```
var query = from book in books.AsParallel().WithDegreeOfParallelism(3)
    where book.Quantity > 12250
    select book;
return query;
```

The preceding code will use only three processors of the machine. Execute them, and you'll find that you get the same output as in the case of the previous code.

Summary

In this chapter, we discussed concurrent programming and concurrency in the real world. We looked at how we can handle various scenarios related to concurrency in our day-to-day life. We looked at collecting conference tickets from serving counters, and we understood what parallel programming and concurrent programming are. We have also covered multithreading, `Async/Await`, `Concurrent` collection, and PLINQ.

In the upcoming chapter, we will get a taste of functional programming using the C# language. We will dive deeper into the concepts that show us how to use C# in .NET Core to perform functional programming.

Questions

The following questions will allow you to consolidate the information contained in this chapter:

1. What is concurrent programming?
2. How does true parallelism happen?
3. What is the race condition?
4. Why should we use a concurrent dictionary?

Further reading

The following book will help you learn more about the topics that have been covered in this chapter:

- *Concurrent Patterns and Best Practices*, by *Atul S Khot*, published by *Packt Publishing*: https://www.packtpub.com/in/application-development/concurrent-patterns-and-best-practices

9
Functional Programming Practices

The previous chapter (Chapter 8, *Concurrent Programming in .NET Core*) introduced concurrent programming in .NET Core, and the aim of the chapter was to take advantage of async/await and parallelism, to make our program more performant.

In this chapter, we will get a taste of functional programming, using the C# language. We will also dive deeper into the concepts that show you how to leverage C# in .NET Core to perform functional programming. The aim of this chapter is to help you understand what functional programming is and how we can use it using the C# language.

Functional programming was inspired by mathematics, and it solves problems in a functional way. In mathematics, we have formulas and, in functional programming, we use math in the form of various functions. The best part of functional programming is that it helps to implement concurrency seamlessly.

The following topics will be covered in this chapter:

- Understanding functional programming
- The inventory application
- Strategy patterns and functional programming

Technical requirements

This chapter contains various code examples to explain the concepts of functional programming. The code is kept simple and is just for demonstration purposes. Most of the examples involve a .NET Core console application written in C#.

> The complete source code is available at the following link: https://github.com/PacktPublishing/Hands-On-Design-Patterns-with-C-and-.NET-Core/tree/master/Chapter9.

To run and execute the code, the prerequisites are as follows:

- Visual Studio 2019 (a Visual Studio 2017 update 3 or later can also be used to run the application).
- Setting up .NET Core
- SQL server (the Express Edition is used in this chapter)

Installing Visual Studio

To run these code examples, you need to install Visual Studio 2017 (or a later version such as 2019). To do so, follow these instructions:

1. Download Visual Studio from the following download link, which includes installation instructions: https://docs.microsoft.com/en-us/visualstudio/install/install-visual-studio.
2. Follow the installation instructions.
3. Multiple versions are available for the Visual Studio installation. Here, we are using Visual Studio for Windows.

Setting up .NET Core

If you do not have .NET Core installed, you need to follow these instructions:

1. Download .NET Core for Windows at https://www.microsoft.com/net/download/windows.
2. For multiple versions and a related library, visit https://dotnet.microsoft.com/download/dotnet-core/2.2.

Installing SQL Server

If you do not have SQL Server installed, you need to follow these instructions:

1. Download SQL Server from the following link: https://www.microsoft.com/en-in/download/details.aspx?id=1695.
2. Find the installation instructions here: https://docs.microsoft.com/en-us/sql/ssms/download-sql-server-management-studio-ssms?view=sql-server-2017.

> For troubleshooting and more information, refer to the following link: https://www.blackbaud.com/files/support/infinityinstaller/content/installermaster/tkinstallsqlserver2008r2.htm.

Understanding functional programming

In simple terms, **functional programming** is an approach to symbolic computation that is done in the same way as solving mathematical problems. Any functional programming is based on mathematical functions and its coding style. Any language that supports functional programming works for solutions for the following two questions:

- What does it need to solve?
- How does it solve it?

Functional programming is not a new invention. This language has existed in the industry for a long time. The following are some well-known programming languages that support functional programming:

- Haskell
- Scala
- Erlang
- Clojure
- Lisp
- OCaml

Functional Programming Practices

> In 2005, Microsoft released the first version of F# (pronounced *EffSharp*—https://fsharp.org/). This is a functional programming language that has a lot of good features that any functional programming should have. In this chapter, we are not going to discuss much F#, but we will be discussing functional programming and its implementation using the C# language.

Pure functions are the ones that strengthen functional programming by saying that they're pure. These functions work on two levels:

- The end result/output will always remain the same for the provided parameters.
- They will not impact the behavior of the program or the execution path of the application, even when they are being called a hundred times.

Consider the following example from our FlixOne inventory application:

```
public static class PriceCalc
{
    public static decimal Discount(this decimal price, decimal discount) =>
        price * discount / 100;

    public static decimal PriceAfterDiscount(this decimal price, decimal discount) =>
        decimal.Round(price - Discount(price, discount));
}
```

As you can see, we have a `PriceCalc` class with two extension methods: `Discount` and `PriceAfterDiscount`. These functions could be called pure functions; both the `PriceCalc` function and the `PriceAfterDiscount` function are meeting the criteria to be `Pure` function; the `Discount` method will calculate the discount based on the current price and discount. In this case, the output of the method will never change for the supplied parameter values. In this way, the product with a price of `190.00` and a discount of `10.00` will be calculated in this way: `190.00 * 10.00 /100`, and this will return `19.00`. Our next method—`PriceAfterDiscount`—with the same parameter values will calculate `190.00 - 19.00` and return the value of `171.00`.

One more important point in functional programming is that functions are pure and convey complete information (also called **functional honesty**). Consider the `Discount` method from the previous code; this is a pure function that is also honest. So, if someone accidentally supplies a negative discount or a discount that is more than its actual price (more than 100%), will this function remain pure and honest? To handle this scenario, our mathematics function should be written in such a way that if someone enters `discount <= 0` or `discount > 100`, then the system will not entertain it. Consider the following code with this approach:

```
public static decimal Discount(this decimal price, ValidDiscount validDiscount)
{
    return price * validDiscount.Discount / 100;
}
```

As you can see, our `Discount` function has a parameter type named `ValidDiscount`, which validates the input we have discussed. In this way, our function is now an honest function.

These functions are as simple as functional programming, but working with functional programming still requires a lot of practice. In the upcoming sections, we will discuss advanced concepts of functional programming, including functional programming principles.

Consider the following code, where we are checking whether the discount value is valid:

```
private readonly Func<decimal, bool> _vallidDiscount = d => d > 0 || d % 100 <= 1;
```

In the preceding code snippet, we have a field named `_validDiscount`. Let's look at what this is doing: `Func` accepts `decimal` as an input and returns `bool` as an output. From its name, you can see that `field` stores only valid discounts.

> `Func` is a type of delegate that points to a method of one or more arguments and returns a value. The general declaration of `Func` is `Func<TParameter, TOutput>`, where `TParameter` is the input parameter of any valid datatype and `TOutput` is the return value of any valid datatype.

Functional Programming Practices

Consider the following code snippet, where we are using the _validDiscount field in a method:

```
public IEnumerable<DiscountViewModel> FilterOutInvalidDiscountRates(
    IEnumerable<DiscountViewModel> discountViewModels)
{
    var viewModels = discountViewModels.ToList();
    var res = viewModels.Select(x => x.Discount).Where(_vallidDiscount);
    return viewModels.Where(x => res.Contains(x.Discount));
}
```

In the preceding code, we have the FilterOutInvalidDiscountRates method. This method is self-explanatory and indicates that we are filtering out invalid discount rates. Let's analyze the code now.

The FilterOutInvalidDiscountRates method returns a collection of DiscountViewModel class for the products that have a valid discount. The following code is of our DiscountViewModel class:

```
public class DiscountViewModel
{
    public Guid ProductId { get; set; }
    public string ProductName { get; set; }
    public decimal Price { get; set; }
    public decimal Discount { get; set; }
    public decimal Amount { get; set; }
}
```

Our DiscountViewModel class contains the following:

- ProductId: This represents the ID of a product.
- ProductName: This represents the name of a product.
- Price: This contains the actual price of the product. The actual price is before any discount, taxes, and so on.
- Discount: This contains the percentage of a discount such as 10 or 3. A valid discount rate should not be negative, equal to zero, or more than 100% (in other words, it should not be more than the actual cost of the product).
- Amount: This contains the product value after any discount, taxes, and so on.

Now, let's jump back to our FilterOutInavlidDiscountRates method and take a look at viewModels.Select(x => x.Discount).Where(_vallidDiscount). Here, you might notice that we are selecting discount rates from our viewModels list. This list contains discount rates that are valid as per the _validDiscount field. In the next line, our method is returning records with valid discount rates.

In functional programming, these functions are also known as **first-class functions**. These are the functions whose values can be used as an input or output for any other function. They can also be assigned to variables or stored in collections.

Go to Visual Studio and open the `FlixOne` inventory application. From here, run the application and you will see the following screenshot:

Product Name	Description	Image	Price (INR)	Discount Rate	Discount (INR)	Net Price (INR)	Category Name	Action
Mango	A juicy mango		40.00	5.00	2.00	38.00	Fruit	Edit | Details | Delete
Apple	Red apple		100.00	10.00	10.00	90.00	Fruit	Edit | Details | Delete
Orange	Fruity oranges		35.00	3.00	1.05	33.95	Fruit	Edit | Details | Delete

The previous screenshot is the **Product Listing** page that is showing all the available products. This is a simple page; you can also call it the **Product Listing** dashboard, where you'll find all the products. From **Create New Product**, you can add a new product, and **Edit** will give you the facility to update an existing product. In addition, the **Details** page will show the complete details of a specific product. By clicking **Delete**, you can remove the existing product from the listing.

Please refer to our `DiscountViewModel` class. We have the option to have multiple discount rates for a product with a business rule, which establishes that only one discount rate is active at a time. To view all the discount rates for a product, click on a discount rate from the preceding screen (**Product Listing**). This will show the following screen:

Functional Programming Practices

Product Name	Price (INR)	Discount Rate	Description	Active?	Remarks, if any
Mango	40.00	5%	Seasonal Discount	Yes	-
Mango	40.00	105%	Wrong discount, should be ignored	No	Discount rate is invalid, hence will not consider in price calculations.

The preceding screen is **Product Discount Listing** that shows the discount listing for the product name **Mango**. This has two discount rates, but only the **Seasonal Discount** rate is active. You might have noticed the remarks column; this is marked as an invalid discount rate because, as per _validDiscount—which is discussed in the previous section—this discount rate does not match the criteria for a valid discount rate.

> Predicate is also a delegate type, similar to Func delegates. This represents a method that validates the set of criteria. In other words, Predicate returns the type of Predicate <T>, where T is a valid datatype. It works if the criteria matches and returns a value of type T.

Consider the following code, where we are validating the **Product Name** to be valid as sentence case:

```
private static readonly TextInfo TextInfo = new CultureInfo("en-US", false).TextInfo;
private readonly Predicate<string> _isProductNameTitleCase = s =>
s.Equals(TextInfo.ToTitleCase(s));
```

In the preceding code, we are using the Predicate keyword, and this analyzes the condition to validate ProductName using TitleCase keyword. If the criteria matches, the result will be true. If not, the result will be false. Consider the following code snippet, where we are using _isProductNameTitleCase:

```
public IEnumerable<ProductViewModel> FilterOutInvalidProductNames(
    IEnumerable<ProductViewModel> productViewModels) =>
productViewModels.ToList()
    .Where(p => _isProductNameTitleCase(p.ProductName));
```

In the preceding code, we have the `FilterOutInvalidProductNames` method. The aim of this method is to pick the products with a valid product name (a `TitleCase` product name only).

Enhancing our inventory application

The project is for a hypothetical situation where a company, FlixOne, wants to enhance an inventory management application to manage its growing collection of products. This is not a new application, as we have already started the development of this application and discussed the initial stage in `Chapter 3`, *Implementing Design Patterns - Basics Part 1*, where we have started developing a console-based inventory system. From time to time, stakeholders will review the application and try to meet end users' requirements. The enhancement is important, as this application will be used by both staff (to manage the inventory) and by customers (to browse and create new orders). The application will need to be scalable, and is an essential system for the business.

As this is a technical book, we will mostly discuss the various technical observations from the development team's perspective and discuss the patterns and practices used to implement the inventory management application.

Requirements

There is a need to enhance the application, and this cannot be achieved in one day. This will require a lot of meetings and discussions. Over the course of several meetings, the business and the development teams discussed the requirements of the new enhancements to the inventory management system. Progress toward defining a clear set of requirements was slow, and the vision of the final product was not clear. The development team decided to pare down the enormous list of requirements to just enough functionality so that a key individual could start to record some inventory information. This would allow for simple inventory management and provide a basis that the business could extend upon. We will work on the requirement and take a **Minimal Viable Product** (**MVP**) approach.

> MVP is the smallest set of features of an application that can still be released and have enough value for a user base.

After several meetings and discussions between management and business analysts, a list of requirements was produced to enhance our FlixOne web application. The high-level requirements are as follows:

- **Implementation of pagination**: Currently, all page listings are not paginated. It is really challenging to view items with large page counts by scrolling down or scrolling up the screen.
- **Discount Rates**: Currently, there is no provision to add or see the various discount rates for a product. The business rules for discount rates are as follows:
    - A product can have more than one discount rate.
    - A product can only have one active discount rate.
    - A valid discount rate should not be a negative value and should not be more than 100%.

Back to FlixOne

In the previous section, we discussed what is required in order to enhance an application. In this section, we will implement these requirements. Let's first revisit the file structure of our project. Take a look at the following snapshot:

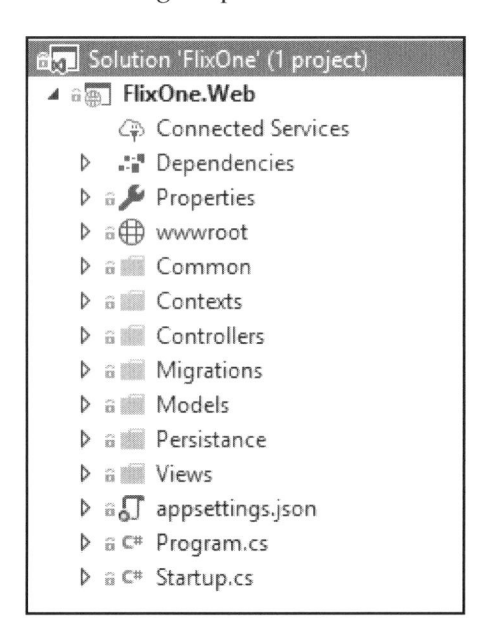

Chapter 9

The previous snapshot is depicting our **FlixOne** web application, having a folder structure as follows:

- **wwwroot**: This is the folder that comes with static contents, such as CSS and jQuery files, which are required for the UI project. This folder comes with the default template provided by Visual Studio.
- **Common**: This contains all the common files and operations related to business rules and more.
- **Contexts**: This contains `InventoryContext`, which is a `DBContext` class that provides `Entity Framework Core` capabilities.
- **Controllers**: This contains all the controller classes of our `FlixOne` application.
- **Migration**: This contains the `InventoryModel` snapshot and initially created entities.
- **Models:** This contains data models, `ViewModels`, that are required for our application.
- **Persistence:** This contains the `InventoryRepository` and its operations.
- **Views**: This contains all the views/screens of the application.

Consider the following code:

```
public interface IHelper
{
    IEnumerable<DiscountViewModel> FilterOutInvalidDiscountRates(
        IEnumerable<DiscountViewModel> discountViewModels);

    IEnumerable<ProductViewModel> FilterOutInvalidProductNames(
        IEnumerable<ProductViewModel> productViewModels);
}
```

The preceding code contains an `IHelper` interface that is holding two methods. We will implement this interface in the following code snippet:

```
public class Helper : IHelper
{
    private static readonly TextInfo TextInfo = new CultureInfo("en-US", false).TextInfo;
    private readonly Predicate<string> _isProductNameTitleCase = s => s.Equals(TextInfo.ToTitleCase(s));
    private readonly Func<decimal, bool> _vallidDiscount = d => d == 0 || d - 100 <= 1;

    public IEnumerable<DiscountViewModel> FilterOutInvalidDiscountRates(
        IEnumerable<DiscountViewModel> discountViewModels)
    {
```

[251]

Functional Programming Practices

```
        var viewModels = discountViewModels.ToList();
        var res = viewModels.Select(x =>
x.ProductDiscountRate).Where(_vallidDiscount);
        return viewModels.Where(x => res.Contains(x.ProductDiscountRate));
    }

    public IEnumerable<ProductViewModel> FilterOutInvalidProductNames(
        IEnumerable<ProductViewModel> productViewModels) =>
productViewModels.ToList()
        .Where(p => _isProductNameTitleCase(p.ProductName));
}
```

The `Helper` class implements the `IHelper` interface. In this class, we have two main, and important, methods: one is to check for a valid discount and the other is to check for a valid `ProductName` attribute.

Before we use this functionality in our application, we should add this to our `Startup.cs` file, as shown in the following code:

```
public void ConfigureServices(IServiceCollection services)
{
    services.AddTransient<IInventoryRepositry, InventoryRepositry>();
    services.AddTransient<IHelper, Helper>();
    services.AddDbContext<InventoryContext>(o =>
o.UseSqlServer(Configuration.GetConnectionString("FlixOneDbConnection")));
    services.Configure<CookiePolicyOptions>(options =>
    {
        // This lambda determines whether user consent for non-essential cookies is needed for a given request.
        options.CheckConsentNeeded = context => true;
        options.MinimumSameSitePolicy = SameSiteMode.None;
    });
}
```

In the preceding code snippet, we have a written statement, `services.AddTransient<IHelper, Helper>();`. With this, we are adding a transient service to our application. We have already discussed the *Inversion of control* section in `Chapter 5`, *Implementing Design Patterns - .Net Core*.

[252]

Consider the following code, where we are using the IHelper class by taking leverage of Inversion of control:

```
public class InventoryRepositry : IInventoryRepositry
{
    private readonly IHelper _helper;
    private readonly InventoryContext _inventoryContext;

    public InventoryRepositry(InventoryContext inventoryContext, IHelper helper)
    {
        _inventoryContext = inventoryContext;
        _helper = helper;
    }

...
}
```

The preceding code contains the InventoryRepositry class, where we can see the use of a proper **Dependency Injection (DI)**:

```
    public IEnumerable<Discount> GetDiscountBy(Guid productId, bool activeOnly = false)
        {
            var discounts = activeOnly
                ? GetDiscounts().Where(d => d.ProductId == productId && d.Active)
                : GetDiscounts().Where(d => d.ProductId == productId);
            var product = _inventoryContext.Products.FirstOrDefault(p => p.Id == productId);
            var listDis = new List<Discount>();
            foreach (var discount in discounts)
            {
                if (product != null)
                {
                    discount.ProductName = product.Name;
                    discount.ProductPrice = product.Price;
                }

                listDis.Add(discount);
            }

            return listDis;
        }
```

Functional Programming Practices

The preceding code is the `GetDiscountBy` method of the `InventoryRepository` class that is a returning collection of the discount model for the `active` or `de-active` records. Consider the following code snippet that is used for the `DiscountViewModel` collection:

```
public IEnumerable<DiscountViewModel> GetValidDiscoutedProducts(
    IEnumerable<DiscountViewModel> discountViewModels)
{
    return _helper.FilterOutInvalidDiscountRates(discountViewModels);
}
```

The preceding code that uses a collection of `DiscountViewModel` is filtering out the products that do not have a valid discount as per the business rule we discussed previously. The `GetValidDiscountProducts` method returns the collection of `DiscountViewModel`.

If we forget to define `IHelper` in our project `startup.cs` file, we will meet an exception, as shown in the following screenshot:

```
An unhandled exception occurred while processing the request.
InvalidOperationException: Unable to resolve service for type 'FlixOne.Web.Common.IHelper' while attempting to activate 'FlixOne.Web.Persistence.InventoryRepositry'.
    Microsoft.Extensions.DependencyInjection.ServiceLookup.CallSiteFactory.CreateArgumentCallSites(Type serviceType, Type implementationType, CallSiteChain callSiteChain, ParameterInfo[] parameters, bool throwIfCallSiteNotFound)
```

The preceding screenshot is clearly saying that the `IHelper` service is not resolved. In our case, we will not face this exception, as we have already added `IHelper` to the `Startup` class.

Until now, we have added helper methods to fulfill our new requirement for discount rates and to validate them. Now, let's add a controller and subsequent action methods. To do so, add a new `DiscountController` controller from **Solution Explorer**. After this, our `FlixOne` web solution will look similar to the following snapshot:

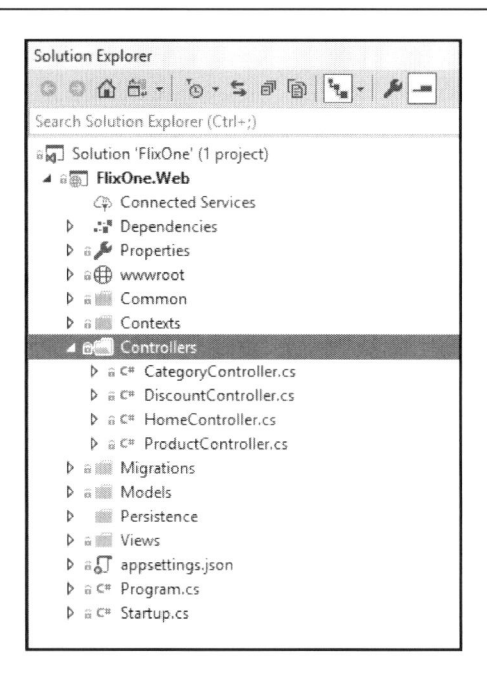

In the preceding snapshot, we can see that our `Controller` folder now has one additional controller, which is `DiscountController`. The following code is from `DiscountController`:

```
public class DiscountController : Controller
{
    private readonly IInventoryRepositry _repositry;

    public DiscountController(IInventoryRepositry inventoryRepositry)
    {
        _repositry = inventoryRepositry;
    }

    public IActionResult Index()
    {
        return View(_repositry.GetDiscounts().ToDiscountViewModel());
    }

    public IActionResult Details(Guid id)
    {
        return View("Index",
_repositry.GetDiscountBy(id).ToDiscountViewModel());
    }
}
```

Execute the application and, from the main screen, click on **Products** and then click on **Product Discount Listing**. From here, you will get the following screen:

Product Name	Price (INR)	Discount Rate	Description	Active?	Remarks, if any
Mango	40.00	5%	Seasonal Discount	Yes	-
Mango	40.00	105%	Wrong discount, should be ignored	No	Discount rate is invalid, hence will not consider in price calculations.
Orange	35.00	3%	Fruit dhamaka	Yes	-
Orange	35.00	32%	Pitch Discount	No	-
Apple	100.00	10%	Special discount	Yes	-
Apple	100.00	2%	Seasonal Discount	No	-
Apple	100.00	125%	Discarded	No	Discount rate is invalid, hence will not consider in price calculations.

The preceding snapshot is depicting **Product Discount Listing** for all the available products. The **Product Discount Listing** has a lot of records; therefore, it requires scrolling up or scrolling down to view items on the screen. To handle this difficult situation, we should implement paging.

Strategy pattern and functional programming

During the first four chapters of this book, we discussed patterns and practices a lot. The strategy pattern is one of the important patterns of **Gang of Four** (**GoF**) patterns. This falls under the behavioral patterns category and is also known as a policy pattern. This is a pattern that is usually implemented with the help of classes. This is also an easier one to implement using functional programming.

Jump back to the *Understanding functional programming* section of this chapter and reconsider the paradigm of functional programming. Higher-order functions are one of the important paradigms of functional programming; using this, we can easily implement a strategy pattern in a functional way.

> **Higher-order functions** (**HOFs**) are the functions that take parameters as functions. They can also return functions.

Consider the following code that shows the implementation of HOFs in functional programming:

```
public static IEnumerable<T> Where<T>
    (this IEnumerable<T> source, Func<T, bool> criteria)
{
    foreach (var item in source)
        if (criteria(item))
            yield return item;
}
```

The preceding code is a simple implementation of the Where clause, in which we used LINQ Query. In this, we are iterating a collection and returning an item if it meets the criteria. The preceding code can be further simplified. Consider the following code for a more simplified version of the preceding code:

```
public static IEnumerable<T> SimplifiedWhere<T>
    (this IEnumerable<T> source, Func<T, bool> criteria) =>
    Enumerable.Where(source, criteria);
```

As you can see, the SimplifiedWhere method produces the same result as the previously discussed Where method. This method is criteria-based and has a strategy to return results, and this criterion executes at runtime. We can easily call the preceding function in a subsequent method to take advantage of functional programming. Consider the following code:

```
public IEnumerable<ProductViewModel>
    GetProductsAbovePrice(IEnumerable<ProductViewModel> productViewModels,
decimal price) =>
    productViewModels.SimplifiedWhere(p => p.ProductPrice > price);
```

We have a method called `GetProductsAbovePrice`. In this method, we are providing the price. This method is self-explanatory, and it works on a collection of `ProductViewModel` with a criteria to list the products that have a product price that is more than the parameter price. In our `FlixOne` inventory application, you can find further scope to implement functional programming.

Summary

Functional programming is all about functions and, predominantly, mathematical functions. Any language that supports functional programming always works on the solution with two main questions: what needs to be solved and how can this be solved? We saw functional programming and its easy implementation using the C# programming language.

We also learned about `Func`, `Predicate`, LINQ, `Lambda`, anonymous functions, closures, expression trees, currying, closures, and recursion. Finally, we looked into the implementation of the strategy pattern using functional programming.

In the next chapter (`Chapter 10`, *Reactive Programming Patterns and Techniques*), we will discuss reactive programming as well as its model and principles. We will also discuss **reactive extensions**.

Questions

The following questions will allow you to consolidate the information contained in this chapter:

1. What is functional programming?
2. What is referential transparency in functional programming?
3. What is a pure function?

10
Reactive Programming Patterns and Techniques

In the previous chapter (Chapter 9, *Functional Programming Practices*), we delved into functional programming and learned about **Func**, **Predicate**, **LINQ**, **Lambda**, **anonymous functions**, **expression trees**, and **recursion**. We also looked at the implementation of the strategy pattern using functional programming.

This chapter will explore the use of reactive programming and provides a hands-on demonstration of reactive programming using the C# language. We will delve into the principles and models of reactive programming and discuss the `IObservable` and `IObserver` providers.

The inventory application will be expanded in two main ways: by reacting to changes and by discussing the **Model-View-ViewModel** (**MVVM**) pattern.

The following topics will be covered in this chapter:

- The principles of reactive programming
- Reactive and IObservable
- Reactive extensions—.NET Rx Extensions
- Inventory application use case—getting inventory with a filter, paging, and sorting
- Patterns and practices – MVVM

Technical requirements

This chapter contains various code examples to explain the concepts of reactive programming. The code is kept simple and is only for demonstration purposes. Most of the examples involve a .NET Core console application written in C#.

> The complete source code is available at the following link: https://github.com/PacktPublishing/Hands-On-Design-Patterns-with-C-and-.NET-Core/tree/master/Chapter10.

Running and executing the code will require the following:

- Visual Studio 2019 (you can also use Visual Studio 2017)
- Setting up .NET Core
- SQL Server (the Express Edition is used in this chapter)

Installing Visual Studio

To run the code examples, you will need to install Visual Studio (the preferred IDE). To do so, you can follow these instructions:

1. Download Visual Studio 2017 or the later version (2019) from the download link mentioned with the installation instructions: https://docs.microsoft.com/en-us/visualstudio/install/install-visual-studio.
2. Follow the installation instructions.
3. Multiple options are available for Visual Studio installation. Here, we are using Visual Studio for Windows.

Setting up .NET Core

If you do not have .NET Core installed, you will need to follow these steps:

1. Download .NET Core for Windows: https://www.microsoft.com/net/download/windows.
2. For multiple versions and a related library, visit https://dotnet.microsoft.com/download/dotnet-core/2.2.

Installing SQL Server

If you do not have SQL Server installed, you can follow these instructions:

1. Download SQL Server from the following link: https://www.microsoft.com/en-in/download/details.aspx?id=1695.
2. You can find the installation instructions here: https://docs.microsoft.com/en-us/sql/ssms/download-sql-server-management-studio-ssms?view=sql-server-2017.

> For troubleshooting and for more information, refer to the following link: https://www.blackbaud.com/files/support/infinityinstaller/content/installermaster/tkinstallsqlserver2008r2.htm.

The principles of reactive programming

These days, everyone is talking about **asynchronous programming**. Various applications are built on RESTful services that use asynchronous programming. The term *asynchronous* is relevant to reactive programming. Reactive is all about data streams, and reactive programming is a model structure that is built around asynchronous data streams. Reactive programming is also known as *the art of programming the propagation of changes*. Let's go back to our example from Chapter 8, *Concurrent Programming in .NET Core*, where we were discussing the ticket collection counters at a big conference.

In addition to the three ticket-collection counters, we have one more counter named the calculation counter. This fourth counter concentrates on counting the collection, and it counts how many tickets are distributed from each of the three counters. Consider the following diagram:

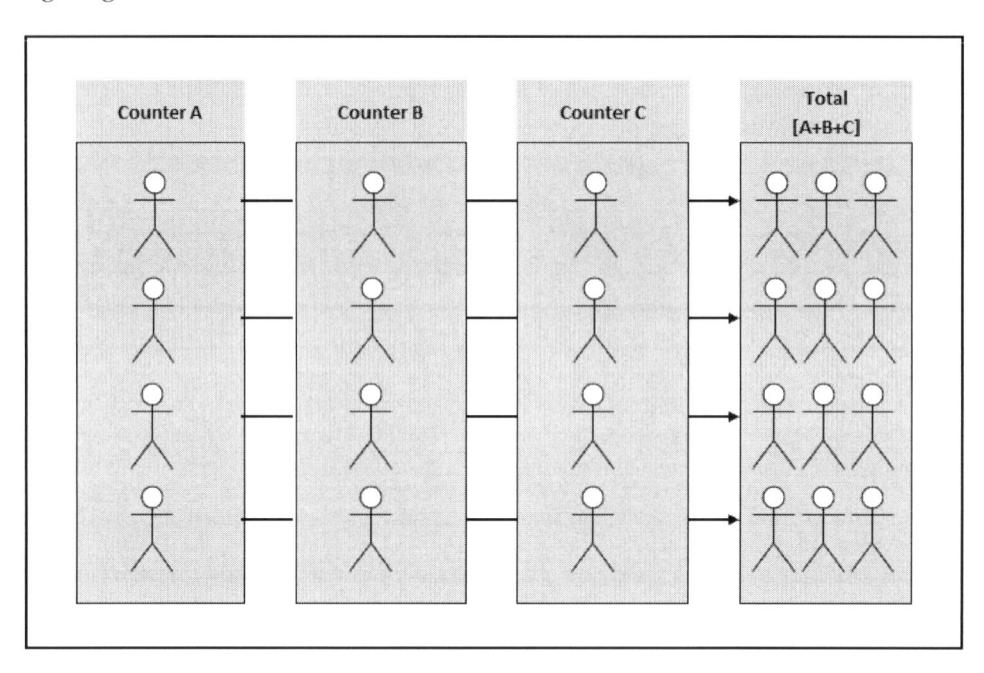

In the preceding diagram, the total of A+B+C is the sum of the remaining three columns; it is 1+1+1 = 3. The **Total** column always shows the sum of rest of the three columns, and it will never show the actual person who is standing in the queue and waiting for their turn to collect the ticket. The value of the **Total** column depends upon the number of the remaining columns. If **Counter A** had two people in a queue, then the **Total** column would have the sum of 2+1+1 = 4. You can also refer to the **Total** column as a computed column. This column calculates the sum as soon as other rows/columns shift their counts (people waiting in the queue). If we were to write the **Total** column in C#, we would choose the computed property, and this would look as follows: `public int TotalColumn { get { return ColumnA + ColumnB + ColumnC; } }`.

In the preceding diagram, data flows from column to column. You can treat this as a data stream. You can create a stream for anything such as click events and hover events. Anything can be a stream variable: user inputs, properties, caches, data structures, and more. In the stream world, you can listen to the stream and react accordingly.

> A sequence of events is called a **stream**. A stream can emit three things: a value, an error, and a signal for completion.

You can easily work with a stream in this way:

- One stream can be the input for another stream.
- Multiple streams can be the input for another stream.
- Streams can be merged.
- Data values can be mapped from one stream to another.
- Streams can be filtered with the data/events that you need.

To understand streams more closely, see the following diagram that represents a stream (a sequence of events):

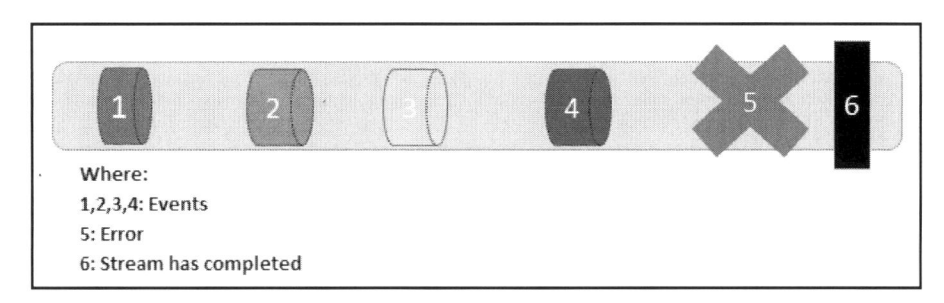

```
Where:
1,2,3,4: Events
5: Error
6: Stream has completed
```

The preceding diagram is a representation of a stream (sequence of events) where we have one to four events. Any of these events can be triggered or someone can click on any of them. These events can be represented by values and these values can be strings. The X sign shows that an error has occurred during the operation where streams are merged or their data is being mapped. Finally, the | sign shows that a stream (or an operation) is complete.

Be reactive with reactive programming

Obviously, our computed property (discussed in the previous section) cannot be reactive or represent reactive programming. Reactive programming has specific designs and technologies. To experience the reactive programming or to be reactive, you can start with documents, available at http://reactivex.io/ and experience it by going through the reactive manifesto (https://www.reactivemanifesto.org/).

> In simple terms, reactive properties are binding properties that react when an event is triggered.

Nowadays, when we deal with various large systems/applications, we find that they are too large to handle at once. These large systems are divided or composed into smaller systems. These smaller units/systems rely on reactive properties. To adhere to reactive programming, reactive systems apply design principles so that these properties can apply to all methods. With the help of this design/approach, we can make a composable system.

According to the manifesto, reactive programming and reactive systems are both different.

On the basis of the reactive manifesto, we can conclude that reactive systems are as follows:

- **Responsive**: Reactive systems are event-based design systems; these systems are quick to respond to any request in a short amount of time.
- **Scalable**: Reactive systems are reactive in nature. These systems can react to changing the scalability rate by expanding or reducing the allocated resources.
- **Resilient**: A resilient system is one that will not stop even if there is a failure/exception. Reactive systems are designed in such a way so that in any exception or failure, the system will never die; it remains working.
- **Message-based**: Any data item represents a message that can be sent to a specific destination. When a message or data item has arrived at a given state, an event emits a signal to notify the subscribers that a message has reached. Reactive systems rely on this message passing.

The following diagram shows a pictorial view of a reactive system:

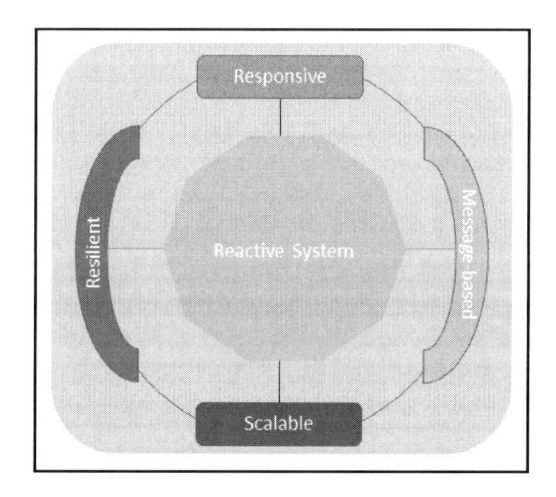

Chapter 10

In this diagram, a reactive system is composed of small systems that are resilient, scalable, responsive, and message-based.

Reactive streams in action

So far, we have discussed the fact that reactive programming is a data stream. In the previous sections, we have also discussed how streams work and how these streams travel in a timely manner. We have seen an example of events and discussed the data streams in a reactive program. Now, let's go ahead with the same example and look at how two streams work with various operations.

In the next example, we have two observable streams of an integer data type collection. Please note that we are using the pseudo code in this section to explain the behavior and the way in which these collections of data streams work.

The following diagram represents two observable streams. The first stream, Observer1, contains numbers **1**, **2**, and **4**, whereas Observer2, which is a second stream, contains numbers **3** and **5**:

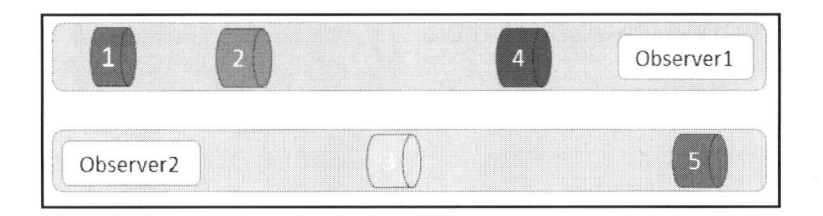

Merging two streams involves combining their sequence elements into a new stream. The following diagram shows a new stream that results when Observer1 and Observer2 are merged:

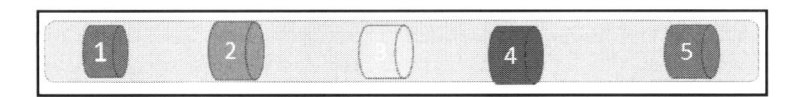

The preceding diagram is only a representation of a stream and is not an actual representation of the sequence of elements in the stream. In this diagram, we have seen that elements (numbers) are in the sequence **1, 2, 3, 4, 5**, but this is not true in a realistic example. The sequence can vary; it could be **1, 2, 4, 3, 5**, or in any other order.

Reactive Programming Patterns and Techniques

Filtering a stream is just like skipping elements/records. You can imagine a `Where` clause in LINQ, which looks something like this: `myCollection.Where(num => num <= 3);`.

The following diagram illustrates a pictorial view of criteria, where we're trying to pick only the elements that are meeting the specific criteria:

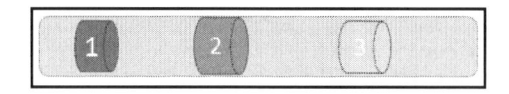

We are filtering our stream and picking only those elements that are <=3. This means we are skipping elements **4** and **5**. In this case, we can say the filter is there to skip elements or to match the criteria.

To understand a map stream, you can imagine any mathematical operation where you would be counting sequences or incrementing numbers by adding some constant values. For example, if we have an integer value of *3* and our map stream is +3, that means we are counting a sequence as *3 + 3 = 6*. You can also correlate this with the LINQ and select and project the output like this: `return myCollection.Select(num => num+3);`.

The following diagram represents a map of the stream:

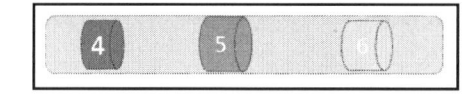

After applying filters with the condition, <= 3, our stream has the elements **1**, **2**, and **3**. Additionally, we applied `Map (+3)` to the filtered stream with the elements **1**, **2**, and **3**, and, finally, our stream has the elements **4,5,6** (1+3, 2+3, 3+3).

In the real world, these operations would occur sequentially or on demand. We have already done this operation of sequences so that we can apply the operations of merge, filter, and mapping in a sequential manner. The following diagram represents the flow of our imaginary example:

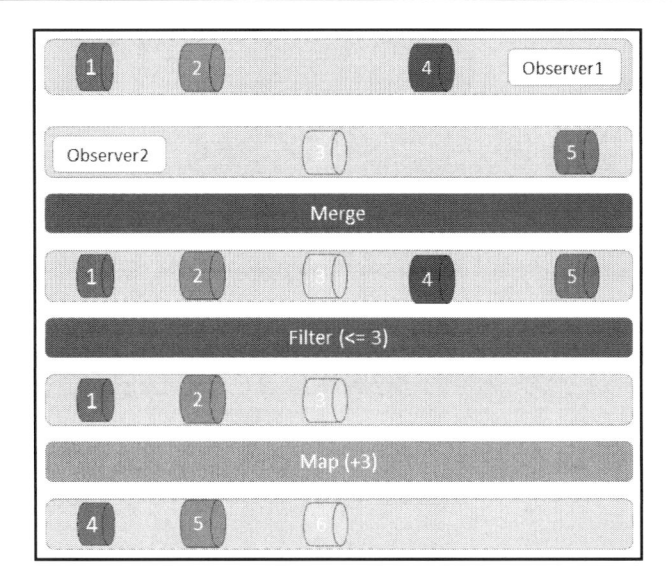

So, we have tried to represent our examples through diagrams, and we have gone through various operations where two streams talk to each other, and we got a new stream, and then we filtered and mapped the stream.

> To understand this better, refer to `https://rxmarbles.com/`.

Now let's create a simple code to complete this example in the real world. First, we will study the code that implements the example, and then we will discuss the output of the stream.

Consider the following code snippet as an example of the `IObservable` interface:

```
public static IObservable<T> From<T>(this T[] source) =>
source.ToObservable();
```

This code represents an extension method of a `T` type array. We created a generic method and named it `From`. This method returns an `Observable` sequence.

> You can visit the official documentation to know more about extension methods here: `https://docs.microsoft.com/en-us/dotnet/csharp/programming-guide/classes-and-structs/extension-methods`.

[267]

Reactive Programming Patterns and Techniques

In our code, we have the `TicketCounter` class. This class has two observers that are actually arrays of the integer data type. The following code shows two observables:

```
public IObservable<int> Observable1 => Counter1.From();
public IObservable<int> Observable2 => Counter2.From();
```

In this code, we apply the `From()` extension method to `Counter1` and `Counter2`. These counters actually represent our ticket counters and recall our example from Chapter 8, *Concurrent programming in .NET Core*.

The following code snippet represents `Counter1` and `Counter2`:

```
internal class TicketCounter
{
    private IObservable<int> _observable;
    public int[] Counter1;
    public int[] Counter2;
    public TicketCounter(int[] counter1, int[] counter2)
    {
        Counter1 = counter1;
        Counter2 = counter2;
    }
    ...
}
```

In this code, we have two fields, `Counter1` and `Counter2`, and they are initialized from the constructor. When the `TicketCounter` class is being initialized, these fields get the values from the constructor of the class, as defined in the following code:

```
TicketCounter ticketCounter = new TicketCounter(new int[]{1,3,4}, new int[]{2,5});
```

To understand the complete code, go to and execute the code by hitting *F5* in Visual Studio. From here, you will see the following screen:

```
Enter comma separated number (0-9):
```

This is the console output and, in this console window, the user has been asked to enter a comma-separated number from 0 to 9. Go ahead and enter a comma-separated number here. Please note that, here, we are trying to create a code that depicts our diagram of data stream representation, which was discussed earlier in this section:

```
Enter comma separated number (0-9): 1,2,4
Enter comma separated number (0-9): 3,5
```

As per the preceding diagram, we have entered two different comma-separated numbers. The first is 1, 2, 4 and the second is 3, 5. Now consider our `Merge` method:

```
public IObservable<int> Merge() => _observable =
Observable1.Merge(Observable2);
```

The `Merge` method is merging two sequences of the data stream into `_observable`. The `Merge` operation is initiated with the following code:

```
Console.Write("\n\tEnter comma separated number (0-9): ");
var num1 = Console.ReadLine();
Console.Write("\tEnter comma separated number (0-9): ");
var num2 = Console.ReadLine();
var counter1 = num1.ToInts(',');
var counter2 = num2.ToInts(',');
TicketCounter ticketCounter = new TicketCounter(counter1, counter2);
```

In this code, the user is prompted to enter comma-separated numbers, and then the program stores these numbers into `counter1` and `counter2` by applying the `ToInts` method. The following is the code of our `ToInts` method:

```
public static int[] ToInts(this string commaseparatedStringofInt, char separator) =>
    Array.ConvertAll(commaseparatedStringofInt.Split(separator), int.Parse);
```

This code is an extension method for `string`. The target variable is of a `string` type that contains integers separated by `separator`. In this method, we are using the built-in `ConvertAll` method that is provided by .NET Core. This first splits the string and checks whether the split value is of an `integer` type. It then returns the `Array` of integers. This method produces the output, as shown in the following screenshot:

```
Counter1:    1    2    4
Counter2:    3    5
```

[269]

Reactive Programming Patterns and Techniques

The following is the output of our `merge` operation:

```
Merge:          1       3       2       5       4
```

The preceding output shows that we now have a final merged observer stream with the elements in sequence. Let's apply a filter to this stream. The following code is our `Filter` method:

```
public IObservable<int> Filter() => _observable = from num in _observable
    where num <= 3
    select num;
```

We have the filter criteria for the number <= 3, which means we will pick only the elements whose values are either less than or equal to 3. This method will initiate with the following code:

```
ticketCounter.Print(ticketCounter.Filter());
```

When the preceding code is executed, it produces the following output:

```
Filter (<= 3):  1       3       2
```

Finally, we have a filtered stream with the elements in the sequence 1,3,2. Now we need to map on this stream. We need a mapped element with `num + 3`, which means we need to output an integer number by adding 3 to this number. The following is our `Map` method:

```
public IObservable<int> Map() => _observable = from num in _observable
    select num + 3;
```

The preceding method will be initialized with the following code:

```
Console.Write("\n\tMap (+ 3):");
ticketCounter.Print(ticketCounter.Map());
```

On execution of the preceding method, we will see the following output:

```
Map (+ 3):      4       6       5
```

After applying the Map method, we have the stream of an element in the sequence of 4,6,5. We have discussed how reactive works even with an imaginary example. We have created a small .NET Core console application to see the power of Merge, Filter, and Map operations on the observables. The following is the output of our console application:

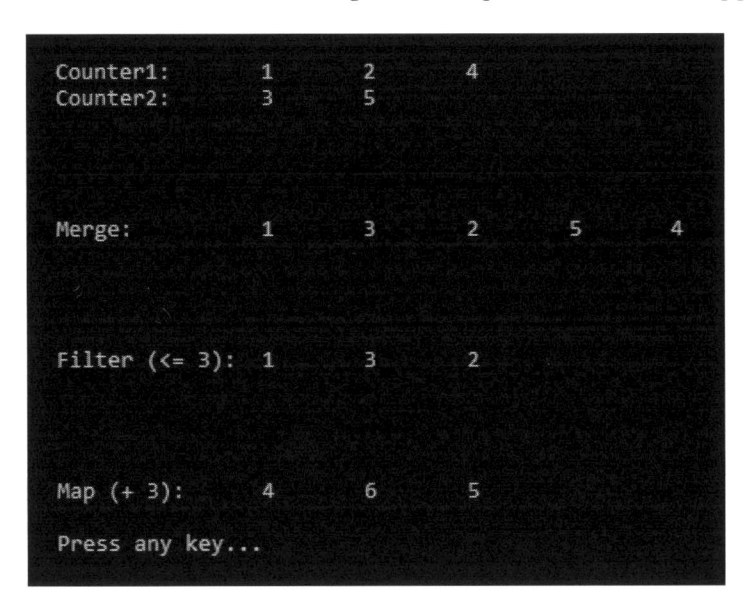

```
Counter1:       1       2       4
Counter2:       3       5



Merge:          1       3       2       5       4



Filter (<= 3):  1       3       2



Map (+ 3):      4       6       5

Press any key...
```

The previous snapshot is telling the whole story of the execution of our sample application; Counter1 and Counter2 are data streams that contain the sequences of data 1,2,4 and 3,5. We have the preceding output for Merge with the result 1,3,2,5,4 Filter (<=3), with the result 1,3,2 and Map (+3) with the data 4,6,5.

Reactive and IObservable

In the previous section, we discussed reactive programming and went through its model. In this section, we will discuss the Microsoft implementation of reactive programming. In response to reactive programming in .NET Core, we have various interfaces that provide a way to implement reactive programming in our application.

Reactive Programming Patterns and Techniques

`IObservable<T>` is a generic interface that is defined in the `System` namespace and declared as `public interface IObservable<out T>`. Here, `T` represents a generic type of parameter that provides notification information. In simple terms, this interface helps us to define a provider for notifications, and these notifications can be pushed for information. You can use the observer pattern while implementing the `IObservable<T>` interface in your application.

Observer pattern – implementation using IObservable<T>

In simple terms, a subscriber registers with a provider so that the subscriber may get notifications related to the message information. These notifications notify the provider that messages have been delivered to subscribers. This information may also be related to changes in operations or any other changes in the method or object itself. This is also known as **state changes**.

> The observer pattern specifies two terms: **Observer** and **Observable**. The observable is a provider also known as the **subject**. The observer is registered with the `Observable/Subject/Provider` types, and the observer will be automatically notified by the provider whenever any changes occur due to the pre-defined criteria/condition, change or event, and so on.

The following diagram is a simple representation of the observer pattern, where the subject is notifying two different observers:

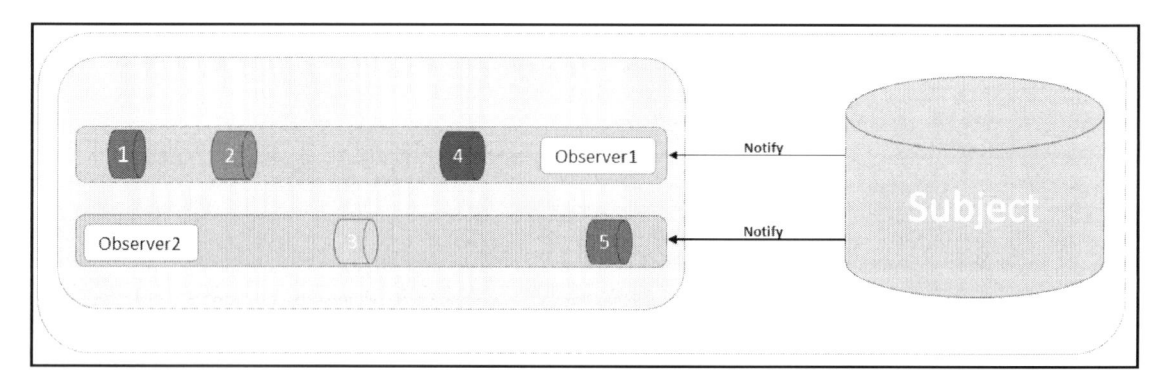

Go back to the `FlixOne` inventory web application from Chapter 9, *Functional Programming Practices*, initiate your Visual Studio, and open the `FlixOne.sln` solution.

Open **Solution Explorer**. From here, you will see that our project will look similar to the following snapshot:

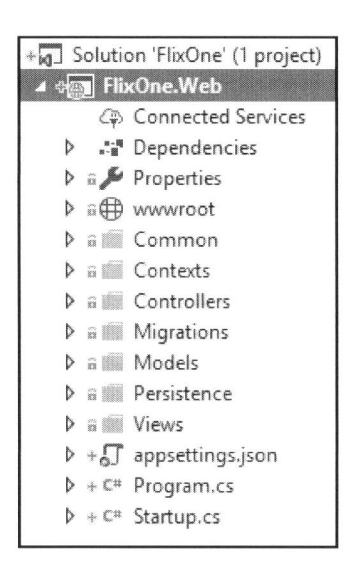

```
Solution 'FlixOne' (1 project)
  FlixOne.Web
      Connected Services
    ▷ Dependencies
    ▷ Properties
    ▷ wwwroot
    ▷ Common
    ▷ Contexts
    ▷ Controllers
    ▷ Migrations
    ▷ Models
    ▷ Persistence
    ▷ Views
    ▷ appsettings.json
    ▷ Program.cs
    ▷ Startup.cs
```

Expand the **Common** folder under **Solution Explorer** and add two files: `ProductRecorder.cs` and `ProductReporter.cs`. These files are the implementation of the `IObservable<T>` and `IObserver<T>` interfaces. We also need to add a new **ViewModel** so that we can report actual messages to the users. To do so, expand the `Models` folder and add the `MessageViewModel.cs` file.

The following code is showing our `MessageViewModel` class:

```
public class MessageViewModel
{
    public string MsgId { get; set; }
    public bool IsSuccess { get; set; }
    public string Message { get; set; }

    public override string ToString() => $"Id:{MsgId}, Success:{IsSuccess}, Message:{Message}";
}
```

`MessageViewModel` contains the following:

- `MsgId`: A unique identifier
- `IsSuccess`: Shows whether the operation has failed or succeeded
- `Message`: A success message or an error message that depends upon the value of `IsSuccess`
- `ToString()`: An override method that returns a string after concatenating all the information

Let's now discuss our two classes; the following code is from the `ProductRecorder` class:

```
public class ProductRecorder : IObservable<Product>
{
    private readonly List<IObserver<Product>> _observers;

    public ProductRecorder() => _observers = new
List<IObserver<Product>>();

    public IDisposable Subscribe(IObserver<Product> observer)
    {
        if (!_observers.Contains(observer))
            _observers.Add(observer);
        return new Unsubscriber(_observers, observer);
    }
    ...
}
```

Our `ProductRecorder` class implements the `IObservable<Product>` interface. If you recall our discussion regarding the observer pattern, you will come to know that this class is actually a provider, a subject, or an observable. The `IObservable<T>` interface has a `Subscribe` method that we need to use to subscribe our subscribers or observers (we will discuss the observer later in this section).

There should be a criteria or a condition so that the subscriber can get notifications. In our case, we have a `Record` method that serves this purpose. Consider the following code:

```
public void Record(Product product)
{
    var discountRate = product.Discount.FirstOrDefault(x => x.ProductId ==
product.Id)?.DiscountRate;
    foreach (var observer in _observers)
    {
        if (discountRate == 0 || discountRate - 100 <= 1)
            observer.OnError(
                new Exception($"Product:{product.Name} has invalid discount
```

```
rate {discountRate}"));
        else
            observer.OnNext(product);
    }
}
```

The preceding is a Record method. We created this method to showcase the power of the pattern. This method is simply checking for the valid discount rates. If discount rate is not valid, as per the criteria/condition, this method would raise an exception and share the product name with an invalid discount rate.

The previous method validates the discount rate as per the criteria and sends a notification about the raised exception to the subscriber upon failure of the criteria. Take a look at the iteration block (the foreach loop) and imagine a situation where we do not have anything to iterate and all the subscribers have been notified. Can we imagine what will happen in this case? The same kind of situation may arise for infinite loop. To stop this, we need something that terminates the loop. For this, we have the following EndRecording method:

```
public void EndRecording()
{
    foreach (var observer in _observers.ToArray())
        if (_observers.Contains(observer))
            observer.OnCompleted();
    _observers.Clear();
}
```

Our EndRecoding method is looping through the collection of _observers and triggering the OnCompleted() method explicitly. Finally, it cleared the _observers collection.

Now, let's discuss the ProductReporter class. This class is an example of the implementation of the IObserver<T> interface. Consider the following code:

```
public void OnCompleted()
{
    PrepReportData(true, $"Report has completed: {Name}");
    Unsubscribe();
}

public void OnError(Exception error) => PrepReportData(false, $"Error ocurred with instance: {Name}");

public void OnNext(Product value)
{
    var msg =
        $"Reporter:{Name}. Product - Name: {value.Name},
```

Reactive Programming Patterns and Techniques

```
    Price:{value.Price},Desc: {value.Description}";
        PrepReportData(true, msg);
}
```

The `IObserver<T>` interface has the `OnComplete`, `OnError`, and `OnNext` methods that we have to implement in the `ProductReporter` class. The purpose of the `OnComplete` method is to notify the subscriber that the job has been done and then flush out the code. Furthermore, `OnError` is invoked when an error occurs during execution, while `OnNext` provides information of the next element in the sequence of a stream.

In the following code, `PrepReportData` is a value addition that gives the user a formatted report about all the operations of the process:

```
    private void PrepReportData(bool isSuccess, string message)
    {
        var model = new MessageViewModel
        {
            MsgId = Guid.NewGuid().ToString(),
            IsSuccess = isSuccess,
            Message = message
        };

        Reporter.Add(model);
    }
```

The preceding method is simply making additions to our `Reporter` collection, which is a collection of `MessageViewModel` classes. Note that, for simplicity purposes, you can also use the `ToString()` method that we have implemented in our `MessageViewModel` class.

The following code snippet shows the `Subcribe` and `Unsubscribe` methods:

```
    public virtual void Subscribe(IObservable<Product> provider)
    {
        if (provider != null)
            _unsubscriber = provider.Subscribe(this);
    }

    private void Unsubscribe() => _unsubscriber.Dispose();
```

The previous two methods tell the system that there is a provider. Subscribers could subscribe to the provider or unsubscribe/dispose of it upon completion of the operations.

[276]

Now it's time to showcase our implementation and see some good results. To do so, we need to make some changes to our existing `Product Listing` page and add a new **View page** to our project.

Add the following link to our `Index.cshtml` page so that we can see the new link to view **Audit Report**:

```
<a asp-action="Report">Audit Report</a>
```

In the preceding code snippet, we added a new link to show the **Audit Report** based on our implementation of the `Report Action` method, which we have defined in our `ProductController` class.

After adding this code, our **Product Listing** page will look as follows:

Product Name	Description	Image	Price (INR)	Discount Rate	Discount (INR)	Net Price (INR)	Category Name	Action
Mango	A juicy mango		40.00	5.00	2.00	38.00	Fruit	Edit | Details | Delete
Apple	Red apple		100.00	10.00	10.00	90.00	Fruit	Edit | Details | Delete
Orange	Fruity oranges		35.00	3.00	1.05	33.95	Fruit	Edit | Details | Delete

© 2019 - FlixOne.Web - Privacy

First, let's discuss the `Report action` method. For this, consider the following code:

```
var mango = _repositry.GetProduct(new Guid("09C2599E-652A-4807-
A0F8-390A146F459B"));
var apple = _repositry.GetProduct(new Guid("7AF8C5C2-FA98-42A0-
B4E0-6D6A22FC3D52"));
var orange = _repositry.GetProduct(new Guid("E2A8D6B3-
A1F9-46DD-90BD-7F797E5C3986"));
var model = new List<MessageViewModel>();
//provider
ProductRecorder productProvider = new ProductRecorder();
//observer1
```

Reactive Programming Patterns and Techniques

```
ProductReporter productObserver1 = new ProductReporter(nameof(mango));
//observer2
ProductReporter productObserver2 = new ProductReporter(nameof(apple));
//observer3
ProductReporter productObserver3 = new ProductReporter(nameof(orange));
```

In the preceding code, we are only taking the first three products for demonstration purposes. Please note that you can modify the code as per your own implementation. In the code, we have created a `productProvider` class and three observers to subscribe to our `productProvider` class.

The following diagram is a pictorial view of all the activities to showcase the `IObservable<T>` and `IObserver<T>` interfaces that we have discussed:

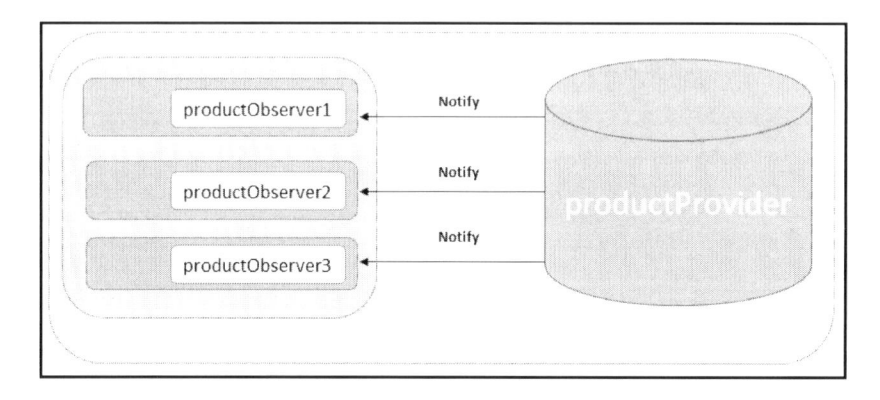

The following code is used to subscribe to `productrovider`:

```
//subscribe
productObserver1.Subscribe(productProvider);
productObserver2.Subscribe(productProvider);
productObserver3.Subscribe(productProvider);
```

Finally, we need to log the report and then unsubscribe:

```
//Report and Unsubscribe
productProvider.Record(mango);
model.AddRange(productObserver1.Reporter);
productObserver1.Unsubscribe();
productProvider.Record(apple);
model.AddRange(productObserver2.Reporter);
productObserver2.Unsubscribe();
productProvider.Record(orange);
model.AddRange(productObserver3.Reporter);
productObserver3.Unsubscribe();
```

[278]

Let's come back to our screen and add the `Report.cshtml` file to **Views** | **Product**. The following code is part of our **Report** page. You can find the complete code in the `Product` folder:

```
@model IEnumerable<MessageViewModel>

    <thead>
    <tr>
        <th>
            @Html.DisplayNameFor(model => model.IsSuccess)
        </th>
        <th>
            @Html.DisplayNameFor(model => model.Message)
        </th>
    </tr>
    </thead>
```

This code will create a header for the columns of our table that shows the audit report.

The following code will complete the table and add values to the `IsSuccess` and `Message` columns:

```
    <tbody>
    @foreach (var item in Model)
    {
        <tr>
            <td>
                @Html.HiddenFor(modelItem => item.MsgId)
                @Html.DisplayFor(modelItem => item.IsSuccess)
            </td>
            <td>
                @Html.DisplayFor(modelItem => item.Message)
            </td>

        </tr>
    }
    </tbody>
</table>
```

Reactive Programming Patterns and Techniques

At this point, we are done with our implementation of the observer pattern using `IObservable<T>` and `IObserver<T>` interfaces. Run the project by pressing *F5* in Visual Studio, click on **Product** in the home page, and then click on the **Audit Report** link. From here, you will see that the audit report of our selected products, as shown in the following screenshot:

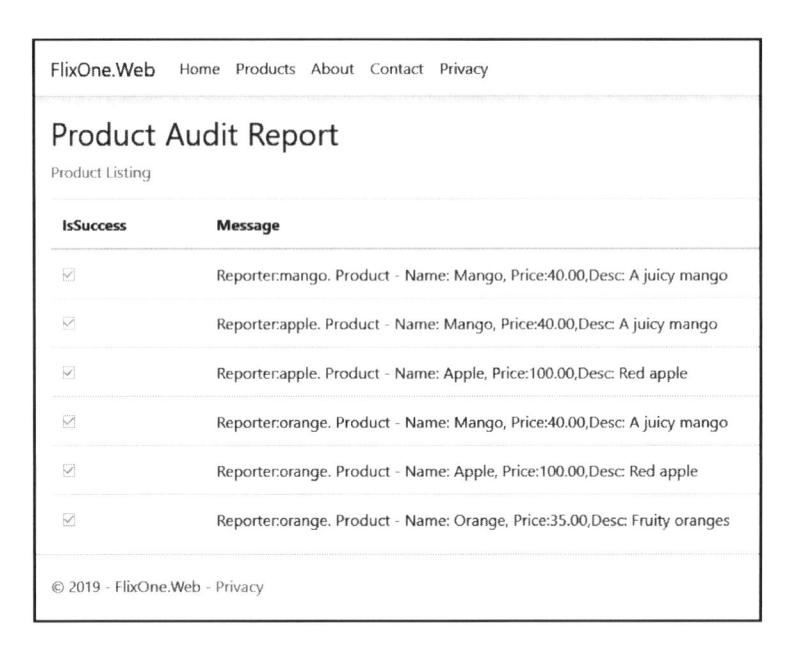

The preceding screenshot shows a simple listing page that shows the data from a `MessageViewModel` class. You can make the changes and modify them as per your requirement. In general, audit reports are coming from a lot of operational activities that we are seeing in the preceding screen. You could also save the audited data in the database and then serve this data accordingly for different purposes such as for reporting to admin and more.

Reactive extensions – .NET Rx extensions

The discussion in the previous session was aimed at reactive programming and the implementation of reactive programming using the `IObservable<T>` and `IObserver<T>` interfaces as an observer pattern. In this section, we will extend our learning with the help of **Rx Extensions**. If you would like to find out more about the development of Rx Extensions, you should follow the official repository at `https://github.com/dotnet/reactive`.

Please note that Rx Extensions are now merged with the `System` namespace, and you can find everything in the `System.Reactive` namespace. If you have experience with Rx Extensions, you should know that the namespace of these extensions has been changed, as follows:

- `Rx.Main` has been changed to `System.Reactive`.
- `Rx.Core` has been changed to `System.Reactive.Core`.
- `Rx.Interfaces` has been changed to `System.Reactive.Interfaces`.
- `Rx.Linq` has been changed to `System.Reactive.Linq`.
- `Rx.PlatformServices` has been changed to `System.Reactive.PlatformServices`.
- `Rx.Testing` has been changed to `Microsoft.Reactive.Testing`.

To initiate Visual Studio, open the `SimplyReactive` project (discussed in the previous section) and open the **NuGet Package Manager.** Click on **Browse** and enter the search term `System.Reactive`. From here, you will see the following results:

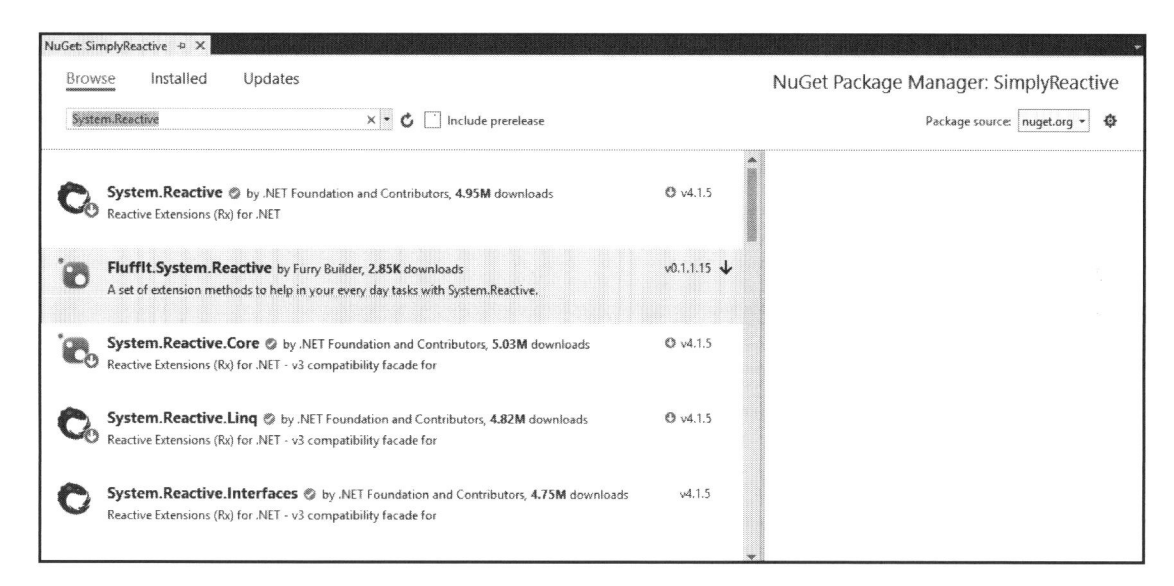

The aim of this section is to make you aware of reactive extensions but not delve into its internal development. These extensions are under the Apache2.0 license and maintained by .NET Foundation. We have already implemented reactive extensions in our `SimplyReactive` application.

Inventory application use case

In this section, we will continue with our FlixOne inventory application. Throughout this section, we will discuss the web application pattern and extend our web application developed in `Chapter 4`, *Implementing Design Patterns - Basics Part 2*.

> This chapter continues looking at web applications that were discussed in the previous chapter. If you skipped the previous chapter (`Chapter 9`, *Functional Programming Practices*), please revisit it to get up to speed with the current chapter.

In this section, we will go through the process of requirement gathering and then discuss the various challenges of development and business with our web application that we developed previously.

Starting the project

In `Chapter 7`, *Implementing Design Patterns for Web Applications - Part 2*, we added features to our FlixOne inventory web application. We extended the application after considering the following points:

- The business needs a rich UI.
- New opportunities demand a responsive web application.

Requirements

After several meetings and discussions with management, **Business Analyst** (**BA**), and presales folks, the management of the organization decided to work upon the following high-level requirements.

Business requirements

Our business team listed the following requirements:

- **Item filtering**: Currently, users are unable to filter items by category. To extend the list-view feature, the user should be able to filter the product item based on its respective category.
- **Item sorting**: Currently, items are appearing in the order in which they have been added to the database. There is no mechanism where a user can sort items based on the item's name, price, and so on.

Chapter 10

> The FlixOne inventory management web application is an imaginary product. We are creating this application to discuss the various design patterns required/used in the web project.

Getting inventory with a filter, paging, and sorting

As per our business requirements, we need to apply a filter, paging, and sorting to our FlixOne inventory application. First, let's start implementing the sorting. To do so, I've created a project and put this project in the `FlixOneWebExtended` folder. Start Visual Studio and open the FlixOne solution. We will apply to sort to our product listing sheet for these columns: `Category`, `productName`, `Description`, and `Price`. Please note that we will not be using any external component for sorting, but we will create our own login.

Open the **Solution Explorer**, and open `ProductController`, which is available in the `Controllers` folder. Add the `[FromQuery]Sort sort` parameter to the `Index` method. Please note that the `[FromQuery]` attribute indicates that this parameter is a query parameter. We will use this parameter to maintain our sorting order.

The following code shows the `Sort` class:

```
public class Sort
{
    public SortOrder Order { get; set; } = SortOrder.A;
    public string ColName { get; set; }
    public ColumnType ColType { get; set; } = ColumnType.Text;
}
```

The `Sort` class contains three public properties as detailed here:

- `Order`: Indicates the sorting order. The `SortOrder` is an enum defined as `public enum SortOrder { D, A, N }`.
- `ColName`: Indicates the column name.
- `ColType`: Indicates the type of a column; `ColumnType` is an enum defined as `public enum ColumnType { Text, Date, Number }`.

[283]

Reactive Programming Patterns and Techniques

Open the `IInventoryRepositry` interface, and add the `IEnumerable<Product> GetProducts(Sort sort)` method. This method is responsible for sorting the results. Please note that we are going to use LINQ queries to apply sorting. Implement this `InventoryRepository` class method and add the following code:

```
public IEnumerable<Product> GetProducts(Sort sort)
{
    if(sort.ColName == null)
        sort.ColName = "";
    switch (sort.ColName.ToLower())
    {
        case "categoryname":
        {
            var products = sort.Order == SortOrder.A
                ? ListProducts().OrderBy(x => x.Category.Name)
                : ListProducts().OrderByDescending(x => x.Category.Name);
            return PDiscounts(products);

        }
```

The following code is handling the case when `sort.ColName` is productname:

```
        case "productname":
        {
            var products = sort.Order == SortOrder.A
                ? ListProducts().OrderBy(x => x.Name)
                : ListProducts().OrderByDescending(x => x.Name);
            return PDiscounts(products);
        }
```

The following code is handling the case when `sort.ColName` is productprice:

```
        case "productprice":
        {
            var products = sort.Order == SortOrder.A
                ? ListProducts().OrderBy(x => x.Price)
                : ListProducts().OrderByDescending(x => x.Price);
            return PDiscounts(products);
        }
        default:
            return PDiscounts(ListProducts().OrderBy(x => x.Name));
    }
}
```

In the previous code, we set the value of the sort parameter as blank if it contains a null value, and then we process it by using switch..case in sort.ColName.ToLower().

The following is our ListProducts() method that gives us the result of the IIncludeIQuerable<Product,Category> type:

```
private IIncludableQueryable<Product, Category> ListProducts() =>
    _inventoryContext.Products.Include(c => c.Category);
```

The preceding code simply gives us Products by including Categories for each product. The sorting order will come from our user, so we need to modify our Index.cshtml page. We also need to add an anchor tag to the header columns of the table. For this, consider the following code:

```
<thead>
    <tr>
        <th>
            @Html.ActionLink(Html.DisplayNameFor(model => model.CategoryName), "Index", new Sort { ColName = "CategoryName", ColType = ColumnType.Text, Order = SortOrder.A })
        </th>
        <th>
            @Html.ActionLink(Html.DisplayNameFor(model => model.ProductName), "Index", new Sort { ColName = "ProductName", ColType = ColumnType.Text, Order = SortOrder.A })
        </th>
        <th>
            @Html.ActionLink(Html.DisplayNameFor(model => model.ProductDescription), "Index", new Sort { ColName = "ProductDescription", ColType = ColumnType.Text, Order = SortOrder.A })
        </th>
    </tr>
</thead>
```

The preceding code show the header columns of the table; new Sort { ColName = "ProductName", ColType = ColumnType.Text, Order = SortOrder.A } is the main way we are implementing SorOrder.

Run the application and you will see the following snapshot of the **Product Listing** page with the sorting feature:

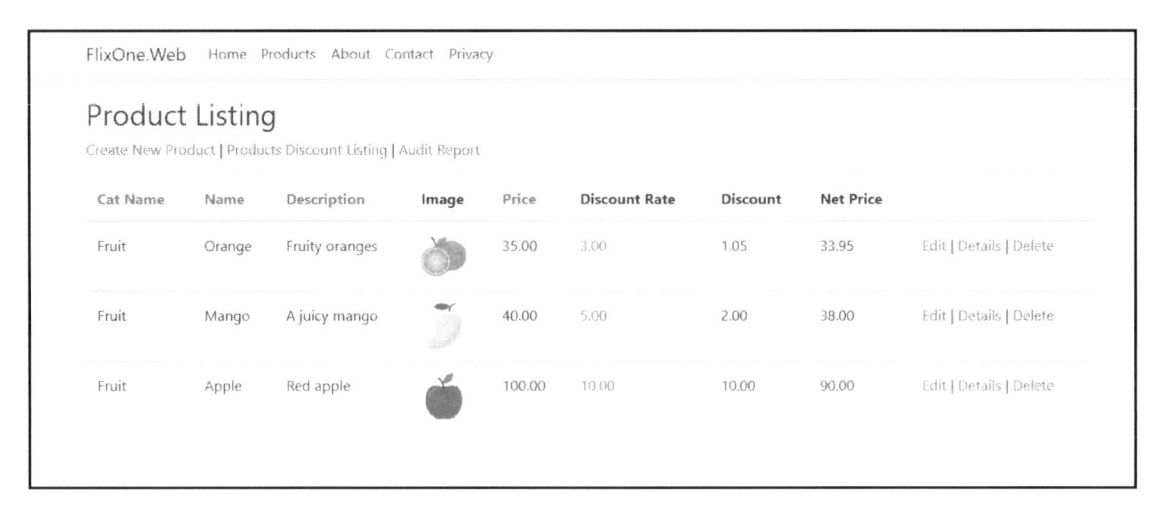

Cat Name	Name	Description	Image	Price	Discount Rate	Discount	Net Price	
Fruit	Orange	Fruity oranges		35.00	3.00	1.05	33.95	Edit | Details | Delete
Fruit	Mango	A juicy mango		40.00	5.00	2.00	38.00	Edit | Details | Delete
Fruit	Apple	Red apple		100.00	10.00	10.00	90.00	Edit | Details | Delete

Now, open the `Index.cshtml` page, and add the following code to the page:

```
@using (Html.BeginForm())
{
    <p>
        Search by: @Html.TextBox("searchTerm")
        <input type="submit" value="Search" class="btn-sm btn-success" />
    </p>
}
```

In the preceding code, we are adding a textbox under `Form`. Here, the user inputs the data/value, and this data submits to the server as soon as the user clicks the submit button. At the server side, the filtered data will returned back and show the product listing. After the implementation of the preceding code, our **Product Listing** page will look like this:

Product Listing

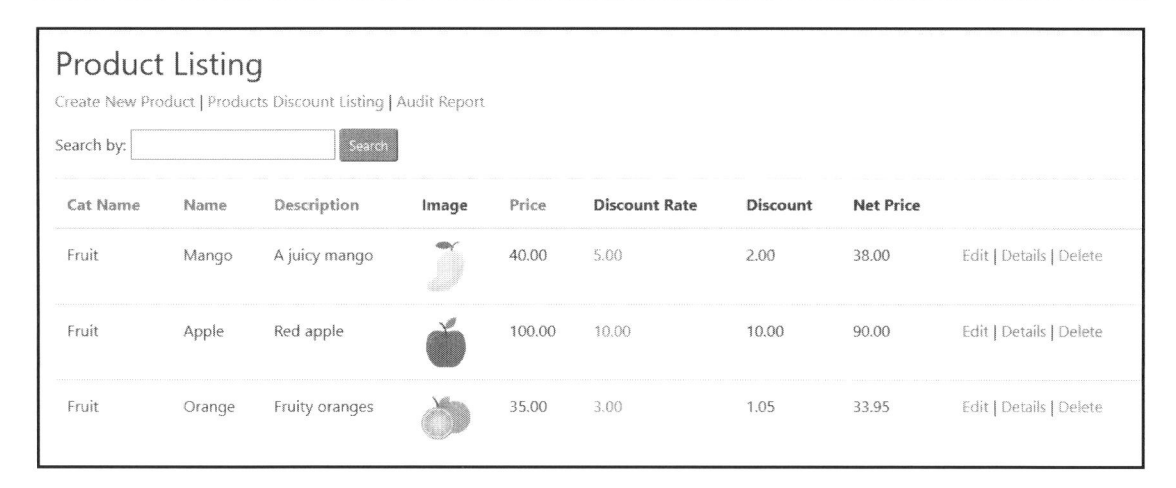

Create New Product | Products Discount Listing | Audit Report

Search by: [_____] [Search]

Cat Name	Name	Description	Image	Price	Discount Rate	Discount	Net Price	
Fruit	Mango	A juicy mango		40.00	5.00	2.00	38.00	Edit	Details	Delete
Fruit	Apple	Red apple		100.00	10.00	10.00	90.00	Edit	Details	Delete
Fruit	Orange	Fruity oranges		35.00	3.00	1.05	33.95	Edit	Details	Delete

Go to the `Index` method in `ProductController` and change the parameters. Now the `Index` method looks like this:

```
public IActionResult Index([FromQuery]Sort sort, string searchTerm)
{
    var products = _repositry.GetProducts(sort, searchTerm);
    return View(products.ToProductvm());
}
```

Similarly, we need to update the method parameters of `GetProducts()` in `InventoryRepository` and `InventoryRepository`. The following is the code for the `InventoryRepository` class:

```
private IEnumerable<Product> ListProducts(string searchTerm = "")
{
    var includableQueryable = _inventoryContext.Products.Include(c =>
c.Category).ToList();
    if (!string.IsNullOrEmpty(searchTerm))
    {
        includableQueryable = includableQueryable.Where(x =>
            x.Name.Contains(searchTerm) ||
x.Description.Contains(searchTerm) ||
            x.Category.Name.Contains(searchTerm)).ToList();
    }

    return includableQueryable;
}
```

Reactive Programming Patterns and Techniques

Now run the project by pressing *F5* from Visual Studio and navigating to the filter/search option in **Product Listing**. For this, see this snapshot:

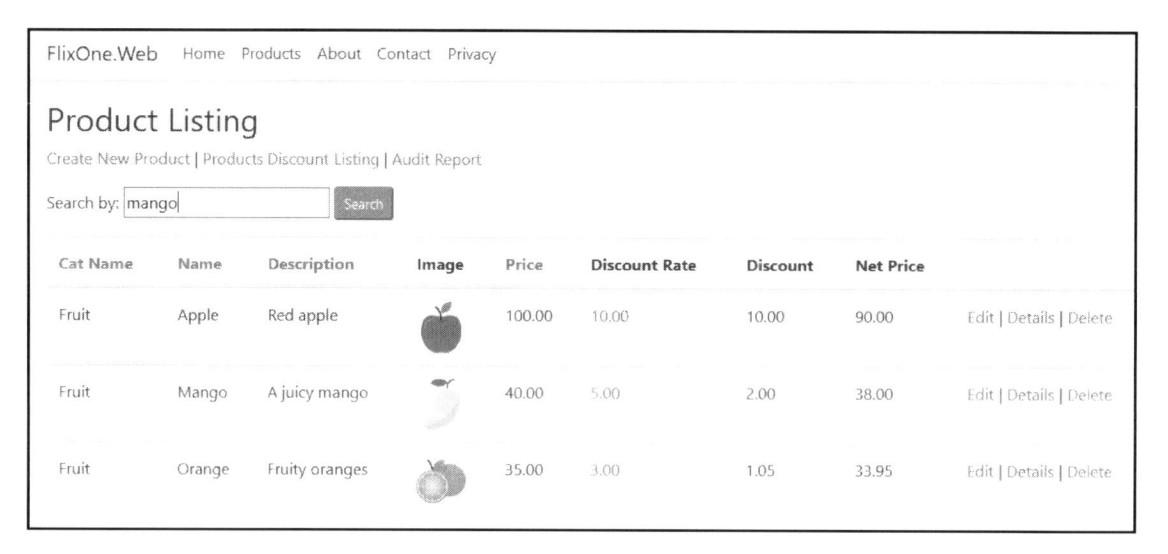

After entering your search term, click on the **Search** button, and this will give you the results, as shown in the following snapshot:

Chapter 10

In the preceding **Product Listing** screenshot, we are filtering our **Product** records with `searchTerm mango`, and it produces single results, as shown in the previous snapshot. There is one issue in this approach for searching data: add `fruit` as a search term, and see what will happen. It will produce zero results. This is demonstrated in the following snapshot:

We do not get any result, which means our search is not working when we are putting `searchTerm` in lowercase. This means our search is case-sensitive. We need to change our code to get it started.

Here is our modified code:

```
var includableQueryable = _inventoryContext.Products.Include(c =>
c.Category).ToList();
if (!string.IsNullOrEmpty(searchTerm))
{
    includableQueryable = includableQueryable.Where(x =>
        x.Name.Contains(searchTerm,
StringComparison.InvariantCultureIgnoreCase) ||
        x.Description.Contains(searchTerm,
StringComparison.InvariantCultureIgnoreCase) ||
        x.Category.Name.Contains(searchTerm,
StringComparison.InvariantCultureIgnoreCase)).ToList();
}
```

[289]

We are ignoring the case to make our search case-insensitive. We used `StringComparison.InvariantCultureIgnoreCase` and ignored the case. Now our search will work with either capital or lowercase letters. The following is the snapshot that produces results using lowercase `fruit`:

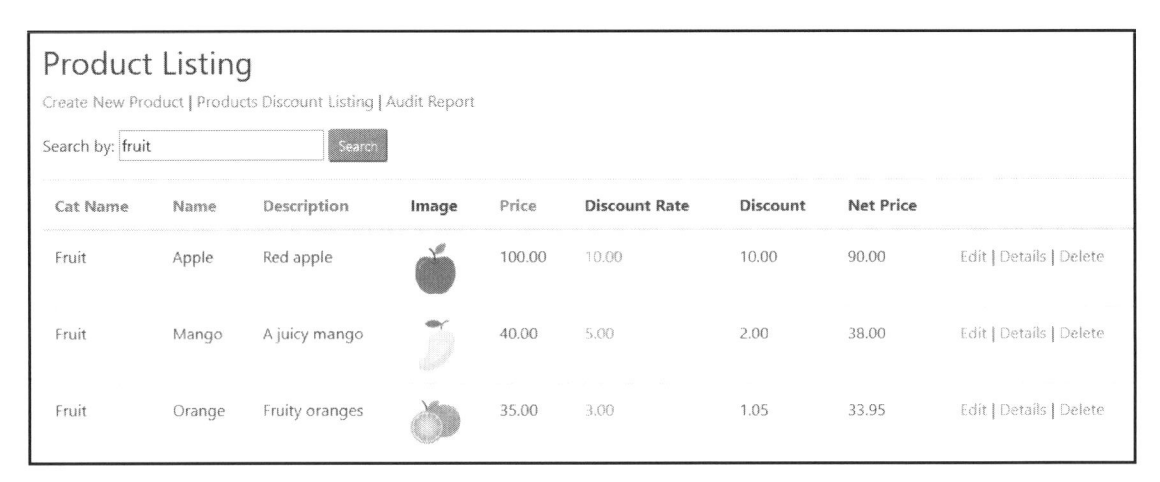

Product Listing

Create New Product | Products Discount Listing | Audit Report

Search by: fruit   [Search]

Cat Name	Name	Description	Image	Price	Discount Rate	Discount	Net Price	
Fruit	Apple	Red apple		100.00	10.00	10.00	90.00	Edit | Details | Delete
Fruit	Mango	A juicy mango		40.00	5.00	2.00	38.00	Edit | Details | Delete
Fruit	Orange	Fruity oranges		35.00	3.00	1.05	33.95	Edit | Details | Delete

In a previous discussion during the FlixOne app extension, we applied `Sort` and `Filter`; now we need to add `paging`. To do so, we have added a new class named, `PagedList` as follows:

```
public class PagedList<T> : List<T>
{
    public PagedList(List<T> list, int totalRecords, int currentPage, int recordPerPage)
    {
        CurrentPage = currentPage;
        TotalPages = (int) Math.Ceiling(totalRecords / (double) recordPerPage);

        AddRange(list);
    }
}
```

Now, change the parameters of the `Index` method of `ProductController` as follows:

```
public IActionResult Index([FromQuery] Sort sort, string searchTerm,
    string currentSearchTerm,
    int? pagenumber,
    int? pagesize)
```

Add the following code to the `Index.cshtml` page:

```
@{
    var prevDisabled = !Model.HasPreviousPage ? "disabled" : "";
    var nextDisabled = !Model.HasNextPage ? "disabled" : "";
}

<a asp-action="Index"
    asp-route-sortOrder="@ViewData["CurrentSort"]"
    asp-route-pageNumber="@(Model.CurrentPage - 1)"
    asp-route-currentFilter="@ViewData["currentSearchTerm"]"
    class="btn btn-sm btn-success @prevDisabled">
    Previous
</a>
<a asp-action="Index"
    asp-route-sortOrder="@ViewData["CurrentSort"]"
    asp-route-pageNumber="@(Model.CurrentPage + 1)"
    asp-route-currentFilter="@ViewData["currentSearchTerm"]"
    class="btn btn-sm btn-success @nextDisabled">
    Next
</a>
```

The preceding code makes it possible to move our screen to the next or the previous page. Our final screen will look like this:

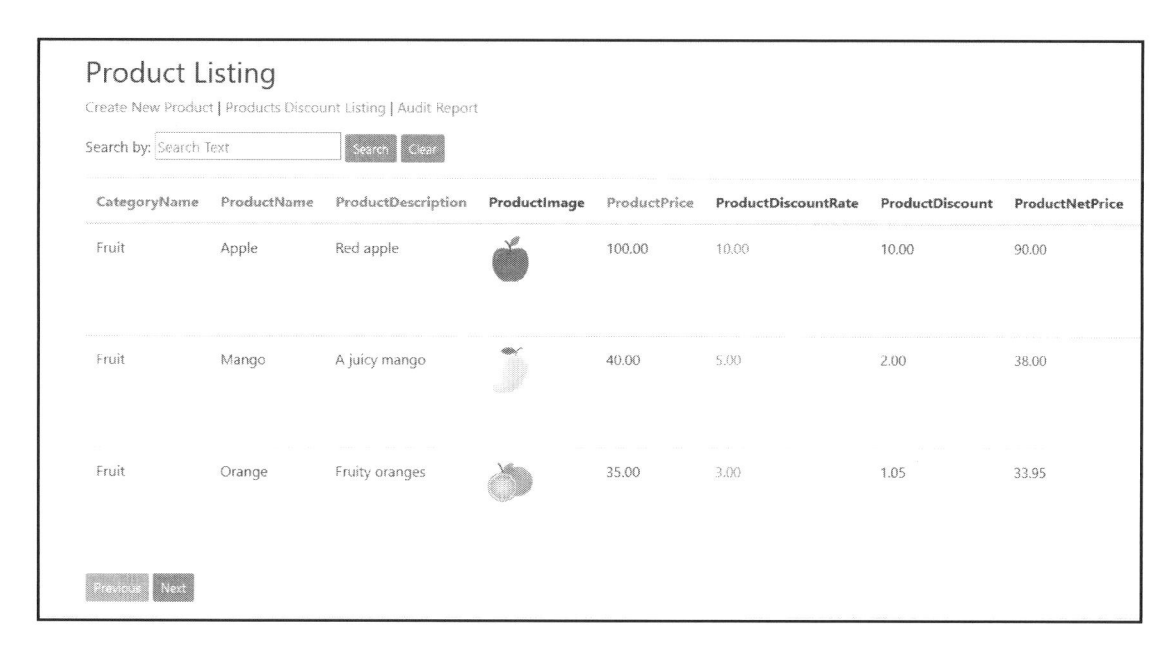

Product Listing

Create New Product | Products Discount Listing | Audit Report

Search by: [Search Text] [Search] [Clear]

CategoryName	ProductName	ProductDescription	ProductImage	ProductPrice	ProductDiscountRate	ProductDiscount	ProductNetPrice
Fruit	Apple	Red apple		100.00	10.00	10.00	90.00
Fruit	Mango	A juicy mango		40.00	5.00	2.00	38.00
Fruit	Orange	Fruity oranges		35.00	3.00	1.05	33.95

[Previous] [Next]

In this section, we have discussed and extended the features of our FlixOne application by implementing `Sorting`, `Paging`, and `Filter`. The aim of this section was to give you hands-on experience with a working application. We have coded our application in such a way that it will directly meet real-world applications. With the preceding enhancement, our application is now capable of giving a product listing that can be sorted, paginated, and filtered.

Patterns and Practices – MVVM

In `Chapter 6`, *Implementing Design Patterns for Web Applications - Part 1*, we discussed the **MVC** pattern and created an application based on this.

Ken Cooper and Ted Peters are the names behind the invention of the MVVM pattern. At the time of this invention, both Ken and Ted were architects at the Microsoft Corporation. They made this pattern to simplify the UI of event-driven programming. Later on, it was implemented in **Windows Presentation Foundation** (**WPF**) and **Silverlight**.

> The MVVM pattern was announced in 2005 by John Gossman. John has blogged about this pattern in context with building WPF applications. The link for this is at `https://blogs.msdn.microsoft.com/johngossman/2005/10/08/introduction-to-modelviewviewmodel-pattern-for-building-wpf-apps/`.

MVVM is considered to be one of the variations of MVC to meet the modern **User Interface** (**UI**) development approach, where UI development is the core responsibility of designer/UI-developers rather than application developers. In this approach of development, a designer who is a graphical enthusiast and is focused on making a UI more attractive may or may not bother about the development part of the application. Generally, designers (UI persons) use various tools to make the UI more attractive. The UI can be made with a simple HTML, CSS, and so on, using rich controls of WPF or Silverlight.

> **Microsoft Silverlight** is a framework that helps to develop applications with a rich UI. Many developers refer to it as an alternative of Flash by Adobe. In July 2015, Microsoft announced that it was no longer supporting Silverlight. Microsoft announced the support of WPF in .NET Core 3.0 during its build (`https://developer.microsoft.com/en-us/events/build`). There is also a blog with more insight into the plan to support WPF found here: `https://devblogs.microsoft.com/dotnet/net-core-3-and-support-for-windows-desktop-applications/`.

The MVVM pattern can be elaborated with its various components as follows:

- **Model**: Holds data and does not care about any business logic in the application. I prefer to refer to this as a domain object because it holds the actual data of the application we are working with. In other words, we can say that a model is not responsible for making the data beautiful. For example, in a product model of our FlixOne application, a product model holds the value of various properties, and these describe a product by its name, description, category name, price, and more. These properties contain the actual data of the product, but the model is not responsible for making behavioral changes to any of the data. For example, it's not the responsibility of our product mode to format the product description to look perfect on the UI. On the other hand, many of our models contain validations and other computed properties. The main challenge is to maintain the pure and cleaned model, which means that the model should resemble the real-world model. In our case, our `product` model is called a **clean model**. A clean model is one that resembles the actual properties of real products. For example, if the `Product` model is storing the data of fruits, then it should show properties such as the color of fruits and so on. The following code is from a model of our imaginary application:

    ```
    export class Product {
      name: string;
      cat: string;
      desc: string;
    }
    ```

    Note that the preceding code is written in Angular. We will discuss Angular code in detail in the upcoming section, *Implementing MVVM*.

- **View**: This is a data representation for the end user to access via the UI. This simply displays the value of the data, and this value may or may not be formatted. For example, we can show the discount rate as 18% on the UI, while it would be stored as 18.00 in the model. The view can also responsible for behavioral changes. The view accepts user inputs; for example, there would be a view that provides a form/screen to add a new product. Also, the view can manage the user input such as the key pressed, detecting a keyword, and more. It could also be an active view or a passive view. The view that accepts the user input and manipulates the data model (properties) according to the user input is an active view. A passive view is one that does nothing. In other words, a view that is not associated with the model is a passive view, and this kind of view is manipulated by a controller.

- **ViewModel**: This works as a middleman between View and Model. Its responsibility is to make the presentation better. In our previous example, where View shows the discount rate as 18% but Model has a discount rate of 18.00, it is the responsibility of View Model to format 18.00 to 18% so that View can display the formatted discount rate.

If we combine all the points discussed, we can visualize the entire MVVM pattern, which would look like the following diagram:

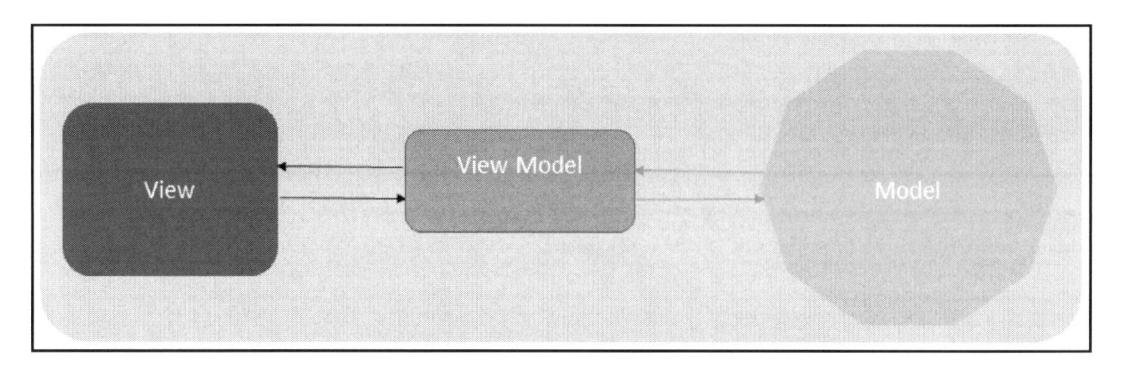

The preceding diagram is a pictorial view of MVVM, and it shows us that **View Model** separates **View** and **Model**. **ViewModel** also maintains the `state` and `perform` operations. This helps **View** to present the final output to the end user. The view is UI, which gets data and presents it to the end user. In the next section, we will implement the MVVM pattern using Angular.

Implementation of MVVM

In the previous section, we understood what the MVVM pattern is and how it works. In this section, we will use our FlixOne application and build an application using Angular. To demonstrate the MVVM pattern, we will use the API built on ASP.NET Core 2.2.

Chapter 10

Start **Visual Studio** and open **FlixOne Solution** from the `FlixOneMVVM` folder. Run the `FlixOne.API` project where you will see the following **Swagger** documentation page:

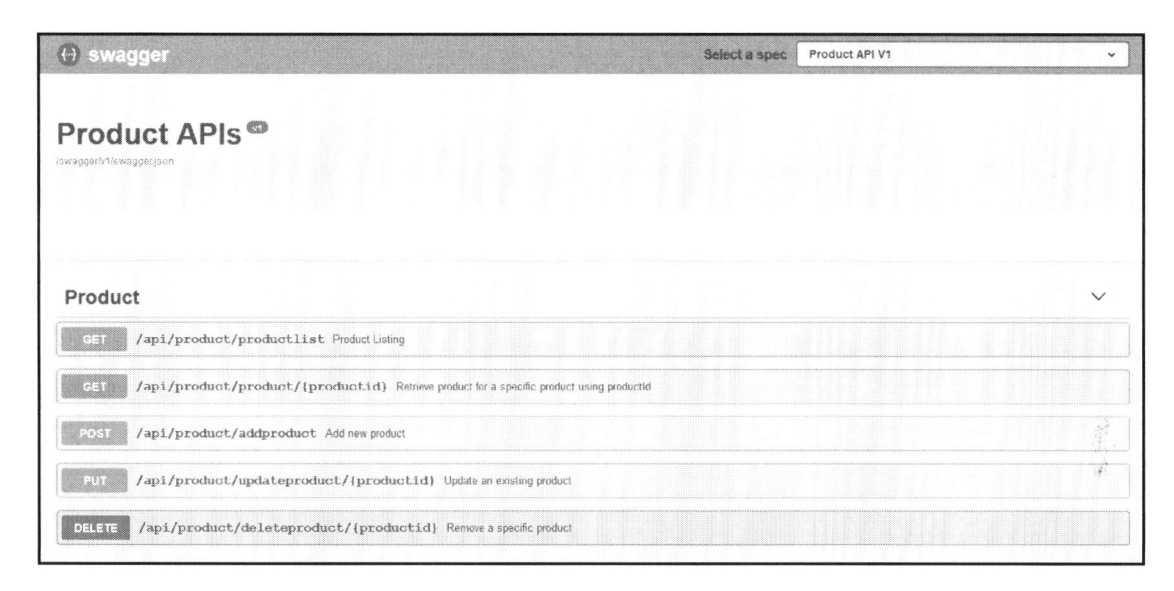

The preceding screenshot is the snapshot of our **Product APIs** documentation, where we have incorporated **Swagger** for the API documentation. If you want to, you can test the API from this screen. If the APIs are returning results, then your project is successfully set up. If not, please check the prerequisites for this project, and also check the `README.md` file from the Git repository for this chapter. We have everything that is required to build a new UI; as discussed previously, we will create an Angular application that will consume our Product APIs. To get started, follow these steps:

1. Open the **Solution Explorer**.
2. Right-click on **FlixOne Solution**.
3. Click on **Add New Project**.

[295]

Reactive Programming Patterns and Techniques

4. From the **Add New Project** window, select **ASP.NET Core Web Application**. Call it **FlixOne.Web** and click **OK**. After doing so, refer to this screenshot:

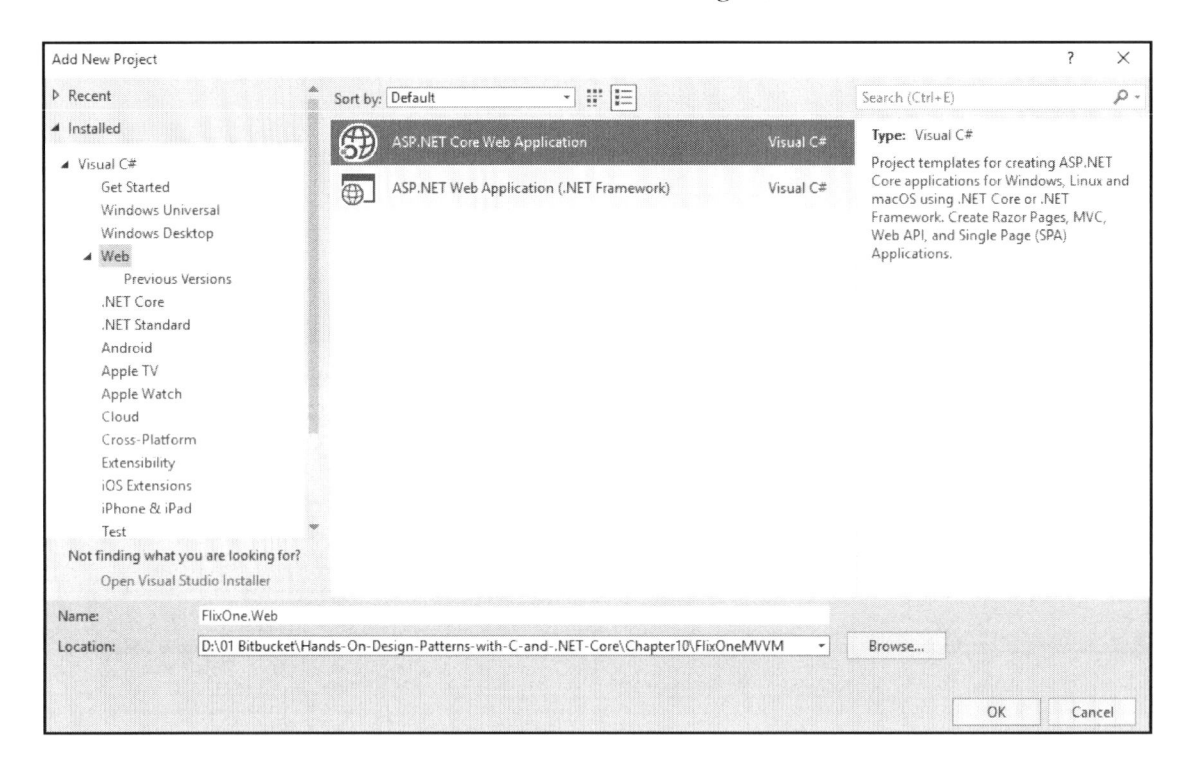

Chapter 10

5. From the next window, select **Angular**, make sure you have selected **ASP.NET Core 2.2**, click **OK**, and refer to this screenshot:

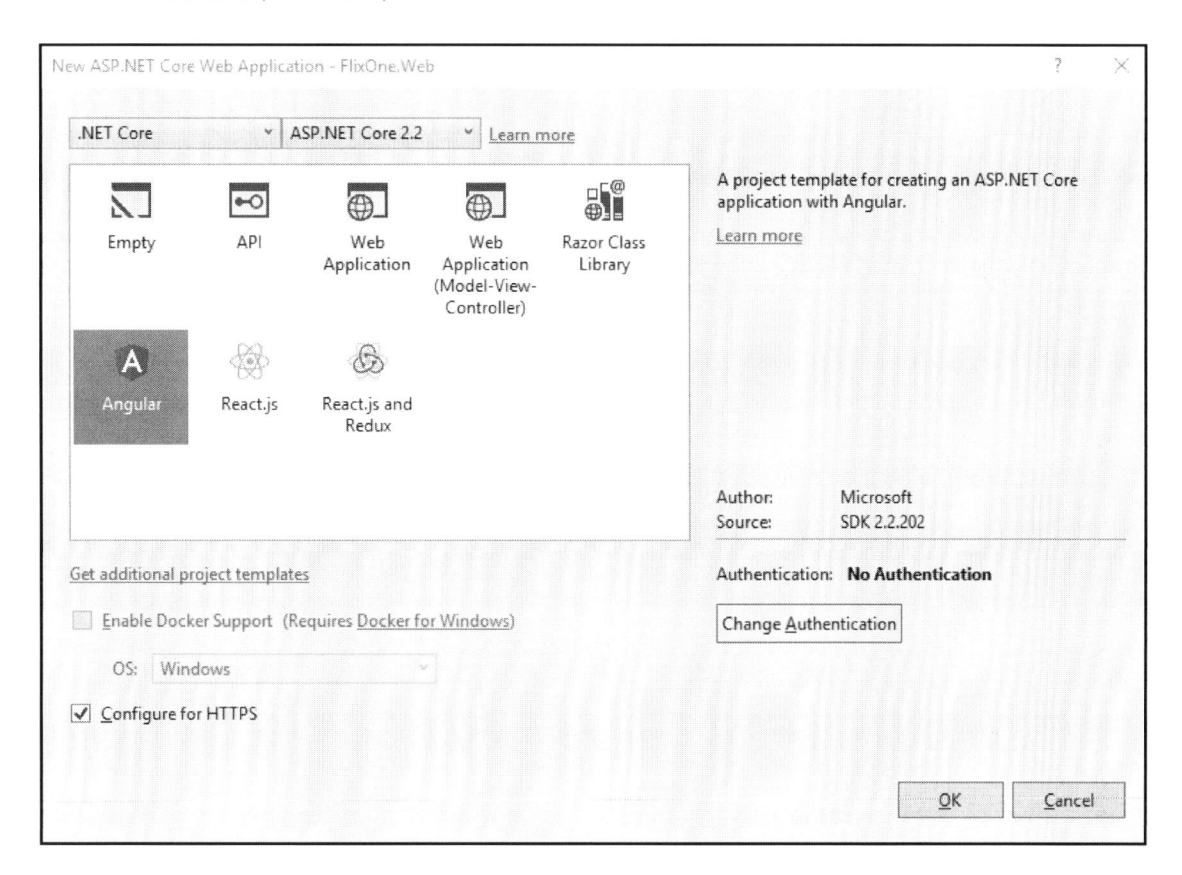

6. Open **Solution Explorer** and you will find the new `FlixOne.Web` project and folder hierarchy, which looks like this:

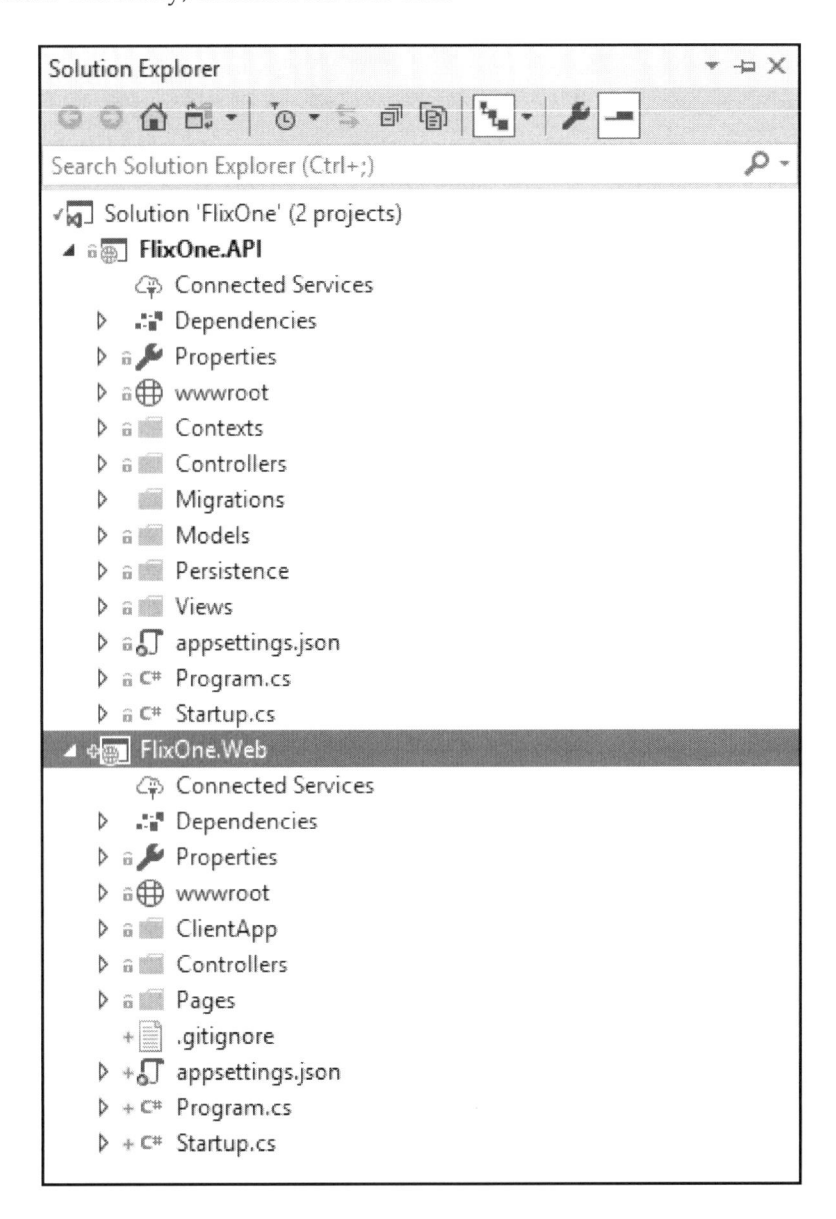

```
Solution Explorer
Solution 'FlixOne' (2 projects)
    FlixOne.API
        Connected Services
        Dependencies
        Properties
        wwwroot
        Contexts
        Controllers
        Migrations
        Models
        Persistence
        Views
        appsettings.json
        Program.cs
        Startup.cs
    FlixOne.Web
        Connected Services
        Dependencies
        Properties
        wwwroot
        ClientApp
        Controllers
        Pages
        .gitignore
        appsettings.json
        Program.cs
        Startup.cs
```

7. From the **Solution Explorer**, right-click on the **FlixOne.Web** project, and click on the **Set as Startup** project, and then refer to the following screenshot:

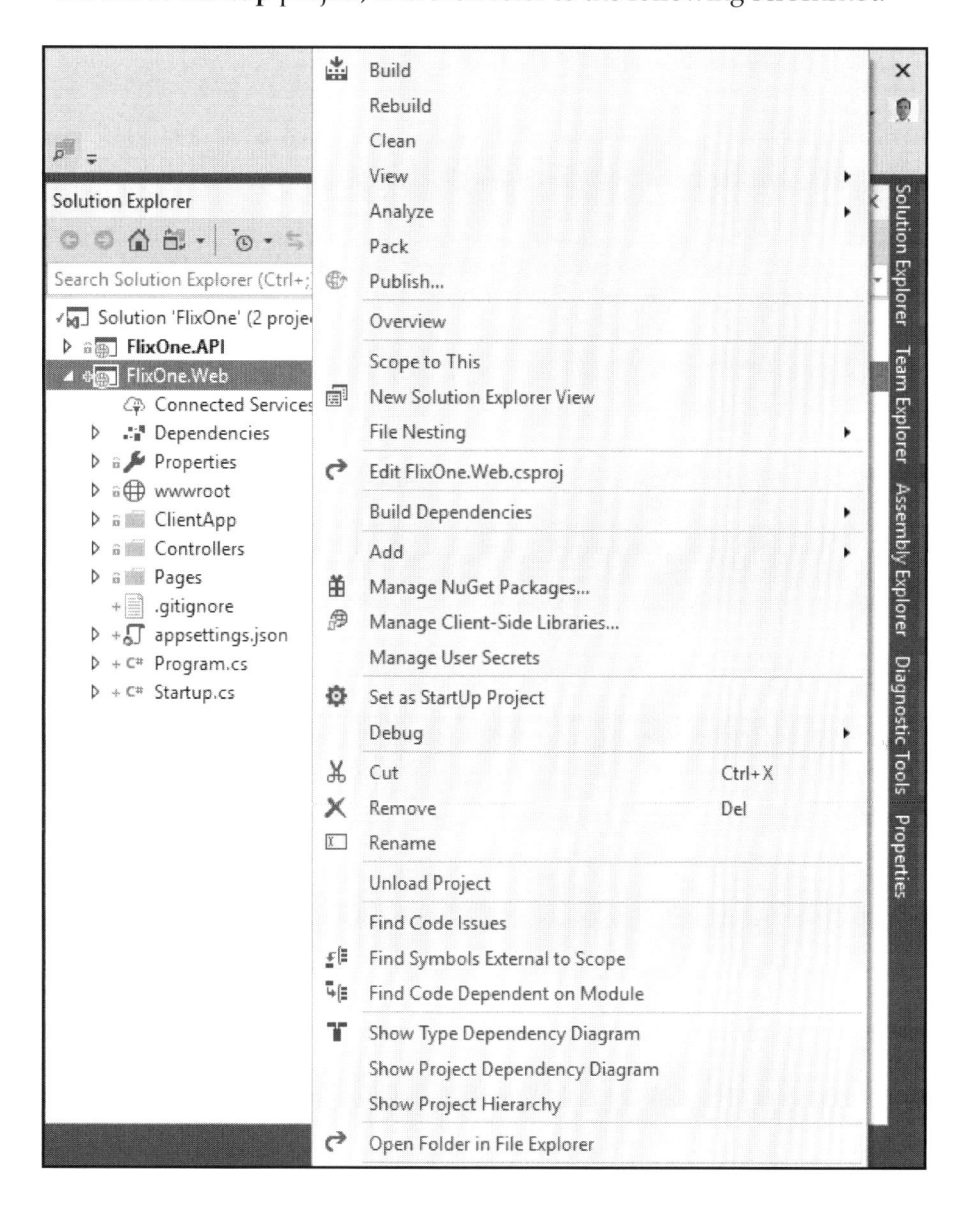

8. Run the `FlixOne.Web` project and see the output, which will look like the following screenshot:

We have set up our Angular app successfully. Go back to your **Visual Studio** and open the **Output** window. Refer to the following screenshot:

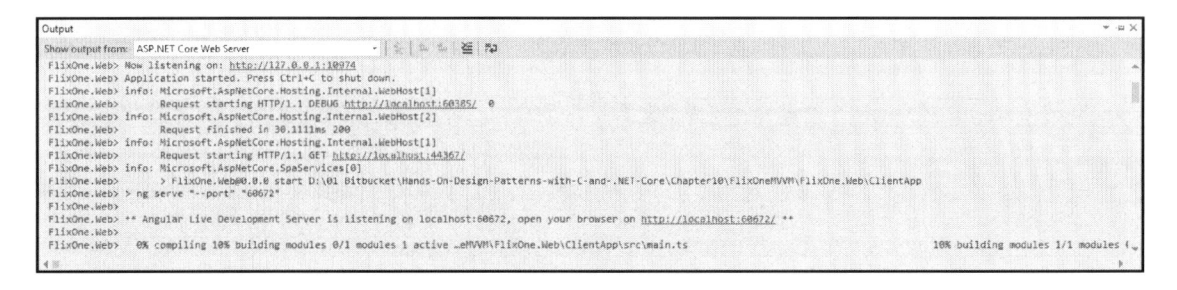

You will find `ng serve "--port" "60672"` from the **Output** window; this is a command that tells the Angular app to listen and serve. Open the `package.json` file from `Solution Explorer`; this file belongs to the `ClientApp` folder. You will notice `"@angular/core":"6.1.10"`, which means our application is built on `angular6`.

The following is the code of our `product.component.html` (this is a view):

```
<table class='table table-striped' *ngIf="forecasts">
  <thead>
    <tr>
      <th>Name</th>
      <th>Cat. Name (C)</th>
```

```
            <th>Price(F)</th>
            <th>Desc</th>
          </tr>
        </thead>
        <tbody>
          <tr *ngFor="let forecast of forecasts">
            <td>{{ forecast.productName }}</td>
            <td>{{ forecast.categoryName }}</td>
            <td>{{ forecast.productPrice }}</td>
            <td>{{ forecast.productDescription }}</td>
          </tr>
        </tbody>
      </table>
```

Run the application from Visual Studio, and click on **Product**, where you will get a **Product Listing** screen similar to this:

Name	Cat. Name	Price	Desc
Microservices Book		655	Building Microservices with .NET Core2.0
Mango		135	A juicy mango

FlixOne.Web — Home Product
Product Listing
Product Listing...

In this section, we have created a small demo application in Angular.

Summary

The aim of this chapter was to get you through the reactive programming by discussing its principles and the reactive programming model. Reactive is all about the data stream, which we have discussed with examples. We extended our example from Chapter 8, *Concurrent Programming in .NET Core*, where we discussed the use case of the ticket collection counter at a conference.

We explored the reactive system during our discussion of the reactive manifesto. We discussed the reactive system through the help of showcasing the `merge`, `filter`, and `map` operations, and how streams work with the help of examples. Also, we discussed the `IObservable` interface and the Rx extensions, using examples.

We carried forward our `FlixOne` inventory application and discussed the use cases to implement the paging and the sorting of inventory data for products. Finally, we discussed the MVVM pattern and created a small application on a MVVM architecture.

In the next chapter (`Chapter 11`, *Advanced Database Design and Application Techniques*), advanced database and application techniques will be explored, including applying **Command Query Responsibility Segregation** (**CQRS**) and a ledger-style database.

Questions

The following questions will allow you to consolidate the information contained in this chapter:

1. What is a stream?
2. What are reactive properties?
3. What is a reactive system?
4. What is meant by merging two reactive streams?
5. What is the MVVM pattern?

Further reading

To learn more about the topics covered in this chapter, refer to the following book. This book will provide you with various in-depth and hands-on exercises for reactive programming:

- *Reactive Programming for .NET Developers*, Antonio Esposito and Michael Ciceri, Packt Publishing: `https://www.packtpub.com/web-development/reactive-programming-net-developers`

11
Advanced Database Design and Application Techniques

In the previous chapter, we learned about reactive programming by discussing its principles and models. We also discussed and looked at examples of how reactive programming is all about data streams.

Database designing is a complex task and needs a lot of patience. In this chapter, we will discuss advanced database and application techniques, including applying **Command Query Responsibility Segregation** (**CQRS**) and ledger-style databases.

Similar to previous chapters, a requirement gathering session will be illustrated in order to determine the **Minimum Viable Product** (**MVP**). In this chapter, several factors will be used to lead the design to CQRS. We will be using a ledger-style approach that consists of increased tracking of changes to inventory levels, as well as wanting to provide public APIs for retrieving inventory levels. This chapter will cover why developers use ledger-style databases and why we should focus on CQRS implementation. In this chapter, we will see why we adapt the CQRS pattern.

The following topics will be covered in this chapter:

- Use case discussion
- Database discussion
- Ledger-style databases for inventory
- Implementing the CQRS pattern

Technical requirements

This chapter contains various code examples to explain the concepts. The code is kept simple and is just for demo purposes. Most of the examples involve a .NET Core console application written in C#.

To run and execute the code, Visual Studio 2019 is a prerequisite (you can also use Visual Studio 2017 to run the application).

Installing Visual Studio

To run these code examples, you need to install Visual Studio (preferred IDE). To do so, follow these instructions:

1. Download Visual Studio 2017 (or version 2019) from the following download link: `https://docs.microsoft.com/en-us/visualstudio/install/install-visual-studio`.
2. Follow the installation instructions that are accessible through the previous link. Multiple options are available for Visual Studio installation. Here, we are using Visual Studio for Windows.

Setting up .NET Core

If you do not have .NET Core installed, you will need to follow these instructions:

1. Download .NET Core for Windows: `https://www.microsoft.com/net/download/windows`.
2. For multiple versions and a related library, visit `https://dotnet.microsoft.com/download/dotnet-core/2.2`.

Installing SQL Server

If you do not have SQL Server installed, you need to follow these instructions:

1. Download SQL Server from the following link: `https://www.microsoft.com/en-in/download/details.aspx?id=1695`.
2. You can find the installation instructions at `https://docs.microsoft.com/en-us/sql/ssms/download-sql-server-management-studio-ssms?view=sql-server-2017`.

> For troubleshooting and for more information, refer to the following link: https://www.blackbaud.com/files/support/infinityinstaller/content/installermaster/tkinstallsqlserver2008r2.htm.

Use case discussion

In this chapter, we will continue with our FlixOne inventory application. Throughout this chapter, we will discuss CQRS patterns and extend the web application that we developed in the previous chapters.

> This chapter continues with the web application that was developed in the previous chapter. If you skipped the previous chapter, please revisit it in order to aid your understanding of the current chapter.

In this section, we will go through the process of requirement gathering, and then discuss the various challenges with our web application.

Project kickoff

In Chapter 7, *Implementing Design Patterns for Web Applications – Part 2*, we extended FlixOne Inventory and added authentication and authorization to the web application. We extended the application after considering the following points:

- The current application is open for all; therefore, any user can visit any page, even restricted pages.
- Users should not access pages that require access or special access rights; these pages are also known as restricted pages or pages with limited access.
- Users should be able to access pages/resources as per their roles.

Advanced Database Design and Application Techniques

In `Chapter 10`, *Reactive Programming Patterns and Techniques*, we further extended our FlixOne Inventory application and added paging, filtering, and sorting to all pages that show listings. The following points were considered while we extended the app:

- **Item filtering**: Currently, users are unable to filter items by their categories. To extend this feature, users should be able to filter product items based on their categories.
- **Item sorting**: Currently, items are appearing in the order in which they have been added to the database. There is no mechanism that enables the user to sort items based on categories such as item name or price.

Requirements

After several meetings and discussions with management, **Business Analyst** (**BA**), and pre-sales staff, management decided to work on the following high-level requirements: business requirements and technical requirements.

Business requirements

On the basis of discussions with stakeholders and endusers, and as per the market survey, our business team has listed the following requirements:

- **Product expansion**: The product is reaching different users. This is a good time to expand the application. The application will robust to expand after having expanded it.
- **Product model**: Being an inventory management application, users should feel freedom (this mean no restriction at model level, without complicated validations) and there should not be any restriction while users are interacting with the application. Every screen and page should be self-explanatory.
- **Database design**: The application's database should be designed in such a way that the expansion should not take much time.

Technical requirements

The actual requirements that meet business needs are now ready for development. After several discussions with business staff, we concluded that the following are the requirements:

- The following are the requirements for the **landing** or **home page**:
    - Should be a dashboard that contains various widgets
    - Should show an at-a-glance picture of the store
- The following are the requirements for the **product page**:
    - Should have the capability to add, update, and delete products
    - Should have the capability to add, update, and delete product categories

> The FlixOne Inventory Management web application is an imaginary product. We are creating this application to discuss the various design patterns that are required/used in web projects.

Challenges

Although we have extended our existing web application, it has various challenges for both developers and businesses. In this section, we will discuss these challenges and then we will find out the solutions to overcome these challenges.

Challenges for developers

The following are the challenges that arose due to a big change in the application. They were also a result of the major extensions associated with upgrading a console application to a web application:

- **No support for RESTful services**: Currently, there is no support for RESTful services because no APIs have been developed.
- **Limited security**: In the current application, there is only one mechanism that can restrict/permit the user from/to gaining access to a particular screen or module of the application: that is, by the login.

Challenges for businesses

The following challenges occur as we adapt a new technology stack, and there are plenty of changes in the code. Therefore, it takes time to achieve the final output, which delays the product, resulting in a loss for the business:

- **Loss of clientele**: Here, we are still in the development stage but the demand for our business is very high. However, the development team is taking longer than expected to deliver the product.
- **It takes more time to roll out the production updates**: Development efforts are time-consuming at the moment and this delays the subsequent activities, leading to a delay in production.

Providing a solution to the problems/challenges

After several meetings and brainstorming sittings, the development team came to the conclusion that we have to stabilize our web-based solution. To overcome these challenges and provide the solution, the tech team and business team got together to identify the various solutions and points.

The following are the points supported by the solution:

- Evolve RESTful webservices—there should be one API dashboard
- Strictly following **Test-Driven Development** (**TDD**)
- Re-designing the **user interface** (**UI**) to meet the user experience expectations

Database discussion

Before we start with the database discussion we have to consider the following points—a big picture of our FlixOne web application:

- One part of our application is inventory management, but another part of it is an e-commerce web application.
- The challenging part is that our application would also serve as a **Point Of Sale** (**POS**). In this part/module, the user can pay for the items they have purchased from offline counters/outlets.
- For the inventory part, we need to address which approach we will be taking to calculate and maintain accounts and transactions, and to determine the cost of any item sold.

- To maintain stock for inventories, various options are available, with the two most commonly used options being **First In First Out** (**FIFO**) and **Last In First Out** (**LIFO**).
- Most of the transactions involve financial data, hence these transactions require historical data. Every record should have the following information: current value, the value before current changes, and the changes made.
- While we're maintaining inventory, we are also required to maintain the items purchased.

There are more points that are important when designing a database for any e-commerce web application. We are limiting our scope for the FlixOne application in order to showcase the inventory and stock management.

Database processing

Similar to the other topics we have covered in this book, there are a large number of databases ranging from basic patterns concerning the schema of a database to patterns that govern how database systems are put together. This section will cover two system patterns, **Online Transaction Processing** (**OLTP**) and **Online Analytical Processing** (**OLAP**). To further understand database design patterns, we will explore a specific pattern, ledger-style databases, in more detail.

> A database schema is another word for the collection of tables, views, stored procedures, and other components that make up a database. Think of this as the *blueprint* of the database.

OLTP

An OLTP database has been designed to handle large numbers of statements that cause changes to the database. Basically, the `INSERT`, `UPDATE`, and `DELETE` statements all cause changes and behave very differently from the `SELECT` statement. OLTP databases have been designed with this in mind. Because these databases record changes, they are typically the *main* or *master* database, meaning that they are the repositories that hold the current data.

> The MERGE statement also qualifies as a statement that causes change. This is because it provides a convenient syntax for the insertion of a record when a row does not exist, and the insertion of an update when a row does exist. It will update when a row does exist. The MERGE statement is not supported in all database providers or versions.

OLTP databases are typically designed to process change statements quickly. This is normally done by the careful planning of table structures. A simple way of viewing this is to consider a database table. This table can have fields for storing data, keys for looking up the data efficiently, indexes to other tables, triggers to respond to specific situations, and other table constructs. Each one of these constructs has a performance penalty. The design of OLTP databases is, therefore, a balance between using the minimum number of constructs on a table versus the desired behavior.

Let's consider a table that records the books in our inventory system. Each book might record the name, quantity, date published, and have references to author information, publishers, and other related tables. We could put an index on all columns and even add indexes for the data in related tables. The problem with this approach is that each index has to be stored and maintained for each statement that causes change. Database designers have to carefully plan and analyze databases in order to determine the optimal combination of adding and, just as importantly, not adding indexes and other constructs to tables.

> A table index can be thought of like a virtual lookup table that provides the relational database with a faster way of looking up data.

OLAP

Databases designed using the OLAP pattern are expected to have more SELECT statements than statements that cause change. These databases usually have a consolidated view of the data of one or more databases. Because of this, these databases are usually not the master database, but a database used to provide reporting and analysis separate from the master database. In some situations, this is provided on infrastructure isolated from other databases so as to not impact the performance of operational databases. This type of deployment is often referred to as a **data warehouse**.

A data warehouse can be used to provide a consolidated view of a system or collection of systems within an enterprise. The data is traditionally fed with slower periodical jobs to refresh the data from other systems, but with modern database systems, this is trending towards near real-time consolidation.

The major difference between OLTP and OLAP is around how the data is stored and organized. In many situations, this would require tables or persistent views—depending on the technology used—to be created in the OLAP database that supports specific reporting scenarios and duplicates the data. In OLTP databases, duplication of data is undesirable as it then introduces multiple tables that need to be maintained for a single statement that causes change.

Ledger-style databases

The ledger-style database design will be highlighted, as it is both a pattern that has been used in many financial databases for decades and it may not be known to some developers. The ledger-style database stems from an accountant's ledger, where transactions were added to a document and the quantities and/or amounts are tallied in order to arrive at a final quantity or amount. The following table shows a ledger of the sale of apples:

Date	Purchaser	Amount	Price
5/05/2019	West Country Produce	100	$ 200.00
5/05/2019	Jim's Freshest	30	$ 60.00
5/07/2019	West Country Produce	-25	-$ 50.00
5/07/2019	Marlborogh Fair	70	$ 140.00
5/07/2019	West Country Produce	12	$ 30.00
5/07/2019	Marlborogh Fair	15	$ 30.00
6/07/2019	Coopers Colective	80	$ 160.00
		282	$ 570.00

There are a couple of things to point out about the example. The **Purchaser** information is written on separate rows instead of erasing their amounts and entering a new amount. Take the two purchases and one credit for **West Country Produce**. This is typically different from many databases in which a single row contains the **Purchaser** information with separate fields for the **Amount** and **Price**.

A ledger-style database takes this concept by having a separate row per transaction, thus removing the UPDATE and DELETE statements and only relying on INSERT statements. This has several benefits. Similarly to a ledger, once each transaction has been written it cannot be removed or changed. If a mistake or a change occurs, such as the credit to **West Country Produce**, a new transaction needs to be written in order to arrive at the desired state. An interesting benefit of this is that the source table now has the immediate value of providing a detailed log of the activity. If we were to add a **modified by** column, we could then have a comprehensive log of who or what made the change and what the change was.

> This example is for a single-entry ledger, but in the real world, a double-entry ledger would be used. The difference is that in a double-entry ledger, each transaction is recorded as a credit in one table and a debit in another.

The next challenge is capturing the final or rolled-up version of the table. In this example, that is that amount of apples that have been purchased and for how much. The first approach could use a SELECT statement that simply performs GROUP BY on the purchaser, as follows:

```
SELECT Purchaser, SUM(Amount), SUM(Price)
FROM Apples
GROUP BY Purchaser
```

While this would be fine for smaller data sizes, the issue here is that the performance of the query would degrade over time as the number of rows increases. An alternative would be to aggregate the data into another form. There are two main ways of achieving this. The first is to perform this activity at the same time as you write the information from the ledger table into another table (or persistent view if supported) that holds the data in an aggregate form.

> A **persistent** or **materialized view** is similar to a database view, but the results of the view are cached. This gives us the benefit of not requiring the view to be recalculated on each request, and it is either refreshed periodically or when the underlying data changes.

The second approach relies on another mechanism that is separate from the INSERT statement to retrieve the aggregated view when required. In some systems, the primary scenario of writing changes to a table and retrieving the result is performed less frequently. In this case, it would make more sense to optimize the database so that writes are faster than reads, therefore limiting the amount of processing required when new records are inserted.

The next section deals with an interesting pattern CQRS that can be applied at the database level. This could be used in the ledger-style database design.

Implementing the CQRS pattern

CQRS simply works on the separation between queries (to read) and commands (to modify). **Command-Query Separation (CQS)** is an approach to **Object-oriented Design (OOD)**.

> CQRS was introduced for the first time by Bertrand Meyer (https://en.wikipedia.org/wiki/Bertrand_Meyer). He mentioned this term in his book, *Object-Oriented Software Construction*, during the late 1980s: https://www.amazon.in/Object-Oriented-Software-Construction-Prentice-hall-International/dp/0136291554.

CQRS does fit well with some scenarios and has some useful factors to it:

- **Model separation**: In modeling terms, we are able to have multiple representations for our data model. The clear separation allows for choosing different frameworks or techniques over others that are more suitable for query or command. Arguably, this is achievable with **create, read, update, and delete (CRUD)**-style entities, although the single data layer assembly often emerges.
- **Collaboration**: In some enterprises, a separation between query and command would benefit the teams involved in building complex systems, particularly when some teams are more suited for different aspects of an entity. For example, a team that is more concerned about presentation could concentrate on the query model, while another team that is more focused on data integrity could maintain the command model.
- **Independent scalability**: Many solutions tend to either require more reads against the model, or more writes, depending on the business requirements.

> For CQRS, remember that commands update data and queries read data.

[313]

Advanced Database Design and Application Techniques

Some important things to note while working on CQRS are as follows:

- Commands should be placed asynchronously rather than as synchronous operations.
- Databases should never be modified with queries.

CQRS simplifies the design with the use of separate commands and queries. Also, we can physically separate read data from write data operations. In this arrangement, a read database could use a separate database schema, or in other words, we can say that it could use a read-only database that is optimized for queries.

As the database uses a physical separation approach, we can visualize the CQRS flow of the application, as depicted in the following diagram:

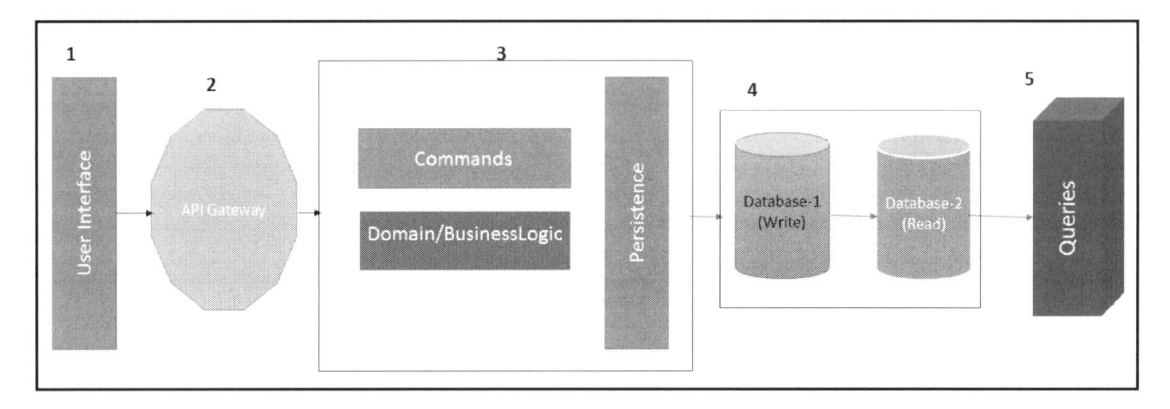

The preceding diagram depicts an imaginary workflow of the CQRS application, in which an application has physically separate databases for write operations and read operations. This imaginary application is based on RESTful web services (.NET Core APIs). No APIs have been exposed directly to the client/end user who is consuming these APIs. There is an API gateway exposed to users, and any requests for applications will come through the API gateway.

> **TIP**
> The API Gateway provides an entry point to groups with similar types of services. You can also simulate it with the facade pattern, which is part of the distributed system.

In the previous diagram, we have the following:

- **User interface**: This could be any client (who is consuming the APIs), web application, desktop application, mobile application, or any other application.
- **API Gateway**: Any request from UI and response to UI is delivered from the API Gateway. This is the main part of CQRS, as business logic can be incorporated by using the Commands and Persistence layers.
- **Database(s)**: The diagram shows two physically separated databases. In real applications, this depends upon the requirements of the product, and you can use the database for both write and read operations.
- Queries are generated with `Read` operations that are **Data Transfer Objects (DTOs)**.

You can now go back to the *Use case* section, in which we discussed the new features/extensions of our FlixOne inventory application. In this section, we will create a new FlixOne application with the features discussed previously using the CQRS pattern. Please note that we will be developing APIs first. If you did not install the pre-requisites, I suggest revisiting the *Technical requirements* section, gathering all of the required software, and installing them onto your machine. If you have completed the pre-requisites, then let's start by following these steps:

1. Open Visual Studio.
2. Click **File | New Project** to create a new project.
3. On the **New Project** window, select **Web** and then select **ASP.NET Core Web Application**.
4. Give a name to your project. I have named our project `FlixOne.API` and ensured that the **Solution Name** is `FlixOne`.

Advanced Database Design and Application Techniques

5. Select the **Location** of your `Solution` folder, then click on the **OK** button as shown in the following screenshot:

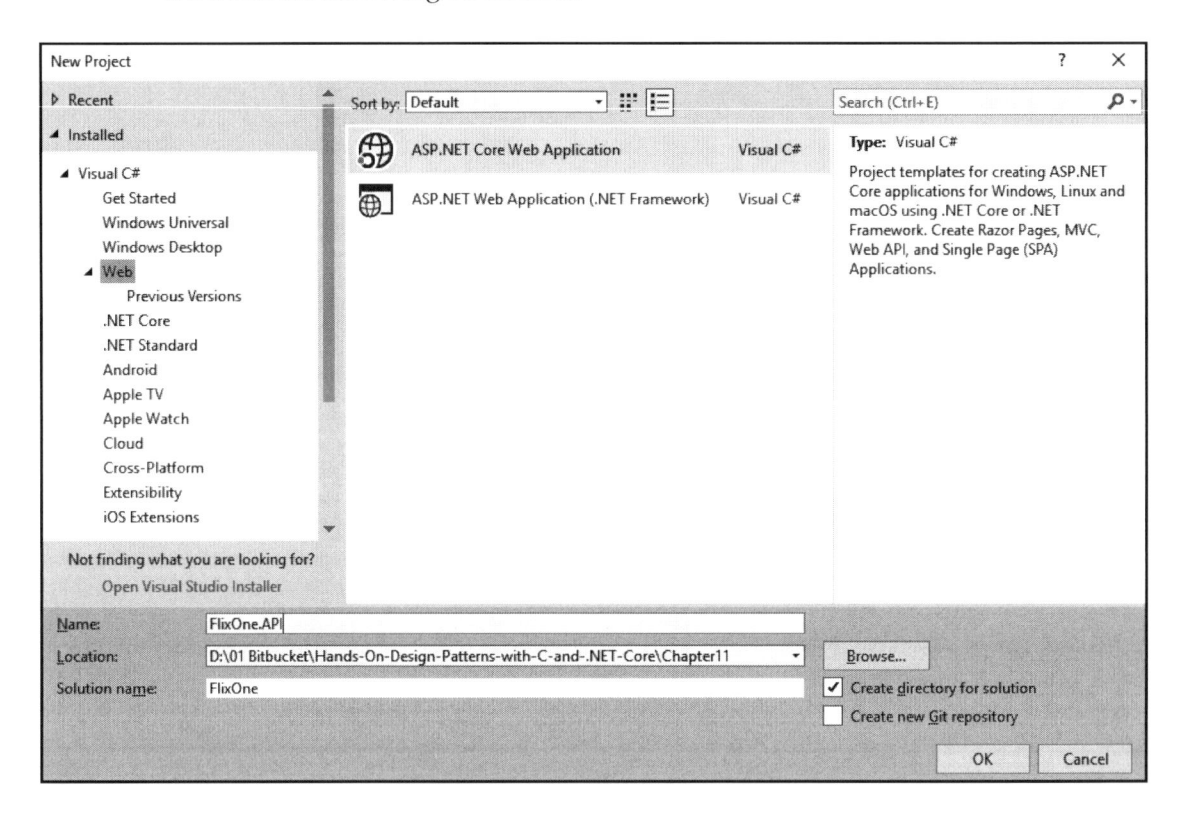

6. Now you should be on the **New ASP.NET Web Core Application - FlixOne.API** screen. Make sure that on this screen, you select **ASP.NET Core 2.2**. Select **Web Application (Model-View-Controller)** from the available templates, and uncheck the **Configure for HTTPS** checkbox, as shown in the following screenshot:

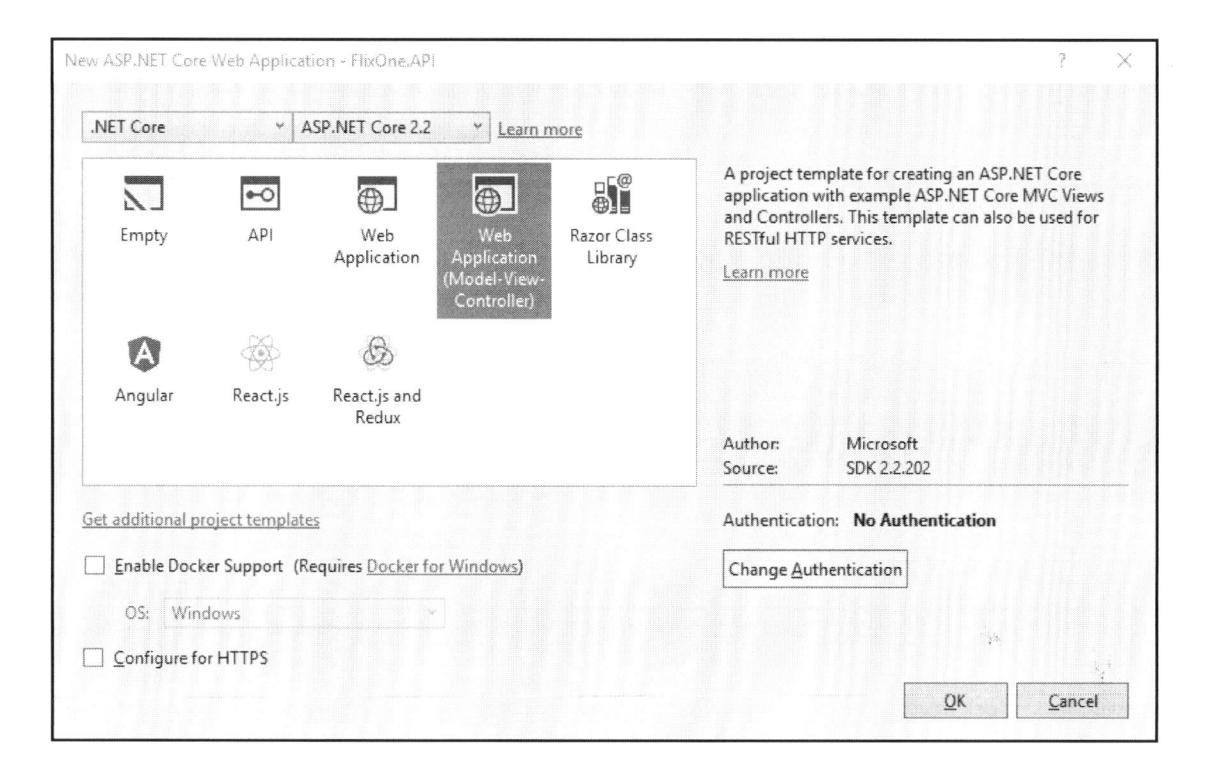

7. You will see a default page appear, as shown in the following screenshot:

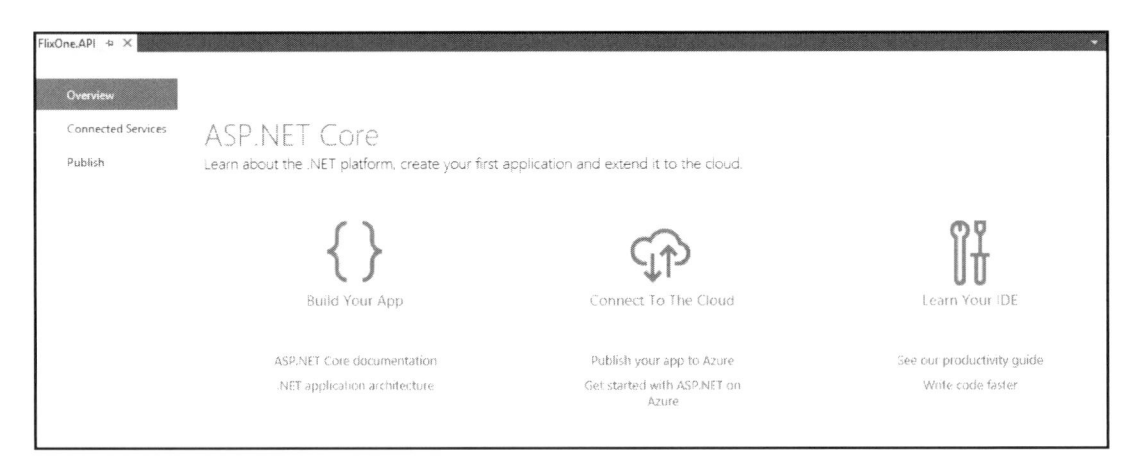

8. Expand **Solution Explorer** and click on **Show All files**. You will see the default folders/files created by **Visual Studio**. Refer to the following screenshot:

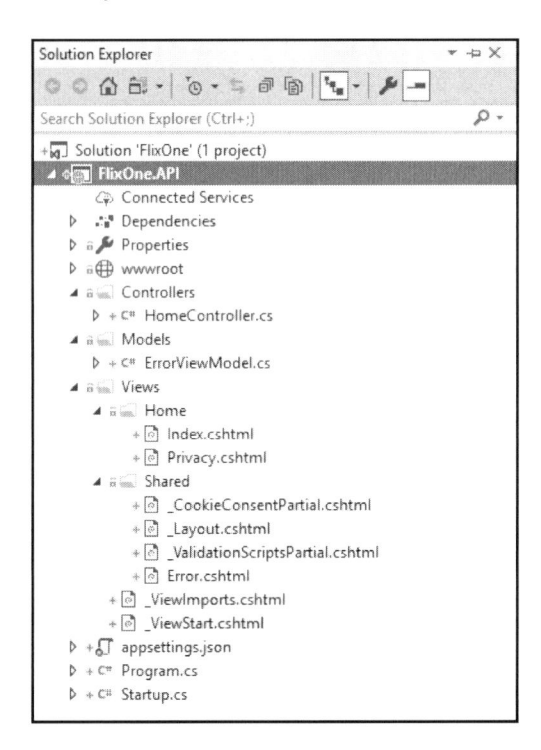

We have selected the **ASP.NET Core Web (Model-View-Controller)** template. Therefore, we have the default folders, **Controllers**, **Models**, and **Views**. This is a default template provided by **Visual Studio**. To check this default template, hit *F5* and run the project. Then, you will see the following default page:

The previous screenshot is the default **Home** screen of our web application. You may be thinking *is it a website?* and be expecting an API documentation page here instead of a web page. This is because, when we select the template, **Visual Studio** adds MVC Controller instead of API Controller by default. Please note that in ASP.NET Core, both MVC Controller and API Controller use the same Controller Pipeline (see the Controller class: `https://docs.microsoft.com/en-us/dotnet/api/microsoft.aspnetcore.mvc.controller?view=aspnetcore-2.2`).

Advanced Database Design and Application Techniques

Before discussing API projects in detail, let's first add a new project to our FlixOne solution. To do so, expand **Solution Explorer**, right-click on the **Solution Name**, and then click on **Add New Project**. Refer to the following screenshot:

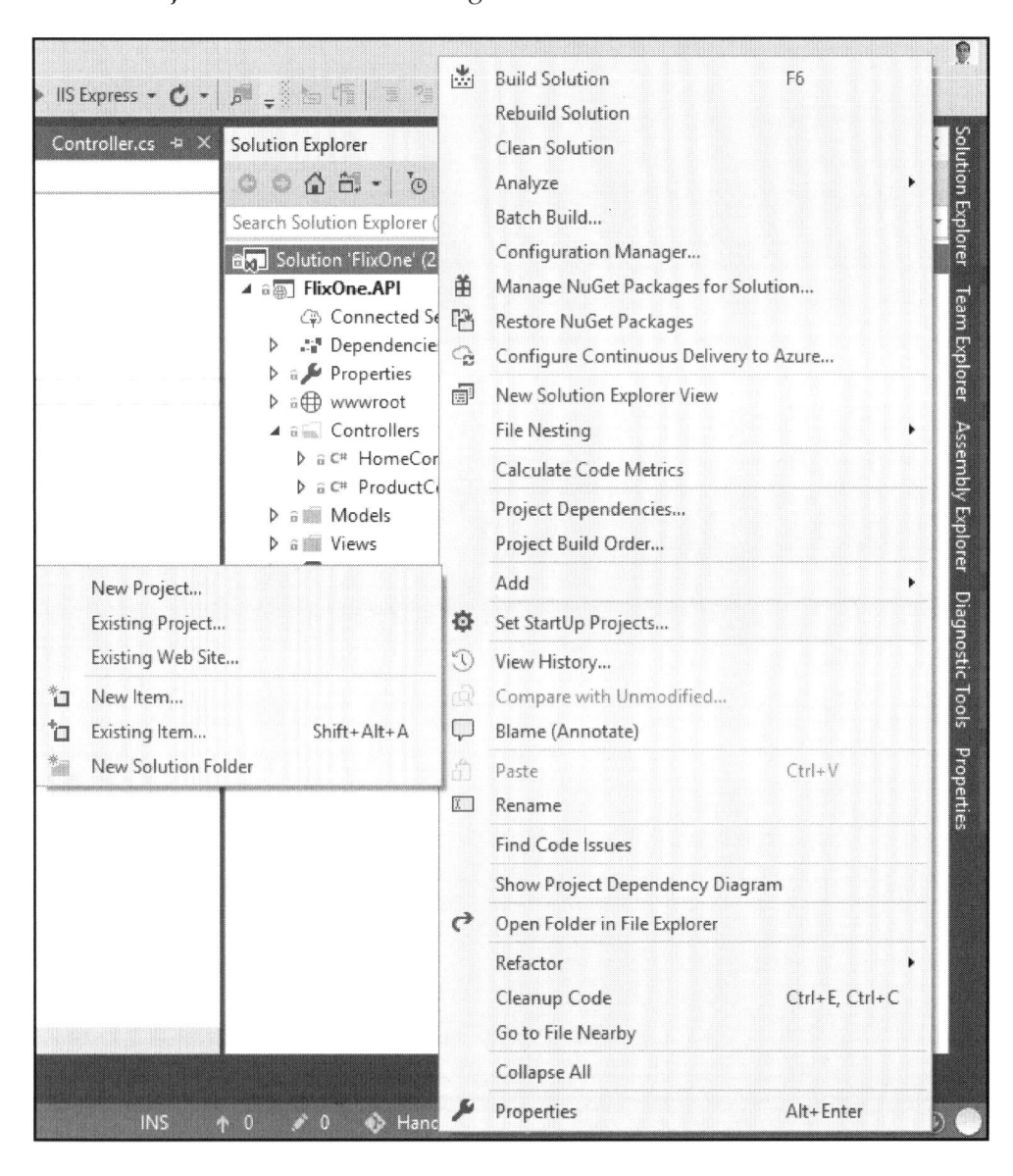

In the **New Project** window, add the new `FlixOne.CQRS` project, and click on the `OK` button. Refer to the following screenshot:

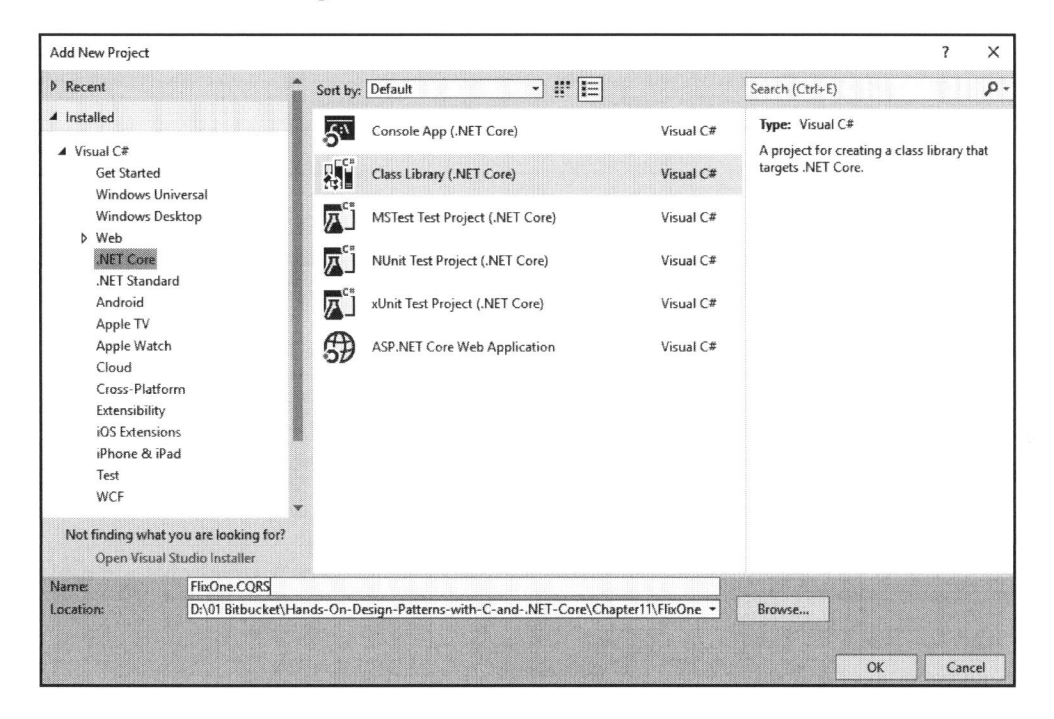

Advanced Database Design and Application Techniques

The previous screenshot is of the **Add New Project** window. On it, select .NET Core and then select the **Class Library(.NET Core)** project. Enter the name `FlixOne.CQRS` and click the **OK** button. A **New Project** has been added to the solution. You can then add folders to the new solution, as shown in the following screenshot:

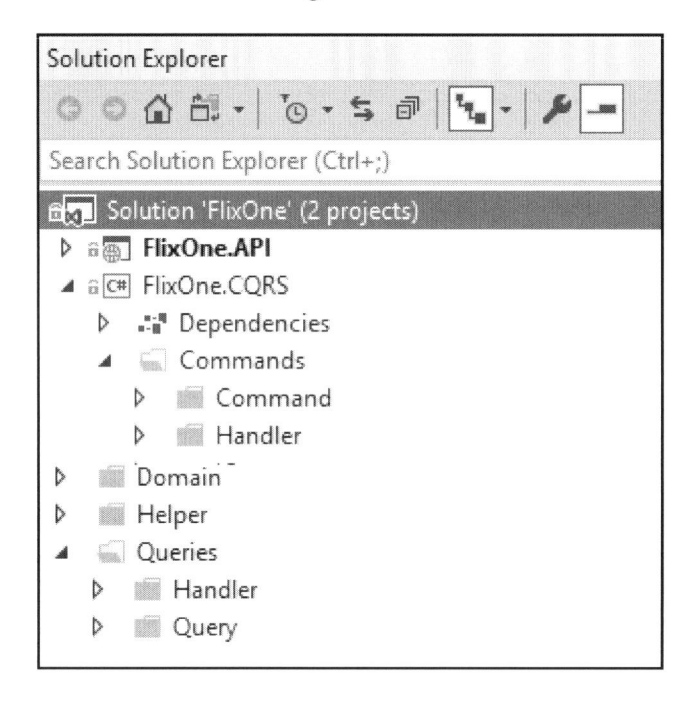

```
Solution Explorer
Search Solution Explorer (Ctrl+;)
  Solution 'FlixOne' (2 projects)
    FlixOne.API
    FlixOne.CQRS
      Dependencies
      Commands
        Command
        Handler
      Domain
      Helper
      Queries
        Handler
        Query
```

The previous screenshot is showing that I have added four new folders: `Commands`, `Queries`, `Domain`, and `Helper`. In the `Commands` folder, I have the `Command` and `Handler` sub-folders. Similarly, for the `Queries` folder, I have added sub-folders called `Handler` and `Query`.

To get started with the project, let's first add two Domain Entities in the project. The following is the required code:

```
public class Product
{
    public Guid Id { get; set; }
    public string Name { get; set; }
    public string Description { get; set; }
    public string Image { get; set; }
    public decimal Price { get; set; }
}
```

The preceding code is a `Product` domain entity that has the following properties:

- `Id`: A unique identifier
- `Name`: A product name
- `Description`: A product description
- `Image`: An image of the product
- `Price`: The price of the product

We also need to add the `CommandResponse` database. This plays an important role when interacting with database/repository, in that it ensures that the system gets a response. The following is the code-snippet of the `CommandResponse` Entity Model:

```
public class CommandResponse
{
    public Guid Id { get; set; }
    public bool Success { get; set; }
    public string Message { get; set; }

}
```

The preceding `CommandResponse` class contains the following properties:

- `Id`: Unique identifier.
- `Success`: With values of `True` or `False`, it tells us whether the operation is successful or not.
- `Message`: A message as a response to the operation. If `Success` if false, this message contains `Error`.

Advanced Database Design and Application Techniques

Now, it's time to add interfaces for a query. To add interfaces, follow these steps:

1. From **Solution Explorer**, right-click on the `Queries` folder, click on **Add**, and then click on **New Item**, as per the following screenshot:

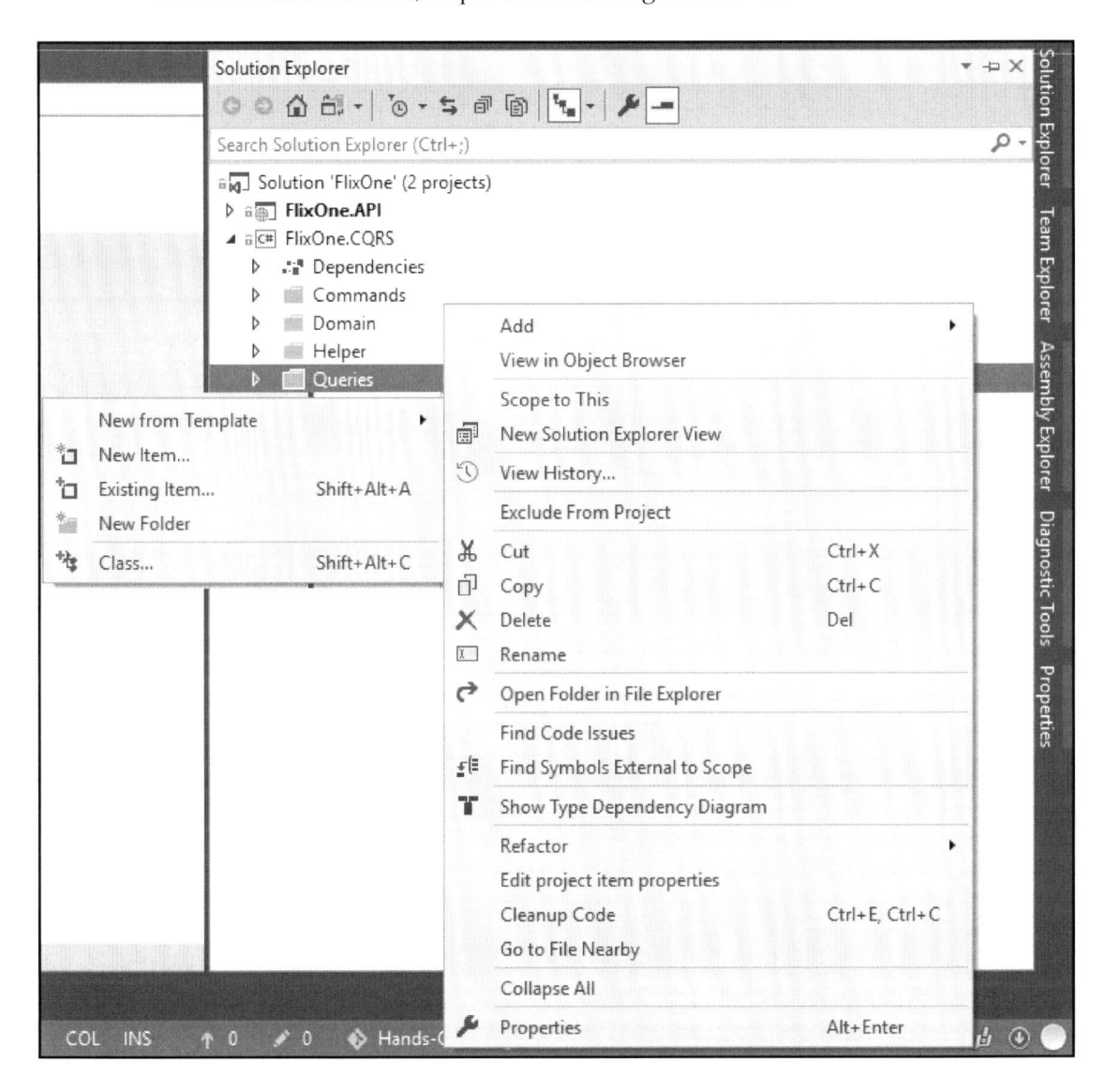

Chapter 11

2. From the **Add New Item** window, choose **Interface**, name it **IQuery**, and click on the **Add** button:

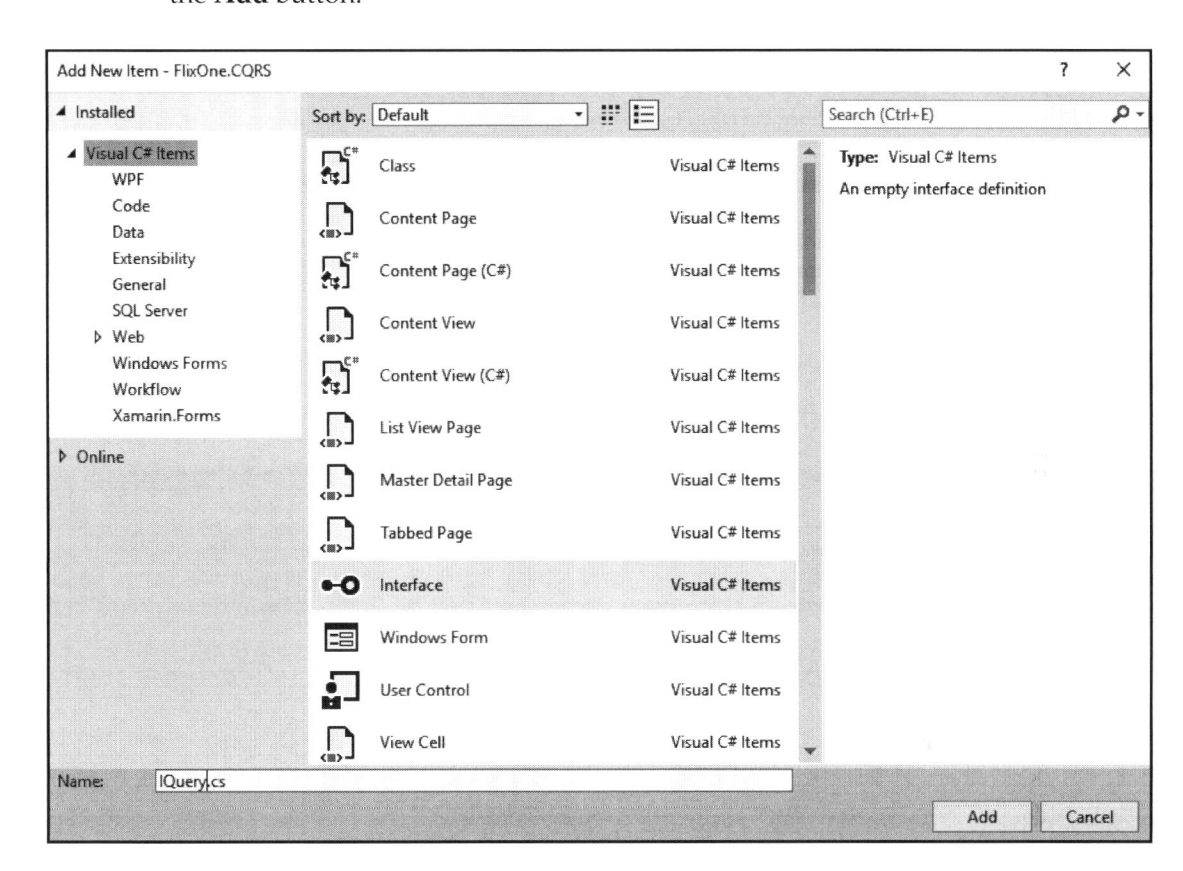

3. Follow the previous steps and add the `IQueryHandler` interface as well. The following is the code from the `IQuery` interface:

```
public interface IQuery<out TResponse>
{
}
```

4. The previous interface works as a skeleton for querying for any kind of operation. This is a generic interface using an `out` parameter of the `TResponse` type.

The following is code from our `ProductQuery` class:

```
public class ProductQuery : IQuery<IEnumerable<Product>>
{
}

public class SingleProductQuery : IQuery<Product>
{
    public SingleProductQuery(Guid id)
    {
        Id = id;
    }

    public Guid Id { get; }
}
```

The following is code from our `ProductQueryHandler` class:

```
public class ProductQueryHandler : IQueryHandler<ProductQuery, IEnumerable<Product>>
{
    public IEnumerable<Product> Get()
    {
        //call repository
        throw new NotImplementedException();
    }
}
public class SingleProductQueryHandler : IQueryHandler<SingleProductQuery, Product>
{
    private SingleProductQuery _productQuery;
    public SingleProductQueryHandler(SingleProductQuery productQuery)
    {
        _productQuery = productQuery;
    }

    public Product Get()
    {
        //call repository
        throw new NotImplementedException();
    }
}
```

The following is code from our `ProductQueryHandlerFactory` class:

```
public static class ProductQueryHandlerFactory
{
    public static IQueryHandler<ProductQuery, IEnumerable<Product>>
Build(ProductQuery productQuery)
    {
        return new ProductQueryHandler();
    }

    public static IQueryHandler<SingleProductQuery, Product>
Build(SingleProductQuery singleProductQuery)
    {
        return new SingleProductQueryHandler(singleProductQuery);
    }
}
```

Similarly to `Query` interfaces and `Query` classes, we need to add interfaces for commands and their classes.

At the point by which we have created CQRS for a product domain entity, you can follow this workflow and add more entities as many times as you like. Now, let's move on to our `FlixOne.API` project and add a new API controller by following these steps:

1. From **Solution Explorer**, right-click on the `Controllers` folder.
2. Select **Add | New Item**.

Advanced Database Design and Application Techniques

3. Select **API Controller Class** and name it `ProductController`; refer to the following screenshot:

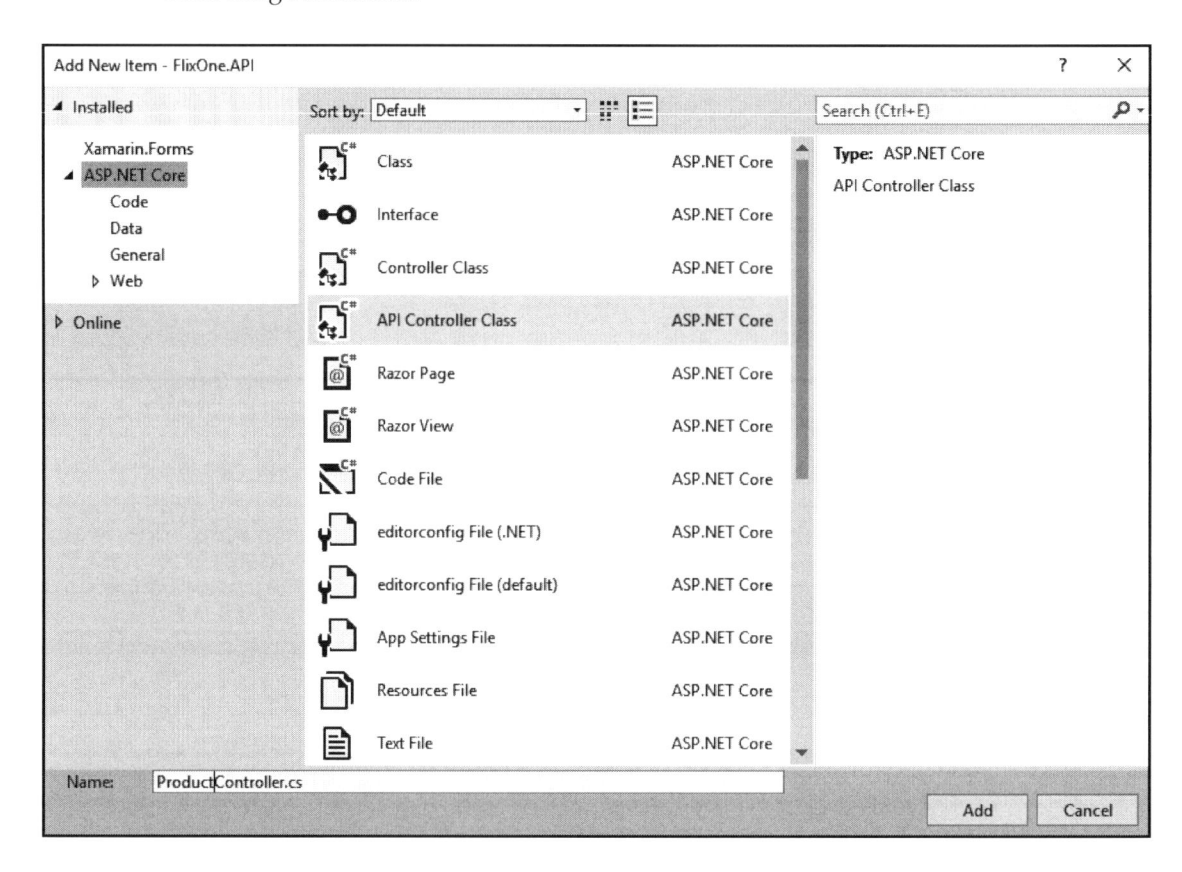

4. Add the following code in the API controller:

```
[Route("api/[controller]")]
public class ProductController : Controller
{
    // GET: api/<controller>
    [HttpGet]
    public IEnumerable<Product> Get()
    {
        var query = new ProductQuery();
        var handler = ProductQueryHandlerFactory.Build(query);
        return handler.Get();
    }

    // GET api/<controller>/5
```

```
[HttpGet("{id}")]
public Product Get(string id)
{
    var query = new SingleProductQuery(id.ToValidGuid());
    var handler = ProductQueryHandlerFactory.Build(query);
    return handler.Get();
}
```

The following code is for saving the product:

```
// POST api/<controller>
[HttpPost]
public IActionResult Post([FromBody] Product product)
{
    var command = new SaveProductCommand(product);
    var handler = ProductCommandHandlerFactory.Build(command);
    var response = handler.Execute();
    if (!response.Success) return StatusCode(500, response);
    product.Id = response.Id;
    return Ok(product);

}
```

The following code is for deletion of products:

```
// DELETE api/<controller>/5
[HttpDelete("{id}")]
public IActionResult Delete(string id)
{
    var command = new DeleteProductCommand(id.ToValidGuid());
    var handler = ProductCommandHandlerFactory.Build(command);
    var response = handler.Execute();
    if (!response.Success) return StatusCode(500, response);
    return Ok(response);
}
```

We have created Product APIs, and we are not going to creates UI in this section. To view what we have done, we will be adding **Swagger** support to our API project.

Swagger is a tool that can be used for documentation purposes, and provides all of the information regarding the API endpoints on one screen, where you can visualize the API and test it by setting parameters as well.

Advanced Database Design and Application Techniques

To get started with the implementation of Swagger in our API project, follow these steps:

1. Open Nuget Package Manager.

2. Go to **Nuget Package Manager** | **Browse** and search for `Swashbuckle.ASPNETCore`; refer to the following screenshot:

3. Open the `Startup.cs` file and add the following code to the `ConfigureService` method:

```
//Register Swagger
           services.AddSwaggerGen(swagger =>
           {
               swagger.SwaggerDoc("v1", new Info { Title = "Product APIs", Version = "v1" });
           });
```

4. Now, add the following code to the `Configure` method:

   ```
   // Enable middleware to serve generated Swagger as a JSON endpoint.
   app.UseSwagger();

   // Enable middleware to serve swagger-ui (HTML, JS, CSS, etc.),
   specifying the Swagger JSON endpoint.
   app.UseSwaggerUI(c =>
   {
       c.SwaggerEndpoint("/swagger/v1/swagger.json", "Product API
   V1");
   });
   ```

We have now completed all of the changes that serve to showcase the power of CQRS in the application. Hit *F5* in **Visual Studio** and open the Swagger documentation page by accessing the following URL: `http://localhost:52932/swagger/` (please note that port number `52932` may vary as per your setting of the project). You will see the following **Swagger Documentation** page:

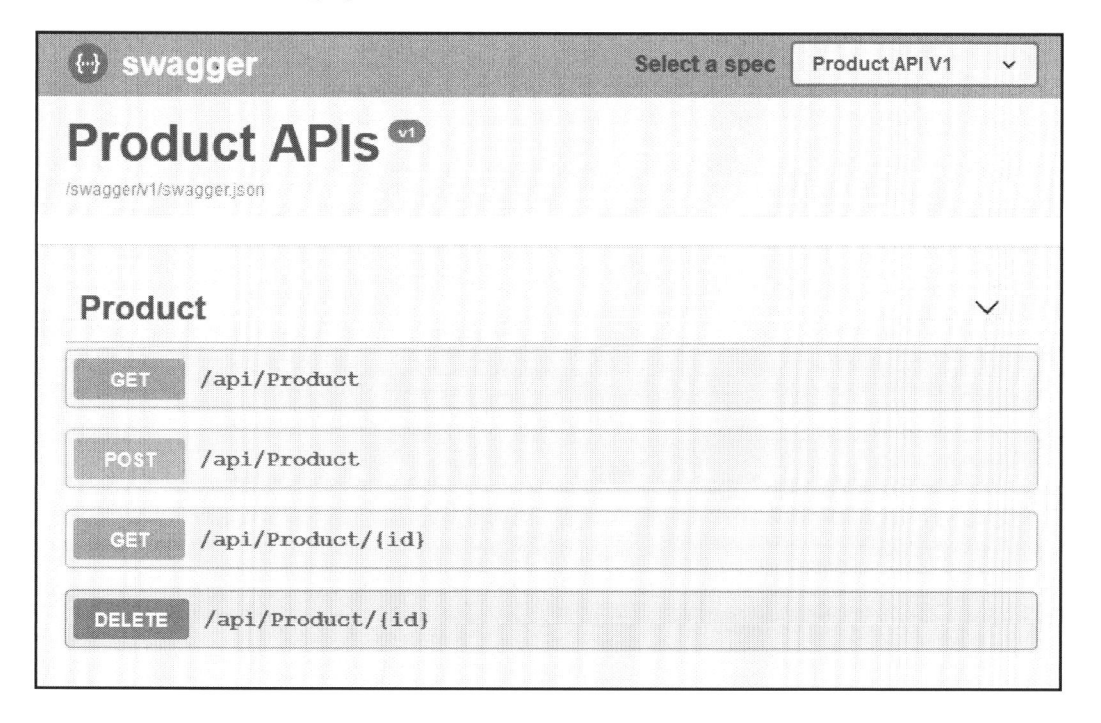

Here, you can test Product APIs.

Summary

This chapter introduced the CQRS pattern, which we then implemented into our application. The aim of the chapter was to go through the database techniques and look at how ledger-style databases work for inventory systems. To showcase the power of CQRS, we have created Product APIs and added support for Swagger documentation.

In the next chapter, we will discuss cloud services and look at microservices and serverless techniques in detail.

Questions

The following questions will allow you to consolidate the information contained in this chapter:

1. What is a ledger-style database?
2. What is CQRS?
3. When should we use CQRS?

12
Coding for the Cloud

The previous chapters explored patterns, from lower-level concepts such as the Singleton and Factory patterns, to patterns for specific technologies such as databases and web applications. These patterns are essential for ensuring the good design of a solution to ensure maintainability and efficient implementation. These patterns provide a solid foundation that allows applications to be enhanced and modified as requirements change and new functionality is added.

This chapter takes a higher-level view of a solution to address concerns involving designing implementing solutions that are reliable, scalable, and secure. The patterns in this chapter often involve environments that contain multiple applications, a repository, and a range of possible infrastructure configurations.

The software industry is continually evolving and with the change comes new opportunity as well as new challenges. In this chapter, we will look at different software patterns for the cloud. Many of these patterns are not new, and existed in on-premises environments. As cloud-first solutions are becoming the norm, these patterns are even more commonplace due to the ease of implementing solutions that do not rely on on-premises infrastructure.

> Cloud-first or cloud-native solutions have been designed to target cloud computing resources, while hybrid solutions have been designed to use both cloud computing resources as well as resources from a private data center.

This chapter defines five key concerns when building solutions in the cloud:

- Scalability
- Availability
- Security
- Application design
- DevOps

We will discuss the key concerns and why they are significant to building cloud solutions. As the concerns are discussed, different patterns will be described that can be applied to address these concerns.

Technical requirements

This chapter does not require any special technical requirements or source code as it is primarily theoretical.

Key considerations when building solutions in the cloud

Making the decision to move to the cloud comes with its own set of problems and challenges. In this section, we will cover five key areas of consideration for building cloud-based solutions. While these are not unique to the cloud, they require special attention when switching to the cloud due to the wide range of technologies and solutions that are available.

The five primary considerations are as follows:

- **Scalability**: This allows for accommodation of increased load or traffic for a growing business.
- **Resilience/availability**: This ensures the handling of failures in a system gracefully with as little impact on the user as possible.
- **Security**: This ensures that private and proprietary data stays that way and is safe from hacks and attacks.
- **Application design**: This refers to the design of applications with special consideration for cloud-based solutions.
- **DevOps**: This is a collection of tools and practices that supports the development and running of cloud-based solutions.

Depending on your business requirements, you may need to look for solutions for some or all of these considerations. It is also in your business's best interest to adopt providers with solutions to problems that you don't anticipate but would make for good contingency planning.

In the following sections, we will discuss these considerations in further detail along with the available solution patterns for them.

> These patterns range from a type of technology to architectural to business processes and a single pattern could address more than one concern.

Scalability

Scalability refers to the ability to allocate and manage resources used by an application in order for the application to maintain an acceptable level of quality under a given workload. Most cloud offerings provide mechanisms for increasing the quality and quantity of resources used by an application. For example, the Azure App Service allows scaling of both the size of the App Service and the number of instances of the App Service.

Scalability can be viewed as demand on a limited number of resources. A resource could be disk space, RAM, bandwidth, or another aspect of software that can be quantified. The demand can range from the number of users, concurrent connections, or another demand that would produce a constraint on a resource. As the demand increases, a strain is placed on the application in order to provide the resource. When the strain affects the performance of the application, this is referred to as a resource bottleneck.

For example, a measure might be the number of users that can access an application before the performance of the application begins to deteriorate. The performance could be set as an average latency on requests being less than 2 seconds. As the number of users increases, the load on the system could then be viewed, and specific resource bottlenecks affecting the performance could be identified.

Workload

In order to determine how to effectively address scaling issues, it is important to understand the workload that the system will be under. There are four main types of workload: static, periodic, once-in-a-lifetime and unpredictable.

A static workload represents a constant level of activity on a system. Because the workload does not fluctuate, this type of system does not require a very elastic infrastructure.

Systems that have a predictable change in workload have a periodic workload. An example would be a system that experiences a surge of activity around the weekends or around the months when income tax is due. These systems can be scaled up to maintain a desired level of quality when the load increases and scaled down to save cost when the load decreases.

Coding for the Cloud

Once-in-a-lifetime workloads indicate systems designed around a specific event. These systems are provisioned to handle the workload around the event and deprovisioned once they are no longer needed.

Unpredictable workloads often benefit from the auto-scale functionality mentioned earlier. These systems have large fluctuations in activity that are either not understood by the business yet or are influenced by other factors.

Understanding and designing a cloud-based application for its type of workload is essential for both maintaining a high level of performance as well as lowering costs.

Solution patterns

We have available three design patterns and one architecture pattern to choose from to enable us to add scalability to our systems:

- Vertical scaling
- Horizontal scaling
- Auto-scaling
- Microservices

Let's review each in more detail.

Vertical scaling

Though it is possible to add physical RAM or an additional disk drive to an on-premises server, most cloud providers support the ability to easily increase or decrease the computing power of a system. This is often with little or no downtime as the system scales. This type of scaling is called vertical scaling and refers to when a resource such as the type of CPU, size and quality of RAM, or size and quality of the disk is altered.

> Vertical scaling is often referred to as *scaling up* while horizontal scaling is often referred to as *scaling out*. In this context, the term *up* refers to the size of the resource while *out* refers to the number of instances.

Horizontal scaling

Horizontal scaling differs from vertical scaling because, instead of altering the size of a system, horizontal scaling changes the number of systems involved. For example, a web application might run on a single server having 4 GB RAM and 2 CPUs. If the server was increased in size to 8 GB RAM and 4 CPUs, then this would be vertical scaling. However, if two more servers were added with the same configuration of 4 GB RAM and 2 CPUs, then this would be horizontal scaling.

Horizontal scaling can be achieved by using some form of load balancing that redirects the requests across a collection of systems as illustrated in the following diagram:

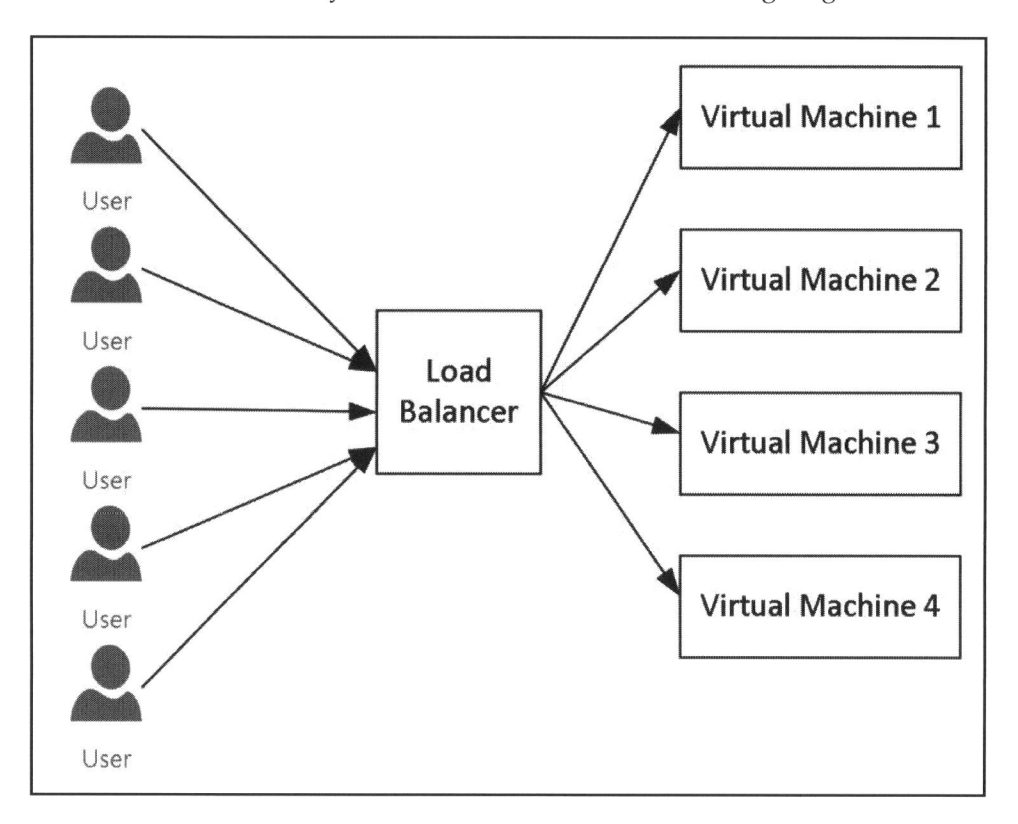

Horizontal scaling is usually preferred in cloud solutions over vertical scaling. This is because, in general, it is more cost effective to use several smaller virtual machines to a single large server to provide the same measure of performance.

For horizontal scaling to be most effective, it does require a system design that supports this type of scaling. For example, web applications designed without sticky sessions and/or state stored on the server work better for horizontal scaling. This is because sticky sessions cause a user's requests to be routed to the same virtual machine for processing and, over time, the balance of the routing across the virtual machines could become uneven and therefore not as efficient as possible.

> **Stateful applications**
> A *stateful* application maintains information about an active session on the server or repository.
>
> **Stateless applications**
> *Stateless* applications are designed to not require information about an active session to be stored on the server or repository. This allows for subsequent requests in a single session to be sent to any server to be handled and not just to the same server for the entire session.

Web applications designed that are stateful require sessions or information to be maintained in a shared repository. Stateless web applications support a more resilient pattern as any server in a web garden or web farm. This allows for a single node in the web application to fail without losing session information.

> A web *garden* is a pattern where multiple copies of the same web application are hosted on the same server, whereas a web *farm* is a pattern where multiple copies of the same web application are hosted on different servers. In both patterns, routing is used to expose the multiple copies as if they were a single application.

Auto-scaling

An advantage of using a cloud provider over on-premises solutions is the built-in support for auto-scaling. As an added benefit to horizontal scaling, the ability to auto-scale an application is often a configurable feature of a cloud service. For example, an Azure App Service provides the ability to set up auto-scale profiles that allow an application to react to conditions. For example, the following screenshot shows an auto-scale profile:

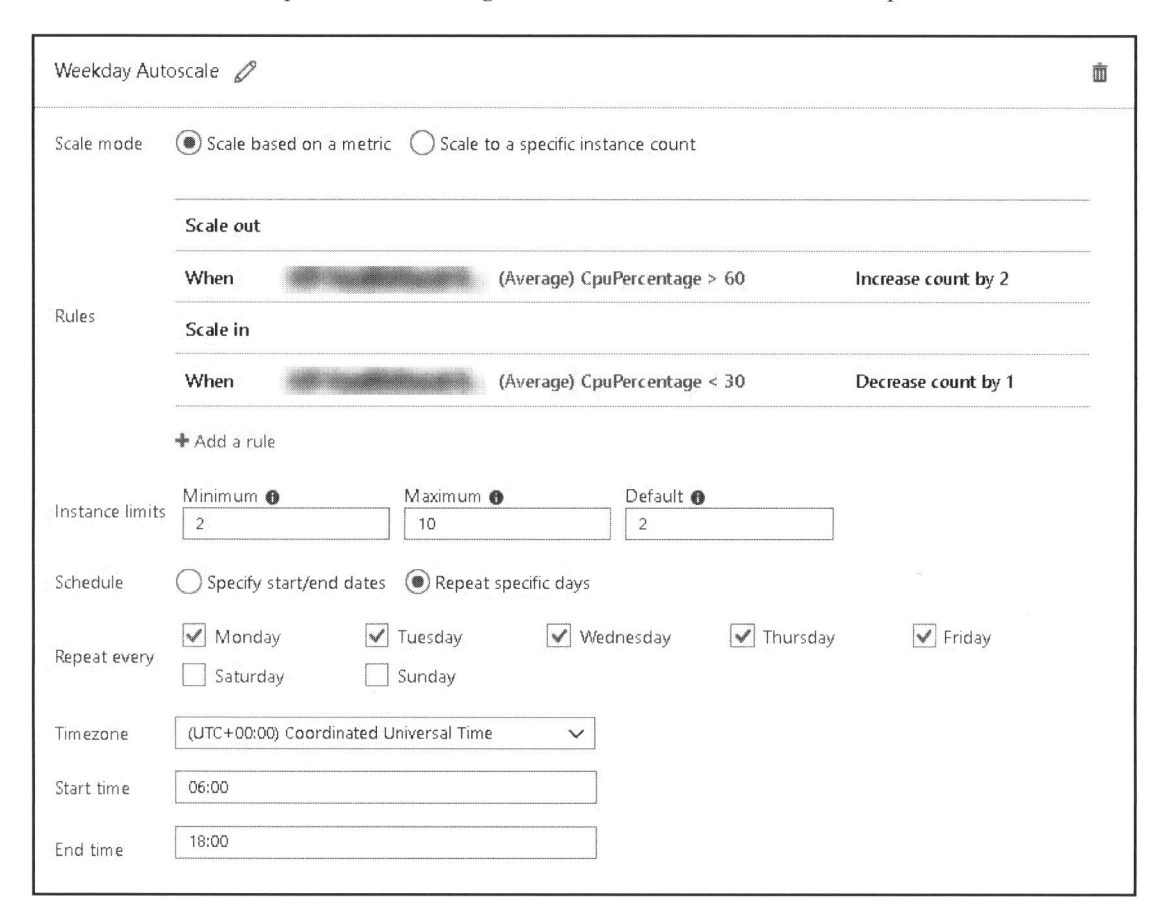

The profile designed for weekdays will increase or decrease the number of app service instances depending on the load on the servers. The load is being measured in CPU percentage. If the CPU percentage is averages above 60%, then the number of instances is increased up to a maximum of 10. Similarly, if the CPU percentage falls below 30%, the number of instances is reduced to a minimum of 2.

> An elastic infrastructure allows for resources to be scaled vertically or horizontally without requiring a re-deploy or downtime. The term is actually more of a degree of elasticity instead of referring to whether a system is *elastic* or *not elastic*. For example, an elastic service could allow for scaling both vertically and horizontally without requiring a restart of the service instances. A less elastic service would allow for scaling horizontally without a restart but would require a restart of the service when the size of the server is altered.

Microservices

There are different interpretations of what microservices means and how it relates to **service-oriented architecture** (**SOA**). In this section, we are going to view microservices as a refinement of SOA and not a new architectural pattern. The microservice architecture extends SOA by adding some additional key principles which require that services must:

- be small - hence the term *micro*
- be built around a business capability
- be loosely coupled with other services
- be independently maintainable
- have an isolated state

Small

Microservices takes the services in SOA farther by reducing them to their smallest possible size. This fits well with some other patterns that we have seen, such as **Keep It Simple Stupid** (**KISS**) and **You Aren't Gonna Need It** (**YAGNI**) from `Chapter 2`, *Modern Software Design Patterns and Principles*. The microservice should only fulfill its requirements and nothing more.

Business capability

By building a service around a business capability, we align our implementation in such a way that, as the business requirements change, our services will be changed in a similar manner. Because of this, it is less likely that change in one area of the business will impact other areas.

Loosely coupled

A microservice should interact with other services across a service boundary using a technology-agnostic protocol such as HTTP. This allows for the microservices to be integrated more easily and, more importantly, not require the rebuild of a microservice when another service changes. This does require a known *service contract* to exist.

> **Service contract**
> A *service contract* is the definition of a service that is distributed to other development teams. **Web Services Description Language** (**WSDL**) is a widely known XML-based language for describing services, but other languages, such as Swagger, are also very popular.

When implementing a microservice, it is important to have a strategy for how the change will be managed. By having a versioned service contract, it is then possible to communicate the change clearly to a client of the service.

For example, the strategy of a microservice used to store an inventory of books could have the following strategy:

- Each service will be versioned and include a Swagger definition.
- Each service will start with version 1.
- When a change is made that requires the service contract to change, the version will be increased by 1.
- The service will maintain up to three versions.
- Changes to a service must ensure that all current versions behave suitably.

The preceding basic strategy does have interesting implications. First of all, the team maintaining a service must ensure that changes do not break existing services. This ensures a new deployment will not break other services while allowing for new functionality to be deployed. The contract does allow for up to three services to be active at a time, thus allowing for a dependable service to update independently.

Independently maintainable

This is one of the most distinguishing features of microservices. Having a microservice able to be maintained independent of other microservices empowers a business to be able to manage the service without impacting other services. By managing a service, we are including both the development as well as the deployment of a service. With this principle, microservices can be updated and deployed with a reduced chance of impacting other services, as well as at a different rate of change from other services.

Isolated state

Isolated state includes both data and other resources that could be shared including databases and files. This is also a distinguishing feature of microservice architecture. By having an independent state, we are reducing the chance that a change in the data model to support one service will impact other services.

The following diagram illustrates a more traditional SOA approach, where a single database is used by multiple services:

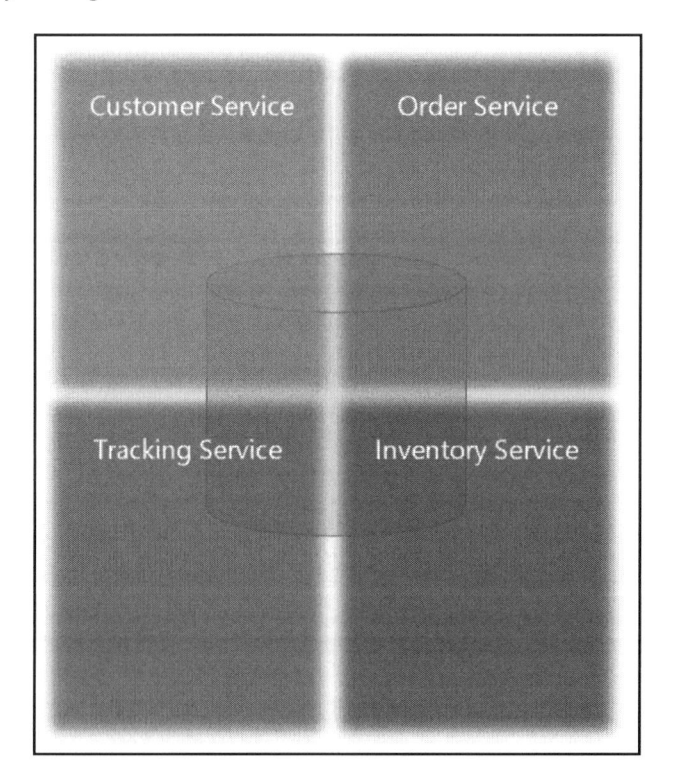

By requiring a microservice to have an isolated state, we would then require a database per service as shown in the following diagram:

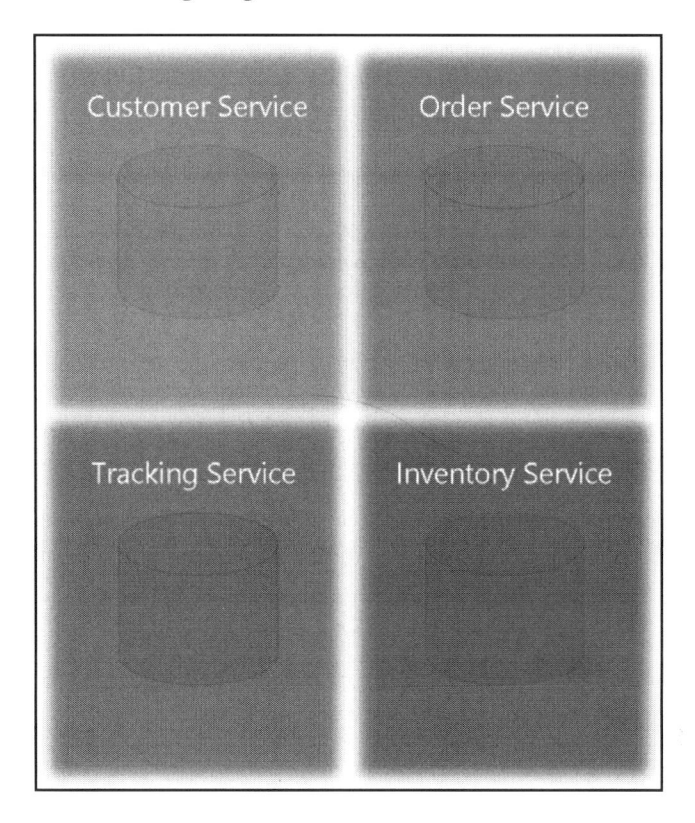

Customer Service	Order Service
Tracking Service	Inventory Service

This has an advantage in that each service can choose the technology that best fits the requirements of the services.

Advantages

The microservice architecture does represent a shift from traditional service design and it does fit well in a cloud-based solution. The advantages of microservices and why they are gaining in popularity might not be immediately obvious. We have touched on how the design of microservices provides advantages for handling change gracefully. From a technical point of view, microservices can be scaled independently both at the service level and at the database.

What might not be clear is the benefit a microservice architecture has to a business. By having small independent services, the business can then look at different ways to maintain and develop microservices. The business now has options to host the services in different ways, including different cloud providers, as best fits the independent services. Likewise, the isolated nature of the services allows for a greater degree of agility in developing the services. As change happens, resources (that is, development team members) can be allocated to different services as required, and, as the scope of service is smaller, the amount of business knowledge required is also reduced.

Resiliency/availability

Resiliency is the ability of an application to handle failure gracefully while availability is a measure of the amount of time the application is working. An application may have a collection of resources and still remain available if one of the resources becomes inoperable or unavailable.

> If an application is designed to handle one or more resources failing without the entire system becoming inoperable, this is referred to as **graceful degradation**.

Patterns apply to both isolate the elements of an application as well as handle the interaction between the elements so that when a failure occurs, the impact is limited. Many of the resiliency-related patterns focus on the messaging between the components within the application or to other applications. The Bulkhead pattern, for example, isolates the traffic into pools so that when one pool becomes overwhelmed or fails, the other pools are not adversely affected. Other patterns apply specific techniques to handle messaging, such as retry policies or compensating transactions.

Availability is an important factor to many cloud-based applications and, typically, availability is measured against a **service level agreement** (**SLA**). In most cases, the SLA stipulates the percentage of time the application must remain operable. Patterns involve both allowing for redundancy of components as well as using techniques to limit the effect of an increase in activity. For example, the Queue-Based Load Leveling pattern uses a queue to limit the effect a spike in activity might have on an application by acting as a buffer between the caller, or client, and the application or service.

> Resiliency and availability are identified here as related cloud solution factors as often a resilient application allows for a strict SLA on availability to be achieved.

Solution pattern

To ensure we have a system that has resilience and availability, our best bet is to look for a provider with a specific architecture. Enter **event-driven architecture** (**EDA**).

EDA is an architectural pattern that uses *events* to drive the behavior and activity of a system. The solution patterns available under it will help us achieve the intended resolutions.

EDA

EDA promotes the concept of having loosely connected producers and consumers where the producers do not have direct knowledge of the consumers. An event in this context is any change ranging from a user logging onto a system, to an order being placed, to a process failing to complete successfully. EDA fits well in distributed systems and allows for highly scalable solutions.

There are many related patterns and approaches to EDA and the following patterns are presented in this section as being directly relevant to EDA:

- Queue-Based Load Leveling
- Publisher Subscriber
- Priority Queue
- Compensating Transaction

Queue-Based Load Leveling

Queue-Based Load Leveling is an effective way of minimizing the impact of occurrences of high demand on availability. By introducing a queue between a client and service, we are able to throttle or restrict the number of requests that are being handled by the service at a time. This allows for smoother user experience. Take the following diagram as an example:

Coding for the Cloud

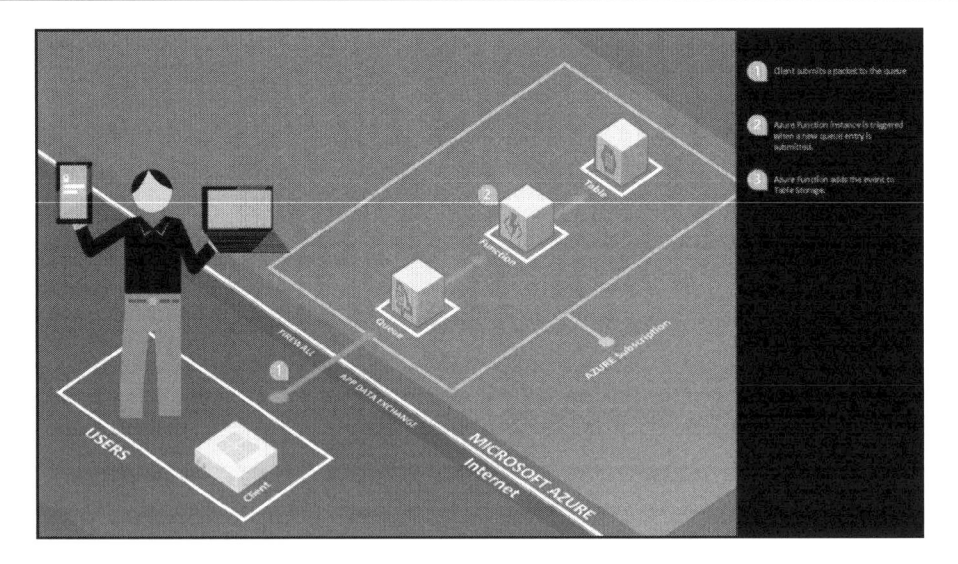

The preceding diagram shows a client submitting a request to a queue to be processed and the result saved to a table. The queue acts to prevent the function from being overwhelmed by a sudden spike in activity.

Publisher Subscriber

The Publisher Subscriber pattern states that there are event publishers and event consumers. Essentially, this is the heart of EDA, as the publishers are decoupled from the consumers and are not concerned about the delivery of events to the consumers, but only with publishing events. The event will contain information that will be used to route the event to interested consumers. A consumer would then register or subscribe to being interested in specific events:

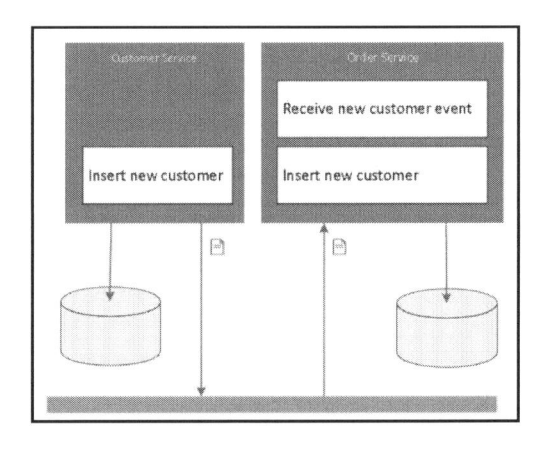

The preceding diagram illustrates a Customer Service and an Order Service. The Customer Service acts as a publisher and submits an event when a customer is added. The Order Service has subscribed to new customer events. When a new customer event is received, the Order Service inserts the customer information into its local store.

By introducing the Publisher Subscriber pattern into the architecture, the Order Service is then decoupled from the Customer Service. An advantage of this is it provides a more flexible architecture for change. For example, a new service could be introduced to add new customers to the solutions that do not require being added to the same repository used by the Customer Service. Also, more than one service could subscribe to the new customer event. Adding a welcome email could more easily be added as a new subscriber, rather than having to build this functionality into a single monolithic solution.

Priority Queue

Another related pattern is Priority Queue, which provides a mechanism for treating similar events differently. Using the new customer example from the previous section, it would be possible to have two subscribers for a new customer event. One subscriber would be interested in the majority of the new customers, while one subscriber would identify a subset of the customers that should be handled differently. For example, new subscribers from rural areas might receive an email with additional information about specialized shipping providers.

Compensating transaction

With distributed systems, it is not always practical or desirable to issue a command as a transaction. A transaction in this context refers to a lower-level programming construct that manages one or more commands as a single action that either all succeeds or all fails. In some situations, a distributed transaction is not supported, or the overhead of using a distributed transaction outweighs the benefits. The Compensating Transaction pattern was developed to handle this situation. Let's use the following as an example based on a BizTalk orchestration:

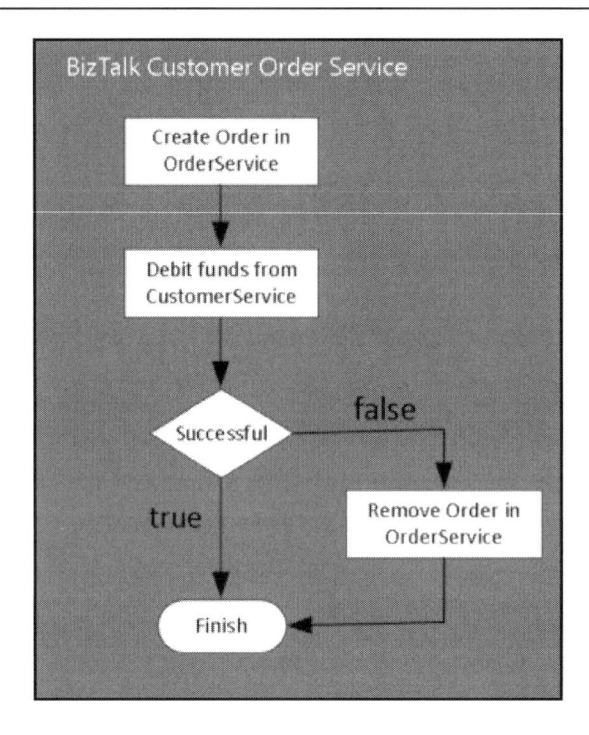

The diagram shows two steps in a process: creating order in an Order Service and debiting funds from a Customer Service. The diagram shows how, first the order is created and then the funds are removed. If the debit of funds does not succeed then the order is removed from the Order Service.

Security

Security ensures an application does not disclose information incorrectly or provide functionality outside of intended use. Security includes both malicious and accidental actions. With cloud applications and increasing use of a wide range of identity providers, restricting access to only approved users is often challenging.

End-user authentication and authorization requires design and planning as fewer applications run in isolation, and it is common for multiple identity providers, such as Facebook, Google, and Microsoft, to be used. In some instances, patterns are used to provide access directly to resources for improved performance and scalability. Furthermore, other patterns are concerned with creating a virtual wall between clients and applications.

Solution patterns

As the industry has become more interconnected, the pattern of using an external party to authenticate users has become more common. The Federated Security pattern has been chosen for discussion here as it is one of the best ways to ensure security in our systems, and most **software-as-a-service (SaaS)** platforms offer this feature.

Federated security

Federated security delegates the authentication of user or service (consumer) to an external party known as an **identity provider** (**IdP**). An application using federated security will trust the IdP to properly authenticate the consumer and provide details about the consumer or claims accurately. This information about the consumer is presented as a token. A common scenario for this would be a web application using a social IdP such as Google, Facebook, or Microsoft.

Federated security can handle a variety of scenarios, from interactive sessions to authentication backend services or non-interactive sessions. Another common scenario is the ability to provide a single authentication experience or **single sign-on** (**SSO**) across a suite of separately hosted applications. This scenario allows for a single token to be acquired from a **security token service** (**STS**) and the same token used to present to the multiple applications without requiring the login procedure to be repeated:

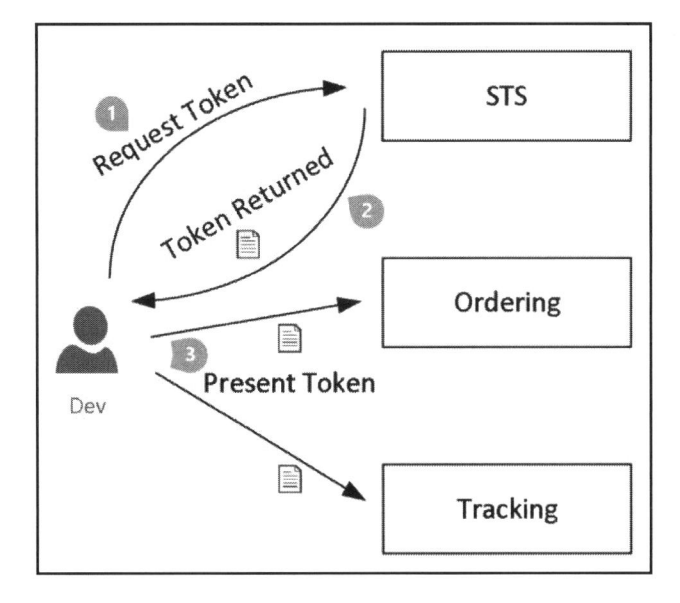

Federated security has two main purposes. First, it simplifies the management of identities by having a single identity store. This allows for identities to be managed in a central and unified manner, making it easier to perform management tasks such as providing the login experience, forgotten password management, as well as revoking passwords in a consistent manner. Secondly, it provides a better user experience by offering users a similar experience across multiple applications as well as requiring only a single form of authentication, instead of needing to remember multiple passwords.

There are several standards for federated security and two widely used ones are **Security Assertion Markup Language (SAML)** and **OpenId Connect (OIDC)**. SAML is older than OIDC and allows for the exchange of messages using an XML SAML format. OIDC is built upon OAuth 2.0 and commonly uses **JSON Web Token (JWT)** for describing the security token. Both formats support federated security, SSO, and many public IdPs such as Facebook, Google, and Microsoft support both standards.

Application design

The design of an application can vary significantly and be influenced by many factors. These factors are not only technical but are influenced by the teams involved in building, managing, and maintaining the applications. Some patterns, for example, work best with small dedicated teams as opposed to a larger number of geographically dispersed teams. Other design-related patterns handle different types of workload better and are used in specific scenarios. Other patterns have been designed around the frequency of change and how to limit the disruption of changes to an application once it has been released to users.

Solution patterns

As almost all on-premises patterns are applicable to cloud-based solutions, the scope of patterns that could be covered is staggering. The Cache and CQRS patterns have been chosen because the former is a very common pattern employed by most web applications and the latter shifts how designers think of building solutions and lends itself well to other architectural patterns such as SOA and microservices.

Cache

Storing information retrieved from slower forms of storage into faster forms of storage, or caching, has been a technique that has been used in programming for decades and can be seen in software such as a browser cache and hardware such as RAM. In this chapter, we will look at three examples: Cache-aside, Write-through Cache, and Static Content Hosting.

Cache-aside

The Cache-aside pattern can be used to improve performance by loading frequently referenced data in a local or faster form of storage. With this pattern, it is the responsibility of the application to maintain the state of the cache. This is illustrated in the following diagram:

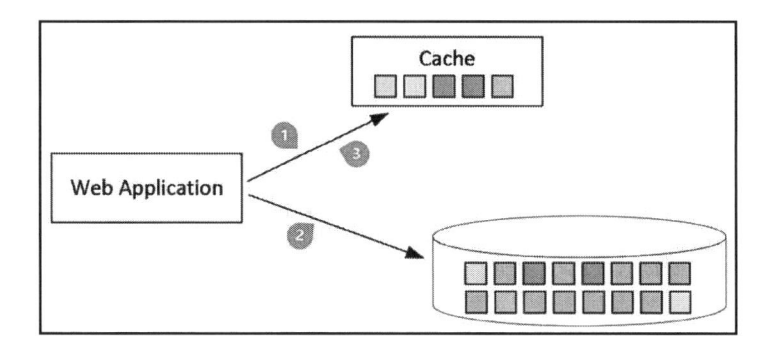

First, the application requests information from the cache. If the information is missing, then it is requested from the data store. The application then updates the cache with the information. Once the information is stored, it will then be retrieved from the cache and used without referencing the slower data store. With this pattern, it is the application's responsibility to maintain the cache, both when there is a cache miss, and when the data is updated.

> The term *cache miss* refers to when data is not found in the cache. In other words, it is missing from the cache.

Write-through cache

The Write-through Cache pattern can also be used to improve performance in a similar manner as the Cache-aside pattern. Its approach differs by moving the management of the cache's content from the application to the cache itself, as shown in the following diagram:

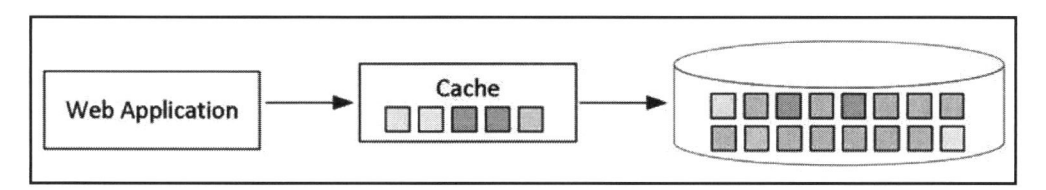

A request is made for a piece of information in the cache. If the data is not already loaded, then the information is retrieved from the data store, placed in the cache, and then returned. If the data was already held, then it is immediately returned. This pattern supports updating the cache by passing the write of the information through the cache service. The cache service then updates the information held, both in the cache and in the data store.

Static Content Hosting

The Static Content Hosting pattern moves static content such as media images, movies, and other non-dynamic files to a system dedicated for fast retrieval. A specialized service for this is called a **content delivery network** (**CDN**), which manages to distribute content across multiple data centers and directs requests to the data center closest to the caller, as shown in the following diagram:

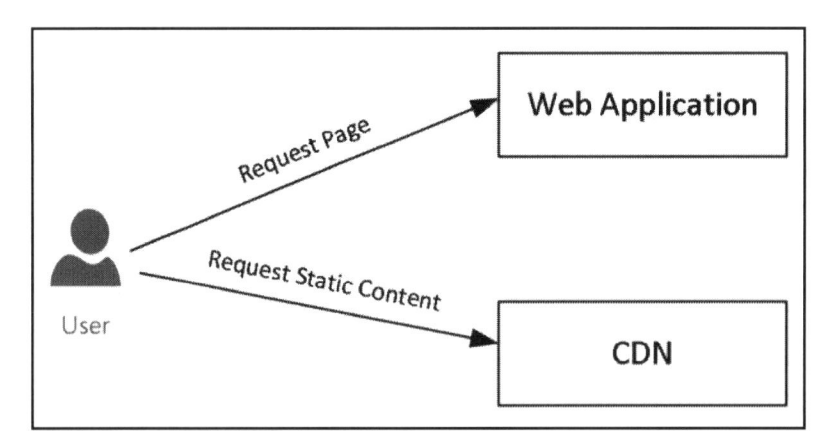

Static Content Hosting is a common pattern for web applications where a dynamic page is requested from the web application and the page contains a collection of static content, such as JavaScript and images, which the browser then retrieves directly from the CDN. This is an effective way to reduce the traffic on the web application.

Command and Query Responsibility Segregation

Command and Query Responsibility Segregation (**CQRS**) is a great software pattern to discuss in more detail as it is conceptually simple and relatively easy to implement but has dramatic implications to both the application and the developers involved. The pattern clearly separates the commands that affect the state of the application from queries that only retrieve data. Simply put, commands such as updates, adds, and deletes are provided in different services from the queries that do not change any data.

You might say *CQRS again!* and we recognize that we have used an example of CQRS in OOP and database design. The same principle does apply to many areas of software development. We are presenting CQRS in this section as a pattern for service design as it leads to some interesting benefits and fits well in modern patterns such as microservices and reactive application design.

> CQRS is based on the object-oriented design presented in the late 1980s by Bertrand Meyer's book, *Object-Oriented Software Construction*: http://se.ethz.ch/~meyer/publications/.

If we revisit Chapter 5: *Implementing Design Patterns - .NET Core*, we illustrated this pattern by splitting our inventory context into two interfaces: IInventoryReadContext and IInventoryWriteContext. As a reminder, here are the interfaces:

```
public interface IInventoryContext : IInventoryReadContext,
IInventoryWriteContext { }

public interface IInventoryReadContext
{
    Book[] GetBooks();
}

public interface IInventoryWriteContext
{
    bool AddBook(string name);
    bool UpdateQuantity(string name, int quantity);
}
```

As we can see, the GetBooks method is separated from the two methods, AddBook and UpdateQuantity, that modify the state of the inventory. This illustrated CQRS within the code solution.

The same approach can be applied at a service level. If we use a service for maintaining inventory as an example, we would break the service between a service for updating the inventory and another service for retrieving the inventory. This is illustrates in the following diagram:

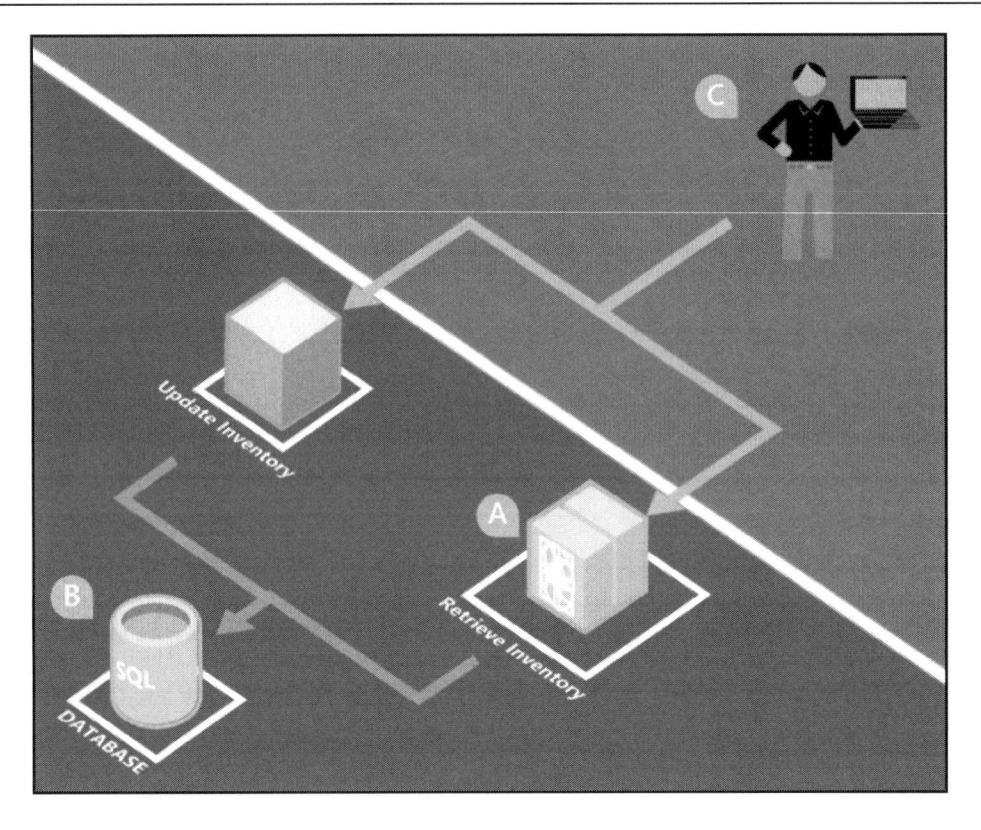

Let's explore CQRS first by looking at the challenges of when it is applied in cloud-based solutions.

Challenges of CQRS

There are significant challenges to using the CQRS pattern with services:

- Consistency
- Adoption

Staleness is a measure of how closely data reflects the committed version of the data. Data, in most circumstances, has the potential to change, so, as soon as a piece of data is read, there is a chance that the data could be updated, making the read data become inconsistent with the source data. This is a challenge with all distributed systems where it is not practical to guarantee the value shown to a user reflects the source value. When the data directly reflects what is stored, we can call the data consistent; when the data does not, it is viewed as inconsistent.

> A common term used in distributed systems is *eventual consistency*. Eventual consistency is used to say a system will over time become consistent. In other words, it will eventually become consistent.

The other more subtle challenge is adoption. Implementing CQRS into an established development team can be met with resistance both from developers and designers who are unfamiliar with the pattern and may lack support from the business for deviating from current design patterns.

So what are the benefits?

Why CQRS?

The following are three compelling factors for using CQRS:

- **Collaboration**
- **Model separation**
- **Independent scalability**

With separate services, we can then maintain, deploy, and scale these services independently. This increases the level of collaboration we can achieve between the development teams.

By having separate services, we can use a model that best fits our service. The command service might use simple SQL statements directly against a database, as that is the most familiar technology to the team responsible, while the team building the query service might use a framework for handling complex statements against the database.

Most solutions tend to have a higher level of reads than writes (or vice versa) so splitting the services along this criterion makes sense in many scenarios.

DevOps

With cloud-based solutions, the data center is remotely hosted and you often do not have full control or access to all aspects of an application. In some cases, such as serverless services, the infrastructure is abstracted away. An application must still expose information about a running application that can be used to manage and monitor an application. Patterns used to manage and monitor are essential for the success of an application by providing both the ability to keep an application running healthily as well as providing strategic information to the business.

Solution patterns

With the availability of commercial packages relating to monitoring and managing solutions, many businesses have gained better control and understanding of their distributed systems. Telemetry and continuous delivery/continuous integration have been chosen to cover in more detail as they have particular value in cloud-based solutions.

Telemetry

As the software industry has evolved and distributed systems involve more services and applications, being able to have a collective and consistent view of a system has become a huge asset. Popularized by services such as New Relic and Microsoft Application Insights, **application performance management** (**APM**) systems use information recorded about applications and infrastructure, known as telemetry, to monitor, manage performance, and view the availability of a system. In cloud-based solutions, where it is often not possible or practical to gain direct access to the infrastructure of a system, an APM allows for telemetry to be sent to a central service, digested, and then presented to operations and the business, as shown in the following diagram:

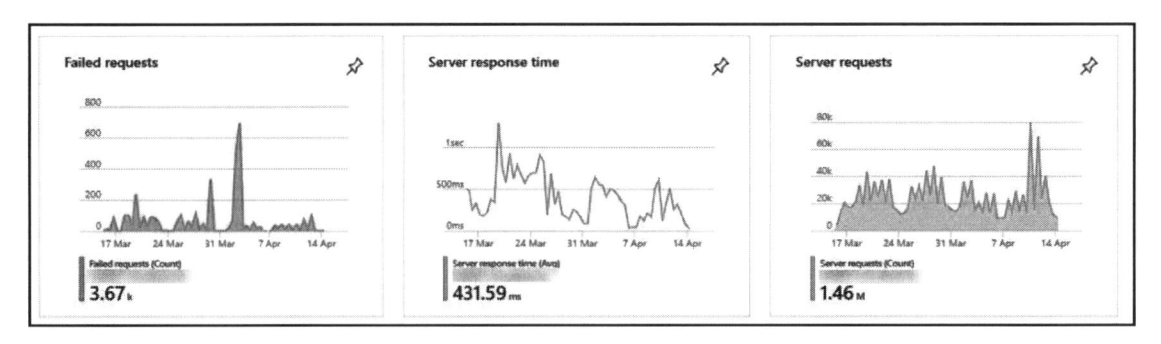

The preceding diagram is taken from Microsoft Application Insights and provides a high-level snapshot of a running web application. At a glance, operations can identify changes in the behavior of the system and react accordingly.

Continuous integration/continuous deployment

Continuous integration/continuous deployment (**CI/CD**) is a modern development process designed to streamline the **software delivery product life cycle** (**SDLC**) by merging changes frequently and deploying those changes often. CI addresses the issues that arise in enterprise software development where multiple programmers are working on the same code base or when a single product is managed with multiple code branches.

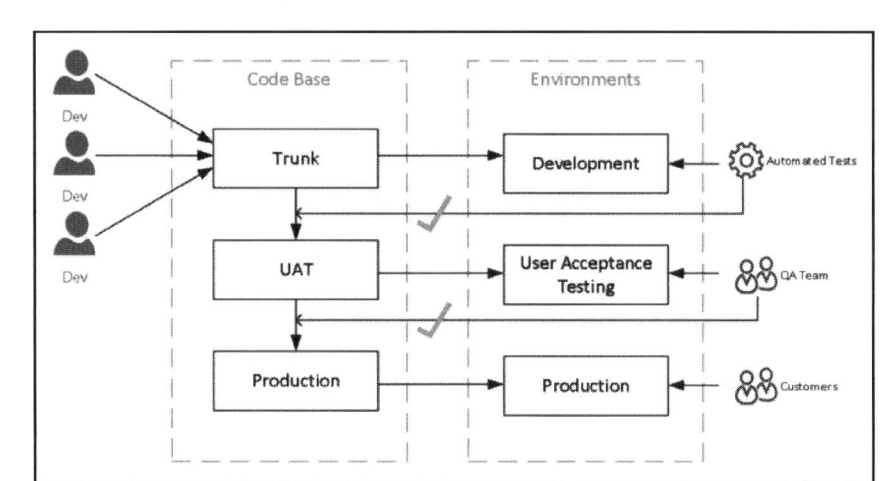

Take a look at the following diagram:

In the preceding example, there are three target environments: Development, **User Acceptance Testing** (**UAT**), and Production. The Development environment is the initial environment where all the changes made to an application are tested together. The UAT environment is used by the **Quality Assurance** (**QA**) team to verify the system is working as intended before the changes are moved to a customer-facing environment, referred to in the diagram as Production. The code base has been broken into three matching branches: the trunk which all changes by the development team are merged into, UAT, which is used to deploy to the UAT environment, and the Production code base, which is used to deploy into the Production environment.

The CI pattern is applied by creating a new build when the code base changes. After a successful build, a suite of unit tests is run against the build to ensure existing functionality has not been broken. If a build is not successful, the development team investigates and either fixes the code base or the unit test so the build then passes.

Successful builds are then pushed to a target environment. The Trunk might be set to push a new build automatically once a day to the Integration environment, while the QA team has requested less disturbance in the environment, so a new build is only pushed once a week after office hours. Production might require a manual trigger to coordinate new releases as to announce the new features and bug fixes in a formal release.

> There is confusion over the terms *continuous deployment* and *continuous delivery*. Many sources differentiate the two terms as to whether the process of deploying is automated or manual. In other words, continuous deployment requires automated continuous delivery.

The trigger to cause a merge between environments and therefore a build to be pushed to an environment, or released, might differ. In our illustration for the Development environment, we have a set of automated tests that are run against new builds automatically. If the tests are successful, then the merge is automatically performed from the Trunk to the UAT code base. The merge between UAT and Production code bases is only performed once the QA team has signed off or accepted the changes in the UAT environment.

Each enterprise will tailor the CI/CD process to fit their particular SDLC and business requirements. A public-facing website, for example, might require a rapid SDLC to stay competitive in the market, whereas an internal application might require a more conservative approach to limit the disruption caused by changing functionality without staff training.

Regardless, suites of tools have been developed to manage the CI/CD process within an organization. Azure DevOps, for example, helps to manage this process by allowing for a pipeline to be built to handle when builds are created and when they are released to environments, including both manual and automated triggers.

Summary

Cloud development requires careful planning, maintenance, and monitoring, and patterns can help achieve highly scalable, reliable, and secure solutions. Many of the patterns discussed in this chapter are applicable to on-premises applications and are essential in cloud solutions. The design of a cloud-first application should consider many factors, including scalability, availability, maintenance, monitoring, and security.

A scalable application allows for fluctuations in system load while maintaining an acceptable level of performance. The load can be measured in the number of users, concurrent processes, amount of data, and other factors in software. The ability to scale a solution horizontally requires a particular type of application development and is a paradigm that is especially significant to cloud computing. Patterns such as Queue-Based Load Leveling are a great technique to ensure solutions remain responsive under an increased load.

Many of the patterns covered in this chapter are complementary. For example, an application following the Command and Query Responsibility Segregation might leverage federated security for providing a single sign-on experience and use an event-driven architecture to handle consistency across the different components of an application.

In cloud-based solutions, there is a near-endless collection of applicable patterns that address different challenges in distributed systems. The patterns presented in this chapter represent a selection chosen for their breadth, as well as how they complement one another. Please see the references to explore other patterns suitable in cloud-based solutions.

What a journey! We have covered patterns from software design patterns used in object-oriented programming and architectural patterns used in cloud-based solutions, to business patterns for more efficient teams and patterns for building successful applications. Though we tried to cover a wide range of patterns, there are bound to be ones that could have, and should have, been added.

With that, thank you from Gaurav and Jeffrey and we hope you enjoyed and gained something from reading *Hands-On Design Patterns with C# and .NET Core*. Please let us know what you think and share with us your favorite patterns.

Questions

The following questions will allow you to consolidate the information contained in this chapter:

1. Most patterns have been developed recently and only apply to cloud-based applications. True or false?
2. An ESB stands for what, and can be used in what type of architecture: EDA, SOA or monolithic?
3. Is Queue-Based Load Leveling primarily used for DevOps, scalability, or availability?
4. What are the benefits of CI/CD? Would it be more beneficial in a large number of globally dispersed teams or a single small team of collocated developers?
5. In a website following Static Content Hosting, does a browser retrieve images and static content directly through a CDN, or does the web application retrieve the information on behalf of the browser?

Further reading

To learn more about the topics covered in this chapter, refer to the following books. These books will provide you with various in-depth and hands-on exercises on the topics that have been covered in this chapter:

- *Azure Serverless Computing Cookbook,* by *Praveen Kumar Sreeram*, published by *Packt Publishing*: `https://www.packtpub.com/in/virtualization-and-cloud/azure-serverless-computing-cookbook`
- *Microservices with Azure,* by *Namit Tanasseri and Rahul Rai*, published by *Packt Publishing*: `https://www.packtpub.com/in/virtualization-and-cloud/microservices-azure`
- *Hands-On Azure for Developers,* by *Kamil Mrzygłód*, published by *Packt Publishing*: `https://www.packtpub.com/virtualization-and-cloud/hands-azure-developers`
- *Building Microservices with .NET Core 2.0 - Second Edition* by *Gaurav Aroraa*, published by *Packt Publishing*: `https://www.packtpub.com/application-development/building-microservices-net-core-20-second-edition`.

Miscellaneous Best Practices

In this book so far, we have discussed various patterns, styles, and code. During this discussion, our aim was to understand the patterns and practices to write neat, clean, and robust code. This appendix will mainly focus on practices. The practice is very important when it comes to adhering to any rule or any kind of coding style. As a developer, you should rehearse coding on a daily basis. According to the old proverb, *practice makes man perfect*.

This is shown through the fact that skills such as playing a game, driving a car, reading, or writing do not come instantly. Instead, we should perfect these skills over time and with practice. For example, when you start driving, you start it slowly. There, you need to remember when to press the clutch, when to press the brake, how far they need to turn the steering wheel, and so on. However, once the driver is well acquainted with driving, then there is no need to remember these steps; they come naturally. This is because of practice.

In this appendix, we will cover the following topics:

- Use case discussion
- Best practices
- Other design patterns

Technical requirements

This appendix contains various code examples to explain the concepts covered. The code is kept simple and is just for demo purposes. Most of the examples in this chapter involve a .NET Core console application written in C#.

To run and execute the code, there are these prerequisites:

- Visual Studio 2019 (however, you can also run application using Visual Studio 2017)

Miscellaneous Best Practices

Installation of Visual Studio

To run the code examples included in this chapter, you need to install Visual Studio or later. To do so, follow these instructions:

1. Download Visual Studio from the following download link: `https://docs.microsoft.com/en-us/visualstudio/install/install-visual-studio`.
2. Follow the installation instructions.
3. Multiple versions are available for Visual Studio. We are using Visual Studio for Windows.

> The example code files for the chapter is available at the following link: `https://github.com/PacktPublishing/Hands-On-Design-Patterns-with-C-and-.NET-Core/tree/master/Appendix`.

Use case discussion

Put simply, a use case is a pre-creation or a symbolic representation of a business scenario. For example, we can represent our login page use case in a pictorial/symbolic representation. In our example, users are trying to log into a system. If the login succeeds, they can enter the system. If it fails, the system informs the users that the login attempt failed. Refer to the following diagram of a **login** use case:

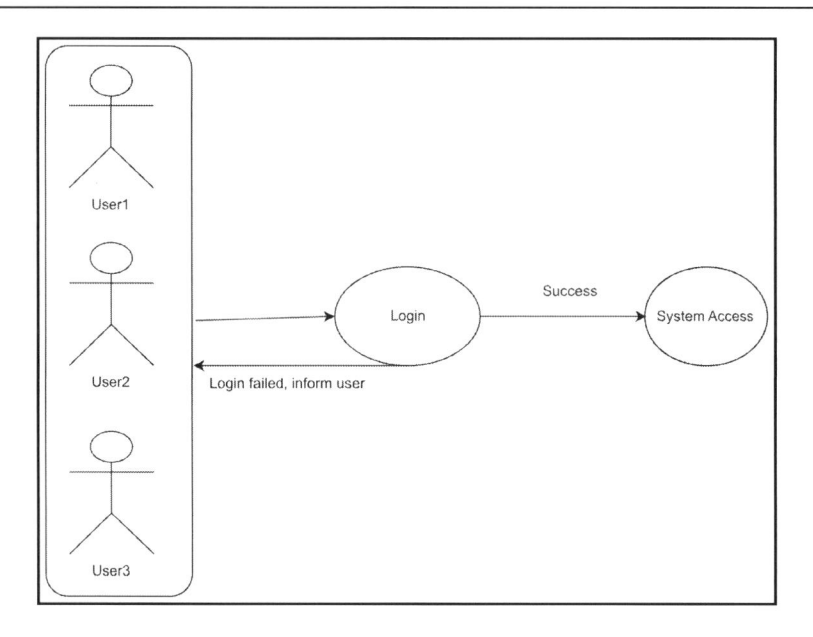

Miscellaneous Best Practices

In the preceding diagram, users called **User1**, **User2**, and **User3** are trying to enter the system using the login functionality of the application. If the login attempt is successful, the user can access the system. If not, the application notifies the user that login wasn't successful and the user can't access the system. The preceding diagram is much clearer than our actual verbose description, where we are describing this diagram. The diagram is also self-explanatory.

UML diagram

In the previous section, we discussed the login functionality with the help of symbolic representation. You might have noticed the symbols that are used in the diagram. The notations or symbols used in the previous diagram are part of a symbolic language called **Unified Modeling Language**. This is a way of visualizing our program, software, or even a class.

> The symbol or notation used in the UML has evolved from the work of Grady Booch, James Rumbaugh, Ivar Jacobson, and the Rational Software Corporation.

Types of UML diagram

These diagrams are divided into two main groups:

- **Structural UML Diagrams**: These emphasize the things that must be present in the system being modeled. This group is further divided into the following different types of diagrams:
    - Class diagram
    - Package diagram
    - Object diagram
    - Component diagram
    - Composite structure diagram
    - Deployment diagram
- **Behavioral UML Diagrams**: These are used to show the functionality of the system and include use case, sequence, collaboration, state machine, and activity diagrams. This group is further divided into the following different types of diagram:
    - Activity diagram
    - Sequence diagram

Miscellaneous Best Practices

- Use case diagram
- State diagram
- Communication diagram
- Interaction overview diagram
- Timing diagram

Best practices

As we have established, practice is a habit that occurs in our daily activities. In software engineering—where software is engineered and not manufactured—we have to practice in order to write good quality code. There may be more points that explain the best practices involved in software engineering. Let's discuss them:

- **Short but simplified code**: This is a very basic thing that does require practice. Developers should use short but simplified code daily in order to write concise code and adhere to this practice in their daily life. The code should be clean and not repeat itself. Clean code and code simplification was covered in previous chapters; if you missed this topic, please revisit Chapter 2, *Modern Software Design Patterns and Principles*. Take a look at the following example of concise code:

    ```
    public class Math
    {
        public int Add(int a, int b) => a + b;
        public float Add(float a, float b) => a + b;
        public decimal Add(decimal a, decimal b) => a + b;
    }
    ```

    The preceding code snippet contains a Math class with three Add methods. These methods are written to calculate the sum of two integer numbers and the sum of two float and decimal numbers. The Add(float a, float b) and Add(decimal a, decimal b) methods are the overloaded methods of Add(int a, int b). The previous code example represents a scenario where the requirements are to make a single method with a output of the int, float, or decimal datatype.

- **Unit testing**: This is an integral part of development when we want to test our code by writing code. **Test-driven development** (**TDD**) is one of the best practices that one should adhere to. We have discussed TDD in Chapter 7, *Implementing Design Patterns for Web Applications - Part 2*.

- **Code consistency**: Nowadays, there are very rare opportunities for a developer to work alone. A developer mostly works in a team, meaning that it is very important for there to be code consistency throughout the team. Code consistency can refer to code style. There are a few recommended practices and coding conversions that developers should use regularly while writing programs.

  There are many ways to declare a variable. Here is one of the best examples for variable declaration:

  ```
  namespace Implement
  {
      public class Consume
      {
          BestPractices.Math math = new BestPractices.Math();
      }
  }
  ```

  In the previous code, we have declared a `math` variable of the `BestPractices.Math` type. Here, `BestPractices` is our namespace and `Math` is the class. If we are not taking `using` directives in the code then it's good practice to have fully namespace qualified variables.

  > Official docs for the C# language describe these conventions very elaborately. You can refer to them here: https://docs.microsoft.com/en-us/dotnet/csharp/programming-guide/inside-a-program/coding-conventions.

- **Code reviews**: Making mistakes is human nature, and this also happens in development. Code review is the first step in practicing writing bug-free code and uncovering the unpredictable mistakes in the code.

Other design patterns

So far, we have covered various design patterns and principles including the best practices to write code. This section will summarize the following patterns and guide you to write quality and robust code. The details and implementation of these patterns are beyond the scope of this book.

We have already covered the following patterns:

- GoF patterns
- Design principles
- Software development life cycle patterns
- Test-driven development

In this book, we have covered a lot of topics and developed a sample application (console and web). This is not the end of the world, there are more things to learn in the world.

We can list more patterns:

- **Space-based architectural pattern**: **Space-based Pattern** (SBPs) are patterns that help with application scalability by minimizing the factors that limit application scaling. These patterns are also known as **cloud architecture patterns**. We have covered many of them in `Chapter 12`, *Coding for the Cloud*.
- **Messaging patterns**: These patterns are used to connect two applications based on messaging (sent in the form of packets). These packets or messages are transmitting using a logical path on which various applications connect (these logical paths are known as channels). There might be scenarios where one application has multiple messages; in that case, not all messages can be sent at once. In a scenario where there are multiple messages, a channel can be called a queue and several messages can be queued up in a channel and can be accessed from various applications at the same point in time.
- **Additional patterns for Domain-Driven Design—layered architecture:** This depicts separation of concerns, where the concept of layered architecture comes in. Behind the scenes, the basic idea for developing an application is that it should be structured into conceptual layers. In general, applications have four conceptual layers:
    - **User interface**: This layer has everything where the end user interacts, this layer accepts the commands and then provides the information accordingly.
    - **Application layer**: This layer is more towards transaction management, data translation, and so on.

- **Domain layer**: This layer sticks to behavior and the state of the domain.
- **Infrastructure layer**: Everything happens here related to repositories, adapters, and frameworks.
- **Containerized application patterns**: Before we dig into this, we should know what containers are. A container is lightweight, portable software; it defines an environment under which software can run. Generally, software that is running inside the container is designed as a single-purpose application. For containerized applications the most important pattern is as follows:
    - **Docker image building patterns**: This pattern is based on the Builder pattern from GoF design patterns, which we discussed in `Chapter 3`, *Implementing Design Patterns-Basics Part 1*. It only describes the setup so that it can be used to build a container. In addition to this, there is a multi-stage image building pattern that provides a way to build multiple images from a single Dockerfile.

Summary

The aim of this appendix was to highlight the importance of practice. In this chapter, we discussed how we can practice enhancing our skills. Once we achieve the skills, there is no need to remember the steps to achieve a specific task. We covered and discussed a few use cases from the real world, discussed best practices from our day-to-day code, and other design patterns that can be used in our daily practice to enhance our skills. Finally, we wrapped up the last chapter of this book and learned that with practice and the adaptation of various patterns, developers can improve their code quality.

Questions

The following questions will allow you to consolidate the information contained in this appendix:

1. What is practice? Take a few examples from our routine and daily life.
2. We can achieve a specific coding skill with practice. Explain this.
3. What is test-driven development and how does it helps developers to practice?

Further reading

We have almost reached the end of this book! In this appendix, we have covered a lot of things related to practice. This is not the end of learning but it is just a beginning, there are more books you can refer to for your learning and knowledge:

- *Hands-On Domain-Driven Design with .NET Core* by *Alexey Zimarev*, published by *Packt Publishing*: https://www.packtpub.com/in/application-development/hands-domain-driven-design-net-core.
- *C# and .NET Core Test-Driven Development* by *Ayobami Adewole*, published by *Packt Publishing*: https://www.packtpub.com/in/application-development/c-and-net-core-test-driven-development.
- *Architectural Patterns*, by *Pethuru Raj, Harihara Subramanian, et al*, published by *Packt Publishing*: https://www.packtpub.com/in/application-development/architectural-patterns.
- *Concurrent Patterns and Best Practices*, by *Atul S. Khot*, published by *Packt Publishing*: https://www.packtpub.com/in/application-development/concurrent-patterns-and-best-practices.

Assessments

Chapter 1 – Overview of OOP in .NET Core and C#

1. **What do the terms late and early binding refer to?**

   Early binding is established when the source code is compiled while late binding is established while the component is running.

2. **Does C# support multiple inheritance?**

   No. The reasoning is that multiple inheritance leads to more complex source code.

3. **In C#, what level of encapsulation could be used to prevent access to a class from outside of the library?**

   The `internal` access modifier can be used to limit the visibility of a class to only within the library.

4. **What is the difference between aggregation and composition?**

   Both are types of association and the easiest way to differentiate the two is by whether or not the classes involved can exist without being associated. In a composition association, the classes involved have a tight life cycle dependency. This implies that, when one class is deleted, the associated classes are also deleted.

5. **Can interfaces contain properties? (This is a bit of a tricky question)**

    It is possible for an interface to define properties, but as an interface does have a body...

6. **Do dogs eat fish?**

    Dogs are lovely but they eat most things they can get in their mouth.

Chapter 2 – Modern Software Design Patterns and Principles

1. **In SOLID, what does the S stand for? What is meant by a responsibility?**

    Single Responsibility Principle. Responsibility can be viewed as a reason for a change.

2. **What SDLC method is built around cycles: Waterfall or Agile?**

    Agile is built around the concept of the development process being conducted in a collection of cycles.

3. **Is the decorator pattern a creational or structural pattern?**

    The decorator pattern is a structural pattern that allows functionality to be divided between classes and is particularly useful to enhance classes at runtime.

4. **What does pub-sub integration stand for?**

    Publish-Subscribe is a useful pattern where processes publish messages and other processes subscribe to receive the messages.

Chapter 3 – Implementing Design Patterns – Basics Part 1

1. **In developing software for an organization, why is it sometimes difficult to determine requirements?**

    There are many challenges to developing software for an organization. An example would be that changes in the organization's industry could cause the current requirements to need to be altered.

2. **What are two advantages and disadvantages of waterfall software development versus agile software development?**

    Waterfall software development provides an advantage over agile software development as it is simpler to understand and implement. In some situations, where the complexity and size of the project is smaller, Waterfall Software Development could be a better option over Agile Software Development. Waterfall Software Development, though, does not handle change well and, by having a larger scope, has more chance of requirements changing before the project is completed.

3. **How does dependency injection help when writing unit tests?**

    By injecting dependencies into a class, a class becomes easier to test as the dependencies are clearly known and more easily accessible.

4. **Why is the following statement false? With TDD, you no longer need people to test a new software deployment.**

    Test-Driven Development helps to improve the quality of a solution by building a clear testing strategy into the software development life cycle. The tests defined, though, might not be complete, so there is still the need for additional resources to validate the delivered software.

Chapter 4 – Implementing Design Patterns – Basics Part 2

1. **Provide an example to show why using a singleton would not be a good mechanism for limiting access to a shared resource?**

   A singleton intentionally creates a bottleneck in an application. It is also one of the first patterns developers learn to use and, because of this, it is often used in situations where limiting access to the shared resource is not required.

2. **Is the following statement true? Why or why not?** `ConcurrentDictionary` **prevents items in the collection from being updated by more than one thread at a time.**

   For many C# developers, realizing that `ConcurrentDictionary` does not prevent items in the collection from being updated by more than one thread at a time is a painful lesson. `ConcurrentDictionary` protects a shared dictionary from being accessed and modified concurrently.

3. **What is a race condition and why should it be avoided?**

   A race condition is when the order of processing of multiple threads can culminate in different results.

4. **How does the factory pattern help simplify code?**

   The factory pattern is an effective way to decouple the creation of objects within an application.

5. **Do .NET Core applications require third-party IoC containers?**

   .NET Core has a powerful Inversion of Control built into the framework. It can be enhanced when required by other IoC containers, but is not required.

Chapter 5 – Implementing Design Patterns – .NET Core

1. **If you are not sure what type of service lifetime to use, what type is it best to register a class as? Why?**

   Transient lifetime services are created each time they are requested. The majority of classes should be lightweight, stateless services, so this is the best service lifetime to use.

2. **In .NET Core ASP .NET solutions, a scope is defined per web request or per session?**

   A scope is per web request (connection).

3. **Does registering a class as a Singleton in the .NET Core DI framework make it thread-safe?**

   No, the framework will provide the same instance for subsequent requests, but does not make a class thread-safe.

4. **Is it true that the .NET Core DI framework can only be replaced with other Microsoft-supplied DI frameworks?**

   Yes, there are many DI frameworks that can be used instead of the native DI framework.

Chapter 6 – Implementing Design Patterns for Web Applications – Part 1

1. **What is a web application?**

   It's a program that uses a web browser and can be accessible from anywhere if available over public network. This works on a client/server architecture and serves the client by taking an HTTP request and providing an HTTP response.

Assessments

2. **Craft a web application of your choice and depict a pictorial view of the working of web application.**

   Refer to the FlixOne application.

3. **What is Inversion of Control?**

   Inversion of Control (**IoC**) is a container to invert or delegate the control. It is based on the DI framework. .NET Core has a built-in IoC container.

4. **What is the UI/Architectural pattern? Which pattern you would like to use and why?**

   The UI Architectural pattern is designed to make a robust user interface to give user a better experience of the application. From the developer's point of view of point, MVC, MVP, and MVVM are the popular patterns.

Chapter 7 – Implementing Design Patterns for Web Applications – Part 2

1. **What are authentication and authorization?**

   Authentication is a process in which a system verifies or identifies the incoming requests through credentials (generally a user ID and password). If the system finds that the provided credentials are wrong, then it notifies the user (generally via a message on the GUI screen) and terminates the authorization process.

   Authorization always comes after authentication. This is a process that allows the authenticated user who raised the request to access resources or data after verifying that they have access to the specific resources or data

2. **Is it safe to use authentication at the first level of a request and then allow incoming requests for restricted areas?**

   This is not always safe. As developers, we should take all necessary steps to make our application more secure. After first a level request, the authentication, the system should also check resource-level permissions.

3. **How you will prove that authorization always comes after authentication?**

   In a simple scenario of a web application, it first validates the user by asking for login credentials and then authorizes the user as per role to access specific resource.

4. **What is Test-Driven Development and why do developers care about it?**

   Test-Driven Development is a way to make sure that code is tested; it is like testing code by writing code. TDD is also known as Red/Blue/Green concepts. Developers should follow it to make their code/program work without any error.

5. **Define TDD Katas. How does it help us to improve our TDD approach?**

   TDD Katas are small scenarios or problems that help to learn to code by practice. You can take the example of Fizz Buzz Kata, where developers should apply coding to learn and practice TDD. If you want to practice TDD Katas, refer to this repository: https://github.com/garora/TDD-Katas.

Chapter 8 – Concurrent Programming in .NET Core

1. **What is concurrent programming?**

   Whenever things/tasks are happening at the same time, we say that tasks are happening concurrently. In our programming language, whenever any parts of our program run at the same time, it is concurrent programming.

2. **How does true parallelism happen?**

   True parallelism is not possible on a single CPU machine because tasks are not switchable, as it has a single core. It only happens on a machine with multiple CPUs (multiple cores).

3. **What is a race condition?**

   The potential for more than one thread to access the same shared data and update it with unpredictable results can be referred to as a race condition.

4. **Why should we use `ConcurrentDictionary`?**

   A concurrent dictionary is a thread-safe collection class and stores key-value pairs. This class has implementation for a lock statement and provides a thread-safe class.

Chapter 9 – Functional Programming Practices – an Approach

1. **What is functional programming?**

   Functional programming is an approach to symbolic computation in the same way as we solve mathematical problems. Any functional programming is based on mathematical functions. Any functional programming style language works on solutions with two terms: what to solve and how to solve?

2. **What is referential transparency in functional programming?**

   In functional programs, once we define the variables, they do not change their value throughout the program. As functional programs do not have assignment statements, if we need to store value, there is no alternative; instead, we define new variables.

3. **What is `Pure` function?**

   The `Pure` functions are the ones that strengthen functional programming by saying that they are pure. These functions work on two conditions:

   - The end result/output will always remain the same for the provided parameters.
   - These will not impact the behavior of the program or the execution path of the application, even if they are being called a hundred times.

Chapter 10 – Reactive Programming Patterns and Techniques

1. **What is a stream?**

   A sequence of events is called a stream. A stream can emit three things: a value, an error, and a signal for completion.

2. **What are reactive properties?**

   Reactive properties are binding properties that react when an event triggers.

3. **What is a reactive system?**

   On the basis of the Reactive Manifesto, we can conclude that reactive systems are as follows:

   - **Responsive**: Reactive systems are event-based design systems because of this design approach; these systems are quick to respond to any request in a short time.
   - **Scalable**: Reactive systems are reactive in nature. These systems can react to change the scalability rate by expanding or reducing the allocated resources.
   - **Resilient**: A resilient system is one that would not stop, even if there is any failure/exception. Reactive systems are designed in such a way that, despite any exception or failure, the system will never die; it remains working.
   - **Message-based**: Any data of an item represents a message and can be sent to a specific destination. When a message or data has arrived at a given state, an event that is a signal is emitted to notify that the message has been received. Reactive systems rely on this message-passing.

4. **What is meant by merging two reactive streams?**

   Merging two reactive steams is actually combining elements of two similar or different reactive streams into a new reactive stream. For example, if you have `stream1`, and `stream2` then `stream3 = stream1.merge(stream2)`, but the sequence of `stream3` would not be in order.

5. **What is the MVVM pattern?**

Model-View-ViewModel (**MVVM**) is one of the variations of **Model-View-Controller** (**MVC**) to meet the modern UI development approach, where UI development is the core responsibility of designer/UI-developers, rather than application developers. In this approach of development, a designer who is more of a graphical enthusiast and is focused on making the user interface more attractive may or may not bother about the development part of the application. Generally, designers (UI persons) use various tools to make the user interface more attractive. The MVVM is defined as follows:

- **Model**: This is also called as a domain object and it holds data only; there is no business logic, validations, and so on.
- **View**: This is a representation of data for the end user.
- **View Model**: This separates View and Model; its main responsibility is to serve end users better stuff.

Chapter 11 – Advanced Database Design and Application Techniques

1. **What is a ledger-style database?**

   This database is meant to insert operations only; there are no updates. Then, you create a view that aggregates the inserts together.

2. **What is CQRS?**

   Command Query Responsibility Segregation is a pattern that segregates the responsibilities between Query (to inserts) and Commands (to updates).

3. **When should you use CQRS?**

   CQRS can be a good pattern to apply for task-based or event-driven systems, especially when the solution is composed of multiple applications and not a single monolithic website or application. It is **a pattern and not an architecture**, so it should be applied in specific cases and not in all business scenarios

Chapter 12 – Coding for the Cloud

1. **Is this a true statement? Most patterns have been developed recently and only apply to cloud-based applications.**

    No, this is not true. Patterns have been evolving as software development changes but many of the core patterns have existed for decades.

2. **What does an ESB stand for? What type of architecture can it be used in: EDA, SOA, or monolithic?**

    It stands for Enterprise Service Bus. It can be used effectively in event-driven architecture and service-oriented architecture.

3. **Is queue-based load leveling is primarily used for DevOps, scalability, or availability?**

    Availability. Queue-based load leveling primarily used to handle large fluctuations in load by acting as a buffer to reduce the chance of an application becoming unavailable.

4. **What are the benefits of CI/CD? Would it be more beneficial in a large number of globally dispersed teams or a single small team of collocated developers?**

    In general, CI/CD helps to identify issues early in the development life cycle by frequently performing merges and deployments. Larger, more complex solutions, tend to show the benefits more than smaller, simpler solutions.

5. **In a website following static content hosting, does a browser retrieve images and static content directly through a CDN or does the web application retrieve the information on behalf of the browser?**

    A content delivery network can be used to improve performance and availability by caching static resources in multiple data centers, allowing for a browser to retrieve content directly from the closest data center.

Appendix A – Miscellaneous Best Practices

1. **What is a practice? Give a few examples from our routine/daily life.**

   A practice may be one or more routine activities. To learn to drive, we should practice our driving. A practice is an activity that is not required to be memorized. There are a lot of examples of practice from our daily life: eating while watching TV shows, and so on. It does not break your rhythm to eat anything while you're watching your favorite TV show.

2. **We can achieve a specific coding skill with practice. Explain this.**

   Yes, we can achieve a specific coding skill with practice. The practice needs attention and consistency. For example, you want to learn Test-Driven Development. To do so, you need to learn it first. You can learn it by practicing TDD-Katas.

3. **What is Test-Driven Development and how does it help developers to practice?**

   Test-Driven Development is a way to make sure that code is tested; it is like we are testing code by writing code. TDD is also known as Red/Blue/Green concepts. Developers should follow it to make their code/program work without any error.

Other Books You May Enjoy

If you enjoyed this book, you may be interested in these other books by Packt:

Hands-On Domain-Driven Design with .NET Core
Alexey Zimarev

ISBN: 9781788834094

- Discover and resolve domain complexity together with business stakeholders
- Avoid common pitfalls when creating the domain model
- Study the concept of Bounded Context and aggregate
- Design and build temporal models based on behavior and not only data
- Build graphical user interfaces using JavaFX
- Explore benefits and drawbacks of Event Sourcing
- Get acquainted with CQRS and to-the-point read models with projections
- Practice building one-way flow UI with Vue.js
- Understand how a task-based UI conforms to DDD principles

Other Books You May Enjoy

Hands-On Network Programming with C# and .NET Core
Sean Burns

ISBN: 9781789340761

- Understand the breadth of C#'s network programming utility classes
- Utilize network-layer architecture and organizational strategies
- Implement various communication and transport protocols within C#
- Discover hands-on examples of distributed application development
- Gain hands-on experience with asynchronous socket programming and streams
- Learn how C# and the .NET Core runtime interact with a hosting network
- Understand a full suite of network programming tools and features

Leave a review - let other readers know what you think

Please share your thoughts on this book with others by leaving a review on the site that you bought it from. If you purchased the book from Amazon, please leave us an honest review on this book's Amazon page. This is vital so that other potential readers can see and use your unbiased opinion to make purchasing decisions, we can understand what our customers think about our products, and our authors can see your feedback on the title that they have worked with Packt to create. It will only take a few minutes of your time, but is valuable to other potential customers, our authors, and Packt. Thank you!

Index

.NET Core CLI tools 70
.Net Core service lifetimes
  about 135
  FlixOne 136, 137, 138
  scope 142, 143
  scoped 135
  singleton 136
  transient 135
.NET Core web application, challenges
  about 186
  challenges for businesses 187
  challenges for developers 186
  solution, obtaining for 187
.NET Core web application, requisites
  about 185
  business requisites 185
  technical requisites 186
.Net Core web application
  creating 161
.NET Core web application
  extending 185
.Net Core web application
  project, kicking off 161
  requisites, developing 162
.Net Core, features
  about 126
  CatalogService 128, 129
  IServiceCollection 126, 127
  IServiceProvider 129, 130
.NET Core
  reference 33
  setting up 242

A

abstract class 22
Abstract Factory design pattern
  about 76, 77
  InventoryCommand abstract class 77, 78, 80
access levels
  internal 25
  private 25
  protected 25
  protected internal 25
  public 25
access modifiers
  about 89, 90
  reference 89
AddInventoryCommand 111, 112
AddInventoryCommandTest 114, 115
aggregation 20
Agile SDLC
  about 57, 58
  advantages 57
anonymous functions 259
application design 350
application design, solution patterns
  about 350
  Cache 350
  Command and Query Responsibility Segregation (CQRS) 352, 353, 354
application performance management (APM) 356
association 20
async method 228
asynchronous programming 225, 227, 228, 261
authentication
  about 188, 189, 191, 193
  implementing 193, 195, 196, 198, 200, 202, 203, 204
authorization

about 188, 189, 191, 193
  implementing 204, 206, 208, 210, 212
availability 212
await method 228, 229

B

behavioral pattern
  Chain of Responsibility 42
  chain of responsibility 43, 45, 46
  command 42
  interpreter 42
  iterator 42
  observer 42
  strategy 42
  Template Method 42
  visitor 42
block structures 17
Business Analyst (BA) 65, 185, 282, 306
Business Process Framework (eTOM) 53
business requisites
  item filtering 282
  item sorting 282

C

Cache
  about 350
  Cache-aside pattern 351
  Static Content Hosting pattern 352
  Write-through Cache pattern 351
Canonical Data Model (CDM) 52
CatalogService 128, 129
challenges, use case
  for business 308
  for developers 307
  solution, providing 308
class 18
clean model 293
cloud-based solutions
  building, consideration 334
code duplication
  causes 34
Command Query Responsibility Segregation (CQRS)
  about 145, 303, 352, 353
  challenges 354

collaboration 313
  independent scalability 313
  model separation 313
  need for 355
  reference 313
Command-Query Separation (CQS) 313
composition 21
concurrency 223, 225
concurrent collections 230, 231
confidentiality 212
considerations, cloud-based solutions
  application design 334
  DevOps 334
  resilience/availability 334
  scalability 334
  security 334
console application 130, 131
construction-related patterns examples
  Correlation Identifier 51
  Expiration 51
  Message Sequence 51
  Return Address 51
constructor injection (CI) 144
content delivery network (CDN) 352
continuous deployment (CD) 356
continuous integration (CI) 356
Create Read Update Delete (CRUD) operations 188, 313
creational patterns
  Abstract Factory pattern 38
  builder pattern 38
  Factory Method pattern 38
  Prototype pattern 38
  singleton pattern 38
CRUD pages
  implementing 170, 171, 172, 174, 175, 176, 178, 179, 180, 181

D

data warehouse 310
database 308
database processing 309
deferred execution 237
Dependency Injection (DI) 126
dependency injection principle (DIP) 85

dependency inversion principle (DIP) 85, 87
design patterns 11
design principles
  about 33
  Don't Repeat Yourself (DRY) 33
  Keep It Simple Stupid (KISS) 34
  Minimum Viable Product (MVP) 34
  SOLID 35
  You Aren't Gonna Need It (YAGNI) 34
DevOps 355
DevOps, solution patterns
  about 356
  continuous deployment (CD) 356, 358
  continuous integration (CI) 356, 358
  telemetry 356
Don't Repeat Yourself (DRY) 33
Dynabook
  reference 15
dynamic polymorphism
  about 27
  inheritance polymorphism 28
  interface polymorphism 28

E

EffSharp
  reference 244
Electronic Data Interchange For Administration, Commerce and Transport (EDIFACT) 53
encapsulation 25
Enterprise integration patterns
  reference 49
  topology 49
enterprise service bus (ESB) 50
event-driven architecture (EDA)
  about 345
  Compensating transaction 347, 348
  Priority Queue 347
  Publisher Subscriber 346, 347
  Queue-Based Load Leveling 345
expression trees 259

F

factory pattern
  about 120, 121
  unit tests 121

First In First Out (FIFO) 309
first-class functions 247
FlixOne
  about 250, 253, 255, 256
  folder structure 251
  unit tests 139, 140
for loop 17
Func 259
functional honesty 245
functional programming
  about 243, 246, 248, 257
  programming languages 243

G

Gang of Four (GoF) patterns
  about 37, 256
  behavioral pattern 42
  creational patterns 38
  structural patterns 38
generics 29
GetInventoryCommand 118
GetInventoryCommandTest 119
Globally Unique Identifier (GUID) 194
graceful degradation 344

H

has-a relationship 20
Hash-Based Message Authentication Code (HMAC) 194
hierarchical inheritance 25
high-level requirements, inventory application
  discount rates 250
  pagination implementation 250
Higher order functions (HOFs) 257
Hospitality Industry Technology Integration Standards (HITIS) 53
hub-and-spoke (hub) 50
hybrid inheritance 25
HyperText Transfer Protocol (HTTP) 163

I

identity provider (IdP) 349
IInventoryContext 144
IInventoryReadContext 145
IInventoryWriteContext 146

implementation factory
  about 144
  IInventoryContext 144
  IInventoryReadContext 145
  IInventoryWriteContext 146
  InventoryCommand 148
  InventoryCommandFactory 147, 148
implicit inheritance 25
IMS Question and Test Interoperability specification (QTI) 53
Information Management System (IMS) Global Learning Consortium (GLC) 53
inheritance polymorphism 28, 29
inheritance
  about 14, 23
  hierarchical inheritance 25
  hybrid inheritance 25
  implicit inheritance 25
  multilevel inheritance 25
  multiple inheritance 24
  single inheritance 23
  types 23
integrated development environment (IDE) 70, 184
integration 49
integration pipeline
  additional patterns 52
  categories 51
  messaging 51
  routing pattern 54, 55
  transformation pattern 52, 53
integrity 212
interface 15, 22
interface polymorphism 28
interface segregation principle (ISP) 36, 85
inventory application
  enhancing 249
  FlixOne 250, 253
  obtaining, with filter 283, 285, 287, 290, 292
  obtaining, with paging 283, 285, 287, 290, 292
  obtaining, with sorting 283, 285, 288, 290, 292
  project, business requisites 282
  project, initiating 282
  project, requisites 282
  requirements 249
  use case 282
InventoryCommand abstract class 77, 78, 80
InventoryCommand unit tests
  about 88
  access modifiers 89
  Helper TestUserInterface 91, 92
  QuitCommand 93
InventoryCommand
  about 148
  factory, implementing function used 148, 150
  services, using 152, 153, 154
  third-party containers, using 155, 156
InventoryCommandFactory 147, 148
InventoryCommandFactoryTests 123, 124
Inversion of Control (IoC) 87, 126
IObservable
  about 271
  observer pattern 272, 274, 275, 277, 279, 280
IServiceCollection 126, 127
IServiceProvider 129, 130
item filtering 306
item sorting 306

J

JSON Web Token (JWT) 350

K

Keep It Simple Stupid (KISS) 34, 340

L

Lambda 259
Last In First Out (LIFO) 309
ledger-style database 311, 312
LINQ 237, 259
Liskov substitution principle (LSP) 36, 83

M

materialized view 312
microservices
  about 340
  advantages 343
  business capability 341
  independently maintainable 342
  isolated state 342, 343

loosely coupled 341
small 340
Microsoft Unit Test (MSTest) framework 70
Minimal Viable Product (MVP) 249
Minimum Viable Product (MVP)
  about 34, 65, 303
  advantage 66
  fitting, with future development 67
  requisites 65, 66, 67
Model View Controller (MVC) 183
Model View Presenter (MVP) 183
Model-View-ViewModel (MVVM) 259
multi-threading 225, 227, 228
multilevel inheritance 25
multiple inheritance
  reference 24
MVC pattern 292
MVVM pattern
  about 292
  implementing 294, 297, 299, 300
  Model 293
  practices 292
  View 293
  ViewModel 294

O

Object Management Group (OMG) 22
Object Relational Mapping (ORM) 111
Object-oriented Design (OOD) 313
object-oriented programming (OOP) 11, 15, 16, 31, 77
objects 18, 19, 20
observer pattern 272, 273, 275, 277, 279, 280
One-Time Passwords (OTPs) 194
Online Analytical Processing (OLAP) 309, 310
Online Transaction Processing (OLTP) 309, 310
open/closed principle (OCP) 35, 82
OpenId Connect (OIDC) 350

P

parallel programming 223
parallelism 225
pattern CQRS
  implementing 313, 314, 315, 317, 318, 319, 320, 321, 322, 323, 325, 327, 328, 330, 331

persistent view 312
Point Of Sale (POS) 308
polymorphism
  about 26
  dynamic polymorphism 27
  static polymorphism 27
Predicate 259
procedural call 17
procedural programming 17
processes 98
Proof of Concept (PoC) 67

Q

Quality Assurance (QA) 357

R

race condition 98
reactive extensions 280
reactive manifesto
  reference 263
reactive programming
  about 263
  principles 261, 262
  reactive streams 265, 266, 269, 270
reactive systems
  message-based 264
  resilient 264
  responsive 264
  scalable 264
recursion 259
repository pattern 99
resiliency/availability 344
resiliency/availability, solution pattern
  about 345
  event-driven architecture (EDA) 345
routing pattern
  aggregator 54
  Content-based Routing 54
  Message Filtering 54
  Scatter-Gather 54
  splitter 54
Rx Extensions 280

[391]

S

scalability, solution patterns
  about 336
  auto-scaling 339
  horizontal scaling 337, 338
  microservices 340
  vertical scaling 336
scalability
  about 335
  workload 335
Secure Hash Algorithm (SHA) 194
security 348
Security Assertion Markup Language (SAML) 350
security token service (STS) 349
security, solution patterns
  about 349
  federated security 349, 350
service contract 341
service level agreement (SLA) 344
Service Locator Pattern (SLP) 87
service-oriented architecture (SOA) 340
signature 22
Silverlight 292
Simula
  reference 15
single inheritance 23
single responsibility principle (SRP) 35, 81, 82
single sign-on (SSO) 349
singleton pattern
  about 97
  AddInventoryCommand 111, 112
  GetInventoryCommand 118
  processes 98
  race condition 108, 109, 110, 111
  repository pattern 99
  threads 98
  unit tests 100, 101, 102, 104, 105, 106, 107, 108
  UpdateQuantityCommand 115
Smalltalk
  reference 15
software delivery product life cycle (SDLC) 356
software development life cycle (SDLC)
  about 55
  Agile approach 57

  Waterfall approach 56
software patterns
  about 37
  GoF patterns 37
software-as-a-service (SaaS) 349
SOLID principles
  about 35, 81, 231, 235, 238
  dependency inversion principle (DIP) 37, 85, 87
  interface segregation principle (ISP) 36, 85
  Liskov substitution principle (LSP) 36, 83
  open/closed principle 35
  single responsibility principle (SRP) 35, 81, 82
SQL Server
  installing 243
state changes 272
static polymorphism 27
strategy pattern 256
structural patterns
  adapter pattern 38
  bridge pattern 38
  composite pattern 38
  decorator pattern 38, 39, 41
  facade pattern 38
  flyweight pattern 38
  proxy pattern 38
structured programming 17
subject 272
Subject Matter Expert (SME) 65
subroutines 17

T

Task Parallel Library (TPL) 231, 235, 238
Test-Driven Development (TDD)
  about 69, 183, 221, 231, 235, 238
  initial unit test definitions 74, 75
  projects, setting up 71, 72, 73
  reasons, for selecting 69, 70
  reference 212
TestInventoryContext 112, 113
threads 98
transformation-related patterns
  Canonical Data Model 52
  Content Enricher 52
  Message Translator 52
tuple

reference 79

U

Unified Modeling Language (UML) 13, 22
unit tests, factory pattern
   case-insensitive text commands 125
   UnknownCommand 122
UpdateQuantityCommand 115
UpdateQuantityCommandTest 117
use case
   about 305
   business requisites 306
   challenges 307
   project kickoff 305
   requisites 306
   technical requisites 307
User Acceptance Testing (UAT) 357
User Experience (UX) 187
User Interface (UI) 183, 292

V

View Model 294
Visual Studio
   installing 242

W

Waterfall SDLC
   deployment phase 56
   design phase 56
   development phase 56
   requirements phase 56
   testing phase 56
web application
   coding 165, 167, 168, 170
   crafting 162
   working 163, 164
Web Services Description Language (WSDL) 341
web test project
   creating 212, 215, 217
while loop 17
Windows Presentation Foundation (WPF) 292

X

X12 EDI (X12) 53

Y

You Aren't Gonna Need It (YAGNI) 34, 340

Printed in Great Britain
by Amazon